Uniform

Uniform

Clothing and Discipline in the Modern World

Edited by Jane Tynan and Lisa Godson

BLOOMSBURY VISUAL ARTS
LONDON · NEW YORK · OXFORD · NEW DELHI · SYDNEY

BLOOMSBURY VISUAL ARTS
Bloomsbury Publishing Plc
50 Bedford Square, London, WC1B 3DP, UK
1385 Broadway, New York, NY 10018, USA

BLOOMSBURY, BLOOMSBURY VISUAL ARTS and the Diana logo are trademarks of
Bloomsbury Publishing Plc

First published in Great Britain 2019

Copyright © Jane Tynan, Lisa Godson and contributors, 2019

Jane Tynan and Lisa Godson have asserted their right under the Copyright, Designs and Patents Act, 1988, to be identified as Editors of this work.

For legal purposes the Acknowledgments on pp. xiv and 103 constitute an extension of this copyright page.

Cover design by Adriana Brioso

Cover image: Do Ho Suh, *High School Uni-Form*, 1997. Fabric, plastic, stainless steel, casters. 300 parts total. 701 × 551.2 × 137.2 cm (276 × 217 × 54 inches).
(© Do Ho Suh. Courtesy the artist; Lehman Maupin Gallery, New York, Hong Kong and Seoul; and Victoria Miro, London/Venice)

All rights reserved. No part of this publication may be reproduced or transmitted in any form or by any means, electronic or mechanical, including photocopying, recording, or any information storage or retrieval system, without prior permission in writing from the publishers.

Bloomsbury Publishing Plc does not have any control over, or responsibility for, any third-party websites referred to or in this book. All internet addresses given in this book were correct at the time of going to press. The author and publisher regret any inconvenience caused if addresses have changed or sites have ceased to exist, but can accept no responsibility for any such changes.

A catalogue record for this book is available from the British Library.

A catalog record for this book is available from the Library of Congress.

ISBN: HB: 978-1-350-04555-2
ePDF: 978-1-350-04557-6
eBook: 978-1-350-04556-9

Typeset by RefineCatch Limited, Bungay, Suffolk

To find out more about our authors and books, visit www.bloomsbury.com and sign up for our newsletters.

Contents

List of Illustrations   vii
Notes on Contributors   x
Acknowledgments   xiv

1   Understanding Uniform: An Introduction
     Jane Tynan and Lisa Godson   1

Part One: Uniforming Political Movements

2   The Public Order Act: Defining Political Uniform in 1930s
     Britain   *Annebella Pollen*   25

3   Revolutionary Culture, Girl Power, and the Red Guard Uniform
     During the Chinese Cultural Revolution   *Li Li*   49

Part Two: Uniforming Institutions

4   Uniform Adoption in English Public Schools,
     1830–1930   *Kate Stephenson*   67

5   Dissolving Vatican Uniform Hegemony: The Marist Road to
     Dress Freedom   *William J. F. Keenan*   87

Part Three: Uniforming Leisure

6   Fashionably Rational: The Evolution of Uniformed Leisure
     in Late Nineteenth-Century Britain   *Geraldine Biddle-Perry*   109

7   Uniformity in Fashion Practices During the Modernization
     Period in Turkey   *F. Dilek Himam*   135

Part Four: Uniforming Workers

8   Uniforming the Corporate Body in the City of
     London   *Samira Guerra*   161

9   A Cast of Thousands: Martin Grant and the New Qantas
    Uniform   *Prudence Black*   179

Part Five: Uniforming Fashion

10 Overalls: Functional, Political, Fashionable   *Djurdja Bartlett*   201

11 Utility Chic: Where Fashion and Uniform Meet   *Jane Tynan*   221

Part Six: Uniforming the Military

12 Military Uniform and Lethal Targeting in International Law
    on Armed Conflict   *Amin Parsa*   239

13 Military Uniforms and Women in the Ulster
    Defence Regiment   *Stephen Herron*   255

    Conclusion   277

Notes   283
Select Bibliography   287
Index   295

Illustrations

1.1 Sunbathing stewardesses at Schiphol Airport, Netherlands, 1962. National Archief, The Netherlands. — 22
2.1 Kibbo Kift men and boys in the 'Touching of the Totems' rite, 1925. © Kibbo Kift Foundation. — 34
2.2 Remodeled Kibbo Kift uniform marking shift in group identity, 1931. © Kibbo Kift Foundation. — 35
2.3 Green Shirts in street marching uniform, 1932. © Kibbo Kift Foundation. — 37
3.1 Song Binbin pins a Red Guard armband on Mao's sleeve, August 18, 1966. Private collection. — 56
3.2 'Be This Kind of Human Being', Poster depicting a Red Guard in the PLA uniform and armband. People's Fine Arts Publishing House (Beijing, 1968). Private collection of author. — 61
4.1 Prince Henry, Duke of Gloucester in Eton College uniform, 1914. Library of Congress, Prints & Photographs Division, George Grantham Bain Collection [LC-DIG-ggbain-15452]. — 80
4.2 Advertisement for Chas. Baker & Co., c.1885 showing Eton and Rugby suits for sale. © British Library Board [Evan. 5193]. — 82
5.1 Arrayed in triumph. Photo collage of 'the Marist Martyrs.' Private collection. — 94
5.2 Full Tridentine battle dress. Private collection. — 97
5.3 Airing post-conciliar differences. Gathering of Brothers attending Marist 'renewal' course early 1974. Private collection. — 99
5.4 Unity in diversity. Marist Brothers Institute Superior General and the Marist General Council, Rome, 1984. Private collection. — 102
6.1 Royal shooting party including King Edward VII, by unknown photographer, c. 1890s. © National Portrait Gallery, London. — 117
6.2 Cyclist in tweed suit beside 'High Ordinary' bicycle with equestrian saddle. London Metropolitan Archive [Image 230832] — 119
6.3 Keir Hardie by Arthur Clegg Weston, c. 1892. © National Portrait Gallery, London — 123

6.4	Young woman in rational dress advertising Elliman's Universal Embrocation. Wiki Commons File:Ellimans-Universal-Embrocation-Slough-Ad.png.	125
7.1	Woman with *ferace* and *yaşmak* from İzmir, Turkey. Apikam archive. Author's collection.	144
7.2	Turkish women with modern head coverings known as *sıkmabaş*. Turkey, *c*. 1920s. Author's collection.	146
7.3	Example of a *Sümerbank* fabric with stylized flower patterns decorated with geometric abstract shapes. Designer unknown, *c*. 1950s. İzmir University of Economics, Faculty of Fine Arts and Design, Tudita archive.	152
7.4	A group of women wearing identical dresses with Westernized hairstyles and make-up. Photographer unknown, *c*. 1940s. Çağla Ormanlar Ok collection.	153
8.1	Male and female business wear. Getty Images [Image reference 612387512]	170
8.2	Uniformity of business wear. Getty Images [Image reference 680449771]	173
9.1	Qantas cabin crew wearing Martin Grant uniform, 2016. Courtesy of Qantas.	182
9.2	Qantas pilots wearing Martin Grant uniform, 2016. Courtesy of Qantas.	194
10.1	Alexander Rodchenko in his *prozodezhda*, 1922. Rodchenko Family Archive. Courtesy of Alexander Lavrentiev.	205
10.2	Thayaht in his *tuta*, 1920. Courtesy of Photographic Archive of Prato Textile Museum [inv. n. 05.05.F06].	214
11.1	Katharine Hamnett Spring/Summer 1997 collection. Photograph by Niall McInerney, Bloomsbury Publishing Plc.	228
11.2	Jean Paul Gaultier, Spring/ Summer 1996 collection. Photograph by Niall McInerney, Bloomsbury Publishing Plc.	231
12.1	Full-length image of British army soldier with gun by graffiti on wall. John Vlahidis/EyeEm. Copyright Getty Images [Image ref: 898334748]	249
13.1	UDR soldiers on parade at Steeple Camp, Antrim, Northern Ireland. Remembrance Sunday, 1970. Photograph by Len Kinley. Wikimedia Commons: File [Soldiers_of_UDR_on_parade_at_Steeple_Camp,Antrim.jpg]	258

13.2 A platoon of UDR soldiers march past Mahon Road Barracks, Portadown, Co. Armagh, Northern Ireland, *c.* 1970s. Photograph by Thunderer. Wikimedia Commons: File [11_UDR_March_Past.jpg]   264

13.3 Ulster Defence Regiment Greenfinch in semi-formal skirt wearing old-style 'flak jacket' body armor, *c.* 1970s. Photograph by Ronnie Gamble. Wikimedia Commons: File [UDR_Greenfinch.jpg]   266

Notes on Contributors

Djurdja Bartlett is Reader in Histories and Cultures of Fashion at the London College of Fashion, University of the Arts London (UAL), UK, and also a member of Research Centre for Transnational Art, Identity and Nation (TrAIN) UAL. Bartlett is author of *FashionEast: The Spectre That Haunted Socialism* (2010), editor of the volume on East Europe, Russia and the Caucasus in the *Berg Encyclopedia of World Dress and Fashion* (2010), and co-editor of *Fashion Media: Past and Present* (2013). Bartlett's new monograph *European Fashion Histories: Style, Society and Politics* (2020) has been funded by an Arts and Humanities Research Council Fellowship grant. Bartlett is also editor of a new book on *Fashion and Politics* (2019).

Geraldine Biddle-Perry is a cultural historian and lectures at Central Saint Martins, University of the Arts London, UK. Her work considers questions of self in a range of cultural historical contexts but focuses on the self-conscious fashioning of modern bodies through popular consumption. She has edited notable collections looking at the symbolic and social significance of hair, including *Hair: Styling, Culture and Fashion* (2008) and *A Cultural History of Hair* (2018) and has published journal articles on fashion and oral history, club cycling and social aspiration in the nineteenth-century, the history of sports and leisure retailing in Britain, and British Olympic ceremonial uniforms. More recently she published a monograph *Dressing for Austerity: Aspiration, Leisure and Fashion in Post-war Britain* (2017) that is an important new contribution to the history of post-war Austerity Britain.

Prudence Black is a lecturer in the School of Humanities at Adelaide University and a Research Associate in the Department of Gender and Cultural Studies at the University of Sydney, Australia. Her award-winning book relating to uniforms and the aviation industry was *The Flight Attendant's Shoe* (2011). She has published mainly in the areas of design, modernism, fashion, aviation, and workplace culture. Her latest book, *Smile, Particularly in Bad Weather* (2017) is about the gendered and industrial relations history of flight hostesses and flight attendants.

Lisa Godson is Director of the MA in Design History and Material Culture at the National College of Art and Design, Dublin and Research Fellow at Trinity

College Dublin, Ireland. Recent publications include *Making 1916: Visual and Material Culture of the Easter Rising* (co-edited with Joanna Brück, 2015); *Modern Religious Architecture in Germany, Ireland and Beyond: Influence, Process and Afterlife since 1945* (co-edited with Kathleen James-Chakraborty, 2019) and *How the Crowd Felt: Ceremonial Culture in Ireland, 1922–49* (2020). Her research on modernist architecture in Africa was the basis of the award-winning documentary *Build Something Modern* and she was research collaborator on the Irish Pavilion at the Venice Biennale Arte 2017.

Samira Guerra is an independent scholar. She completed degrees in Social Anthropology at the University of Bern in Switzerland and Fashion Critical Studies at Central Saint Martins in London, UK. Her research interests include the uniformed body in corporate environments and aesthetic labor in the banking industry, with a particular focus on gender and power relations.

Stephen Herron is a military anthropologist and Research Fellow at the Senator George J. Mitchell Institute for Global Peace, Security and Justice at Queen's University Belfast, Northern Ireland. Herron acted as co-investigator on a project which examined how counterinsurgency warfare impacts the post-deployment reintegration experiences of British land based military personnel. This research, the first of its kind, has led to his current role as co-investigator on a major project which examines former soldiers experiencing 'negative transitioning,' such as those who have been in prison, homeless, or under mental health supervision.

F. Dilek Himam is Assistant Professor at the Faculty of Fine Arts and Design, İzmir University of Economics, Turkey. She has degrees from Uludağ University (1999) and the Department of Sociology at Ege University (2005) and a PhD from the Faculty of Fine Arts at Dokuz Eylül University (2012). Her academic interests lie in contemporary fashion and dress history, fashion theory, material culture studies, museology studies, and gender studies.

William J. F. Keenan is a freelance sociologist and independent researcher. Following a lengthy university academic career, he maintains his interest in higher education as Visiting Professor in Cultural Religion at Liverpool Hope University, UK; through participation in academic conferences; and by serving as External Examiner and Programmes Assessor at a number of institutions across the sector. He is on the editorial boards of a number of academic journals, including the *Journal of Contemporary Religion* and *Implicit Religion*. He is a Trustee of the Centre for the Study of Implicit Religion and Contemporary Spirituality.

Dr Keenan's scholarly interests are in cultural religion and spiritual traditions; university cultures; dress codes and fashion movements. He is particularly interested in the transdisciplinary exploration of mutations and transitions of religio-cultural traditions across modernity and postmodernity. His publications include: *Dressed to Impress: Looking the Part* (2001); *Materializing Religion: Expression, Performance and Ritual* (co-edited with Elisabeth Arweck; 2006); and, with colleagues at the International Centre for Social Ethics, Salzburg, he co-edited: *Decent Work and Unemployment* (2010) and *Resilience and Unemployment* (2012). He has contributed numerous articles to edited collections and has published extensively in a range of academic journals, including: *Journal of Contemporary Religion; European Journal of Social Theory; Body & Society; Theory, Culture & Society; Archive for the Psychology of Religion; Fashion Theory; British Journal of Sociology*; and *Implicit Religion*.

Li Li is Associate Professor of Chinese and Asian Studies at the University of Denver, US. She earned her PhD at the University of California (2007) and early publications include translations of English poetry and criticism. Her more recent research is focused on modern, contemporary Chinese literature, popular culture and media studies, especially social and semiotic constructions of women in Chinese literary and visual culture. Her book *Memory, Fluid Identity, and Politics of Remembering: The Representation of the Chinese Cultural Revolution in English-speaking Countries* (2016) investigates many complex cultural and socio-political issues involved in remembering and representation in a cross-country, cross-cultural environment. Her co-edited volume *The Making and Re-making of China's "Red Classics": Politics, Aesthetics, and Mass Culture* (2017) explores how the revolutionary canon was created in the Maoist Era and how it has been re-imagined during the reform period.

Amin Parsa is a Vetenskapsrådet-funded international Post Doctoral Fellow jointly at the Department of Sociology of Law at Lund University, Sweden, and the Centre for the Politics of Transnational Law at Vrije University, Amsterdam, Netherlands. He holds a doctoral degree in public international law from Lund University in Sweden. His research dealt with the legal consequences of the use of technologies of target visualization by US military in counterinsurgency operations in Iraq and Afghanistan.

Annebella Pollen is Principal Lecturer and Academic Programme Leader in the History of Art and Design at the University of Brighton, UK. She researches art, craft, dress, design, and photography across a range of periods and case studies.

Her books include *The Kindred of the Kibbo Kift: Intellectual Barbarians* (2015, with accompanying exhibition at Whitechapel Gallery); *Mass Photography: Collective Histories of Everyday Life* (2015); *Dress History: New Directions in Theory and Practice* (2015, co-edited with Charlotte Nicklas); and *Photography Reframed: New Visions in Contemporary Photographic Culture* (2018), co-edited with Ben Burbridge). She is currently writing a commissioned history of the British Council's visual arts collection and continues her work on dress and dissent.

Kate Stephenson is Associate Lecturer at the University of York, UK, and a Senior Writer for *The Art Story*. She completed her PhD on the history of British school uniform in 2016. In this she situated the development of school uniform within a contextual framework of social, fashionable and educational change with a particular focus on the nineteenth and twentieth centuries. She also holds a Masters in Art History from the University of St Andrews. She has diverse research interests within the fields of dress history and the history of childhood and is currently working on the history of fancy-dress costumes in the United Kingdom.

Jane Tynan is Senior Lecturer in Cultural and Historical Studies at Central Saint Martins, University of the Arts London, UK. Her research concerns visual and material aspects of war and conflict, law and order, with a focus on uniforms and the body. Recent publications include *British Army Uniform and the First World War* (2013) and chapters for *Thinking Through Fashion* (2015), *A Cultural History of Law* (2019) and *Fashion and Politics* (2019). She is series editor for *Palgrave Studies in Fashion and the Body*.

Acknowledgments

The editors would like to thank the copyright holders for permission to reproduce the images in this book. All reasonable attempts have been made to trace copyright holders of images and to obtain their permission for the use of copyright material. The publisher apologizes for any errors or omissions in copyright acknowledgement and would be grateful if notified of any corrections that should be incorporated in future reprints or editions of this book.

As editors we are grateful to Frances Arnold at Bloombury for her encouragement and support in realizing the project. Our gratitude also goes to the authors, who have creatively and constructively responded to our feedback on their work. We are delighted to share their original research and insights. Thanks must also go to University of the Arts London, whose support gave one of the editors a short period of research leave in which to work on the book. Finally, we are very grateful to the Victoria Miro Gallery and the artist Do Ho Suh for giving us permission to use the cover image.

1

Understanding Uniform: An Introduction

Jane Tynan and Lisa Godson

In Hermann Broch's *The Sleepwalkers* (1932), the protagonist Joachim von Pasenow ponders the qualities of military uniform:

> ... it is the uniform's true function to manifest and ordain order in the world, to arrest the confusion and flux of life, just as it conceals whatever in the human body is soft and flowing, covering up the soldier's underclothes and skin ... Closed up in his hard casing, braced in with straps and belts, he begins to forget his own undergarments, and the uncertainty of life ...[1]

In this account, uniform gives the wearer a sense of certainty by acting as an agent of the external forces of power and control; the protective covering conceals his imperfections to make his body feel invincible. In the novel, the Prussian lieutenant's uniform is a coded representation of his inhibited personal life. For von Pasenow, it offers the perfect protection against chaos, instability, and human entanglements. The way the uniformed body mediates between an ideal ordering and the messy reality of the modern world is the key focus of this volume of essays.

This book is about uniform and focuses on the period from the mid-nineteenth century, when this form of clothing became a significant part of public life. The word uniform means 'uni-form' (one form, all alike) and dates from the sixteenth century, arising from the French *uniforme*, or Latin *uniformis* (Langner 1965). In the book, we offer a range of perspectives on the social meaning of uniforms, why they were adopted by various groups, and what they articulate about cultures of late modernity. We are specifically concerned with uniform clothing, or uniform tendencies in various areas of fashion and dress. Modernity, according to geographer David Harvey, saw a diffusion of material practices with the construction of machines, transport and communication systems, bridges, and buildings (1990: 27). Uniform was one of modernity's material practices; it represented resistance to tradition and the embrace of rationality. The rise of uniform was, amongst other things, a response to profound changes in the experience of time and space in Western capitalism.

In this book, we understand sartorial uniformity not just as an outward emblem of power and authority, but also as an embodied social practice that involves the mutual constitution of objects and subjects. In the wearing of prescribed dress such as uniform, this relationship between subjectivity and artefact is thrown into even sharper relief. While much dress history of the modern period is concerned with fashion change and consumer choice, studying uniform calls into question this very focus on the self-consciously fashioned body. There has been notable research on the cultural significance of uniform within various institutional and cultural contexts (Joseph 1986; McVeigh 2000; Craik 2005) but few collections draw together this range of perspectives on the topic. As the subject of a special issue of *Journal of Design History* in 2011, uniform is described in the editorial as a research topic presenting "a maze of interdisciplinary components and interconnections expanding far beyond the field of dress" (Yagou 2011: 101). Exhibitions too have dealt with the cultural significance of uniform, in particular *Uniform: Order and Disorder* shown at the Museum of Modern Art in New York (2001), which drew attention to its range of representations in art, fashion, cinema and popular culture. There is room, however, for a more searching analysis of what uniform means to the modern world. Our interdisciplinary approach highlights uniform as a category of dress that has enabled distinct forms of social organization.

The proximity of uniform to the body demands perspectives that take account of its social, cultural, economic and political contexts. Here, we are less interested in the objects created for consumer culture and instead we focus on design as a means of exercising and contesting power. The lack of certainty about what constitutes uniform offers us a rich seam to mine; we ask what it is and what it does, but we also reflect on its failures. We ask what version of modernity the image of the uniformed citizen represents. In the subsequent chapters various scholars explore how uniforms have been designed, worn and understood through case studies primarily from the twentieth century but within contexts emergent since the mid-1800s. We consider why, at this particular moment in history, uniform was adopted widely to negotiate new relationships between public and private worlds.

A range of scholars have contributed to the volume. They work in a wide number of fields including sociology, art and design history, anthropology, literary and cultural studies, fashion history, politics and law, and international relations. The contributors bring from their disciplines distinctive analyses that might extend our understanding of what uniform means to the formation of the modern world. This unusually broad disciplinary basis indicates how the study of uniform transcends fashion history to touch on questions of identity and power in a range of contexts. From political movements to religious institutions, the book covers uniforms for leisure, fashion, and sports and explores transport, military, and school uniforms in various regions including China, Australia, Turkey, United Kingdom, and Russia.

Through the twelve essays we draw attention to the critical role of clothing in the formation of collective disciplines. The potential for fashion to reinforce or undermine wider social hierarchies is increasingly recognized across various academic disciplines. Uniforms are, however, often sidelined in these debates, despite the fact that they are implicated in creating images of classed, raced, and gendered bodies with the power to reinforce ideology and to form social attitudes. By presenting various case studies, we consider how uniforms work to shape human behavior and action, in various geographical regions and historical periods. Uniforms are complex, and their interpretation calls for a multi-disciplinary approach capable of revealing the many faces of uniformity in cultures of modernity.

The volume is divided into six short sections that each address an aspect of regulatory dress. In the first, Annebella Pollen and Li Li discuss the uniforming of political movements; in Pollen's essay "The Public Order Act: Defining Political Uniform in 1930s Britain," she describes the almost bewildering array of colored-shirt organizations that arose in the interwar period and offers a close reading of legislative attempts to regulate their perceived threat. This points up some of the complexities of uniform: as Pollen writes, "a set of garments associated with orderliness and discipline sits at the very centre of concerns about public disorder" and the continued enforcement of the Act against far less formal 'uniforms' shows enduring unease with massed bodies in standardized dress. This unease was potently materialized by the quasi-military clothing worn by young women of the Chinese People's Liberation Army (PLA) as discussed by Li in "Revolutionary Culture, Girl Power and the Red Guard Uniform during the Chinese Cultural Revolution." The author discusses how their uniforms helped shape an alliance between teenage girls and the leader Mao Zedong "and thus became the symbol of the Cultural Revolution," in particular in depictions of the Guard engaged in acts of violence and destruction.

In addressing how uniforms operate in institutions, William J. F. Keenan and Kate Stephenson show how the use of regulatory dress not only asserts group identity but also emphasises the endurance of that identity by positing uniform against the vagaries and changing codes of fashionable dress. In his study of the clerical garb of the Marist Brothers, a teaching congregation of the Roman Catholic Church, Keenan emphasizes the uniformity of their dress as bespeaking "resistance to secular modern fashion and free choice dress ideology" to denote a disdain for worldliness and its materialist temptations. In "Uniform Adoption in English Public Schools, 1830–1930," Stephenson similarly notes that the dress of pupils was regulated partly in "prevention of ostentatious display," with allegiance to the institution privileged over individual taste and self-expression. While uniform dress within these institutions worked, as Stephenson notes, to "foster a corporate sense of superiority of elites," elements of public school uniform itself came to be imitated by the wider society, with the 'Eton' collar and 'Rugby' suit lending sartorial respectability to those who may have been excluded from such schools due to class and income. Thus, the legibility of uniform worked not only for those who were full members of an institution, but also carried its values to the wider culture.

If most of the essays in the book focus on uniform as specialist clothing, then the section on uniforming leisure deals with the more widespread social adoption of codified dress. F. Dilek Himam discusses this in "Uniformity in Fashion Practices during the Modernization Period in Turkey" in relation to Kemalist reforms that equated uniformity in appearance with social, technological and economic progress. From state-sponsored textile factories producing specified designs to an emphasis on a limited range of clothing items, Himam demonstrates how the 'imagined community' of modernizing Turkey was given material force by the sartorial homogeneity of its citizens. The regulatory mechanisms of modernity were also apparent in the 'evolution of uniformed leisure' in late nineteenth-century Britain as observed by Geraldine Biddle-Perry. Echoing the sense that uniform is the ultimate rationalization of appearance, she argues that the neat division of time into work and leisure and the concomitant rationalizing of dress helps us understand the apparent contradiction of a leisure 'uniform' being mobilized "to distinguish leisure time, space, and bodies" as free from the constraints of everyday life "while at the same time being compelled to take these as their reference point."

People at work operate within the constraints of dress codes and demands for conformity from their employers, which forms the basis of the section on uniforming workers. Samira Guerra's ethnographic study of uniforming the corporate body in the City of London looks in particular to the ways in which the business suit has become globalized and is "closely tied to notions of authority, professionalism, legitimacy, integrity and power." However, as those values are traditionally attached to masculinity, women in corporate environments tend to navigate a course *between* uniformity and fashionability on the job. Longevity underpins the approach taken by those who design the clothing of airline staff as explored by Prudence Black in her essay "A Cast of Thousands: Martin Great and the New Qantas Uniform." If the utopian approach to overall design is to disavow fashion, with the Qantas uniform both long-lasting fashionability and iconicity were carefully considered. As in other cases, it is not only the garments that need to be regulated but the general demeanor and presentation of those who wear them, as outlined in the guide book that staff received along with their new uniform to warn against "no handlebar or horseshoe moustaches (the outline of the upper lip must be visible), no backpacks, no chewing gum and jackets must be worn more regularly, including to and from work."

The interplay of fashion and uniform is implied in many of the essays and often presented as oppositional sartorial strategies, but in the section uniforming fashion Jane Tynan and Djurdja Bartlett explicitly address this relationship, described by Tynan as "the pressure to fit in versus the attraction of being distinctive." While rationalization may have been implicit in the leisure clothing adopted in the late nineteenth century, it was an overt value in the utopian schema a few decades later, most distinctively those of the Constructivists in the new Soviet Union. Bartlett traces overalls as "functional, political, fashionable" from the utilitarianism of the Bolsheviks in the 1920s through the dance floors of Manhattan fifty years later to the present day, where a group of progressive artists have tried to reclaim overalls as an "ungendered mono-garment to replace all clothes in perpetuity." The contemporary appropriation of uniform by fashion design and media is explored by Tynan as a particular form of 'capitalist kitsch' that in an uncertain world fetishizes the uniform aesthetic as a stable social system where hierarchy and status are more easily 'read.'

As discussed later in this introduction, uniform is probably most readily associated with military clothing, which is addressed by last section of the book. In the penultimate essay, Amin Parsa discusses the ways in which military uniform is central to the foundational principle of the legal distinction between civilians and combatants in international law on armed conflict. Parsa demonstrates how the visibility and contrast of uniform and non-uniform can mean the difference between life and death as it operates to realise the "ambitions of laws of armed conflict's most significant principle in protecting civilians during war." In the final essay on uniformed women in the Ulster Defence Regiment, Stephen Herron considers how a locally recruited regiment of the

British Army during the conflict in Northern Ireland routinely sexualized women in uniform through popular representation, a form of symbolic violence that not only "reinforced the dominant position of men as leaders and protectors" but also called into question the legitimacy of female combat, and indeed whether women can wear uniform in this most conventionally masculine sphere.

Uniform: history

This portion of the introduction now turns to provide a very summary historical overview of uniform and considers how the essays in this volume relate to recent scholarship on fashion studies, design history, visual and material culture, and other areas of the humanities and social sciences.

The European sumptuary tradition of the Middle Ages was an early example of uniformity in dress, whereby appearance—and thereby consumption—was regulated according to social hierarchies. While codification was important in dress cultures of subsequent periods, the emergence and proliferation of uniform followed the militarization of civil society and is associated with post-seventeenth century historical developments. In particular, the uniform was key to the development of techniques to discipline the body between the end of the seventeenth century and the beginning of the nineteenth centuries (Roche 1994: 256). Uniforms also gave patriotic nationalists new ways to express citizenship based on collective power, as demonstrated by the dress of the French Revolution.

The nineteenth century saw a range of occupations in various regions adopting uniforms, including police, transport and service workers, shop assistants, and nurses. With the rise of industrialized societies, both fashion and uniform were facilitated by mass production techniques and new patterns of consumption. This was a society where clothing was a clear reflection of a person's class and status. As state, society and nation converged towards the end of the nineteenth century uniform became part of a modern culture increasingly concerned with regulating time, space, and bodies. As outlined below, this phase of modernity included more homogenous masculine dress codes, concomitant with the rise in occupational and institutional uniforms and greater regulation in military dress. At this point the uniform moved from being a form of dress that created a spectacle of massed bodies to one that enabled their surveillance by a state ever more interested in regulation. In their influential book *The Invention of Tradition*, historians Eric Hobsbawm and Terence Ranger argued that the wearing of uniforms was, at the turn of the twentieth century, instrumental in constructing the invented traditions of class and nationhood (1983). Taking this as a high point in terms of the historical significance of uniform, the book focuses on examples from 1850 to present day.

In the early twentieth century, the massing together of uniformed political movements was often permitted, enabling the growth of very real threats to the status quo. The tumultuous period between the two world wars again saw the rise of uniformed movements that gave material expression to alternative political values, or engaged in brinkmanship through shows of strength disguised as ceremonial occasions, which were lent both legitimacy and menace by their uniform. In this period various groups took up uniform with enthusiasm, from dress reformers to fascists, sporting clubs to religious groups. Since the mid-twentieth century, though uniforms for work and leisure have to some extent been casualized, they remain an integral part of public life. As outlined in the conclusion to this book, the use of uniform to variously intimidate, discipline or show solidarity is germane to contemporary culture and is likely to remain a point of contention and debate into the future.

Uniform: clothing

People use clothes for identity work, which according to anthropologist Daniel Miller "plays a considerable and active part in constituting the particular experience of the self, in determining what the self is" (2010: 40). Clothing is about expressing or concealing principles and emotions, but creativity in acts of body adornment can also be evidence of the drive to *make* in a material culture sense (Schwarz 1979: 30). Contemporary fashion historians have looked to the dynamics of fashion to understand how coercive and creative aspects of clothing and adornment reflect current social values (Wilson 1987; Breward 2003). Fashion is a form of communication (Barnard 2002; Barthes 2006) that also has a material reality (Küchler and Miller 2005; Woodward 2007) and, as such, has been embraced as a rich source for the study of social identity (Entwistle 2000; Crane 2000; Miller 2010). In a wide range of academic disciplines, fashion and clothing are now regarded as significant cultural forms that can be used to interpret aspects of the history, experience, and representation of the body.

It is striking that fashion studies—a field where various disciplines converge to consider the significance of fashion and clothing to the formation of social identities—has been less inclined to encompass uniform. As industrial societies developed complex systems of sartorial signs, the uniform could perform "a role opposite that of fashionable clothing, with its implications of self-enhancement" (Crane 2000: 89). For various reasons, such everyday clothing has been less likely to attract the interest of historians and sociologists of fashion. As object and cultural practice, however, uniform has the potential to offer multiple perspectives on human behaviour and forms of social organization. By engaging with 'history from below,' scholars have found in clothing a good source for understanding the meaning of various patterns of human organization (Sharpe 1991: 25). We argue that the powerful *image* and *materiality* of uniform gives it a special place in the distinctive visual and material culture of nineteenth and twentieth century modernity. Uniform also has an intriguing relationship with fashion; differences between uniform and fashion are at times subtle, and at other times, stark. This collection of essays on uniform owes much to developments that have seen fashion studies expand and reach out to a wide variety of academic disciplines including social and cultural history, cultural studies, politics, sociology, gender studies, art history, design history, and material culture studies.

This book is specifically concerned with how uniform visualizes and embodies what it means to be modern. We make a distinction between uniform and fashion but we also take account of how sartorial uniformity has been incorporated into the grammar of fashion. Uniforms too are 'fashioned' to fit the variety of purposes to which they are put. Cultural and dress historians have defined fashion as a provisional means of stabilizing identity, a practice primarily concerned with pleasure and self-expression (Wilson 1987; Lipovetsky 1994; Lehmann 2000). In contrast, modern uniform was designed not for pleasure, but rather for utility. However distinct systems of dressing fashion and uniform are, both promote body discipline and transformation. Fashion is not about seeking durable solutions to the problem of the body. Uniform, on the other hand, often involves an assertive traditionalism counter to the contingency of fashion. Sociologists of fashion and the body draw attention to the various ways in which clothing is activated by political, social, and temporal contexts (Featherstone 1991; Entwistle 2000; Crane 2000). If fashion and uniform can be defined by their respective contexts, then it is perhaps unexpected to find that they are inextricably linked. The origin of modern dress lies in the development of uniform; standardized sizing arose with the first attempts to create standard military issue, an innovation that was key to the evolution of ready-to-wear clothing (Tonchi 2010). Studying uniform presents unique challenges and joys, not least because its meanings are elusive and multivalent, but also because uniform is always about the body and its transformations. Indeed, the various transformations that uniforms undergo illustrate how the material and discursive converge when the body is placed at the heart of historical investigation (Canning 1999). On the surface, this book might be about uniform but it is fundamentally concerned with examining the significance of sartorial uniformity to the history of the body.

In many of the essays in the book uniform is understood to be a gendered object. Techniques governing the wearing of uniform are commonly formed around a masculine ideal (Craik 2005) and have been used as a tool to authenticate masculinity within the military institution (Colville 2003). Encoded in uniform design is a distinctly military masculinity, which is invariably white, able-bodied, and European. Does the uniform, though, always construct a masculine appearance? In fashion, the masculine is commonly subordinated to the feminine, through a traditional division of labor that has constructed consumption as a woman's role (Veblen 1994; Sparke 1995). This is one of the problems vexing those who research uniform. If the study of fashion is primarily concerned with cultural practices associated with women, then how do we understand uniform, which is routinely linked to masculine spaces such as the military? This binary thinking limits our understanding of what uniform can mean for the performance of gender. Questions of gender surface regularly in discussions of uniform, particularly concerning the outward construction of military masculinities, but this has also drawn attention to the military's difficulty with uniforming women (Herbert 1998; Craik 2005). There are examples, though, of uniforms designed specifically *for* women, primarily for the purposes of creating a regulated environment. Nursing uniform has gained attention as a gendered object and practice, where reform resulted in the creation of a new uniform designed to give occupational dignity and credibility to the women who undertook those roles (Schuessler Poplin 1994; Bates 2011). Here, uniformity was neither military nor was it masculine, but instead was advanced as a solution to the problem that fashionable dress might pose for a new profession anxious to be taken seriously.

Other scholars draw attention, not to uniform itself, but to patterns of uniformity, particularly the fashion for a man to assert himself through "standardisation and through control over his body" (Reynaud 2002: 401). Linked historically with the "Great Masculine Renunciation," a term invented by the psychologist John Carl Flügel, the adoption of austere and uniform clothing habits in the nineteenth century is attributed to a new industrial economy and gendered division of labor (Breward 1999). British dress reform between the wars also promoted a simple, readable masculinity rooted in the physical body (Burman 1995), illustrating how patterns of uniformity in dress enabled normative performances of gender. This book argues for a wider understanding of dress that might re-frame questions about everyday clothing practices, in particular those that fall outside fashion. Are uniforms shaped by a hegemonic masculinity rooted in myths about the powerful male body? Or can meanings designed into uniform be re-created and transformed by new contexts and uses? Uniforms have, arguably, retained a masculine image through their militarization, to such an extent that women in military uniform are often perceived to be destabilizing their own femininity. There are, however, many examples of women wearing uniforms that were neither masculine nor military in origin, amongst them nursing and domestic service. Discussions of uniform commonly explore questions of gender and sexuality, not least because uniforms can be enlisted to promote a normative understanding of the body. This book grapples with questions about the political role of regulation clothing, in particular how it disciplines bodies to adopt gender, nationality, race, and sexuality positions.

Uniform: discipline

This collection of essays situates sartorial prescription within a complex network of normalizing standards and discursive practices. As outlined by the discussion so far civilian uniforms are military in origin. Military uniform, however, is a relatively recent phenomenon: until the 'military revolution' in the 1600s there was a reluctance to regulate soldiers' clothing. Generals and Admirals had colorful regalia, leaving their subordinates to wear whatever clothes they had to hand in order to distinguish them from the enemy. Naval and merchant seamen had no official uniform before the mid-nineteenth century and were supplied with 'slops' by the Royal Navy, a distinctive form of clothing that made them recognizable (Styles 2007: 49). By that time, the army did provide a uniform and from the 1700s uniform regulations were strictly enforced. The officer corps, slow to adopt uniform, wished instead to retain signs of distinctiveness, particularly where motifs carried ideas of honor associated with medieval armory. Since the nineteenth century, the dominant aesthetic in military clothing balances the official desire to maintain morale with practical concerns about visibility. During the Napoleonic Wars, military uniforms were primarily about spectacle but sumptuous clothing designed to intimidate the enemy quickly disappeared with the technological warfare of the twentieth century.

From the early twentieth century, surveillance practices on the battlefield ensured that uniforms would thereafter be designed for utility. The instrumentality of standardized clothing made it easier "to shape the physique and the bearing of a combative individual" (Roche 1994: 229), which inspired utilitarian reformers who saw in the military body an efficiency that could usefully be transposed to civil society. This focus on the care of the body reflected an increased interest in hygiene, cleanliness, and uniformity in the military, which was inspiring significant changes in uniform design. Increased uniformity is concomitant with the rise of the nation state and its forms of standardization, bureaucracy and centralized systems of organization. In this sense the uniform is hegemonic; it establishes and legitimizes state or corporate power through control over the body. In the military, it is the uniform that transforms civilians into soldiers, that enables them to escape their personal identity to meet the challenge of performing military tasks (Ben Ari and Lomsky Feder 1999). The recent "aesthetic turn" in International Relations scholarship, has changed the terms of academic debate on geopolitics, to include consideration of aesthetic practices (Bleiker 2001). This, amongst other developments, has given impetus to debate on the uniforming of citizens and its role in political discourse.

As Antonio Gramsci described in his theory of cultural hegemony, political control is exercised through a combination of persuasion and force (1971). The overt formality and restrictive qualities of the typical uniform suggest that it manages both appearance and human behaviour; its *image* persuades and its *materiality* forces. This was well understood in the military and a policy of regulation in the eighteenth and nineteenth centuries that standardized military dress (Byrde 1979) anticipated technological changes that by the start of the twentieth century saw the establishment of functional camouflage designs on the battlefield. The industrialization of war meant the end of spectacular and ritual aspects of warfare, and with it brightly colored uniforms, which were no longer effective on the battlefield (Giddens 1985: 223). Drab colors and functional uniform design transformed the military body through the adoption of a tactical rather than fashionable appearance (Tynan 2013a). With the move to a new functional camouflage dress, uniform design became integral to modern warfare but these changes in military organization, at the end of the nineteenth and the start of the twentieth century, also signaled a new instrumentalism in everyday life. More uniforms on the street reflected a new rationalizing and militarizing of civil society.

The study of uniform offers insights into the institutional rules and regulations encoded in specific designs; uniform is a special form of clothing that marks status much more visibly than other forms of dress (Joseph 1986: 67). Sociologists in particular who conceptualize the body as a project in modernity (Featherstone

1991; Shilling 1993; Canning 1999) highlight how we can analyze forms of power through the body and its adornments. As any kind of public procession demonstrates, uniforms can transform a group of soldiers, music bands, workers, police, or schoolchildren into a dazzling pageant. Whether commemorating a military victory, independence from an oppressor, or marking a religious festival, the spectacle of synchronized movement owes much to the aesthetic impact of uniform clothing. As anthropologist Luke Freeman observes of the parade he witnessed for Malagasy Independence Day, this display of "the physical apparatus of the state in full" ensures that the "glorious regalia of state create a stunning figure so that the president himself does not need to be one" (2007: 290). The pageantry of uniformed citizens in synchronized formations offer a physical and spatial manifestation of the unity created by certain types of authority, all to exhibit the leader's power. Uniform is widely recognized as a technique for the most potent visual displays that constitute the spectacle of state power.

For philosopher Michel Foucault, the body was central to understanding the operation of institutional power (2001; 1991), making the surface qualities of the body significant to the workings of a disciplinary society. Foucault argued that the body became the focus for practices of improvement and transformation in the eighteenth century (1991: 198–202). Uniform clothing was an integral part of this technology of normalization to position people within a network of relations (Foucault 1991:146), to brand them public property and to regulate their behavior. Most importantly, though, the uniform represents the power and control of the institution that sets it to work; it is one part of a whole aesthetic system to regulate environments, be it in the school, workplace or prison.

Military and other kinds of uniforms are critical to modes of regulation and control associated with colonialism. Historically, uniforms worn by soldiers, police, and colonial officials were useful in order to establish imperial authority. In various institutions uniformity promotes ideas of order, stability, and discipline but in the colonial context uniform had a special significance. Images are critical to sustaining power and authority, and do so by assigning values to people; codifying the violent other as benign soldier could normalize the colonial encounter. The colonial policeman in particular blended military and civilian roles to become the most "visible symbol of colonial rule" (Anderson and Killlingray 1991: 2). Uniform, here as elsewhere, was a visible display of power and control. In India, revisions to dress that followed the suppression of the Indian Mutiny of 1857–8 signified changes in the colonial campaign, and resulting adaptations to uniform reflected the more complex forms of power that were taking hold. The British effectively transformed their colonial strategy from ruling as outsiders to insiders, evident in how their visual symbols changed to incorporate more 'Indian' features (Cohn 1983). This was not benign and neither was the change confined to dress, but in this period various attempts were made to naturalize colonial power, by giving British Indian people access to their own culture through European ideas. From 1860, therefore, a move away from Western-style uniforms meant that "the dress uniforms of Indians and English included turbans, sashes, and tunics thought to be Mughal or Indian" (Cohn 1983: 183). This objectified vision of India was present in the design of colonial uniforms; what apparently signified exchange and co-operation was in reality the establishment of British imperial authority through small acts of incorporation.

Uniforms were instrumental to how Europeans established control over South Asian and African peoples. Uniforms, which represent softer forms of control, offer important insights into cultural aspects of colonialism and while these perspectives have been somewhat neglected, there are some notable exceptions (Cohn 1983; Renne 2004; Streicher 2012). Clothing, and uniforms in particular, are the codification of ritual idiom; in colonial India the British were careful to construct their authority through uniform and its representations. By tracing the imperial reconfigurations of military uniforms in Thailand's southern provinces, in the late nineteenth and twentieth century, Ruth Streicher highlights how they demarcated boundaries essential to the performance of the gentlemanly state, in that "dressing in uniform is integral to modern statehood for it signifies that practices performed by soldiers are not defined as violence but can be fashioned as 'civilized force'." (2012: 472) This brings us close to the persuasive qualities of uniform clothing illustrating how bodies can be fashioned to legitimize extreme actions. It is precisely the uniform's abstraction from violence that allows it to escape critique, which authorizes its use while maintaining an image of 'civilized force.' Here and elsewhere, image manipulation allowed the appearance of gentlemanly soldiering to be passed off as fashionable progress.

In Nigeria, where khaki uniforms were part of the strategy to establish the colonial state, other forms of traditional dress associated with pre-colonial rule "were used by the British in reinforcing their political authority in colonial Nigeria" (Renne 2004: 137). Paradoxically, military leaders who dressed in khaki might find themselves visibly supported by wealthy traditional rulers dressed in *agbadas* (robes); this combined native and colonial authority represented the political elite in colonial Nigeria in the late nineteenth and twentieth century.

The phrase 'khaki to agbada' described the transition from military to civilian rule at the end of the colonial period in terms that emphasized the move away from uniform. If uniform clothing played a role in establishing imperial authority, how then was anti-imperial conflict embodied and performed? The revolutionary period in Ireland saw the nationalist Irish Volunteers, founded in 1913, first creating uniforms modeled on those worn by the British army but the nature of the conflict caused them to move away from regulation clothing. They were allowed drill and exercise, partly as a sop to growing tensions with the loyalist Ulster Volunteers, but were in fact in training for revolutionary action that erupted with the 1916 Easter Rising. In a period when the militarizing of society in Britain and Ireland was at a height, the authorities were undisturbed by such outward shows of force. Once the conflict began, though, it became clear that rebels had to use less conspicuous forms of clothing to escape the gaze of the authorities. If uniforms demarcate boundaries essential to the performance of the gentlemanly state, then the 1916 rebels in Ireland re-defined ideas of what modern statehood might look like. Being creative with their uniform gave the insurrectionists a role in establishing the visual signifiers of anti-colonial struggle at the start of the twentieth century. The unusual uniform aesthetic adopted by rebel groups in the insurrection called into question the legitimacy of the apparent 'civilizing' force of imperialism.

If military uniforms have been used to dress up colonial violence through performances of gentlemanly virtue, do imperial notions of gender, race and ethnicity inform conventional uniform design? Not always. Uniform can also signify the wearer's lack of power. In military contexts, uniforms might be a show of power, but as studies of prison uniform reveal, regulated clothing can also be designed to humiliate and control the wearer. Prison uniform has been a critical part of the system to control inmates to project the power of the penal establishment on the incarcerated body through reform and humiliation (Ash 2009). In the military context, uniform confers on the wearer the power to perform statehood, but in the prison regulation clothing marks the body as state property. Police uniform is caught between the two: conceived to balance the demands of social control with the needs of public service, the idea of the uniformed constable was conceived to visibly perform state power while also making them subject to scrutiny by the public and the authorities. In the newly industrialized cities, the desire for a more "policed society" found uniformed police an ideal solution, whereby "images of law" would penetrate everyday life (Brogden 1987). Uniformed police were introduced in the 1800s as part of a system of surveillance that sought control by increasing the visibility of civilian bodies and law enforcement on the streets of expanding cities. Forms of policing power emerging in the nineteenth century were attempts to comprehend society panoptically (McMullan 1998: 104) consistent with Foucault's conception of a 'disciplinary society.' The history of policing reveals how the clothing of these new police forces, including the London Metropolitan police, were modeled on those first adopted for harsh militia-style policing in the colonies (Tynan 2019). This was about creating illusions, primarily the illusion that state, society, and nation were one, making distinctive military-style uniforms critical to the invention of modern policing.

Nowhere is the illusion of uniformity more evident than in the aesthetics of fascism in the first half of the twentieth century. Uniforms such as the black shirt of Italian fascism were part of the regimes' specific construction of citizenship (Falasca-Zamponi 2002). Here, as elsewhere, clothing had transformative power but the appropriation of body uniformity had sinister motives for fascist leaders who used it to mobilize eugenics discourses. Implicit in these discourses was the message that unhealthy, uncivilized bodies were in need of reform, hence, the standardization of bodies in 1930s Italy sought to erase differences of class, gender, and geography through the widespread use of civil uniforms (Paulicelli 2004: 24) to put on display a disciplined social body. The drive to uniform society clearly has a dark side, and extreme cases bring us closer to understanding the attractions body uniformity holds for ethnonationalists, and why these political projects exalt idealized bodies. Uniformity constitutes an overlooked but nevertheless significant vocabulary of both conformity and subversion. In this book, we explore how uniforms embody political control, but also how they give insurgents legitimacy; in various ways we use the study of uniform to consider the interconnected concerns of dress, gender, and citizenship.

Uniform: the modern world

The nineteenth century is pivotal to understanding the development of uniform and fashion, a duality that reflected the competing possibilities presented by mass-production. The age of the bourgeoisie in Western Europe gave prominence to the contest of "the individual and the anonymous crowd, dandyism and uniformity, distinctiveness and conformism" (Perrot 1994: 4). It was the era of the ready-made, which saw the increased regulation of dress for workers in the United States (US) and Britain (de Marly 1986; Kidwell and Steele 1989). Mass clothing production first stimulated by the demand for military uniforms concentrated the labor force but also, more importantly, standardized sizing (Green 1997: 29–31). While historians find little evidence of civilian uniforms in eighteenth-century England (Styles 2007), they proliferate in the nineteenth century (Richmond 2013). British railway companies started to issue uniform clothing regulations along with the liveries issued to workers twice a year (de Marly 1986: 126). From the 1820s to the end of the century, railway workers and police officers were conspicuously uniformed, which represented the increased interest in codified dress in various industrialized economies (Richmond 2013). Workplace uniforms and dress codes were used as a form of social control to indicate rank in organizational hierarchies (Crane 2000: 5). Uniforms made social class differences explicit in the workplace and employers became convinced of their value in the creation of corporate identities.

If modernity transformed the body into an observer and an object of vision (Crary 1990), this recoding of reality contributed to the creation of the uniformed citizen. A new visual culture demanded a kind of truth of appearances, to objectify the body as a unit of labor and a social self to be made and remade. Uniform and fashion, regulation and self-expression, existed side by side, a complex duality made possible by modernity. Uniformity was the aesthetic system that most resembled the new technologies of mass production. The tape measure transformed custom tailoring into a system of mass production (Zakim 2003); similarly geometry, used for cutting, and machine-sewing for making-up, mechanized all aspects of the process for making clothes (Forty 1986). Science and technology were increasingly governing the production of modern bodies (Breward 2001: 165–81) and the modernist search for universal forms was a symbolic reflection of mass-production (Woodham 1997). In art, design, and architecture, the machine aesthetic became inseparable from the machinery that created it. Why then has uniform not been a focus of particular interest for design and cultural historians? The answer may lie in the place uniform occupies; neither part of consumer culture nor properly belonging to design culture. The state might appear to be anti-consumption (Fine 2002: 176–86) but this misconception is in part attributable to the way commodities, such as uniform, come to the market. Their consumption is predicated not on consumer sovereignty, but on more official forms of power and control. The study of uniform has been slow to flourish, as a result, despite the fact that uniformity became a fashionable aesthetic within modernism. For women's fashion, Chanel's little black dress is thought to exemplify the simplicity, functionality, and indeed masculinity of modernist design.

The real significance of modern, streamlined uniform lies in its aesthetic of standardization and the attention it draws to the body; this appeals to a corporate culture keen to project an image of unity and authority. It started with the standardization of railway staff clothing in the nineteenth century, but now a whole branch of business studies focuses on organizational aesthetics. Sartorial uniformity is now demanded in various work environments including business, retail, hospitality and the transport industry. Historically, uniform marked out work/leisure distinctions but more recently the push to commodify labor sees dress codes at the center of academic and media debates on work cultures. A focus on the style of the service encounter in the workplace to appeal to customers' senses has been termed "aesthetic labour" (Nickson et al. 2001: 170). The uniform's abstraction from the coercive aspects of the job has made it critical to these new forms of discipline and control in the workplace. Despite compromising the agency of the wearer, the uniform is nonetheless promoted as essential to the operation of workplace duties. At work, uniform is about image management and brand identity, which is why scholars of organizational studies now see evidence of aesthetic labor in clothing, appearance, and uniform practices (Warhurst and Nickson 2007). In an effort to create a science of the management of corporate identity, many companies have looked to aesthetics to embody the desired corporate image. Workers are styled and transformed by clothing, grooming, and behavior management to *materialize* the corporate aesthetic. Much new research in the area concerns whether managing the self-presentation techniques of workers produces the desired—and undesired—service encounter. Questions about what happens when workers deviate from the uniform or dress code are of particular interest to scholars of organizational aesthetics. Debates on aesthetic labor, concerned with how uniforms make workers symbol-bearers of organizations, are increasingly exploring questions around the suppression of individual identity and official attempts to mask aspects of gender, sexuality, or race in the workplace. Everyday contestations of workplace dress codes constitute challenges to the very notion that uniform is an idealized form of dress.

Georg Simmel viewed fashion as a reflection of the widespread desire in the modern world to combine uniformity with social differentiation in habits of dress (Simmel 1904). This conflicting desire in our social environment illustrates the various challenges we face in understanding the social and cultural meanings of uniform. When is a uniform a uniform? The complex duality of 'dandyism and uniformity' that characterizes the modern age can in part be explained by the competing opportunities presented by mass-production. It was, however, also the era when more scientific forms of people management emerged and the rationalization of time and labor became fashionable. In other words, uniform in the modern sense is part of a cultural shift that standardized clothing to fit with the utilitarian social reform projects to build prisons, schools and hospitals. But the focus on the care of the body reflected the increased interest in hygiene, cleanliness, and uniformity that dominated official efforts to tackle poverty and despair in the nineteenth century. While capitalism had its critics, on the whole public health and social reform programs turned their attention away from larger systemic issues and inequalities to instead govern the micro-territory of the body. The uniform was instrumental to such projects, whereby attempts were made to govern bodies through discipline, control, and standardization techniques. Regulation in dress reflected the discipline and control various agencies sought over bodies, particularly those threatening the status quo: the poor, the vagrant, dissidents, women, and young people. These official attempts to use uniforms to discipline and control populations might perhaps be read as representing the dark side of modernity.

Given its sinister past, why does uniform still so fascinate today in film and popular culture? If uniform gains its power through a sense of dominance, authority, and the right to seize power, why is it copied so enthusiastically in fashion design and eroticized in popular media? Does the seduction of uniform perhaps lie in its secret codes? Uniform styles meaningful to institutional settings have had a history of symbolic transformation from work to leisure (Biddle-Perry 2014), from sacred to profane (Keenan 1999) and from military to civilian (Tynan 2013b). Are these transformations a sign that the uniformed citizen is now a fragile outsider and figure of fun? Or does it instead offer insights into just how durable uniform codes have become? It is striking that no matter how much uniform codes are manipulated and subverted they endure in ever more inventive forms into the twenty-first century. Institutions might come and go, but uniform as a category of dress and mode of self-presentation survives. As new institutions and organizations form, there is still an expectation that citizens dressing the part will populate them. An old uniform, though, does hold certain poignancy; only then is it exposed as an empty sign. Once divested of its authority an outmoded uniform can reveal the instability and redundancy of the traditional institution from whence it came.

References

Anderson, D. and D. Killingray, eds (1991), *Policing the Empire: Government, Authority and Control, 1830–1940,* Manchester: Manchester University Press.

Ash, J. (2009), *Dress Behind Bars: Clothing as Criminality,* London: IB Tauris.

Barnard, M. (2002), *Fashion as Communication,* London: Routledge.
Barthes, R. (2006), *The Language of Fashion,* Oxford: Berg.
Bates, C. (2011), "'Their Uniforms All Esthetic and Antiseptic': Fashioning Modern Nursing Identity, 1870–1900," in I. Parkins and E. M. Sheehan (eds), *Cultures of Femininity in Modern Fashion,* Durham, NC: University of New Hampshire Press, 151–79.
Ben Ari, E. and E. Lomsky Feder (1999), *The Military and Militarism in Israeli Society,* Albany, NY: SUNY Press.
Biddle-Perry, G. (2014), "The Rise of the World's Largest Sports and Athletic Outfitter: A Study of Gamage's of Holborn, 1878–1913," *Sport in History,* 34 (2): 295–314.
Bleiker, R. (2001), "The Aesthetic Turn in International Political Theory," *Millennium: Journal of International Relations,* 30 (3): 509–33.
Breward, C. (1999), *The Hidden Consumer: Masculinities, Fashion and City Life 1860–1914,* Manchester: Manchester University Press.
Breward, C. (2001), "Manliness, Modernity and the Shaping of Male Clothing" in J. Entwistle and E. Wilson (eds.), *Body Dressing,* Oxford: Berg, 165–81.
Breward, C. (2003), *Fashion,* Oxford: Oxford University Press
Brogden, M. (1987), "The Emergence of the Police: The Colonial Dimension," *British Journal of Criminology,* 27 (1): 4–14.
Burman, B. (1995), "Better and Brighter Clothes: The Men's Dress Reform Party, 1929–1940" *Journal of Design History,* 8 (4): 275–90.
Byrde, P. (1979), *The Male Image: Men's Fashion in England 1300–1970,* London: Batsford.
Canning, K. (1999), "The Body as Method? Reflections on the Place of the Body in Gender History," *Gender and History,* 11 (3): 499–513.
Colville, Q. (2003), "Jack Tar and the Gentleman Officer: The Role of Uniform in Shaping the Class- and Gender-Related Identities of British Naval Personnel, 1930–1939," *Transactions of the RHS,* 13: 105–29.
Craik, J. (2005), *Uniforms Exposed: From Conformity to Transgression,* Oxford: Berg.
Crane, D. (2000), *Fashion and Its Social Agendas: Class, Gender and Identity in Clothing,* Chicago: University of Chicago Press.
Crary, J. (1990), *Techniques of the Observer: On Vision and Modernity in the Nineteenth Century,* Cambridge, MA: MIT Press.
de Marly, D. (1986), *Working Dress,* London: Batsford.
Entwistle, J. (2000), *The Fashioned Body,* Cambridge: Polity.
Falasca-Zamponi, S. (2002), "Peeking Under the Black Shirt: Italian Fascism's Disembodied Bodies," in W. Parkins (ed.), *Fashioning the Body Politic,* Oxford: Berg, 145–65.
Featherstone, M. (1991), *The Body: Social Process and Cultural Theory,* London: SAGE Publications.
Fine, B. (2002), *The World of Consumption,* 2nd edn, London: Routledge.

Forty, A. (1986), *Objects of Desire: Design and Society 1750–1980*, London: Thames and Hudson.

Foucault, M. ([1977] 1991), *Discipline and Punish: The Birth of the Prison*, London: Penguin.

Foucault, M. ([1964] 2001), *Madness and Civilization: A History of Insanity in the Age of Reason*, London: Routledge.

Freeman, L. (2007), "Why are some people powerful?" in R. Astuti, J. Parry, and C. Stafford (eds), *Questions of Anthropology*, Oxford: Berg, 281–306.

Giddens, A. (1985), *The Nation-State and Violence*, Cambridge: Polity Press.

Gramsci, A. (1971), *Selections from the Prison Notebooks of Antonio Gramsci*, New York: International Publishers.

Green, N. L. (1997), *Ready-to-Wear and Ready-to-Work: A Century of Industry and Immigrants in Paris and New York*, Durham, NC: Duke University Press.

Harvey, D. (1990), *The Condition of Postmodernity*, Oxford: Blackwell.

Herbert, M. S. (1998), *Camouflage Isn't Only for Combat: Gender, Sexuality and Women in the Military*, New York: New York University Press.

Hertz, C. (2007), "The Uniform: As Material, As Symbol, As Negotiated Object," *Midwestern Folklore*, 32 1 (2): 43–58.

Hobsbawm, E. and T. Ranger, eds (1983), *The Invention of Tradition*, Cambridge: Cambridge University Press.

Joseph, N. (1986), *Uniforms and Nonuniforms: Communication Through Clothing*, Westport, CT: Greenwood Press.

Keenan, W. (1999), "From Friars to Fornicators: The Eroticization of Sacred Dress," *Fashion Theory*, 3 (4): 389–410.

Kidwell, C. and V. Steele (1989), *Men and Women: Dressing the Part*, Washington D.C.: Smithsonian Institution Scholarly Press.

Küchler, S. and D. Miller, eds (2005), *Clothing as Material Culture*, Oxford: Berg.

Langner, L. (1965), "Polity: Clothes and Government," in E. Roach and J. B. Eicher (eds), *Dress, Adornment and the Social Order*, New York: John Wiley, 124–37.

Lehmann, U. (2000), *Tigersprung*, Cambridge, MA: MIT Press.

Lipovetsky, G. (1994), *The Empire of Fashion: Dressing Modern Democracy*, Princeton, NJ: Princeton University Press.

McMullan, J. (1998), "The Arresting Eye: Discourse, Surveillance and Disciplinary Administration in Early English Police Thinking," *Social and Legal Studies*, 7 (1): 97–128.

McVeigh, B. (2000), *Wearing Ideology: State, Schooling and Self Presentation in Japan*, Oxford: Berg.

Miller, D. (2010), *Stuff*, Cambridge: Polity Press.

Nickson, D, C. Warhurst, A. Witz, and A. M. Cullen (2001), "The Importance of Being Aesthetic: Work, Employment and Service Organization" in A. Sturdy, I. Gruglis, and H. Willmott (eds), *Customer Service: Empowerment and Entrapment*, Basingstoke: Palgrave Macmillan, 170–90.

Paulicelli, E. (2004), *Fashion Under Fascism: Beyond the Black Shirt,* Oxford: Berg.
Perrot, P. (1994), *Fashioning the Bourgeoisie: A History of Clothing in the Nineteenth Century,* Princeton, NJ: Princeton University Press.
Renne, E. P. (2004), "From Khaki to Agbada: Dress and Political Transition in Nigeria," in J. Allman (ed.), *Fashioning Africa: Power and the Politics of Dress* Bloomington, IN: Indiana University Press, 125–43.
Reynaud, E. (2002), "Manly Aesthetics," in S. Jackson and S. Scott (eds), *Gender: A Sociological Reader,* London: Routledge, 401–05 [extract from Holy Virility].
Richmond, V. (2013), *Clothing the Poor in Nineteenth Century England,* Cambridge: Cambridge University Press.
Roche, D. (1994), *The Culture of Clothing: Dress and Fashion in the "Ancien Regime,"* Cambridge: Cambridge University Press.
Schuessler Poplin, I. (1994), "Nursing Uniforms: Romantic Idea, Functional Attire or Instrument of Social Change?," *Nursing History Review,* 2: 153–67.
Schwarz, R. A. (1979), "Uncovering the Secret Vice: Toward an Anthropology of Clothing and Adornment," in J. M. Cordwell and R. A. Schwarz (eds), *The Fabrics of Culture: The Anthropology of Clothing and Adornment,* The Hague: Mouton Publishers, 23–46.
Shilling, C. (1993), *The Body and Social Theory,* London: SAGE Publications.
Sharpe, J. (1991), "History from Below," in P. Burke (ed.), *New Perspectives on Historical Writing,* Cambridge: Polity Press, 24–41.
Simmel, G. (1904), "Fashion," *International Quarterly,* 10: 130–55.
Sparke, P. (1995), *As Long as It's Pink: The Sexual Politics of Taste,* London: Pandora.
Streicher, R. (2012), "Fashioning the Gentlemanly State: The Curious Charm of the Military Uniform in Southern Thailand," *International Feminist Journal of Politics,* 14 (4): 470–88.
Styles, J. (2007), *The Dress of the People: Everyday Fashion in Eighteenth-century England,* New Haven, CT: Yale University Press.
Tonchi, S. (2010), "Military Style," in V. Steele (ed.), *The Berg Companion to Fashion,* Oxford: Berg, 507–08.
Tynan, J. (2013a), *British Army Uniform and the First World War: Men in Khaki,* Basingstoke: Palgrave Macmillan.
Tynan, J. (2013b), "Military Chic: Fashioning Civilian Bodies for War," in K. McSorley (ed.). *War and the Body: Militarisation, Practice and Experience,* London: Routledge, 78–89.
Tynan, J. (2019), "Codes: Police Uniform and the Image of Law Enforcement," in I. Ward (ed.) *A Cultural History of Law in the Age of Reform,* Vol. 5, London: Bloomsbury, 55–71.
Veblen, T. ([1899] 1994), *Theory of the Leisure Class,* London: Dover.
Warhurst, C. and D. Nickson (2007), "Employee Experience of Aesthetic Labour," *Work, Employment and Society,* 21 (1): 103–20.
Wilson, E. (1987), *Adorned in Dreams: Fashion and Modernity,* Berkeley, CA: University of California Press.

Woodham, J. (1997), *Twentieth Century Design,* Oxford: Oxford University Press.
Woodward, S. (2007), *Why Women Wear What they Wear,* Oxford: Berg.
Yagou, A. (2011), "Foreword: Uniforms in Design-Historical Perspective," *Journal of Design History,* 24 (2): 101–04
Zakim, M. (2003), *Ready-Made Democracy: A History of Men's Dress in the American Republic 1760–1860,* Chicago: University of Chicago Press.

Figure 1.1 Sunbathing stewardesses at Schiphol Airport, Netherlands, 1962. National Archief, The Netherlands.

Part One

Uniforming Political Movements

This section addresses how the uniforming of political movements has been perceived and addressed by state authorities, and how standardized dress emboldens and gives force to political aspirations. Regulatory dress in the modern period most typically denotes centralized power; in relation to political settings, the authority to command uniformed bodies is generally the purview of the state and its agents. As such, the implicit threat of non-state actors to governance is greatly heightened when members appear in uniform. As Li Li describes in relation to female Red Guards in the Cultural Revolution in China, this threat is emphasized and disseminated through the circulation of images.

In the early twentieth century, the massing together of uniformed political movements was often permitted, enabling the development of very real threats to the status quo, often at times when civil authorities were preoccupied. Within a highly militarized society, these organizations tended to test the boundary between militia and paramilitary. The tumultuous period between the two world wars again saw the rise of uniformed movements that gave material expression to alternative political values, or engaged in brinkmanship through shows of strength disguised as ceremonial occasions, which were lent both legitimacy and menace by their uniform. Attempts to legislate against the wearing of political uniform, generally expressed in relation to public order and assembly, might be read as measures to ensure physical and symbolic acquiescence to the authority of the state. It also comes in the wake of violence on the part of uniformed political movements as discussed by Annebella Pollen; in 1930s Britain, this most directly related to riots emerging out of the actions of the black-shirted British Union of Fascists. In Ireland, an attempt to introduce a parliamentary Act restricting the wearing of uniform in the early 1930s was similarly conceived as a riposte to the militaristic Army Comrades Association (colloquially, the 'Blueshirts'). Other nation-states similarly have laws whose origins lie in specific historic experience with uniformed political organizations. In Germany, for example, section § 86a of the *Strafgesetzbuch* (Criminal Code) forbids the use of symbols, including uniform, of unconstitutional groups, whereas in France the lack of legislation suggests that uniform is not believed in itself to carry a militant threat, and yet the wearing of reservist uniform at political demonstrations is forbidden. French law also forbids the wearing of facial coverings, and while this has generally been discussed in relation to the so-called 'burqa ban,' it is also invoked in terms of lack of individuation, making it difficult to identify and prosecute dissidents at political protests. Conversely, the First Amendment to the American Constitution that guarantees freedom of expression and assembly means that 'uniformed' political organisations are more widely tolerated even if they constitute a clear threat to the rights of others, such as the white supremacist organization, the Ku Klux Klan. As discussed in these two essays, uniforms animate ideas of transformation and control that can be particularly persuasive, demonstrating how uniform creates opportunities for the release of forces that might otherwise lie dormant.

2

The Public Order Act: Defining Political Uniform in 1930s Britain

Annebella Pollen

In a 1933 speech reported in the press as "The Age of Shirts," G. K. Chesterton sought to rationalize a newly emerging sight on the streets of British cities. "It occurs to me", he wrote, "that what is happening today has always happened at intervals in human history. There are moments when a civilisation begins to stagger and grow bewildered," he explained, "People rush about. They form groups. They wear peculiar kinds of shirts." ("Gossip of the Day" 1933: 10). To Chesterton, the formation of political sects defined by distinctive attire was part of an enduring tradition. Another contemporary summary exploring the rise of uniforms on the streets of Britain found historical parallels in centuries-old European battle narratives: "During the English Civil Wars Cavaliers and Roundheads were easily distinguished by their clothing," it was noted. Equally, the same report observed that the red and white roses of the Houses of Lancaster and York respectively operated by dressed distinction; the colored shirts of the Camisards in the religious wars in France under Louis XIV and the red blouses of Garibaldi's troops during the Italian wars of liberation were also name-checked (*Meetings, Uniforms and Public Order* 1937: 6). Yet, while such approaches positioned the street skirmishes of the 1930s as part of a predictable continuity, many others, including Members of Parliament, felt that the rise of organized violence between rival political groups in clashing bodies as well as shirts required new interventions for new times. These debates crystallized in the passing of the British Public Order Act of 1936 which, in its opening salvo, banned the wearing of political uniform in public places. The Act still stands (1 Edw. 8 & 1 Geo. 6 c. 6).

Under the auspices of the Act political uniform was never clearly defined; indeed, the core difficulty of articulating its object was a central point of contention in the formation of the initial Bill and its later implementation as law. As such, the Act offers a pertinent focus for exploring the challenges and limits for understanding uniform as a category more broadly. While the Act was partly structured to dismantle the ascendant power of the British Union of Fascists ('the Blackshirts') by attacking a central aspect of their collective identity, the ruling also had a wider knock-on effect on other 'shirted' organizations of diverse purposes, resulting in a variety of legal outcomes tested through telling court cases. This essay examines the broader purposes of the Act and its wider reaches and explores in particular the opposing fortunes of two lesser-known green-shirted organizations that came within its reach. Drawing on parliamentary reports, Home Office correspondence, institutional literature, and press reaction, the essay explores the philosophical debates that played out around the meaning of uniform at the formation of the Act, the creative clothing strategies employed in reaction to the ban, and its legacy for political organizations in the present day.

A foreign force

The emergence of colored shirts as the dress choice for a novel form of political street action was observed from the early 1930s; some contemporary observers even considered it to be a part of the experience of urban modernity alongside trends for sport, the emergence of high-speed transport and electric light (Coupland 2004: 101). The British Union of Fascists (BUF), formed in October 1932 and led by Sir Oswald Mosley, adopted from the outset the black shirt that had been made emblematic of Italian fascist politics by Benito Mussolini from the early 1920s. Initially in a design that buttoned at the neck and shoulder, the striking garment was frequently likened to a fencing shirt. Especially when combined with a high black belt, tight black leggings and angled black beret, it undoubtedly signalled the group's ambitions to become a "trained and disciplined force" (Coupland 2004: 100–01). Although, as noted above, a variety of British historic groupings with political intentions had long expressed allegiance through collective garb, in the 1930s this particular manifestation of political uniform was largely seen as a continental import. As will be shown, discussion in the press often highlighted the emergence of political uniforms as un-British in character; a by-product of foreign feeling and method. Alongside Italians in black shirts, brown-shirted German National Socialists were becoming familiar sights in news media. As such, the green-, blue-, and red-shirted uniformed campaign groups on home territory were considered alien in the first attempts to legislate against them.

In his 1934 effort to introduce a bill of prohibition, Commander Locker-Lampson stated: "The appearance of uniforms in British public life must mean the gradual extinction of government by consent, and the substitution of government by coercion." It was "this new spirit of foreign force in our affairs" that the Bill was meant to counter ("Party Uniforms" 1934: 7). Despite the precedent set by Holland, Switzerland, and Sweden in introducing similar bans, it was not until 1936 that such a Bill was approved in Britain. Regular street violence during the autumn of that year, including the famous Battle of Cable Street where black-shirted fascist groups attempted to forcibly process through the Jewish East End of London and were met by a major counter-offensive, resulting in unprecedented and unsustainable levels of policing. Public meetings and political speakers on the streets frequently finished in physical fights. 'Political organizations', the euphemistic term mostly intended to describe fascist and communist formations, were increasingly adopting highly organized tactics. Marching bands, drum corps, and uniformed parades with flags created a quasi-military aesthetic that sometimes functioned as a front for political violence. As one contemporary source put it:

> The rise of bodies trained to act with military precision, which might even in time, through their influence over the undisciplined masses and the glamor which their uniforms and public display shed around then, make an attempt to seize power in the State by revolutionary means, perhaps by the use of armed force, seemed to reasonable and moderate men of all parties to call for suppression at the very outset.
> *Meetings, Uniforms and Public Order* 1937: 4

Early attempts at enforcing a ban were thrown out by the force of counter-arguments, including the risk, noted by Lord Winterton, that it might represent "the greatest possible advertisement for Sir Oswald Mosley's movement," resulting in "cheap ready-made martyrdom" ("Party Uniforms" 1934: 7). As will be discussed below, parliamentary debates raised core concerns: the need to create a wider principle would mean that other smaller uniformed organizations who posed no threat to public order would be outlawed alongside those that the Act was designed to hit hardest. There was also the fundamental and thorny issue of how political uniform might be defined.

"Seven shades of shirt"

Although the Public Order Act was drafted to deal with serious acts of violence and disorder, the fact that its first clause dealt with matters of clothing meant that some of the parliamentary and press discussions adopted a playful tone about its possible execution. For example, Commander Locker-Lampson's statement that he did not want to prohibit the wearing of shirts, or as the press put it that "he did not want people to go about in singlets" ("Party Uniforms" 1934: 7) provided much amusement in the House. Satirical writers also made great play with the Act's comic potential, including its legislation against particular colors. 'Richardson,' in the *Yorkshire Evening Post*, wrote of the palette:

> Quite a number of organisations in this country can now be identified by the distinctive colour of the shirts chosen by members. [...] This distinctive coloured shirt idea is a good one – it is nice to be able to see, at a glance, a man's political opinions, and avoid getting a sock on the ear for saying the wrong thing – and there is sure to be a run on the few remaining colours. There are not many left, and they are rapidly being snapped up. The Purple Shirt Publicans has already been reserved, while it is only a matter of days before we hear of Tangerine Shirt Tram-drivers, the Ultramarine Shirt Unitarians, the Brown Shirt Bookbinders and the Orange Shirt Organ-grinders.
>
> "Gossip of the Day" 1933: 10

Another columnist, writing for the *Dundee Courier*, noted, "Red shirts provoke bulls and Conservatives; blue shirts provoke Socialists and Communists; green shirts are certain to inflame Orangemen; and orange shirts bring out the worst that is in Celtic Hibernian nature. Nothing is safe but what the artists call the broken colours" ("What is a Uniform?" 1937: 4).

The Star newspaper delineated "seven shades of shirt" worn in Britain by political organizations in November 1936. These were black shirts by the British Union of Fascists and the Imperial Fascist League; blue by the Kensington Fascists (an off-shoot of the BUF); gray by the United Empire Fascist Party; red by the Independent Labour Party Guild of Youth; green by Social Credit economic reformers; brown (khaki) by Communist Youth organizations, and white "by a political body in Manchester" (cited in *Meetings, Uniforms and Public Order* 1937: 7). In Home Office internal documentation, a clutch of blacklisted organizations, pre-designated as both political and uniformed, was the Act's first formal target. Their overlapping list of groups included the British Union of Fascists, the Imperial Fascist League, the Italian Fascisti, the Social Credit Party, the Young Communist League, Young Pioneers (a children's organization within the Communist Party), the Independent Labour Party Guild of Youth, and the Legion of Blue and White Shirts (an anti-Fascist and anti-Communist Jewish organization). Each of these groups was written to in advance of the Act becoming law, and the Secretary of State advised that any person publicly wearing uniform signifying his association with those organizations "should be regarded by the Police as offending against the prohibition in Section 1 of the Act" (Home Office 1936: 2).

Some groups responded to say that the Act did not apply to them as they had disbanded, in the case of the Young Pioneers (Gollan 1936); they were non-political, in the case of the Italian Fascists, who claimed to be involved only in "benevolent and social work" (Camagna 1936); or that their garments were not a uniform but an outfit worn for "rambles, for sports purposes, and on week-end outings," in the case of the Independent Labour Party Guild of Youth (Brockway 1936). Surprisingly, others expressed gratitude for the ruling. For example, the Imperial Fascist League wrote to the Commissioner of Police to thank him: "so many of our members are unable to afford to buy the uniforms we had to adopt to compete with other bodies," adding that they were loath to shatter the Home Secretary's illusions that they were a uniformed body and requested that the Commissioner "keep this aspect 'dark'" (Ridout 1936). Among those who did not deny their political purpose and valued their uniform as part of their propaganda purpose, there was understandable anxiety about the detail of the prohibition. How could satisfactory adaptations be made to keep a collective identity but remain on the right side of the law? What constituted a political uniform, exactly? Frustratingly, there was no definition given.

Vaguely nebulous

In the frivolous spirit noted above, members of the House of Parliament grappled with the lexicon of clothing. While failing to take it seriously, they nonetheless acknowledged its slippery, polysemic character. As one unnamed contributor to parliamentary discussions is reported to have stated, "It was impossible to lay down a hard and fast rule as to when garments ended and uniforms began" ("Kilt is not under political uniform ban" 1936: 5).

Must a uniform be a complete outfit? Would a tie with political insignia count? What about a rosette, badge, armband, sash? What about ceremonial regalia? Is traditional dress worn by a Scottish nationalist campaigning for Home Rule a political uniform? Must a political uniform be a formal dress shirt? And what was to be done about "ladies who wore black blouses out of sympathy with the leader of the Fascists" ("Parliamentary Sketch" 1936: 9)? At times the lack of certainty seemed to smack of a failure of nerve. The Attorney-General likened uniform to an elephant: you can't define it, but you know what it is when you see it (*Meetings, Uniforms and Public Order* 1937: 10). This side-step meant that magistrates must decide in court if "striped hatbands, monocles of blue glass, or large iron rings in their noses" could constitute political apparel on the wrong side of the law (*Meetings, Uniforms and Public Order* 1937: 9).

Although there was some frustration by prosecutors that the Act was "vaguely nebulous" on its central point ("Political Uniform Test Case" 1937: 5), there was also some admiration for the deliberately perverse strategy. The *Bystander* journalist A. G. Macdonell celebrated it as a "characteristically British" piece of common sense. "It is a perfectly good way out of a difficult legal technicality," he added (1936: 271). The deliberately open-ended response was also a pre-emptive strike to counter the "ingenious devices" that had been deployed by the Nazis when their uniform had been prohibited by German authorities. It was noted that they simply changed their allegiance to a new form of hat or buttonhole flower (*Meetings, Uniforms and Public Order* 1937: 10). After much deliberation, in the final detail of the Act it was given to the courts to decide on a case-by-case basis. In the absence of a statutory definition, magistrates were to refer to the 'ordinary meaning' of the term in everyday usage. "It appears from the definition given in standard dictionaries," the Home Office advised police, that "'uniform' connotes some dress or at any rate the substantial part of some dress." Further, "the dress or part of the dress must be distinctive of, and peculiar to, the class of persons wearing it" (Home Office 1936: 1). The Act allowed maximum flexibility, but there were inevitably many gray areas.

Suppressing the rainbow

Parliamentary debate on the Public Order Bill on November 23 and December 7, 1936, resolved that a uniform need not comprise a full set of garments. Singular items could be considered; a tie alone would not be considered uniform, but a shirt might. Certain shirts, however, were considered more uniform than others. Some of these rulings were convenient for the BUF, who drew on the preparatory discussions of the Attorney General and the Home Secretary in the House of Commons. They hung in particular onto the following words that seemed to allow fascists to continue to sport a distinctive livery: "If in future they merely wear a black shirt and otherwise wear diverse clothes, some flannels, other corduroys, and so on, it is most improbably that any court will hold that they are wearing a Blackshirt" (cited in Francis-Hawkins 1936). The BUF saw a way to keep a form of black shirt through this concession, supported by the fact that similar garments, in their words, "can be bought in any shop, and have been worn for long past by some members of the public in no way associated with this organization" (Francis-Hawkins 1937). In a seeming contradiction, however, the Commissioner of Police in London told Independent Labour Party members that the red shirts and blouses of the Guild of Youth would be treated as a breach of the law (Brockway 1936). Here, the wearing of colored shirts as ideological devices was also confused by their rising popularity as everyday wear in interwar fashion. As a journalist for the *Evening News* noted in 1933:

> Red Shirts have become very popular. In one sense they have become too popular. Red shirts are being sold to the general public in such large numbers that they are not so distinctive as a political badge as they used to be. Some shirt shops in the West End look like branches of the Guild of Youth. They aren't, of course.
>
> "The Age of 'Shirts'" 1930: 7

In a gesture of leniency, the Act allowed the wearing of political emblems on ordinary clothes to escape the definition of uniform. It also permitted the wearing of political uniform for special occasions (although special dispensation needed to be granted, and Home Office records for 1937 show that most requests, especially those by the BUF, were denied). The wearing of uniform by non-political groups continued. For the purposes of the Act, the latter included uniformed organizations "such as the Salvation Army, the Boy Scouts, the Church Lads' Brigade, Commissionaires, hospital nurses, and other similar bodies" (Home Office 1936: 1). Many of these groupings had the additional protection of the Chartered Associations (Protection of Names and Uniforms) Act of 1926, which permitted designated members to wear a formally recognized set of garments and insignia; this applied, for example, to St John Ambulance, Girl Guides, and Boy Scouts. While some of the groups considered non-political might seem to have distinctive ideological aims and purposes sometimes informed by a religious, imperialist, or military ethos, the term 'political' in the Act was largely applied to formal party political groupings rather than leisure and occupational organizations. While this was an attempt to designate different organizations as eligible or otherwise for prosecution, in practice there were issues of clarity demonstrated by the protracted internal discussions within the Home Office files about whether disparate organizations—from the Labour Party Male Voice Choir and the Loyal Orange Institution to the Quaker Land Corps of agricultural volunteers—could come under the Act's jurisdiction. What was and was not political was arrived at with a similar fuzziness to the Act's other avoidances. In a court case following its passage into law, as the case for the defense put it, "the word 'political' is as difficult to define as the word 'uniform'" ("R. v. Taylor, Hawthorn, Ward" 1937: 6).

With the passing of the Act on January 1, 1937, however, prosecutions followed almost immediately. Some cases seemed cut and dried. The BUF, for example, abandoned their stylized fencing garb but their sympathizers continued to dress in ordinary black garments, sometimes decorated with fascist insignia. Within a month of the Act's passing, a man was arrested in Leeds for selling copies of the BUF newspaper, *Action*, while wearing a peaked cap with two BUF cap badges, a black shirt, and black tie. While he argued that he was selling a newspaper and was thus merely identifying himself as a news vendor rather than a party member, the court was not convinced. During his prosecution, the fascist complained, "What about the Green Shirts with their green berets?" ("Political Uniform Test Case" 1937:5) Those who wore green shirts on the streets of 1930s Britain were a complicated case, and their fortunes were more varied than those of the Blackshirts. As such, they offer a lesser-known but rich narrative of uniform and its complex trajectories and purposes.

"The Lilywhite Boys, Clothed all in Green-O"

Carrying drums, banners, and flags, green-shirted brigades marched in synchronized formation around Britain's urban centers on a regular basis in the 1930s. Smartly turned out, and including women as well as men, the group had an original repertoire of rousing songs and striking insignia. Sometimes cryptic in meaning, their banners variously read, "Would the Maggot Starve because the Apple was too Big?" and "Demand the Wages of the Machine!" Their visual fashioning and declamatory addresses shared a quasi-military style with the fascists, but their politics were wholly opposed.

The Green Shirt movement for Social Credit, later the Social Credit Party of Great Britain and Ireland (1935–51), campaigned for radical economic reform in a period of deep financial crisis. They espoused the Social Credit system of Major C. H. Douglas, a complex form of economic redistribution that included the payment of a National Dividend to every citizen, and the welcoming in of a leisure society. Global finance was the enemy for these reformers, who saw the money system as a corrupt and mystifying force conspiring to introduce scarcity in an age of plenty. The methods of the group were in some ways conventional for campaigners of the period, including the production of printed literature, the delivery of rousing speeches from street rostrums, and banner-laden parades. However, in other ways they were highly idiosyncratic. The group burned effigies of the Governor of the Bank of England, dressed as robots to show the potential for mechanized labor, and threw painted bricks through the windows of 10 and 11 Downing Street (Drakeford 1997; Pollen 2015). These agit-prop techniques were supported by highly invested organizational signs including a double K 'key' symbol, said to signify the twin aims that the group wished to unlock—prosperity and leisure—and a green shirt.

While economics was a pressing topic for all social reformers responding to the new conditions of the 1930s, the Social Credit system was a distinctive contribution to the mix. It was underpinned by a complex mathematical formula that few could understand, but for those intrigued enough to want to know more it was far from clear why an economic system should be promoted through ritualized performances, a songbook of original folksongs, the carrying of blazing torches, and a uniformed presence. For those with longer memories, however, the background of the organization's leader helped explain certain symbols and styles. John Hargrave, the charismatic podium speaker and the chief orchestrator of the Social Credit Party's visual aesthetic and public methods, was a novelist, illustrator, and long-standing layout man for an advertising agency. Highly knowledgeable about persuasion and propaganda through his professional experience at the cutting edge of commercial techniques, he also knew first-hand what made a compelling leader, having first risen to second-in-command in the Boy Scouts in the 1910s and then to the head of his own organization, the Kindred of the Kibbo Kift, from 1920. A decade at the helm of a green shirted "youth group for all ages" had honed his interest in social reform techniques that incorporated pageantry and collective participation, mysticism and personal magnetism (Pollen 2015).

Kibbo Kift, whose name meant 'proof of strength,' started life as a pacifist splinter group of the Scouts, but from the outset their covenant required members to commit to campaigns for personal mental, physical, and spiritual fitness, and for social, educational, and economic reform, alongside global ambitions for world government and world peace. With high-profile support from leading figures in the arts and sciences, but with a membership only a few hundred-strong, the daily practices at Kibbo Kift meetings and camps were a blend of self-developmental primitivist practices adapted from the roots of scouting and hands-on political actions including child-centered education, craft manufacture, and anti-war demonstrations. At all events, a specific costume had to be worn. Hargrave had a keen sense of personal style and a wide knowledge of avant-garde design. As such, Kibbo Kift wardrobes variously included priestly robes and scanty exercise attire—always homemade. The core camping and hiking kit was, importantly, all in green (Figure 2.1). Men wore green jerkins and shorts, a combination of a Native American hunting shirt upper with the bottom half of the scouts. Drama was provided through the addition of green pointed hoods or cowls, floor-length cloaks, and for women, Valkyrie-like suede helmets over a green two-piece. Hargrave felt the color green to have deep symbolic importance for those who venerated nature; he called it "the sharp, brilliant vert of the first thrusting leaf-spears of the vernal equinox" (Hargrave n.d.).

As Kibbo Kift began to develop political philosophies, and particularly as they made the economic theories of Major Douglas ever more central, their so-called 'habit' became more uniform in appearance, in both senses of the word. By the time the organization entered its second decade, no closer to achieving its lofty aims and with seriously dwindling numbers in the low hundreds, Hargrave resolved to refocus on economic reform alone. With a dramatic flourish, in 1931 his organization cast aside camping and craft and became instead a mouthpiece for financial change. This sudden shift caused inevitable rifts among those who were unable to follow their leader's new direction. However, Hargrave was keen

Figure 2.1 Kibbo Kift men and boys in the 'Touching of the Totems' rite, 1925. © Kibbo Kift Foundation.

to reassure those that remained that this was not a U-turn in proceedings, but a natural development that had been planned all along. As such, he regularly revisited the group's philosophy to reframe it to this new end, and carefully retained key elements of continuity from the earlier organization into its later development. The endurance of the green shirt was central.

A new model army

From 1931, Hargrave also created a new streamlined urban identity for his followers (Figure 2.2). His men were now sharp-shouldered in white buckskin-belted tunics with asymmetrical fastenings, rakish caps, tailored shorts, and cable-knit knee socks. The earlier hoods remained, but were now lined with white silk. The outfit was professionally produced rather than hand-cut and glued. Economic reform might not need a uniform, but Hargrave defended its

Figure 2.2 Remodeled Kibbo Kift uniform marking shift in group identity, 1931.
© Kibbo Kift Foundation.

inclusion as an essential part of group technique. He asserted, "Kinsmen must bear in mind that the public will form its opinion of the efficiency and capabilities of The Kindred from the impression it receives of Kinsmen in habit" ("Kincouncil Decrees and Notices: Men's Habit" 1931: 1). For any who saw a core contradiction in the group's origins as anti-war scouts, Hargrave asserted that their military style and comportment was akin to the Royal Army Medical Corps, with whom he had served in the First World War. They must pursue their Social Credit aims with a similar "unarmed military technique," and as such, they aimed to become "a New Economic Corps. A military, or soldierlike, formation and method is forced upon us because the British People (whether it knows it or not) is at war. It is an economic war, but war nevertheless" (Hargrave 1931: 3).

Initially, the 'green habit' demonstrated the group's roots in Kibbo Kift, which had achieved plentiful press attention in Britain, largely due to its striking appearance, and also some success abroad through Hargrave's publications on woodcraft techniques of outdoor living (see, for example, Hargrave 1919). Hoping to transfer these associations to his 'New Model Army,' he claimed: "Before long, whenever the old English hunting green is worn, the public will know that it stands FOR THE BRITISH PEOPLE AGAINST INTERNATIONAL FINANCE!" ("Welcome to the Green Shirts" 1931: 3). In order to achieve a smooth transition from a camp and campaign group into a full political party, however, several years of compromises and transformations were made.

The first was that the highly stylized outfit of 1931 proved too expensive for most, and Hargrave intended to create a mass movement. Off-the-shelf green shirts replaced the tailored tunic. The hood, shorts, and knee socks that had marked a connection to the hiking years were also hard to explain to the new recruits who came to economic reform from different backgrounds. In particular, Hargrave sought allegiance with the League of Unemployed, which included large numbers of jobless men in the north of England and leaders with economic reform sympathies. These men were supplied with free green shirts to wear so they could maintain an organized appearance and show their connection as an associated group, with costs covered by Hargrave's advertising director employer, Colin Hurry, a wealthy Social Credit supporter. In time, to boost numbers, these associate members were brought into the fold as part of a wider Social Credit 'movement,' and the informal nickname they had acquired as the 'Green Shirts' was adopted as an official addition. By 1933, this title completely replaced the hard-to-understand term 'Kibbo Kift.'

Although the second version of Green Shirt 'kit' (Figure 2.3) consisted of a dark green shirt ('blouse pattern'), a black leather belt with brass buckle, and

Figure 2.3 Green Shirts in street marching uniform, 1932. © Kibbo Kift Foundation.

a dark green beret (with badge on left), to be worn with "ordinary gray flannel trousers," this was not essential to begin with: "the Green Shirt, worn with any kind of trousers, is all that is necessary to make a start" ("Come On, The Green Shirts!" 1933: 3). Through the supply of mass-produced green shirts for followers, Hargrave was able to cheaply build numbers across the country and to multiply the organization's visual presence. As he asserted, somewhat optimistically, "there is no doubt that we begin to succeed in giving political significance to the colour known as 'hunting green', or Kin green" ("Welcome to the Green Shirts" 1931: 3). The shade was carefully managed by Hargrave. He emphasized that it was "a dark 'bottle' green, very like Lincoln green and Kendal green" ("Welcome to the Green Shirts" 1931: 3) and elsewhere warned against "sage green, olive green, or any dull green paint or fabric" (Hargrave 1935: 3). The green must be bright; as Hargrave put it, in typical evangelical tones, "It is the outward and visible sign of LIFE BREAKING OUT of the Grave of the Living Dead" (Hargrave 1935: 3). Drums, flags, banners, and printed matter were all produced in striking green, with white and black highlights. Hargrave argued:

> If we wish to have an effect upon anyone – educated or uneducated – we must first of all open their mind through one of the five senses. You must know how to play on their emotions, and the best method is to show them things, not ideas.
>
> You must be seen and heard. Every colour has its own emotion – green has a very particular one; it is automatic and an idea is attached to it. It sounds abstract but for the Green Shirt Movement for Social Credit it is very important.
>
> "Replacing the Loss of Propaganda Power" 1934: 4

Because of the centrality of "soldierly smartness" to the Green Shirts ("Kincouncil Decrees and Notices" 1931: 1), it was inevitable that they would come under the jurisdiction of the Public Order Act, even though they did not align themselves with communism or fascism and proposed an alternative direction. Undoubtedly, the aims of the Green Shirts were political, not least as they made the transition in 1935 from a campaign group to a formal party. In the last month of 1936, on the eve of the Act becoming law, Green Shirts campaigned inside and outside the Houses of Parliament, arguing for their orderliness and good reputation, and protesting the 'un-Britishness' of the Bill. Principal among their concerns was how they would convey their message without their display techniques. As always, members were encouraged to obey the law. They were told, through their official gazette, "We do not want martyrs – yet! Better to have Green Shirts on the streets than in prison" ("The Public Order Act, 1936" 1936: 3). But a core consideration was "What are we to do to compensate for the loss sustained under the Act?" (Tacey 1937: 2) In many ways, for Green Shirts, their medium was their message. Without it, they were economic theory alone.

After the Act was passed, Charles Tacey, the Green Shirts' Director of Propaganda reflected,

> We used the uniform as a 'magnet' to draw the eyes of the public. We are now deprived of utilising this method of attraction and so must develop others to replace it. While the uniform could be displayed publicly every Green Shirt in uniform was a living advertisement for Social Credit. Heads were turned and interest quickened whenever a 'shock trooper' walked down a street.
>
> TACEY, 1937: 2

Drums, flags, and banners were not outlawed by the Act, and the Green Shirts adopted a similar strategy to Blackshirts in their adoption of ordinary colored shirts and ties, and the continued use of badges, street meetings, and parades. As with the Blackshirts, however, they were also charged with breaches of the Act, and—as will be discussed below—green-clad members came twice before court.

"There are shirts and shirts!"

The first charge was at Camberwell in London in April 1937. A civilian lodged the initial complaint to the police, noting that a speaker at a Social Credit Party rally wore a green shirt, with a green collar and tie, which featured "small interwoven inscriptions of the Movement" (the double K). He also wore gray flannel trousers and a dark belt. In court, the magistrate was shown the shirt-and-tie ensemble worn on the day of arrest alongside the former uniform of the organization before the ban. As the case for the defense summarized, "There are shirts and shirts!" He noted that "the recognised uniform of the Party, with its pleated pockets and silver buttons and all the rest of it [...] is what you might call a blouse-shirt." By this, he signaled the stylized nature of the garment and its separation from everyday wear: "It is not the sort of shirt that any of us would wear unless we were connected with some peculiar body who wore such things." He concluded, "it is impossible to say a man wearing a green shirt is wearing uniform" ("Camberwell, April 1937"). The case was dismissed.

In a second incident in Luton in April 1936, permission had been granted for the Social Credit Party to hold an outdoor meeting. Two group members were accused of wearing party emblems, and the prosecution reminded them that it was not necessary to be wearing a full uniform to fall under the Act's reach. On the day, thirty-four men and women had assembled with drums, flags, buttonhole badges, arm badges, and ties. They had set up a rostrum with flags and paraded. Torches were lit, songs sung, speeches made. Mid-way through the meeting, a police officer suggested that the speaker was in uniform, and three Green Shirt men—Ward, Taylor, and Hawthorn—were arrested and charged. In court it was noted that "Ward was dressed in a green jersey, green shirt, green tie, fawn raincoat of military pattern and an armlet with the reversed K and the ordinary K sign. Taylor was wearing an ordinary suit, green tie, green armlet with the double K and a badge with a similar sign in the lapel of his jacket." With recourse to the dictionary definition of uniform, the defense put an argument that what his clients were wearing was neither distinctive nor uniform (one wore a "sweater" and one an everyday shirt). One of the accused said the shirt was a sports shirt purchased some time before for a sea-trip. He claimed to merely like the color: "My room at home is decorated in green" ("R. v. Taylor, Hawthorn, Ward" 1937). The magistrate again dismissed the case.

Press reports afterwards showed some disappointment with the ready acquiescence of the accused in Public Order Act trials. As journalist D. B. Wyndham Lewis reflected, on the Green Shirts, "They didn't put up a very impressive show in court. They seemed to us a shade too anxious to explain away their greenery." He argued that Green Shirts "surely ought to show the same grim fire-eyed defiance when up before the beak for wearing Social Credit colors as they did when they marched recently to Trafalgar Square to demonstrate sympathy for the Spanish Reds?" In both cases, he lamented a "notable absence of devilry when up against the authorities. It doesn't ring true after the manifestos" (Wyndham Lewis 1937: 545). It is true that there was a discrepancy between the tenor of the claims on the printed page and Green Shirt behavior in court. In the pages of his magazine, Hargrave proclaimed that his group were practicing "guerrilla" tactics in a "Holy War" against corporate finance (Hargrave 1937: 2). Following the uniform ban, however, the eschatological fervor of the group was undoubtedly dampened. In a last hurrah that showed Hargrave's ad-man's innovation, a May Day Demonstration in 1938 saw: "a contingent marched in formation carrying their green shirts on poles." The accompanying posters declared: "Shirt or No Shirt – Social Credit is Coming!" As Hargrave gloated, "the 'banned' uniform went on parade, and the authorities dare not make such fools of themselves as to arrest a contingent of shirts with no men in them! There's going to be more of this" (1938: 3).

There was, however, to be little more. A series of blows to the Green Shirt cause, including a break with Major Douglas over his anti-Semitism, an unsuccessful attempt by Hargrave to apply Social Credit to a province in Canada, and the coming war meant that the fervour of the Green Shirts-without-Shirts dwindled during the conflict. The group was of insufficient numbers and popularity to have much impact when briefly revived subsequently, and in 1951 it closed entirely. The banning of political uniforms had destabilized the popularity of the BUF, but it incidentally played a role in demolishing the Social Credit Party. Hard-line Social Credit loyalists looked back in later years with a revisionist view that made the Act all about them. As one former member put it in 1979, it was "a measure ostensibly aimed at the Fascist Blackshirts, but which also conveniently (for the authorities) struck at the Social Credit Party, increasingly seen by the Money Power as the real danger for their established order" (Elwell-Sutton 1979: 5). Imagined power and imagined threats were embodied in a battle over a uniform that could not even be defined.

Children in costume

Home Office files contain extensive correspondence with and about another green-shirted organization that had rather different experiences at the hands of the authorities. In February 1937, the leader of the children's organization, Woodcraft Folk, sought advice about whether members in organizational clothing would be at risk from the Public Order Act ("Woodcraft Folk International Camp at Brighton" 1937). Specifically, their enquiry related to their planned international summer camp, to be held over three weeks on the south coast of England. The Home Office was torn: was this a political organization, and was it uniformed? Woodcraft Folk described their aims as educational, and specifically referred to their dress as "costume" (Pollen 2016). The organization had been formed in 1925 as a direct splinter group of Kibbo Kift, following a 1924 dispute about ideological approach and organizational method. Its green outfit, based around rustic hand-crafted fringed jerkins and shorts, rucksacks, and decorated leather belts, shared much with the early attire of Kibbo Kift, but its status in relation to the jurisdiction of the Public Order Act was less clear cut. In the Home Office's initial estimation, Woodcraft Folk were "a socialist counterpart of the Scouts movement" whose "avowed objects include active opposition to War and to Fascism" but they were aware that there was some absurdity of applying the Act to clothes worn by children under fifteen, "unless", they hesitated, *"there is a very strong and clear political element"* ("Woodcraft Folk International Camp at Brighton" 1937; italics in original). What would constitute 'strong and clear?' Special Branch had followed Woodcraft Folk since at least the early 1930s; their report to the Home Office had found little political activity beyond a general alliance with progressives and pacifists.

The event organizer, Henry Fair, informed the Home Office that up to 2,000 international children would also be attending in their various organizational uniforms, including the blue shirts and red neckerchiefs of the European Red Falcons, who were directly aligned to Socialist Education International. Home Office staff asked among themselves: should permission be granted, and on what basis? There was some reluctance. The application seemed innocuous, but the possible repercussion of any precedent was cause for concern: "how can we deal with an application for uniform in camp by the Young Communist League, the Young Fascisti, or the Young Pioneers?" ("Woodcraft Folk International Camp at Brighton" 1937). The Woodcraft Folk's socialist interests meant that they could not be simply described as non-political, like Boy Scouts, who were exempt from the Act. The final compromise was to not "upset the plans for a children's camp, by insisting that they must not wear their green jerkins and shorts," and permission was granted "on the condition that no person wearing the uniform shall attend any meeting of a political nature, or take part in a procession in the nature of a political demonstration" ("Woodcraft Folk International Camp at Brighton" 1937).

Political jerkins

In August, however, with camp proceedings well underway, *Daily Telegraph* and *News Chronicle* carried reports emphasizing the political nature of the event ("Red Flag" 1937; "Youth's Challenge to Fascism" 1937). Children were claimed to be flying the red flag, making clenched fist salutes and singing the *Internationale*. A new file was opened. Had the Act been breached? The Home Office noted, "There can be no doubt now that the people at this camp are members of political organizations" ("Woodcraft Folk International Camp at Rottingdean" 1937). The fascists also went down to investigate. In an inflammatory report in their news sheet, *Action*, entitled "Home and Foreign Reds in Public Order Act Evasion. Will the Government Act?" A. K. Chesterton complained:

> ...while patriotic Britons are forbidden to wear the uniform of their political creed, and immediately command the attention of the police should they appear even in an undress black shirt, hordes of Reds and Pinks from all over Europe are at this moment assembled upon the Downs at Overdene [sic] Camp, near Brighton, wearing two distinct uniforms and giving the Communist salute.

He fantasised:

> Suppose we had invited a German S.A. man, with a sprinkling of Hitler Jugend and Italian Ballila, to our encampment at Selsey; suppose we had then labelled it a 'children's camp'; suppose we had ourselves dressed in green or blue or any other colour of shirt or jerkin; suppose we had marched through Chichester thus attired, giving the Fascist salute—how long would we have found ourselves out of jail? Twenty-four hours at the most. Yet Jews, aliens and Reds are allowed to do all these things with impunity.
> CHESTERTON 1937: 11

The Chief Commissioner of Police was more measured in his appraisal. He noted in internal correspondence that there was 'left wing sympathy' in the camp, and that red flags flew, but they did so alongside the multi-colored flags of the cooperative movement. No political speeches were made, and the only complaints were about the volume of the loudspeakers, not the content of the announcement. A band played on the Level (a public park in the town) but no political speeches were made; the inoffensive uniform of the band was "white cricket shirts, short blue trousers and blue blazers" ("Woodcraft Folk International Camp at Rottingdean" 1937). Despite the organization's conformity to police requirements, the apolitical status of the camp was nevertheless on shaky ground, from both right and left perspectives. The *Daily Worker*, for example, claimed it as "a splendid training ground for future fighters for a Socialist Europe" ("Well Done Woodcraft" 1937).

In the end, no prosecution was made, but Woodcraft Folk took the threat to their legal status seriously, choosing to keep their 'costume' as an important part of their collective identity but progressively emphasising their educational purposes over political aims (Davis 2000). They could not have both. These priorities endure, although for different reasons. With around 15,000 current members, Woodcraft Folk's non-party political interests are a core component of its charitable status (Woodcraft Folk 2011). While the organization still takes part in anti-war parades and other pacifist protests, it advises its members never to appear in Woodcraft Folk attire at political demonstrations. When protest becomes politics with a capital P, the organization's status is put at risk. Woodcraft Folk was undoubtedly founded on socialist sympathies, but these have become increasingly diffuse and are no longer party political. Curiously, despite the fact that most members now opt not to wear a green shirt, or even a casual T-shirt with the organization's logo, in recent times, 'costume' has been redesignated in order for the organization to be eligible for support through government funding schemes. Woodcraft Folk is now recognized as a "uniformed youth group" alongside Police Cadets, the Boys' Brigade, and the Scout Association, organizations to which they were once ideologically opposed (Woodcraft Folk 2015). Both political status and the definition of uniform are evidently mutable, dependent on circumstances, and remain in the eye of the beholder.

The fabric of intimidation

The mixed fates of green-shirted organizations under the Public Order Act reveal the mobility and flexibility of both terms in the loaded phrase 'political uniform.' Clothing has a complex terminology, and words such as kit, costume and habit have their own distinctive meanings that are not simply synonymous. When is a shirt a blouse, a sweater, or a jerkin? It was on these points of detail that fortunes rested in 1937. Uniforms are perhaps the most coded of all clothes, freighted with declamatory signification. They perform allegiance, belief, and identity, yet they are also, as Jennifer Craik puts it, "ambiguous masks" (2005: 6).

When do fabric and buttons become political? As the above examples have shown, uniformed political identity can be performed, subverted or denied according to slight variations in cut, color, and cloth. Clothes can suggest multiple meanings to different viewers in the same instant, while identical garments can mean entirely different things in altered circumstances. In some cases these differences were enough to carry prison sentences, and yet the object at the very center of the legislation repeatedly slipped out of view. The power of uniform is such that it can simultaneously be the subject of legal protection and prosecution. A set of garments associated with orderliness and discipline sits at the very centre of concerns about public disorder; these multiple contradictions demonstrate political uniform's complexity and, ironically, its lack of uniformity.

The Public Order Act of 1936 was controversial at the time of its devising and was riddled with contradictions in its implementation. The opening clause is less than twenty-five words long, but it required three hours of parliamentary discussion, and was approved only after eighty-six amendments ("Party Uniforms" 1936: 8). More than eighty years on, it retains its force. Recent prosecutions under the Act have taken place against Britain First, a far-right group that describes itself as a "patriotic political party" (Britain First 2018). On the most recent occasion, in 2016, members processed through Luton town center on a so-called 'Christian Patrol.' Their leader, Paul Golding, carried a large cross, and handed out inflammatory anti-Islam literature. Dressed in green zip-up fleece jackets and beanie hats, each emblazoned with the Britain First insignia of crown, Union Jack, and a golden lion, the massed bodies were undoubtedly uniform in appearance and political in purpose. Despite fleeces being most commonly associated with casual outdoor wear and middle-aged comfort, the prosecution described them as 'intimidating.' Golding pleaded guilty to the charges and received a substantial fine (Mortimer 2016). Almost a century later, a law originally designed to curb the uniformed violence of the BUF continues to be utilized. That Britain First wear green instead of black, and fleece instead of formal wear, is of no consequence. What indicates comfort in one context can signal conflict in another. The flexibility of the Act acknowledges that political uniform continues to take multiple shapes and forms.

References

Britain First. Available online: https://www.britainfirst.org/ [accessed January 4, 2018]

Brockway, F. [Secretary, Independent Labour Party] letter to Commissioner of Police, December 30, 1936. The National Archives MEPO 3/2513 Public Order Act 1936: Instructions to Police.

Camagna, C. [Secretary, Fascio di Londra], letter to Commissioner of Police, December 30, 1936. The National Archives MEPO 3/2513 Public Order Act 1936: Instructions to Police.

"Camberwell, April 1937" [typed report of a 1937 Green Shirt court case]. Correspondence and papers concerning the Public Order Act, 1936. Youth Movement Archive, London School of Economics Library, Kibbo Kift papers YMA/KK/56.

Chartered Associations (Protection of Names and Uniforms) Act 1926, c.26 Regnal. 16 and 17 Geo. 5. Available online: https://www.legislation.gov.uk/ukpga/Geo5/16-17/26 [accessed January 4, 2018]

Chesterton, A. K. "Home and Foreign Reds in Public Order Act Evasion. Will the Government Act?" *Action* 78, August 14, 1937: 11

"Come On, The Green Shirts!" *The Broadsheet: The Official Gazette of the Kibbo Kift* 83, February 1933: 3–4.

Coupland, P. M (2004), "The Black Shirt in Britain: The Meanings and Function of Political Uniform," in J V Gottlieb and T P Linehan (eds), *The Culture of Fascism: Visions of the Far Right in Britain,* London: I. B. Tauris, 100–15.

Craik, J. (2005), *Uniforms Exposed: From Conformity to Transgression,* Oxford: Berg.

Davis, M. (2000), *Fashioning a New World: A History of the Woodcraft Folk,* Loughborough: Holyoake Books.

Drakeford, M. (1997), *Social Movements and their Supporters: The Green Shirts in England,* Basingstoke: Macmillan.

Elwell-Sutton, L. P. (1979), "Foreword," in John Hargrave, *The Confession of the Kibbo Kift,* rev. ed., London: William Maclellan, 1–7.

Francis-Hawkins, N. [Director General, British Union of Fascists and National Socialists], letter to Commissioner of Police, December 19, 1936. The National Archives, MEPO 3/2513 Public Order Act 1936: Instructions to Police.

Francis-Hawkins, N. [Director General, British Union of Fascists and National Socialists], letter to Commissioner of Police, January 1, 1937. The National Archives, MEPO 3/2513 Public Order Act 1936: Instructions to Police.

Gollan, J. [Secretary, The Young Communist League of Great Britain], letter to Commissioner of Police, December 29, 1936. The National Archives, MEPO 3/2513 Public Order Act 1936: Instructions to Police.

"Gossip of the Day: 'The Age of Shirts,' (1933), *Yorkshire Evening Post,* May 19: 10.

Hargrave, J. (1919), *Tribal Training,* London: Pearson.

Hargrave, J. (1931), "Unarmed Military Technique," *The Broadsheet: The Official Gazette of the Kibbo Kift,* 66, September: 3–4.

Hargrave, J. (1935), "Break Through Apathy! With Colour, Sound, Movement," *The Broadsheet: Official Gazette of the Green Shirt Movement for Social Credit,* 113, November: 2–3.

Hargrave, J. (n.d.), "Green" [unpublished autobiographical fragment], Youth Movement Archive, London School of Economics Library, Hargrave Collection, Box 28.

Hargrave, J. (1935), "Logic Alone is Not Enough. Do Not Neglect the Power of Pageantry," *The Broadsheet: Official Gazette of the Green Shirt Movement for Social Credit*, 106, April: 2–3.

Hargrave, J. (1937), "Green Shirts without Uniform," *The Broadsheet: Official Gazette of the Social Credit Party of Great Britain and Northern Ireland*, 129–30, April–May: 2–3.

Hargrave, J. (1938), "Social Credit is Coming!" *The Broadsheet: Official Gazette of the Social Credit Party of Great Britain and Northern Ireland*, 136, March–April: 2–3.

Home Office, Public Order Act [official advice document circulated to police], December 24, 1936. The National Archives, MEPO 3/2513 Public Order Act 1936: Instructions to Police.

"Kilt is not under political uniform ban" (1936), *Aberdeen Press and Journal*, November 24: 5.

"Kincouncil Decrees and Notices: Men's Habit" (1931), *The Broadsheet: The Official Gazette of the Kibbo Kift*. 65, August: 1.

Macdonell, A. G. (1936), "The Passing Hour: Comments and Asides," *The Bystander*, November 18: 271.

Meetings, Uniforms and Public Order: All About the New Act (1937), London: Jordan and Sons.

Mortimer, C. (2016), "Britain First could be 'finished'," *The Independent*, August 12. Available online: https://www.independent.co.uk/news/uk/politics/britain-first-high-court-bid-luton-mosque-islamophobia-racism-a7186446.html [accessed January 4, 2018]

"Parliamentary Sketch: Public Order Bill. Difficulty of Defining a Political Uniform" (1936), *The Scotsman*, November 24: 9.

"Party Uniforms: House Reject Bill for Prohibitions" (1934), *Yorkshire Post*, May 17: 7.

"Party Uniforms: Knotty Problem of their Definition" (1936), *Yorkshire Post*, November 24: 8.

"Political Uniform Test Case. Question of Badges in Cap. Act 'Vaguely Nebulous,' says Prosecutor" (1937), *Evening Telegraph*, January 27: 5.

Pollen, A. (2015), *The Kindred of the Kibbo Kift: Intellectual Barbarians*, London: Donlon Books.

Pollen, A. (2016), "Who are these folk all dressed in green? Reflections on the first fifty years of Woodcraft Folk costume evolution," in P Harper, J Helm, J Nott, A Pollen, M Pover and N Samson (eds), *A People's History of Woodcraft Folk*, London: Woodcraft Folk, 40–45.

Public Order Act, 1936, 1 Edw. 8 & 1 Geo. 6 c.6. Available online: http://www.legislation.gov.uk/ukpga/Edw8and1Geo6/1/6/contents/enacted [accessed January 4, 2018]

"R. v. Taylor, Hawthorn, Ward" [typed report of a 1937 Green Shirt court case], Correspondence and papers concerning the Public Order Act, 1936, Youth Movement Archive, London School of Economics Library, Kibbo Kift papers, YMA/KK/56.

"Red Flag and Clenched Fist at Sussex Camp" (1937), *Daily Telegraph*, August 14.

"Replacing the Loss of Propaganda Power" (1934), *The Broadsheet: Official Gazette of the Green Shirt Movement for Social Credit*, 92, February: 4.

Ridout, P. J. [Imperial Fascist League], letter to Commissioner of Police, December 28, 1936.
Tacey, C. A. (1937), "The Public Order Act, 1936," *The Broadsheet: Official Gazette of the Social Credit Party of Great Britain and Northern Ireland*, 127, January: 2–3.
"The Age of 'Shirts'," (1933), *Evening News*, May 16: 7.
The National Archives, MEPO 3/2513 Public Order Act 1936: Instructions to Police.
"The Public Order Act, 1936" (1936), *The Broadsheet: Official Gazette of the Social Credit Party of Great Britain and Northern Ireland*, 126, December: 3.
"Welcome to the Green Shirts" (1931), *The Broadsheet: The Official Gazette of the Kibbo Kift*, 68, November: 3.
"Well Done, Woodcraft" (1937), *Daily Worker*, August 11.
"What is a Uniform?" (1937), *Dundee Courier and Advertiser*, 1 January: 4
Woodcraft Folk (2011), "Woodcraft Folk and Political Activity." Available online: https://www.woodcraft.org.uk/sites/default/files/Woodcraft%20folk%20and%20political%20activity%20web%20edit_0.pdf [accessed January 4, 2018]
"Woodcraft Folk. International Camp at Brighton: Wearing of uniform by children at", Sub-file 697904, Home Office, 8 Feb 1937, The National Archive, HO 45/24999 Disturbances: Public Order Act 1936: Wearing of political uniforms.
"Woodcraft Folk International Camp at Rottingdean, Brighton: Political meetings and propaganda at," Sub-file 697904/9 Home Office, August 14, 1937, The National Archive, HO 45/24999 Disturbances: Public Order Act 1936: Wearing of political uniforms.
Woodcraft Folk (2015), "Uniformed Youth Social Action Fund Announced" http://woodcraft.org.uk/news/united-youth-social-action-fund-announced [accessed January 4, 2018]
Wyndham Lewis, D. B. (1937), "Standing By… A Weekly Commentary on One Thing and Another," *The Bystander*, 16 June: 545.
"Youth's Challenge to Fascism" (1937), *News Chronicle*, August 11.

3

Revolutionary Culture, Girl Power, and the Red Guard Uniform During the Chinese Cultural Revolution

Li Li

In the Chinese Great Proletarian Cultural Revolution (1966–76), the most iconic visual images of this 'ten-year turmoil' are those of the Red Guards, especially girl-Red Guards, dressed in the quasi-military uniforms of the Chinese People's Liberation Army (PLA): a grass-green jacket and a pair of loose pants of the same color, soft cloth cap with red star insignia, belt with broad metallic buckles, as well as a red armband to indicate their respective branches. The image of the Red Guards donning this self-invented uniform and engaging in fanatically destructive actions gave rise to shocking effects, then and now, for millions of people who lived through the Cultural Revolution.

As scholars have observed, clothes have historical and cultural significance; they are social constructions of embodied identity. Military uniforms in particular originate from the organizational need to distinguish armies from other social groups, and the emblem of this distinctive group further "lends itself to a variety of controls" to reinforce conformity and to suppress individuality in an organization (Joseph 1986: 65). In general, the socio-historical meanings of clothes "are embedded in, and altered by, the appearance in which they are founded, in social situations, and in larger cultural/historical contexts framing space and time" (Kaiser 1998: 29). In light of these scholarly approaches, this chapter explores the historical context under which the Red Guards devised their dress practices and considers the socio-political functions of this practice in advancing the agendas of Mao Zedong, the leader of the Cultural Revolution. It starts with an examination of the larger historical backdrop to the rise of military culture in China by retracing the origin of the modern military uniform in the turn of nineteenth-to-twentieth century, calling attention to the centrality of militarism in various revolutionary campaigns and its significance in shaping

Chinese revolutionary culture and female identity. It then moves on to investigate how the PLA uniform helped to shape the alliance between the Red Guards and Mao, and thus became the symbol of the Cultural Revolution. The last section investigates the reasons why those of the Red Guard generation were fascinated with the PLA uniform, and here I argue that it was the prevailing revolutionary aesthetic and collective psychological state that turned this generation into utopian rebels. The donning of the PLA uniform was a significant means of self-invention and self-promotion; a practice through which urban adolescents not only legitimized their collective action of social rebellion, but also mobilized themselves to realize a larger-than-life social identity they could hardly achieve in everyday life.

Militarism and women in the Chinese revolutionary tradition

In his study of ancient uniform in the West, Daniel Roche notes that the "birth of uniform in the seventeenth century should [thus] be seen as part of the social transformation of armies, when princes, to reduce their dependence on the feudal nobility, increasingly resorted to cash or wages (*solde*) to pay conscripted troops or mercenaries" (Roche 1994: 225). The rise of uniform in nineteenth-century China, in contrast, resulted not from social transformations within, but primarily from a series of wars imposed by the colonial powers. "Chinese culture is often thought of as favoring literary over martial skills—hence the saying 'good iron is not beaten into nails; good men are not made into soldiers'" (Finnane 1999: 119). For the majority of the Qing dynasty (1644–1912), during which time the Manchurians held sway, the military uniform was not so different from civilian dress of the time: loose trousers, robes similar to that of the Chinese gentry class, and cone-shaped hats. China's catastrophic defeat by Britain in the Opium Wars (1839–42 and 1856–60) for the first time made nationwide military reform urgent. Its subsequent loss to Japan in 1894 further intensified the pressure for wide-ranging institutional reforms proposed as a key strategy for 'self-strengthening'. In 1904, China's first New Army eventually emerged, in which the soldiers practiced German-style military drills and wore German-style uniforms with narrow-legged pants, body-fitting coats, and peaked caps.

The birth of the New Army precipitated widespread changes in traditional culture and society, which made 1905, the year prior to the historic military reforms, a significant turning-point in Chinese history. This was the year in which Imperial Russia was not only defeated by Japan but also went through a failed revolution. Both events attracted enormous attention in China; "the former because it illustrated the potential of an Asian power to gain ascendancy over a European one; the latter because it demonstrated the possibility of popular revolt against imperial rule. Both served to heighten the prestige of the martial ideal" (Finnane 2008: 123). In addition to events external to China in 1905, the Civil Examination system—which had served for more than a century as the pathway to imperial bureaucracy—was abolished as part of constitutional reforms. The vacuum resulting from the interruption of this time-honored civil tradition was then quickly filled by the emerging new-style military schools. Even the conventional schools started to offer a more military-related curriculum for their students, for boys and girls alike. Under these circumstances of traumatic historical events and dramatic social changes, the first decade of the 1900s witnessed a form of military culture steadily seeping into public discourse as both a strategy for national defense and a radical exhortation to revolt against Qing rule in order to restore Han Chinese dominance, just one element of widespread disorder.

The prevailing radical revolutionary sentiments and a rising militarism was intertwined with vehement contestations of social and gender boundaries, often expressed through sartorial practices. The embodiment of these dimensions was probably best exemplified by Qiu Jin (1875–1907), an influential female revolutionary martyr in modern Chinese history. Inspired by revolutionary advocacy against the Manchurian ruling of China, in 1904 Qiu Jin left behind her young children and conservative husband and went to study in Japan, where she joined Chinese revolutionary organizations and also received training in fencing and archery at the Martial Arts Society. To demonstrate her unflagging enthusiasm for revolution, in 1907 Qiu Jin involved herself in a series of military uprisings in China, as well as a failed assassination of the top Manchurian official in Anhui province. She was beheaded publicly in 1907.

One can hardly separate Qiu Jin's revolutionary deeds from her clothing practices. A provocative, self-fashioned cross-dresser, Qiu Jing relentlessly pushed the traditional boundaries for women. In her time, most Chinese women wore headbands to carefully cover their tightened 'bun' hairstyles, loose gowns with high mandarin collars and wide sleeves, and long skirts, all designed to cover their body seamlessly, showing only the points of the shoes covering their bound feet. Qiu Jin, in contrast, not only wore men's clothing in public, but also had no hesitation in displaying a pair of unbound feet. Most strikingly, she occasionally held a sword in her hand when posing for photographers and at public gatherings. Her dramatic cross-dressing style was certainly in the service of revolution and social change but was also a performative act of self-promotion in the most provocative fashion. Her clothing practices represent, on the one hand, women's desire to be equal with men. On the other hand, it is ironic that a woman could receive education, participate in revolution, or receive public attention only when she dressed in men's clothes.

The revolution for which Qiu Jin sacrificed her life ended a few years later, with the overthrow of the Manchurian monarchy. The establishment of the Republic in late 1911, however, did not bring lasting unity and peace to China. The never-ending domestic military confrontations, mostly between the Nationalist Party led by Chiang Kai-shek (1887–1975) and the Communist Party by Mao Zedong (1893–1976), and the devastating Sino-Japanese War (1938–45) saw China disintegrate further. Mao, like generations of other iconoclastic Chinese revolutionaries, believed the emancipation of women—who were suppressed by Confucian gender ethics and traditional family education—was key to the modernization of China. He believed that the inferior position of Chinese women in terms of education, marriage, and social affairs contributed to the backwardness of Chinese society. More interestingly, the issues of women's emancipation and gender equality were often figured by Mao via sartorial appearances, as one of Mao's many remarks show:

> If a woman's head and a man's head are actually the same, and there is no real difference between a woman's waist and man's, why must women have their hair piled up in those ostentatious and awkward buns? Why must they wear those messy skirts cinched tightly at the waist? I think women are regarded as criminals to start with, and tall buns and long skirts are the instrument of torture applied to them by men. There is facial makeup, which is the brand of a criminal: the jewelry on their hands, which constitutes shackles; and their pierced ears and bound feet, which present corporal punishment. Schools and families are their prisons. They dare not voice their pain, nor step out from behind closed doors. If we ask, how they can escape this suffering, my answer is, only by raising a women's revolutionary army.
>
> SCHRAM 1969: 353

Written in 1919, the germinating year of the communist revolution, this remark by Mao not only reflected a commonly held belief among many Chinese revolutionaries that the liberation of women was at the core of the unfolding revolutionary cause, but also employed the then-common rhetoric that used women's clothing and body parts as tropes to evoke the theme of freedom and revolution. What is most significant, however, is Mao's articulation that "only by raising a women's revolutionary army the women can be liberated." (Schram 1969:

353). Mao's belief in violent revolution and military intervention is well known, summarized by his guiding principle "political power grows out of the barrel of a gun," (Mao, 1972: 61) and, in particular, out of the barrels of guns carried by militias in guerrilla warfare. After Mao won the Civil War and established the New China military culture, women wearing military fashion continued to be favored by Mao in promoting the integration of militarism into his country's civilian life. One of his most widely known poems, entitled "Women Militias," reads: "Five-foot rifles, flashing bravely, on the training ground, at break of day; How remarkable the spirit of Chinese women: They love martial dress, not girls' attire."[1]

Mao's fondness for militias, of course, should not be understood only in relation to his personal interest in women wearing military attire, but resulted from his obsession with the ideology of 'continuous revolution' stemming from his communist utopian ideals, as well as fears of the comeback of nationalist rivals in Taiwan and potential subversions of his power by domestic 'class enemies.' If it was the enduring legacy of guerrilla warfare which helped him to gain power, he wanted to use the militia culture to maintain that power. Indeed, uplifting proletarian images and the soldierly loyalty which female militias displayed in Mao's poem reveals his own conception of women in his utopian revolutionary vision.

In fact, the legacy of female liberation activated by the Maoist revolution was canonized by Chinese revolutionary myth in literature, film, and arts, playing a central role in youth education in Mao's China. A quintessential plot of this narrative of liberation involved a woman, either a slave-girl held captive by a ruthless landlord or a victim of aggressive foreign invaders, being liberated and saved by communist agents. Yet, those women often had to overcome the gap between being a woman and being a communist soldier. The former was a natural being, who could spontaneously fight for her own interests; the latter was a disciplined solder, who was always able to prioritize the interests of the proletarian class over her individual revenge. Under the rigorous education of the Chinese Communist Party (CCP), the various heroines ultimately became enlightened communist revolutionaries, who devoted their lives to the liberation of 'class sisters' who were still suffering, as they anticipated the ultimate liberation of all humankind.

Such a prototypical work is *Red Detachment of Women* (1961), first an award-winning film and later adapted into one of the eight original Model Theaters during the Cultural Revolution. The protagonist, Qionghua on film and Qinghua in the Model Theater ballet, was a slave girl who was at the verge of being beaten to death by her sordid landlord, the 'Tyrant of the South,' in punishment for another attempted escape from captivity; fortunately, she was saved by an undercover communist, Hong Changqing. With Hong's guidance and help, she joined the Red Detachment of Women, a regional militia troop under his supervision as he was the male communist party representative. Not long after she joined the detachment, Qionghua encountered the Tyrant of the South. Putting aside the rules she was obliged to obey as a soldier, Qionghua pulled out a handgun and fired at her former master. She was disciplined by the detachment for taking personal revenge and allowed to wear only civilian clothing. Here, uniform is emblematic of the collective cause and reinforces communist conformity. Only following the admonishment of the Party Representative and, later witnessing his heroic death at the hand of the Tyrant of the South, was the slave girl Qionghua eventually transformed into an enlightened revolutionary heroine determined to fight for the liberation of other suffering sisters of the proletarian class. She was in uniform again. A highly dramatized contrast between the attire of *laobaixing* (a common civilian) and that of a communist soldier in this story illustrates the challenges for Chinese people experiencing profound political changes during the Revolution.

To sum up, the slave girl–soldier constructed in Chinese revolutionary myth is a compelling and complex mixture of revolutionary ideology and militarism that also illustrates women's shifting roles. Such stories were often packaged in military attire and appearances. As a core image of Maoist revolutionary culture, this construction signifies the ethical and moral dimensions of revolution as women are liberated from their role as victims of a repressed society. It also shows Mao's belief in military campaigns and the close alliance created between the army and the *laobaixing*, which played a key role in the victory of the Maoist revolution. This construct, embedded in the revolutionary culture, spoke intimately and convincingly to the Red Guard generation, inspiring them to continue pursuing the mission of the Maoist revolution. If some of Mao's political and military strategies proved effective in enabling him to win the battle against the Nationalist Party in the half-century of communist revolution in China, then it is worth noting that Chinese feminism, which started to emerge at the same time, was "the result of the inclusion of women in men's pursuit of a 'Chinese enlightenment'" (Wang 1999: 13).

Dress to perform a new revolution

The meanings of military uniforms in Chinese revolutionary literature not only glorifies the military marvels of communist soldiers in the past but is key to interpreting the political meanings of the Cultural Revolution. Its launch in the notoriously violent 'red summer' of 1966 and the following year visually demonstrates the sharing of dressing practices between the Red Guards and their 'great commander', Mao. The alliance was forged through a series of symbolic interactions, which have been described as pursuing the study of social actions and social objects, underpinned by a belief that "humans fit their 'lines of action' (streams of behavior of social actions) together to make sense of the situations in which they find themselves in" (Kaiser 1998: 39). For Mao, who was at the time desperate to retain his power amid the steady pressures of revisionist colleagues in the CCP, the PLA uniform, which was emblematic of the glorious past of revolutionary and military actions, vindicated his campaign for a "continuous revolution," in which Mao wanted to "create—by means of class struggle—a society with selected roots and memories to the past, created in the present to realize a future utopia of Chinese modernity" (Mittler 2012: 30). For the Red Guards, fitting the lines of Maoist action not only allowed them to make sense of the situation in which they found themselves—that is, to rebel against the rigid status quos and social regulations set by the officials—but, more importantly, to empower themselves to become the front runners in a new social revolution in which they would make their own history.

At the end of May 1966, when the Cultural Revolution was still fermenting in the mind of Mao, who had been sidelined by his political opponents in the Party and was having a long vacation outside Beijing, a small group of students in the middle school attached to Tsinghua University, one of the best-known elite schools in the capital, met secretly in a western suburb of the city. At the meeting, they decided to form an organization to openly denounce the administrators and teachers in their school for repressing their voices. On June 2, members of this group wrote a public manifesto, in which they signed the name of the group 'the Red Guards of Mao Zedong Thoughts.' This was the very first time the term 'Red Guards' appeared in public. To fashion their new group identity, members of this group, who were mostly children of high-ranking communist officials in the military sectors, started to publicly wear the grass-green jackets of the PLA that had been retired by their parents. They also wore a red armband, which was a popular symbol for rebellious peasants and workers in the revolutionary era. After being harshly criticized by school authorities and the city government of Beijing, this group drafted an essay entitled "Long Live the Proletarian Revolutionary Spirit of Rebellion" to defend their acts of rebellion against the authorities. Surprisingly, their essay reached Mao, and he made the unusual gesture of writing an open letter to this group of teenage zealots. In it, Mao offered his support for their rebellion against the bureaucratic administrators who tried to maintain the status quo. Mao's support instilled the early Red Guards with the much-needed encouragement to further defy the authorities, and they were excited about their dress, which would express their newly found freedom.

While the early action of the Red Guards was clearly helpful to Mao in fighting against his political opponents and expanding his own legacy, inspiring and mobilizing millions of teenage students nationwide to participate in his new revolution was a challenge in a pre-mass media era. In the early morning of August 18, 1966, Mao ascended the Tiananmen Gate Tower to meet the mass student rallies, the first of eight organized that summer. Surprisingly, Mao wore a grass-green PLA uniform for this occasion. The most exciting moment occurred when a young female Red Guard in quasi-military uniform from the *All Girl Middle School Attached to Beijing Normal University* named Song Binbin climbed up to the tower and pinned a homemade armband on Mao's shoulder (see Figure 3.1). When Song introduced herself to Mao, he reportedly asked her

Figure 3.1 Song Binbin pins a Red Guard armband on Mao's sleeve, August 18, 1966. Original photo published in *People's Daily*, *Guangming Daily*, and many other newspapers shortly after the event. Private collection. With thanks to Professor Antonia Finnane for permission to use this version.

if *binbin* in her personal name were the same characters as found in a well-known Chinese proverb *wenzhi binbin*, meaning "gentle and polite." When Song answered "yes," Mao said, disapprovingly, "[you should be] *yaowu* (militant), instead" (*People's Daily* 1966). Published in the newspapers the following day, Mao's comment on militancy immediately denoted a behavior that millions of Red Guards, particularly girl Red Guards, were urged to emulate. In the following years the uniform did not remain merely a fashion statement when brutally violent actions were taken against casually defined 'class enemies,' be they 'capitalist roaders,' 'revisionists,' 'antirevolutionary academic authorities,' 'five black elements,' or 'four olds.'[2] Where one beheld grass-green uniforms and red armbands, one witnessed the beating of schoolteachers, the burning of books, the smashing of temples, or the raiding of households.

The newly found political alliance between Mao as commander and his young revolutionary generals was built on the visual identity of their uniforms. Interestingly, while Mao, who was the Chairman of the Communist Party, constitutionally also served as the commander-in-chief of the PLA, like most other party leaders, always appeared in public occasions in a Sun Yat-sen suit. As Mao's appearance on the Tiananmen Gate Tower in PLA uniform in 1966 was to extend his support to the Red Guards, he attempted to convey other messages to the rebellious youngsters. First was a political statement about Mao's alliance with Marshal Lin Biao (1907–71), the then-Minister of Defense who controlled the PLA. During the post-Great Leap Forward period in which Mao was criticized and alienated by a group of more pragmatic party leaders such as China's then President Liu Shaoqi (1898–1969), who advocated for economic gains and the status quo, Lin Biao put every effort into reaffirming Mao's utopian ideals about a pure socialist society of egalitarianism and equality. To help Mao to consolidate his absolute authority, Lin Biao required the army to study Mao's *Little Red Book* as a daily ritual. To keep close to the old army systems during wartime, in 1965 Lin Biao abolished the rank insignia that had been adopted since 1955 and then restored the austere Yan'an-style uniform. Everyone in the army, regardless of rank, was to wear grass-green cotton uniform, a soft cap with a red star insignia, and a flag-shaped red insignia at the corner of the standing collars. It further indicated that the political goal, which Mao tried to achieve in his utopian 'continuous revolution,' was egalitarianism and social equality instead of the hierarchal structure of his opponents. In fact, the divisions of the two political foci and ideologies were made largely visible by the clothing they wore in public following the first rally: whereas Mao and Lin Biao always wore PLA uniforms on public occasions, Liu Shaoqi and his cohorts wore civilian clothing.

Premier Zhou Enlai (1889–1976), a key figure in the Chinese political scene who often served as a mediator between the two groups, switched back and forth between civilian clothing and military uniform. In fact, the self-fashioned and self-serving image of Lin Biao in PLA uniform, always walking one step behind Mao waving his *Little Red Book*, later led to him being selected as the constitutionally designated successor to Mao; while Liu Shaoqi, the constitutionally elected President of the People's Republic of China, was tortured and died in obscurity in a rural town.

It is worth pointing out that although the Red Guard groups crossing the country almost universally embraced the symbolism embedded in the PLA uniforms to fashion their new identity, the fabrics used were not identical at all. The early groups of Red Guards, known as Old Red Guards, or Conservative Red Guards, mostly came from high-ranking military families and thus wore the officially made PLA uniforms their parents used to wear. Faced with groups of other Red Guards emerging in China's major cities, the Old Red Guards started to discriminate against their peers who had no official background; and their uniforms often signaled such distinctions. At the time, access to the official PLA uniform was strictly regulated, obtainable only for those with a certain rank who were serving in or had served in the army. As Antonia Finnane's research shows, the army issued new uniforms twice a year, and soldiers were "supposed to hand in their old ones in exchange, or else pay for them, which they could ill afford. But being in a position to hand out old uniforms was a source of extraordinary social power" (Finnane 2008: 237). Because of these restrictions, the majority of Red Guard uniforms were actually homemade facsimiles. June Chang, an insider of the elite group, writes in her autobiography *Wild Swans*, that among Red Guards, "few owned real PLA uniforms. Some got the old gear through black market trading, and more dyed their clothes green at home" even though the homemade facsimiles often "lacked the haughty air of the elite, and their green was often not quite the right shade" those in the homemade uniforms were sneered at by the children of high officials, as well as by their own friends, as "pseuds" (Chang 1991: 370). The Red Guards with elite backgrounds did not just mock those wearing inferior uniforms, but also developed a 'blood-line theory' to claim their legitimacy as successors to the Maoist revolution. Stating that "if the father's a hero, the son's a great fellow; if the father's reactionary, the son's a rotten egg" (Chan 1985: 133), this theory attempted to exclude their peers of various family backgrounds from participating in the Cultural Revolution, and conflicts between the different divisions soon developed into violent clashes.

In short, interactions between Mao and the Red Guards were largely built through the shared action of donning of the PLA uniform in public. This was critical in both helping to strategize and stage the Cultural Revolution while aiding the Red Guards to realize their own political ambitions. The quasi-military attire of the Red Guards signified the Maoist ideology of equality; but ironically, it also symbolized the political power and social privilege of a special group of teenagers from high-ranking military families over their less-privileged peers. Indeed, the argument about the authenticity of Red Guard uniforms demonstrate the contradictions of the movement as a campaign for social equality and justice.

Fashion a new identity

Growing up in the New China under Mao's leadership, the Red Guards generation was immersed in a revolutionary culture designed to promote the sublime legend of the Maoist revolution. Women's preference for dressing up in masculine and, in particular, militant attire, was inspired by a variety of revolutionary legacies which can be traced all the way back to the revolutionary martyr Qiu Jin in the Republican Revolution, female soldiers of the Red Army in the Long March, the anti-Japanese War, and in regional militias, like the *Red Detachment of Women*, who fiercely fought against local repressive landlords during the Civil War. The body of revolutionary literature and arts created with the guidance of 'revolutionary realism' and 'revolutionary romanticism' often disproportionally featured revolutionary heroes and, especially, deified images of Mao glorifying their upbeat revolutionary spirits and lofty deeds. Stories about the sacrifice these heroes made were also written into textbooks, while living heroes were frequently invited to give talks to, and be interviewed by, school students. This enormous body of state-sanctioned mythologizing about the Maoist revolution had a far-reaching and complex psychological impact on young people. Indeed, for those who grew up in Mao's China, could the stories about the communist revolution, especially those about the emancipation of women, be a legacy to aspire to, a dream to pursue, a burden to bear or to transcend, or all of these? In particular, from whence came the desires and pressures that compelled young women to look like men or soldiers––did it come from the state, from the men, from media, or possibly even from the women themselves?

Sublime revolutionary literature critically shaped the imagination of the Red Guard generation. As brave as they could imagine themselves to be as heroes portrayed in revolutionary fiction and films, the Red Guard generation were in reality disappointed by their enemies being less worthy than those faced by their revolutionary parents. They were inspired by the legendary lives of their parents but their inability to simulate their experiences made them feel inferior. Former Red Guard Rae Yang wrote in her autobiography *Spider Eaters*, "[But] the mental abilities we gained, we were not supposed to apply elsewhere, in reality" (Yang 1997: 115). The Cultural Revolution provided this generation with a rare opportunity to prove their own worthiness by acting like heroic historical figures. The PLA uniforms gave the girl Red Guards especially a blueprint for acquiring what they lacked- equality with their parents- by demonstrating their ability to carry on a new revolution, as well as enjoying equality with their male counterparts, by acting as ruthlessly against class enemies as the boys. Their feelings of pride were vividly reconnected in Yang's autobiography:

> People in the street noticed our new costume: faded army uniforms that had been worn by our parents, red armbands, wide canvas army belts, army caps, the peaks pulled down low by girls in the style of the boy...Some people smiled at us. Some waved their hands. Their eyes showed surprise, curiosity, excitement, admiration...We are not only girls and boys, we are Red Guards!
>
> YANG 1997: 122

In this case, the identity-claiming nature of cross-dressing provided girls with the pleasure of transgressing the gender boundaries set by convention, in doing what the boys could do, and even surpassing them. From this perspective, we might best understand Emily Honig's finding that the excessive violence that girl Red Guards imposed on their teachers was the result of the "style (rather than content) of fierce militant behavior that women sought to emulate" (2002: 264). In this light, Red Guard girls' fondness for cross-dressing was neither socialist androgyny nor masculinization. The fashion for the militarization of women's clothing, together with their rough manner, bold behavior, robust bodies, and grinning facial expressions were forms of self-invention as revolutionary successors, and as historical subjects (Figure 3.2).

The Red Guards' self-molding during the Cultural Revolution was affirmed and supported when they saw Mao appearing in the same cotton uniform. In the eyes of massed Red Guards in Tiananmen Square, the visual image of Mao in that uniform might have had an enormous impact on their collective psychology. Despite the omnipresent deification of Mao in all forms of literature and arts, to most of the Red Guards he was only a remote and abstract figure prior to his appearance at the Tiananmen Gate Tower; therefore, as Ban Wang remarks:

Figure 3.2 'Be This Kind of Human Being', Poster depicting a Red Guard in the PLA uniform and armband. Inspired by Iron Blossom, a heroine of the revolutionary model opera *The Red Lantern*. People's Fine Arts Publishing House (Beijing, 1968). From author's private collection.

the infantile affective attachment, as shown in emotional ties and bodily closeness to the parents, was not quite as apparent or intense. During Mao's views of mass rallies, the youngsters somehow took a drastic turn. The infantile libidinal impulsion, which had been repressed and remained unconscious, came to the fore with enormous strength and intensity.

WANG 1997: 205

Indeed, millions of Red Guards were thrilled to behold, with their own eyes, Mao, a god-like figure ascending the Tiananmen Gate Tower at the moment of sunrise, basking in the vast, glorious rays of the sun, to the lofty melody of the revolutionary creation myth 'The East is Red,' wearing the same uniform and armband as them. Thus, sartorial identification with Mao aroused a collective narcissism among the Red Guards. To be sure, this was not only a demonstration of the Red Guards' zealousness and worship of their great leader, but it was also a display of their celebration of a possible fulfillment of repressed desire. In this light, the mimesis of fashion functions as a trope of "craving for authority through imitation, the secret wish that one person can somehow take the place of parents and other authority figures" (Wang 1997: 205). This impulse for self-establishment proved to be so strong that, on many occasions, it turned to violently removing the earlier authority figures such as teachers and parents. The employment of the quasi-uniform on the popular scene thus reinforced the idea that body and material dress could not be separate; rather, a particular sartorial discourse became a social force in the unstable process of making a new political order and pushing ideological frontiers in the Cultural Revolution.

Conclusion

The conspicuous dress practices of the Red Guards during the Cultural Revolution were symbolic. They illustrated the imbrications of militarism, radical social change, and gender reconfiguration emergent in the historical moment of the painful birth of modern China, particularly its persistent struggle in the Mao era, which resulted in the Cultural Revolution. The Red Guards' practice of donning PLA uniform embodies the influence of more than half a century of revolutions and wars; the lasting enchantment of Maoist utopian ideals, particularly gender equality in the case of girl Red Guards; the libidinal discharge of repressed energy in the form of social rebellion; and self-promotion to be the frontrunners in Mao's 'continuous revolution.' The most intriguing aspect of these dress practices is not how they addressed the already constituted sphere of 'real politics,' but how the drive to wear uniform created symbolic interactions between the Red Guards and Mao, to operate as instruments of identity transformation, and finally to constitute a new political and social reality.

References

Chan, A. (1985), *Children of Mao: Personality Development and Political Activism in the Red Guard Generation,* Seattle, WA: University of Washington Press.

Chang, J. (1991), *Wild Swans: Three Daughters of China,* New York: Simon & Schuster.
Finnane, A. (1999), "Military Culture and Chinese Dress in Early–Twentieth Century," in V. Steele and J. Major (eds), *Chinese Chic: East Meets West,* New Haven, CT: Yale University Press, 119–31.
Finnane, A. (2008), *Changing Clothes in China: Fashion, History, Nation.* New York: Columbia University Press.
Honig, E. (2002), "Maoist Mappings of Gender: Reassessing the Red Guards," in Brownell S. and J. Wasserstrom (eds), *Chinese Femininities/Chinese Masculinities,* Berkeley, CA: University of California Press, 255–69.
Joseph, N. (1986), *Uniforms and Nonuniforms: Communication Through Clothing,* New York: Greenwood Press.
Kaiser, S. (1998), *The Social Psychology of Clothing: Symbolic Appearance in Context,* New York: Fairchild Publications.
Mao, Z. (1969), *Mao zhuxi shici (The Poems by Chairman Mao),* Beijing: Renmin Chubanshe.
Mao, Z. (1972), *Mao Zhuxi Yulu* (Quotations from Chairman Mao Tse-Tung), Peking: Foreign Language Press.
Mittler, B. (2012), *A Continuous Revolution: Making Sense of Cultural Revolution Culture,* Cambridge, MA: Harvard University Press.
People's Daily (1966), August 18.
Roche, D. (1994), *The Culture of Clothing: Dress and Fashion in the "Ancient Regime,"* (trans. Jean Birrell), Cambridge: Cambridge University Press.
Schram, S. R. (1969), *The Political Thought of Mao Tse-tung,* New York, Washington, DC, and London: Frederick A. Praeger Publishers.
Wang, B. (1997), *The Sublime Figure of History: Aesthetics and Politics in Twentieth-century China,* Stanford, CA: Stanford University Press.
Wang, Z. (1999), *Women in the Chinese Enlightenment: Oral and Textual History,* Berkeley, CA: University of California Press.
Yang, R. (1997), *Spider Eaters: A Memoir,* Berkeley, CA: University of California Press.

PART TWO

Uniforming Institutions

As explored in this section, the wearing of uniform clothing as a device for institutional socialization, concerns not only its outward expression but is also about internalizing the values of an organization. Uniforming members of an institution might be presented as an attempt to instil pride or *esprit de corps* in them, but it also denotes the power exerted over the person, and the ceding of their subjectivity. This is not only symbolic, but as these essays demonstrate, in corporeal terms the wearing of specific elements of uniform can shape bearing, gait, and activity. For the duration of time that uniform is worn, the individual materially takes on the broader corporate character of the institution, and thus it is the institution rather than the character of the wearer that is communicated by the uniformed body. With long-standing organizations, the temporal dimension might be cast in terms of 'tradition' whereby the uniform is a point of connection to contemporary peers but also links individuals to those who have worn the institutional uniform in the past and those likely to wear it in the future. As discussed elsewhere in this volume, this sets uniform against the ever-quickening cycle of fashionable clothing, whereby longevity suggests the naturalness of institutional values in contrast with the pace of modernity. This might be expressed as an explicit turn away from worldliness, as discussed by William J. F. Keenan in his essay on religious dress.

Institutional uniforming can also be read as an attempt to mitigate against the mutability of the modern body and its perceived excesses. This is perhaps one reason for the rise of uniformed youth organizations in the late nineteenth and early twentieth century in the wake of the establishment of public school uniform, as discussed in this section by Kate Stephenson. For example, the highly influential boy scout movement (from 1908) was primarily concerned with the production of ideal and self-disciplined citizens at a time when adolescence was identified as a specific and problematic stage of life, and the scout's uniform figured as an important aspect of their shaping. For the scouting movement, the ideology of muscular Christianity made visible markers of physical prowess desirable and thus they favoured rational forms of dress.

That same impulse concerning the power of uniform to discipline and shape young bodies and minds is present in more recent instances of institutional uniforming, for example in the case of contemporary cultures of school uniform in Britain. A brief survey of newspaper reports that address school uniform in Britain over the past decade demonstrates the overwhelming significance attached to adhering to specific clothing codes within institutions that champion self-regulation and obedience. It is notable that this emphasis on uniform is predicated on the visuality and visibility of young people, and uniforms act as a material corollary to concerns about discipline and self-regulation. What is clear is that institutional uniforms are read as a distinctive sign of discipline, morality, and authority, not only within organizations but also by the wider society.

4

Uniform Adoption in English Public Schools, 1830–1930

Kate Stephenson

Although school uniforms have been in existence from the 1550s onwards, they were confined, at first, to charitable institutions and had little impact beyond these establishments. Their use in the public schools of the nineteenth and early twentieth century, therefore represented a crucial step in that they created a uniform model that was widely imitated throughout the rest of the education system by girls' public schools, grammar schools and, later, by state education. The model was also exported to schools throughout the British Empire creating a public school aesthetic on a global scale. This chapter will explore the multifaceted factors at work in boys' public schools between 1830 and 1930, and investigate how they promoted and affected school uniform implementation and development.

In Britain, the term 'public school' was originally used to denote grammar schools founded or endowed for public use and subject to public management. From the nineteenth century, however, it indicated an elite secondary school, initially one of seven designated under the Public Schools Act of 1868. These were Charterhouse, Eton, Rugby, Harrow, Shrewsbury, Westminster, and Winchester, and as institutions they were known for educating the sons of the gentry. As the century progressed, the term was extended to encompass a range of fee-paying secondary schools which took pupils from beyond the local constituency and usually offered boarding facilities. These catered to both the middle and upper classes.

In general, the initial adoption of uniform at these schools can be attributed to practical considerations, particularly on the sports field. The subsequent widespread implementation of uniforms, however, demonstrates a clear correlation with the development of complex ideological practices associated with the schooling process in the public schools. These practices centered on the establishment of a new, national definition of what a public school was, how it operated and what it sought to achieve—the public school ethos (Curtis and Boultwood 1966: 80–85). This definition included an emphasis on sport, manliness, morality, and the maintenance of established class hierarchies (Wardle 1974: 34–35).

Sport and the introduction of uniform clothing

At Harrow in 1828 Lionel Montmorency, writing in *The Harrovian* recorded "exquisites in green surtouts and silver buttons" and "little V, with his hands in his pockets, and a dusky red handkerchief round his neck" (Montmorency 1828: 10–13) and this picture was fairly representative of clothing worn in the public schools around this date. All activities, including sport, were carried out in such fashionable outfits, the only concession made being the removal of coat and hat.

In the eighteenth century, games such as rugby, football, cricket, and the sport fives were well established at the public schools (although some of these, particularly rugby and football were yet to be fully codified and rules varied from institution to institution). They were, however, organized by the boys themselves; masters usually took little notice, often viewing them with detachment and sometimes distrust. From the mid-nineteenth century, this outlook began to change as team games were promoted as a means of improving school discipline and as an outlet for the less academically gifted pupils (Mangan 1986a: 10). Gradually sport ceased to be merely a channel for the mediation of indiscipline, but started to be encouraged for other reasons. Games began to be considered as a character-forming emblem of the wider ethos, administering a moral education through sport and teaching boys to lead and obey (Mangan 1986b: 18; McDevitt 2004: 10).

This growth in frequent and organized games sessions meant that everyday garments were no longer suitable for sport. They failed to provide the freedom required for vigorous exercise and expensive clothing was ruined by mud and sweat. At first, older clothes were worn on the sports field, but these too were found unsatisfactory (Cunnington and Mansfield 1969: 49–50). As team games became increasingly regulated, the ability to identify teams from one another was also required for both players and spectators. This practical element was particularly important in fast-moving sports and explains why uniforms were initially adopted for large team games and fast-paced activities. *Routledge's*

Handbook of Football, published in 1867, recommends placing teams in differing clothing, as this prevented: "confusion and wild attempts to run after and wrest the ball from your neighbour. I have often seen this done, and heard the invariable apology of 'I beg your pardon, I thought you were on the opposite side'" (*Routledge's Handbook of Football* 1867: 59).

A rudimentary football uniform including white trousers and black gaiters worn with colored jerseys and caps (usually a pill-box, skull cap, or knitted brewer's cap) was adopted at Harrow from the late 1830s, and from around 1840 onwards Winchester denoted affiliation by placing competing school teams in different colored striped jerseys—red and white on one side and blue and white on the other (Cunnington and Mansfield 1969: 49). Uniforms also began to emerge on the river: at the first Oxford and Cambridge boat race in 1829, the Oxford team wore dark blue striped jerseys, canvas trousers and black straw hats whilst Cambridge were attired in white shirts and pink sashes (Cunnington and Mansfield 1969: 289). Many of the garments adopted were modifications of upper-class casual and country styles of the period with the exception of the ubiquitous jersey, which probably originated in the clothing of fisherman and other outdoor workers and was embraced for its sheer practicality (Compton 2010: 55–56).

These new sporting garments were often brightly patterned and colored. In *Recollections of Rugby,* written in 1848, 'An Old Rugbeian' recounts how:

> Considerable improvement has taken place within the last few years, in the appearance of a match, not only from the great increase in the number of boys, but also in the use of a peculiar dress, consisting of velvet caps and jerseys. The latter are of various colours and patterns, and wrought with many curious devices.
>
> An Old Rugbeian (R.H. HUTTON) 1848: 131

These 'curious devices'—stripes, quarters, stars, crosses, and fleurs-de-lis were culturally prevalent due to the Medieval revivalism of the period; they were also, more importantly, simple to identify and reproduce. After an initial period of exuberance where clashing colors and designs were randomly adopted by players, decoration became gradually streamlined and specific colors or patterns began to be consistently associated with certain sports, schools, clubs, or houses. Wearing colors was an easy and distinctive way of showing allegiance and this process of codification can be seen as a reflection of the greater affiliation of boys with school and house which occurs during this period.

As games became an increasingly important part of the curriculum, sports clothing continued to develop in formality and specificity. By the end of the nineteenth century, teams wore uniform outfits, which were different for each sport and included whites for tennis and cricket with the adoption of striped blazers for many activities (Holt 2006: 365). This is articulated by Arthur Ponsonby, the British politician and writer, in his social commentary *The Decline of Aristocracy* in which he suggests that boys attending public school "must be fitted out with suits appropriate for each occupation, designed and cut on an approved pattern" (Ponsonby 1912: 191).

Being adept at sport also began to be viewed as the embodiment of the new Victorian notions of masculinity. The concept of muscular Christianity laid an increasing stress on the connection between religious certainty and physical strength meaning that the ability to do the right thing (as dictated by a pervasive Christian morality) was demonstrated by toughness and excellence at games (Cunningham 2006: 144; Hall 2006: 7–8). Boys strove to appear athletic and to do well at games, and prefects were chosen based on how closely they resembled this athletic and behavioral ideal. Boys consequently sought visible markers of their athletic prowess and prestige both on and off the sports field and clothing was the easiest method of communication. Initially pupils were awarded the privilege of flannels, which allowed preferred boys to play games in flannel trousers instead of ducks (a type of canvas trousers). Later, players were rewarded with specifically patterned caps, jerseys, ties, decorated blazers, or other privileges such as the right to wear knickerbockers or studs. For instance, at Charterhouse, cricket caps for excellence in school or house games were awarded from 1849, and football caps from 1861 (Tod 1901: 99–101). The demonstration of allegiance through sporting clothing and the demarcation of hierarchy through the signifiers of sporting prowess are part of a much wider trend of both group and personal identity creation in the public schools and in many ways sporting clothing acts as a precursor of later developments in this area.

Uniform and the public school ethos

The mid-nineteenth century was a period of large-scale wealth creation and this was responsible for a swift and significant growth in the size of the middle classes. These new businessmen and professionals defined themselves by a rigid and gender-specific moral code borrowed from Anglican religious principles in which the home was central and ideas of masculinity and femininity were closely tied to roles and responsibilities (Evans 2001: 347–48; Tosh 2007: 11–12). This middle class was not a unified mass, however, but contained many gradations of wealth, from the rich business elite through to lower-middle class shopkeepers and clerks. The focus here is the upper middle classes and the 'middling sort'; business and factory owners, physicians, lawyers, and others of similar status who could afford to maintain a large house and multiple servants (Tosh 2007: 12-13). These men demanded increased admission to status and political leverage through their money and one of the most accessible routes to social mobility was through education (Mangan 1986a: 128-129; Power et al. 2003: 7). The public schools (initially defined as the seven schools designated under the Public Schools Act of 1868 and noted above) were the education of choice for the sons of gentry and gentlemen and it was to these schools that the new upper middle classes sought admission and were, on the whole, given access (Gathorne-Hardy 1977: 26-8).

Although there were exceptions, conditions at these schools in the early nineteenth century were generally unpleasant and often brutal, particularly with regards to corporal punishment; beatings were frequent and this climate of aggression and violence was passed down to the regularly unsupervised boys who replicated it amongst themselves (Gathorne-Hardy 1977: 67). Around the middle of the century, conditions started to improve and the public school ethos began to emerge and develop. This ethos is difficult to articulate precisely but involved a strong emphasis on sport and the importance of games in teaching moral lessons of teamwork, leadership, and the management of physical discomfort. This tied in closely with the Victorian construction of manliness which was characterized by the traits of courage, fortitude, and decency, along with ideals of patriotic and military duty (Tosh 2002: 455). The ethos is also associated with an increasingly structured school environment with the organization of the institution into sub-units such as houses, societies, and teams (Wilkinson 1963: 15).

In general terms this change in the *modus operandi* of the public schools can be attributed to behavioral, structural, and moral reforms taking place in society, but it may also be viewed as the development of class exclusion processes which prevented the lower echelons of the middle classes from accessing a public school education. Having gained entry to the advantages that a public school education brought, the upper middle classes were reluctant to extend the privilege to others. Public schooling, therefore, became a method of policing the established class system through limitation of access and institutions sought to separate themselves from other educational establishments of a lesser status (Gathorne-Hardy 1977: 228). Schools were selective in their intake and the 'correct' methods of thought and behavior could be reinforced in pupils, a process in which uniform and clothing, along with other aspects of the public school ethos, played an important role. Public schools consequently became the places where gentlemen were made, initiating boys into manhood and preparing them for the future (Tosh 2005: 197). Those without such an education could not partake in the careers and activities reserved for these elite groups, particularly jobs in the rapidly growing British Empire.

Potential pupils who did not meet the correct upper-middle-class criteria were excluded in a number of ways, both practical and social. In the former category, the lower middle classes could be excluded financially through high fees and the costs of clothing and equipment. Schools were often in rural locations which necessitated complicated transport arrangements; the need for boys to board at the school further contributed to the expense. Additionally, entry-level requirements included a familiarity with classical subjects and this meant that boys were expected to have been suitably taught. On the social front, exclusion was implemented through the creation and maintenance of a clear distinction between pupils and non-pupils through dress, school practices, and everyday norms. The latter two forms of distinction are closely tied to the public school ethos, the development of which can be viewed as a combination of methods for the communication of appropriate ideals and complex ritualistic behavior which was hard for those outside the system to imitate. New rituals and expected behaviors were created and later justified as 'traditional' even within a short period of being introduced. Such a designation also served to emphasise the history of an institution placing it in a category of veneration and historical maturity.

The adoption of uniform can be seen as the most obvious way of differentiating between types of school, physically distinguishing public school pupils from non-attendees, although the development of structural differences such as houses, along with slang, complicated hierarchical codes, special celebrations, and other unique actions were equally exclusive. These changes served to create distinct communities with their own rules and social norms and reinforced a more subtle differentiation; a mental distinction on both sides of 'them and us.' This worked to "foster a corporate sense of superiority of elites—particularly when these had to be recruited from those that did not already possess it by birth or ascription," notably the upper middle classes (Hobsbawm 1983: 10).

In most schools, the greatest excesses of fashion were initially prohibited, usually in the period 1850–70, when gaudy ties, decorative waistcoats and fancy socks were banned and then stricter dress codes were introduced later. The Clarendon Report, published in 1864, was the culmination of a Royal

Commission investigation into the seven public schools in England (along with two day schools—St. Paul's and Merchant Taylors') in the wake of complaints regarding the management of Eton (*Report of Her Majesty's Commissioners, Vol I-IIII* 1864). This marks an early but key period in both the growth of the public school ethos and the initial stages in the control of school clothing, and as such the Report gives a unique overview of this process in a selection of schools. The Report consisted of questionnaires concerning the administration and structure of each school, followed by a series of interviews with masters and current and former pupils. Of the nine schools surveyed, there are direct or indirect references to dress in five. Clothing, as with all aspects covered by the report, is dealt with most completely at Eton. It is regularly asserted that Eton was the first public school to implement uniform in 1820, adopting its famous jackets in mourning for George III (see Cooper 2012: 122 or Snodgrass 2015: 233). This is clearly not the case as an interview with the headmaster Rev Balston in 1862 records little in the way of regulated clothing:

> 3613. (Lord Clarendon.) One more question, which bears in some degree upon other schools, namely with regard to the dress. The boys do not wear any particular dress at Eton ?—No, with the exception that they are obliged to wear a white neckcloth.
>
> 3614. Is the colour of their clothes much restricted?—We would not let them wear for instance a yellow coat or any other colour very much out of the way.
>
> 3615. If they do not adopt anything very extravagant either with respect to colour or cut you allow them to follow their own taste with respect to the choice of their clothes ?—Yes.
>
> 3616. (Lord Lyttelton.) They must wear the common round hat ?—Yes.
>
> 3617. (Lord Devon.) How far down in the school does the wearing of the white neckcloth go?—It does not extend to those who wear turn down collars.
>
> 3618. Do many of the boys wear stick ups ?—Yes, and they must then wear a white tie.
>
> *Report of Her Majesty's Commissioners, Vol III, Evidence Part 1* 1864: 116

Thus, with the exception of "the common round hat" (a top hat) and a white neckcloth, boys were allowed to dress much as they chose, and similar situations are apparent at Westminster and Rugby where there was no formal regulation of clothing but certain items were prohibited (*Report of Her Majesty's Commissioners, Vol III, Evidence Part 1* 1864: 367-75; *Report of Her Majesty's Commissioners, Vol IV, Evidence Part 2* 1864: 252). As the sons of wealthy families, pupils' garments are likely to have been fashionable in style and cut. This clothing, however, was not allowed to be too outlandish in appearance and this prevention of ostentatious display and encouragement of conservative dress was the forerunner of uniform in many establishments and marks the early stages in the regulation of clothing.

From this point forward the adoption of uniform took several routes, varying from school to school. The most common method was via a gradual process of increasingly strict dress codes. In other schools, uniform was imposed from above over a relatively short period of time and this is often seen in newer establishments. In a few interesting cases, uniform was introduced through boy-led designations of status and pupils conformed through peer pressure, a process which represented pupils actively partaking in the formation of the schools' unique appearance and exclusions processes. This is the case at both Harrow and Eton.

Uniform design

Public schools sought to create a uniform appearance that fell within the narrow limits of social and sartorial acceptability, but discernibly differentiated the school from other institutions both of the same social standing and those of a different class. Despite the creation of forums, such as the Headmasters' Conference (formed in 1869) and an increase in the number of inter-school sporting fixtures which provided greater opportunities for the informal exchange of ideas, schools remained fiercely protective of their autonomy and this makes broad generalizations difficult. This was particularly true with regards to areas of internal management such as curriculum and uniforms (Percival 1969: 1–3).

During the early to mid-nineteenth century there was a sobering of male attire; colors became darker, textures more limited, and decoration increasingly subtle. Simplicity rather than flamboyance became stylish and this steadily developed into a general distaste for significant singularity in appearance (Kuchta 2002: 177–8). This is not to say that masculine fashion was not important and increasingly prominent male consumers demonstrated their individuality through distinctive items, but overall changes to the fashionable silhouette were more gradual and the palette of colors used were more conservative than in women's dress. For the upper and middle classes neat, well-cut simplicity began to define masculinity. School uniforms reflected this, with pupils most commonly dressed in black, navy, and dark green in conservatively cut and fashionable styles and with little in the way of visible decoration. Particularly prominent were versions of the top hat and tails model (seen at Eton) as these reflected normal youth dress practices when they were adopted. Such styles were also practical for pupils as dark colors did not show dirt easily and fancy trimmings were easy to damage and hard to launder in quantity.

This conservatism operated alongside an increasing informality in clothing. As the precursor to day uniforms, sporting clothing naturally influenced uniform design. As menswear became gradually less formal in the late-nineteenth and twentieth centuries, such sporting styles were adopted for a greater range for situations. Consequently an item that had previously only been correct wear on the river became acceptable attire in other locations, including schools. In fact, such garments often became suitable for children prior to being generally acknowledged as conventional adult wear, as children were usually granted a greater degree of freedom from formal constraints (Shannon 2006: 187–8). This is particularly true of the blazer that started as rowing and cricket wear but became standard uniform for many schools from the early twentieth century. This was influenced by Stowe School, which opened in 1923 and sought to compete academically with the established public schools, but also to move away from archaic systems and practices. Stowe rejected the Eton aesthetic and instead placed boys in gray flannel suits during the week and blue serge suits on Sundays. The success of this approach caused other institutions to move to blazers and jackets, creating the shirt, blazer, and tie model that we know today (Guppy 1978: 58).

The Volunteer Movement of 1859 established local volunteer rifle and artillery forces to assist in the event of an invasion threat. Whilst foreign military campaigns were a normality, having a military presence in the community was, in some areas, novel. Their impact was felt in a variety of ways including an increased interest in, and awareness of, their operational activities and this was reflected in clothing through fashions for military detailing and styles. For example, Zouave jackets and bodices became fashionable for women in 1859 in imitation of the oriental-style jackets worn by the Zouaves, a light infantry regiment of the French army and these retained their popularity for some decades, passing into children's wear (Waugh 2011: 228). In the 1850s military frogging and braiding became a popular decoration and this reappeared as "Hussar" decoration in the 1880s (Waugh 2011: 147). In the wake of the Volunteer Movement, cadet corps were founded at many schools reflecting this public interest and allowing pupils to gain relevant training prior to taking up military careers. Eton was one of the first schools to establish such a corps in 1860. Specific uniforms along military lines were created, in this instance gray tunics with pale blue facings, but at other schools different adaptations of military dress were worn (Maxwell Lyte 1889: 474–5). This participation in cadet corps allowed the normalization of military activities and styling from an early age and ensured that the military aesthetic and the meanings it conveyed were understood within the public school system.

A direct military influence can be seen in the design of some school uniforms and the most prominent of these is Wellington College. The impetus for Wellington originated with Prince Albert, who sought to create a school for orphaned sons of military personnel and his ideas were heavily influential throughout the foundation process. Opening in 1859, the school was part military academy on German lines and part public school, and the uniform, which had been designed with input by Prince Albert himself, had strong military overtones. It consisted of a dark green jacket with brass buttons, plaid trousers, and a postman's cap emblazoned with red piping and a gilt crown, an outfit that appears to have been partly based on the dress of Scottish regiments (Newsome 1959: 58–64).

It is likely that this militarization had an impact on school dress in other public schools as well and this can be seen in military detailing—colored piping, insignia, and some styles of hat. The decorative, brightly colored military uniforms of the Victorian era were closely associated with overt displays of manliness and this appropriation of military design may be viewed as a reflection of the comparable cultures of masculinity within the commissioned ranks of the armed forces and in the public schools (Walton 2010: 41–3). The use of uniform in a military context and in schools is similar in many other ways, including the identification with corps, units and houses which was highlighted through uniform differences (Hughes Myerly 1996: 67). Parallels can also be drawn between the systems of hierarchy and sporting honors developing in public schools at this time and the notion of insignia in use by the armed forces.

Collective identity

Once uniforms had become established, they were increasingly regulated and obedience to strict dress codes were carefully policed by staff and, more prominently, by pupils. Closed groups tend to promote conformity and the tight-knit environment of the public school was no exception; as distinctiveness was frowned upon new boys found the pressure to conform overwhelming and these pressures were extended to the newly codified uniforms (Gathorne-Hardy 1977: 112–14). Writing in *Some People* about his time at Marlborough around 1900, Harold Nicolson describes this attitude in a conversation between himself and

Marstock, an excellent sportsman and a respected member of the school community:

> "Oh why, *oh why* will you persist in being different to other people? I give you up; you simply refuse to be the same." He paused and looked at me with real perplexity in those open eyes. "*I think you must be mad,*" he concluded solemnly. I went to my room determined ... I must pull myself together: it was only a question of being careful: if one was terribly careful one could succeed in being exactly the same. My whole energy during the terms that followed was concentrated on achieving uniformity.
>
> NICOLSON 1947: 35

Thus both the public school ethos and uniforms became self-sustaining, transmitting values and reinforcing the group mentality which they had played a part in creating. Despite some of these traditions being very recently implemented, the result was an increased emphasis on collective identity and uniforms became an outward fulfilment of both practical and ideological functions within the public schools (Synott and Symes 1995: 141). Uniforms, therefore, not only physically distinguished the pupils from others, but reinforced group identity and consequently helped to cement institutional values, by mentally distinguishing them as well. Boys were subsumed into the collective whole, subsequently adopting its beliefs, and uniforms represented an outward manifestation of the acceptance of these values.

Paradoxically, collective identity was also reinforced by a degree of carefully controlled divergence in uniform. Items such as house ties, sports colors, and badges for prefects all served to emphasize the notion of belonging to a community and being part of its hierarchy. When status was demonstrated by a difference in dress, it was easy for other members of the community to see when an individual was promoted or demoted (Davidson 1990: 21). Restrictions also allowed a system of privileges to be implemented in which the removal of a rule became a reward for good behavior, progression within the school or sporting accomplishment, providing a channel of control. Writing in 1929 but reflecting on his time at Charterhouse in the early 1900s, Robert Graves sums up these differences:

> The social code of Charterhouse rested on a strict caste system; the caste marks, or post-te's, being slight distinctions in dress. A new boy had no privileges at all; a boy in his second term might wear a knitted tie instead of a plain one; a boy in his second year might wear coloured socks; the third year gave most of the main privileges – turned down collars, coloured handkerchiefs, a coat with a long roll,

and so on ... but peculiar distinctions were reserved for the bloods. These included light-gray flannel trousers, butterfly collars, jackets slit up the back and the right of walking arm-in-arm.

GRAVES 1960: 43

These physical demonstrations of hierarchy were often developed by the boys themselves, and became increasingly elaborate towards the end of the nineteenth century. The higher up you were, the more freedom in dress was allowed, with "bloods" (usually used to refer to a senior member of an institution who excelled at games) the most highly privileged of all (Holt 1993: 81).

Emulation

As methods of exclusion developed at the established institutions, new schools opened which emulated these processes, consequently allowing families who could not access the higher status schools to give their sons a similar education. This can explain the widespread proliferation of middle-class boarding schools in the second half of the nineteenth century, creating an increasingly competitive educational marketplace and allowing some of these new institutions to gain prestige and status, in the words of Eric Hobsbawm:

> The tendency of the aspiring to imitate the institutions of the arrived made it desirable to draw a line between the genuine ... elites and those equals who were less equal than the rest. The reason for this was not purely snobbish. A growing national elite also required the construction of genuinely effective networks of interaction.

HOBSBAWM 1983: 295

Despite the creation of divisions between institutions, the numbers of acknowledged public schools increased towards the end of the nineteenth century as more schools developed a serious claim to the status, examples include Marlborough (1843), Lancing (1848), Hurstpierpoint (1849), and Haileybury (1862). The importance placed on the process of public schooling for the creation of gentlemen, a practice originally intended to exclude non-elites, ultimately allowed greater mobility to the middle classes through these new schools. The pervasion of the public school ethos to some extent replaced the importance of family background with that of institutional affiliation in the assigning of class; the substitution of the school badge for the family crest in essence reversing the intentions of the more established schools (Gathorne-Hardy 1977: 100–02).

That uniform played an important role in designation of status is indicated by a widespread interest in it and emulation both within the school system and in a more general sense in children's fashion. This fits into a wider picture of class emulation, with the middle classes of the late nineteenth century imitating the dress, as well as the home furnishings and personal items, of the upper classes. Easy imitation was assisted by the rise of the ready-made clothing industry and other mass production techniques, which enabled the creation and purchase of cheaper copies of upper-class styles (Perrot 1994: 85–6). This allowed members of the middle class to dress, at least, superficially in the same manner as those of higher rank. Goods and clothing, therefore, both denoted and disguised status, operating as visible markers of class culture. Initially items differentiated the upper classes and then, once imitated, disguised the disparity between classes except to a knowledgeable observer who could determine telltale differences in quality and appearance. Referencing the work of Douglas and Isherwood in her book *Middle Class Culture in the Nineteenth Century*, Linda Young states that:

> The consumption of goods, which at face value many seem a private or idiosyncratic choice, is seen on the scale of society as a force for social cohesion, a group-controlled pressure to conform to certain values and behaviours ... consumption is about power: the power to reinforce group associations, to include and exclude group relationships, to assert dominance and inculcate subordination.
>
> YOUNG 2003: 161

The rhetoric employed here in the discussion of consumer choice and social imitation, closely mirrors that associated with school uniforms and their role in creating and maintaining group identity and clear parallels may be drawn between the two.

Consequently, some public schools of a later foundation date implemented a rigid uniform code from the first—new schools were keen to present themselves in the same class and model as established institutions and so borrowed the appearances of prestige from their older contemporaries, sometimes imitating uniforms directly. As more schools opened, these new establishments were increasingly in competition with each other to win pupils. This resulted in greater scrutiny from parents as they chose where to educate their sons. Schools that could present the most correct public school image were more likely to attract pupils and increase their income and social standing (Gathorne-Hardy 1977: 100–02).

The status of public schools also meant that to resemble a public schoolboy, despite not attending such an institution, came to be seen as a mark of rank and new fashions of the mid-nineteenth century for boys were imitative of the normal wear of public school pupils, a process which is exemplified by the widespread adoption of the Eton jacket, a style of short, square, single-breasted jacket or "bumfreezer" that eventually became synonymous with the lower years at Eton (Cunnington and Buck 1978: 172–8) (see Figure 4.1). In the late 1840s J. Nicholls, owner of a Regent Street department store, produced and advertised a new design, the Eton jacket. At this date the style was by no means uniform wear at Eton (as evinced by Balston's comments in 1862), although the

Figure 4.1 Prince Henry, Duke of Gloucester, in Eton College uniform, 1914. He is wearing the traditional cropped jacket that was, by this point, uniform wear for lower years at the school. Library of Congress, Prints & Photographs Division, George Grantham Bain Collection [LC-DIG-ggbain-15452].

shape was widely worn by Eton schoolboys (McConnell 1967: 162). Nor was the style in any way exclusive to Eton, but was normal dress for upper class boys of school age. One must assume, therefore, that Nicholls chose to use the aristocratic reputation and widespread recognition of Eton to increase sales by allowing families to buy into the social prestige of the institution. In the early 1860s, manufacturers trying to build on the success of the Eton jacket also produced the Rugby and Harrow jackets. Such styles are listed in an 1860 advertisement for B. Hyam, a manufacturer associated with outlet shops in Manchester, Liverpool, Glasgow, and Dublin: "HYAM'S RUGBY, HARROW & ETON JACKET SUITS. Three Entire New Styles, becoming in design, serviceable for school or dress wear, and admirably adapted for Young Gentlemen" ("Advertisement—B. Hyam and the Spring" 1860). This was clearly a similar, although less successful, attempt to use the name of public schools to sell clothing as neither Rugby or Harrow had a formal school uniform in place at this stage (see Figure 4.2).

Eton jackets (and to some extent Rugby suits) continued to be widely worn for the next thirty to forty years, becoming best wear for the children of families that could afford it and even spread abroad, making a particular impact in America. The Eton jacket was generally worn with a stiff, wide, turned-down collar which became known as an 'Eton' collar. These items were considerably less expensive than the jackets and consequently, filtered downwards through the class system becoming a marker of respectability amongst lower middle class families who could not afford the whole ensemble (Ewing 1977: 114–16).

The public school aesthetic was also taken up in the twentieth century by girls' public schools and grammar schools. Girls' schools gradually adopted the trappings of boys' public school life from the sports ethic to the internal organization in an attempt to demonstrate similarity and consequently academic parity. School uniforms were no exception and increasingly masculine items were added to girls' uniform lists in imitation of those worn at boys' schools, notably shirts and ties. A similar pattern was seen within the new secondary establishments involving county, grammar, and high schools founded to meet middle-class demand. These, too, borrowed their uniform styles from the public schools, aping their status and communicating this to potential attendees.

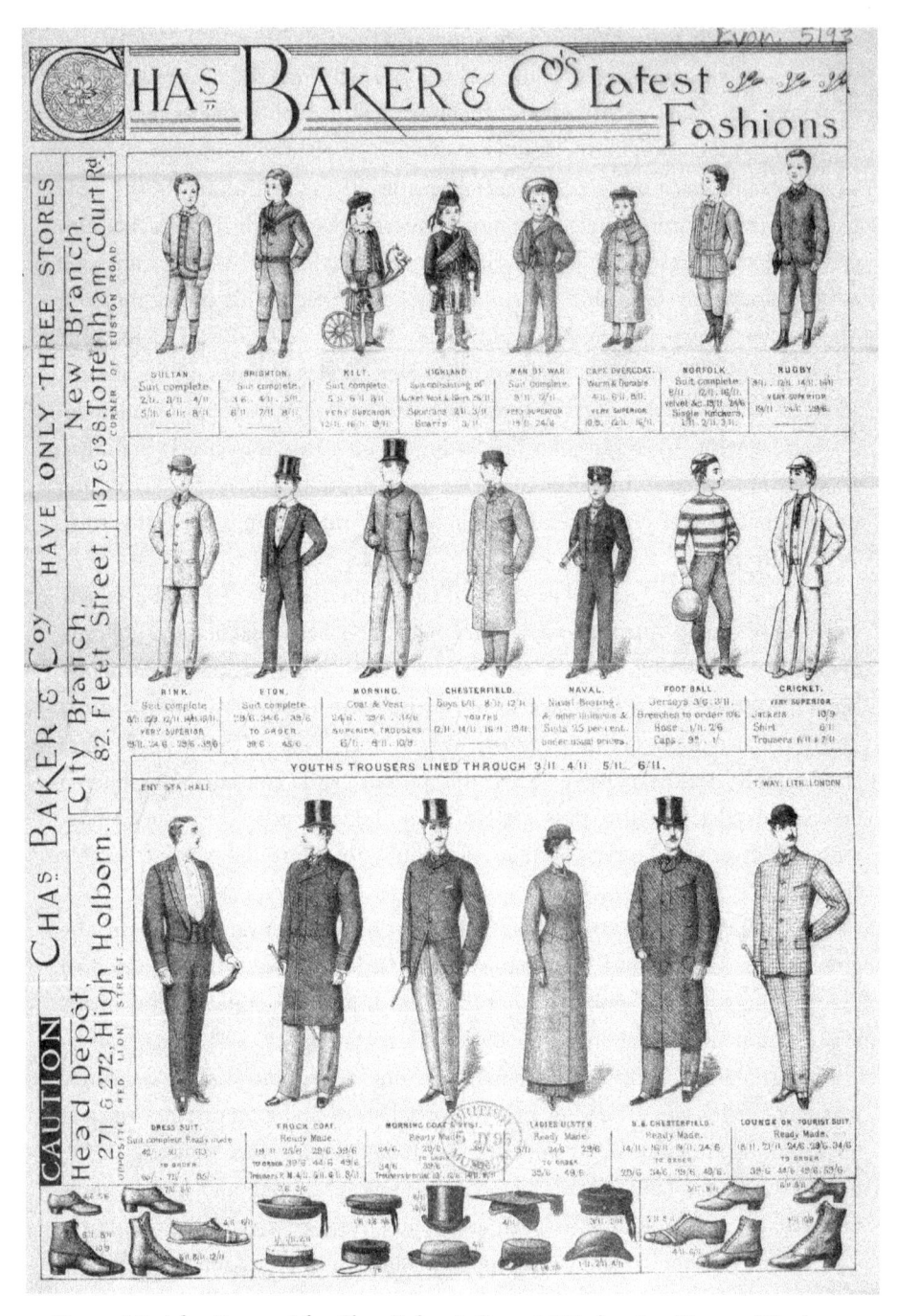

Figure 4.2 Advertisement for Chas. Baker & Co., *c.* 1885, showing Eton and Rugby suits for sale. © British Library Board [Evan. 5193].

Conclusion

Throughout this chapter the intricate linkage between the public school ethos and school uniform has been evident, with each reactive to the other. For example, the increase in the importance of organized games in the schooling process meant that proper sports clothing and the creation of team strips became a practical necessity. On the other hand, the significance of collective identity and allegiance to school and house was both reflected in uniform practices and reinforced by them. Uniform also visibly expressed facets of the public school ethos, projecting a socially appropriate image of class, masculinity, and morality. In this manner uniform was used as a tool to reinforce class boundaries, distinguishing public schools from other less elite establishments as well as promoting internal cohesion, which further excluded those outside the system.

Later in the nineteenth century an established, and sometimes anachronistic, school uniform also became a symbol of tradition communicating the venerable history of the oldest institutions and further emphasising the difference between the older schools and new foundations which aspired to the title of public school. Public school uniforms consequently became a status symbol to the middle classes and were widely imitated in both fashion and other educational establishments. This eventually resulted in some of these schools being elevated to the same rank as the more elite schools. In this way, school uniforms were a victim of their own success, their visibility and prominence made them easily imitable and they eventually became widespread throughout a range of educational institutions, but also within the middle classes at large. In opposition to its original intentions, school uniform became a tool through which the middle classes could display a similar appearance to the elite and this increased prevalence was paralleled with a change in meaning as school uniforms moved from being markers of status to merely signs of respectability.

References

"Advertisement—B. Hyam and the Spring" (1860), *Liverpool Mercury,* March 6.
An Old Rugbeian (R. H. Hutton) (1848), *Recollections of Rugby,* London: Hamilton and Adams.
Compton, R. (2010), *The Complete Book of Traditional Knitting.* New York: Dover Publications Inc.

Cooper, T. (2012), *Head on the Block,* Beauchamp: Matador.
Cunningham, H. (2006), *The Invention of Childhood,* London: BBC Books.
Cunnington, P. and A. Buck (1978), *Children's Costume in England 1300–1900,* London: A & C Black.
Cunnington, P. and A. Mansfield (1969), *English Costume for Sports and Outdoor Recreation; From the Sixteenth to the Nineteenth Centuries,* London: A&C Black.
Curtis, S. J. and M. E. A. Boultwood (1966), *An Introductory History of English Education Since 1800,* Foxton: University Tutorial Press.
Davidson, A. (1990), *Blazers, Badges and Boaters: A Pictorial History of School Uniform,* Horndean, Hants: Scope Books.
Evans, E. J. (2001), *The Forging of the Modern State: Early Industrial Britain, 1783–1870,* London: Routledge.
Ewing, E. (1977), *History of Children's Costume,* London: B.T. Batsford Ltd.
Gathorne-Hardy, J. (1977), *The Public School Phenomenon 597–1977,* London: Hodder & Stoughton.
Graves, R. (1960), *Goodbye to All That,* London: Penguin Books.
Guppy, A. (1978), *Children's Clothes 1939–1970: The Advent of Fashion,* Poole: Blandford Press.
Hall, D. E. (2006), *Muscular Christianity: Embodying the Victorian Age,* Cambridge: Cambridge University Press.
Hobsbawm, E. (1983a), "Introduction: Inventing Traditions," in E. Hobsbawm and T. Ranger (eds), *The Invention of Tradition,* Cambridge: Cambridge University Press, 1–14.
Hobsbawm, E. (1983b), "Mass-Producing Traditions: Europe, 1870–1914," in E. Hobsbawm and T. Ranger (eds), *The Invention of Tradition,* Cambridge: Cambridge University Press, 263–308
Holt, R. (1993), *Sport and the British; A Modern History,* Oxford: Clarendon Press.
Holt, R. (2006), "The Amateur Body and the Middle-class Man: Work, Health and Style in Victorian Britain," *Sport in History,* 26 (3): 352–69.
Kuchta, D. (2002), *The Three-Piece Suit and Modern Masculinity; England, 1550–1850,* Berkeley, CA: University of California Press.
McConnell, J. D. R. (1967), *Eton: How it Works,* London: Faber and Faber.
McDevitt, P. F. (2004), *May the Best Man Win: Sport, Masculinity, and Nationalism in Great Britain and the Empire, 1880–1935,* New York: Palgrave Macmillan.
Mangan, J. A. (1986a), *Athleticism in the Victorian and Edwardian Public School: The Emergence and Consolidation of an Educational Ideology,* London: The Falmer Press.
Mangan, J. A. (1986b), *The Games Ethic and Imperialism: Aspects of the Diffusion of an Ideal.* Middlesex: Viking.
Maxwell Lyte, H. C. (1889), *A History of Eton College, 1440–1884,* London: Macmillan and Co.
Montmorency, L. (1828), "Scenes at a Public School; First Day at Harrow," *Harrovian* I (1), 10–15.

Myerly, S. H. (1996), *British Military Spectacle; From the Napoleonic Wars through the Crimea,* Cambridge. MA: Harvard University Press.
Newsome, D. (1959), *A History of Wellington College, 1859–1959,* London: John Murray.
Nicolson, H. (1947), *Some People,* London: Pan Books Ltd.
Percival, A. C. (1969), *The Origins of the Headmasters' Conference,* London: John Murray.
Perrot, P. (1994), *Fashioning the Bourgeoisie: A History of Clothing in the Nineteenth Century,* Princeton, NJ: Princeton University Press.
Ponsonby, A. (1912), *The Decline of Aristocracy,* London: T Fisher Unwin.
Power, S, T. Edwards, G. Whitty and V. Wigfall (2003), *Education and the Middle Classes,* Buckingham: Open University Press.
Report of Her Majesty's Commissioners Appointed to Inquire into the Revenues and Management of Certain Colleges and Schools and the Studies Pursued and Instruction Given Therein; with an Appendix and Evidence, Vol. III. Evidence Part 1 (1864), London: Printed by George Edward Eyre and William Spottiswoode.
Report of Her Majesty's Commissioners Appointed to Inquire into the Revenues and Management of Certain Colleges and Schools and the Studies Pursued and Instruction Given Therein; with an Appendix and Evidence, Vol. IV. Evidence Part 2 (1864), London: Printed by George Edward Eyre and William Spottiswoode.
Routledge's Handbook of Football (1867), London: G. Routledge and Sons.
Shannon, B. (2006), *The Cut of His Coat: Men, Dress and Consumer Culture in Britain 1860–1914,* Athens, OH: Ohio University Press.
Snodgrass, M. E. (2015), *World Clothing and Fashion: An Encyclopaedia of History, Culture and Social Influence,* London: Routledge.
Synott, J. and C. Symes (1995), "The Genealogy of the School: an Iconography of Badges and Mottoes," *British Journal of Sociology of Education,* 16 (2): 139–52.
Tod, A. H. (1901), *Charterhouse,* London: George Bell and Sons.
Tosh, J. (2002), "Gentlemanly Politeness and Manly Simplicity in Victorian England," *Transactions of the Royal Historical Society,* 6 (12): 455–72.
Tosh, J. (2005), *Manliness and Masculinities in Nineteenth-Century Britain. Essays on Gender, Family and Empire,* Harlow: Pearson Education Limited.
Tosh, J. (2007), *A Man's Place: Masculinity and the Middle-Class Home in Victorian England,* New Haven and London: Yale University Press.
Walton, S. (2010), *Imagining Soldiers and Fathers in the Mid-Victorian Era: Charlotte Yonge's Models of Manliness,* Farnham: Ashgate.
Wardle, D. (1974), *The Rise of the Schooled Society; the History of Formal Schooling in England,* London: Routledge and Kegan Paul.
Waugh, N. (2011), *The Cut of Women's Clothes 1600–1930,* Abingdon: Routledge.
Wilkinson, R. H. (1963), "The Gentleman Ideal and the Maintenance of a Political Elite: Two Case Studies: Confucian Education in the Tang, Sung, Ming and Ching Dynasties; and the Late Victorian Public Schools (1870–1914)," *Sociology of Education,* 37 (1): 9–26.
Young, L. (2003), *Middle-Class Culture in the Nineteenth Century: America, Australia and Britain,* Basingstoke: Palgrave Macmillan.

5

Dissolving Vatican Uniform Hegemony: The Marist Road to Dress Freedom

William J. F. Keenan

Beware of all enterprises that require new clothes.
HENRY DAVID THOREAU, *Walden or, Life in the Woods* (1878[1854]: 27)

Introduction: dress signs of religious time

The dress codes of religious orders and congregations provide a well-stocked wardrobe in which to study the history and transformations of the ancient genre of corporate uniform, the religious habit. Sacred dress is the ultra-traditional counter-modern clothing mode. It bespeaks resistance to secular modern fashion and free choice dress ideology. From the mid-nineteenth-century to the 'aggiornamento' of the Second Vatican Council (1962–5), the Roman Catholic Church's extensive program of modernization generally known as Vatican II, the prescribed ecclesiastical costumes of professional religious virtuosi were regulated top to toe within a tight-knit framework of centralized dress controls established and monitored by the Vatican acting through its agents, the Religious Superiors. Following Vatican II, the stranglehold of the bureaucratic regime of religious body-self-discipline through dress was relaxed and religious communities—"the Pope's divisions," as Stalin called them (see Churchill 1948: 105)—entered upon an as-yet unfinished period of sacred uniform deregulation.

Based on their own archival record, this chapter traces the sartorial career of the Marist Brothers religious order over the modern era; it shows how the hegemonic sartorial empire of the Church was, at different points, accepted and accommodated to, and, subsequently, challenged and changed, in this case by the

Brothers themselves. In the Marist example, we obtain a close-up view of ways in which powerful corporate bodies, such as the Catholic Church, employ the 'soft power' of dress to promote transpersonal ideological interests. Prevailing theological 'fashions' are given sartorial expression in the context of the surrounding secular modern society, sometimes as signs of opposition to 'the world' and its materialist values; sometimes, as of late, as a medium of engagement and rapprochement with 'the signs of the times.'

The 'crisis' of sartorial uniformity in the face of the awakening of personal 'autonomization' within the strategically influential professional religious corps of the Church represents an important indicator of significant shifts in power and authority in contemporary religious and ecclesiastical life. It demonstrates, too, that uniform dress codes, even in the most traditional of contexts, are not necessarily immutable and fixed by traditions and cultures.

A clash of principles

The philosophical conundrum, as variously found in Thomas Hobbes, John Locke, Jean-Jacques Rousseau, and Voltaire, concerning the challenge of integrating, within the same intellectual, political, and ethical framework, the principles of Liberty and Equality, has its sartorial expression in the dress history of the Marist Brothers religious fraternity, a teaching congregation of the Roman Catholic Church. 'Tridentine' Catholicism generally refers to an adherence to the regulations ushered in by the Council of Trent, a reformist body which met intermittently from 1545 to 1563. For most of its history, Tridentine Catholicism, as fervently opposed to the French Revolution as its advocates were passionately in favor, exercised hegemonic control over the body-selves of its affiliated 'religious,' the members of religious orders and religious congregations. Somatic governance loomed as a uniform dress code.

The Founder of the Marist Brothers, the Marist priest Père Marcellin Joseph Benedict Champagnat (d. 1840), was born in the fateful year 1789. He was the son of a devout Catholic mother of ten children, Marie-Thérèse, and of the Jacobin Jean-Baptiste Champagnat, "a local revolutionary leader" (Furet 1856; Chastel 1948; Farrell 1983: 237), who, during the 'Terror,' served as Deputy Mayor of Marhles in the Lyonnais region of eastern central France. One can only imagine how the Champagnat family of ideologically divided parents, multiple siblings, and two enclaustrated sisters, as well as, occasionally, recusant priests, given domestic shelter in this time of rabid anti-clericalism (McGraw 1983: 116), negotiated their Sunday dinner conversations. Marcellin was to take the "Marian" road adopted by his fervent mother (Sester 1991). How the principles of the French Revolution eventually caught up with the successors of Père Champagnat is, perhaps, part of the irony of history, even the "cunning of reason" (Hegel 1959: 209).

The community of religious Brothers Marcellin Champagnat established in 1817 at the village of Lavalla near Saint-Étienne were initially formed as catechists and elementary schoolteachers for poor children of peasant families. The Little Brothers of Mary, so-called, were grounded in the principles and precepts of traditional Catholicism in every particular; religious dress codes included. However, both that faith and its religious dress material expressions have undergone a number of mutations over the period of Marist evolution within the Church. The Marist dress code is a site in which the conflicting standpoints of Catholic traditionalism and progressive secular modernism vied for pre-eminence.

This chapter tells the story of the liberalization of the uniform religious dress regulations of this now globalised religious order. The focus here is on three transformative moments in Marist dress history, each stage representing a decisive shift in the Brothers' sartorial identity in the Church and within the wider society. Stage 1: 'Livery'—the 'charismatic' period of patrimonial authority (1817–62); Stage 2: 'Uniform'—the 'hegemonic' period of centralized Tridentine power (1863–1962); Stage 3—the 'emancipatory' period of Vatican 11 'liberalization' (1963–present).

A tale of dress liberty

Based on the Marists' archives, this chapter traces the sartorial career of the order over the modern era. The hierocratic sartorial empire of the Church was, for a century from 1862, accepted by members of the Marist congregation without question. As with any other uniform—including military, corporate, professional, and educational—the formal religious dress of the Brothers, the religious habit, symbolized group identity and collective belonging. It depersonalized the individual monk, rendering his personal dress choice void; thus incorporating the "body-self" (Turner 1996) of the religious 'actor' within the religious *Gemeinschaft*, an act of obeisance to the normative order of the group and the authority of Religious Superiors. To "their dress" (Bogatyrev 1937), the Brothers added a 'Marian' spiritual inflection.

As a sign of opposition to 'the world' and its secular, materialist values, the religious habit, with its symbolic articulation of the canonical virtues of Poverty, Chastity, and Obedience, served as a veritable sartorial *cordon sanitaire* between the body-self of the professed religious virtuosi and the 'world.' The Benedictine Boulding (1980: 123) commented: "The habit is a 'sacrament' of our incorporation into the great 'sacrament of monastic life … an eschatological sign." By means of "garments of holiness," the religious body-self is "sacralized," "set apart and forbidden" in Durkheim's (1915: 47) terms. At the same time, the religious dress sign can assume quite 'this-worldly' dimensions. The Tridentine sumptuary law of the Church, for example, made religious institutes, in effect, "uniformed organizations" (Joseph 1986) whose members "wore ideology" (McVeigh 2000). In this sense, sociological considerations trumped theological ones.

To put the matter in Weberian-Foucauldian terms: through the governmental principle of subsidiarity, the leadership and management strata of the religious orders and religious congregations, the Religious Superiors, acting on behalf of the Roman Church as a centralized "caesaro-papist" bureaucracy, exercised their legalistic power and pervasive control over the everyday lives of the membership, to administer, surveil, and discipline, on behalf of the Vatican "panopticon," a "hegemonic" (Anderson 2017) religious uniform regime. In effect, throughout the four centuries and more of Tridentine Church history, the formal religious organizations of Roman Catholicism became, in matters of dress-code regulation, Goffmanesque 'total institutions.' This authoritarian 'carceral' spirit exposed that 'other face' of the 'uniform,' the side that invoked repression rather than veneration. All uniforms have this "duality," writes Jennifer Craik (2005).

The complexity and layering of the religious dress sign in terms of *both* its variety of material forms *and* in terms of its multiplicity of theo-spiritual meanings is an under-researched aspect of "the religious life of dress" (Mayer-Spillman *et al* 2012; Hume 2013). The Marist case helps advance our knowledge of dynamic historical relationships between 'material bases' of clothing and their 'ideological superstructures' within a 'little tradition.'

Foundation livery, 1817–62

While at a seminary in Lyon, Marcellin Champagnat—the Founder of the Marist Brothers—became a member of The Society of Mary, a newly created community of priests devoted to the Virgin Mary, under whose spiritual inspiration they sought to take part in the post-Revolution project of the Christian reconversion of France (*patria Mariae*). The presiding genius of the group was the wayward figure of Father Jean-Claude Courveille (Zind 1969, vol. II: 763–4; Balko 1981; Farrell 1983: 196). Courveille proposed a costume for the Brothers that would reflect his somewhat secular counter-vision of their role and status within the Marist Society. His image of the 'Little Brothers' was of a basically secular body of trainee primary level classroom assistants, a 'service class' duly subordinate to the priests within the parishes of the vicinity. To that end, he designed an outfit that would reflect this secularized definition of the Brothers' menial professional standing but, at the same moment, boost his own status as a celebrity in the region with his personal retinue.

Following the local Archbishop's permission in 1824 for the new community to wear a distinctive costume, the mercurial Courveille appears to have stepped in immediately with his design suggestion. For a religious priest, by all accounts Father Courveille himself was a non-conventional dresser. According to one source (Avit 1972: 48) this flamboyant figure: "[D]ressed himself in a rather ornate long blue cloak, took on all the airs of an abbot, and passed himself off as the superior at every opportunity." Hosie (1967: 76) comments: "[H]e played the role magnificently in his Marist religious habit: a top hat, a sweeping sky-blue cloak and a swaggering cane."

Champagnat's understanding of the rationale for the Brothers was wholly different and always deeply religious. More at home with stonework than books (Balko 1976; Bellone 1982), but deeply suffused with Marian piety (Chastel 1948; Coste 1963; Gibson 1971), Champagnat's dress sense can be described as 'spiritual.' It was rooted in the ecclesiastical tradition of the religious habit as a sacramental sign of the consecrated body set apart for divine service. Courveille and Champagnat, men of highly different personalities, styles, and outlooks, were the contenders for control of the formative stages of the Marist Brothers' dress tradition. Out of the conflict of their competing dress design ideas and styles, the one secular in inspiration and appeal, the other religious in intent and derivation, would emerge the shape and spirit of Marist dress history in its infancy.

By contrast with Courveille's unmistakable urbanity, everything about Father Champagnat betokened the countryman. One contemporary, Brother Laurent (in McMahon 1988: 135) remarked: "When he came in at evening, it often happened that he was in tatters, all covered with sweat and dust." This disregard for appearances when hard physical graft needed to be done coincided with one of the periodic waves of fashion-consciousness that occasionally sweeps through the clergy. McMahon writes (1988: 135):

At this period, too, some clerics had unfortunately been affected by a movement towards ostentation in dress – one of the accompaniments of the Bourbon restoration. To them, Champagnat's style of priestly conduct was quite an affront. His manual labour, his working clothes, his living a common life with the Brothers were just not the done thing.

Brother Jean-Baptist Furet, Champagnat's first hagiographer and contemporary, speaks of him as "a rough-hewn Christian" and refers to his appearance (Furet 1856: 259, 279, and 446–7) in such terms as "craggy," "swarthy," and "virility of features." Sester (1981: 721) calls him "a man of the mountains." Furet, both an actor in and a recorder of the unfolding costume drama of the nascent Marist Brothers religious order, put his version of the Champagnat impress on Marist foundation garments as follows:

> In 1828, Father Champagnat completed the costume of the Brothers … [T]he Father gave the Brothers the soutane, the mantle, the three-cornered hat, and the white rabat. When they made their vows, he added a cord, for the vow of Obedience, and a brass cross, set in ebony, for those who made Profession.
>
> He also arranged that the soutane, which up to that time, had been buttoned, should be fastened with hooks and eyes, to about midway down, and that the remainder should be sewn. Several reasons induced him to make this alteration, the principal of which were that, arranged in this manner, it was more modest, and consequently, more befitting their state; it was more easily kept neat and tidy; for the buttons, after some time, became worn and soiled, disfigured the soutane.
>
> FURET 1856: 164

Champagnat's more prosaic dress design, in contrast to the more 'dandified' style of Courveille, showed the clear religious intent of the aspiring Marist movement and signalled to the Church and the world that the fraternity had every intention of becoming a 'sponsored organization' of the powerful Tridentine Roman Church. Champagnat's religious dress conception of "the Livery of Mary," as he referred to it (Keenan 2006), went deep into the sub-soil of Counter-Reformation Catholicism. Moreover, it was rooted in a more "primitive" (Crawley 1931) "mystical" dress sensibility that was never far from the surface of "Catholic piety" (Douglas 1973; McSweeney 1987). Champagnat believed that "the livery of Mary" was imbued with "kerygma," spiritual power (Keenan 2009), that protected its wearers from anticlerical attacks, and all-but guaranteed them "a good death" (Keenan 1998: 10). However, his formation as a priest was suffused with the ascetic, 'rigorist' values of the pre-Revolution 'Ultramontane' Church. Counter-modern

'Fortress Catholicism' and strict religious uniform codes were homologous. In time, the 'mystical' would give way to the 'legal-rational' within the dress sense of the Marist Brothers Institute. On Champagnat's death in 1840, his successor as Superior-General, Frère François, secured Vatican 'approbation' of the Institute in 1863, by which time the Brothers were fully 'at home' in their unmistakably 'clerical' clothing. The century of Vatican-approved Marist 'uniform' was at hand.

Tridentine uniform, 1862–1962

As Nathan Joseph (1986: 131) puts it "[T]he modern uniform is closely linked to the central tendency of our age—an increasingly pervasive bureaucratization." In the Tridentine incarnation of religious life, this insight readily applies to the 'uniformization' of the religious habit. Marist dress regulation is a case in point. The 'Restoration' era in post Revolution France was highly supportive of this 'Ultramontanist' or 'Papalist' model of Church life in which the religious orders and congregations played a spearhead role in what, in effect, was a grand countermodern offensive by 'the Church Militant.' The Marist Society—the tripartite organization of priest, Brothers, and Sisters—founded at a Lyonnais seminary in 1816 embraced this vision and mission with gusto. In this enterprise, securing Vatican approbation of the religious dress code was a sure sign of having arrived. Uniform dress recognition went hand in hand with incorporation as an official sponsored religious organization of 'the embattled Church.' The religious 'uniform' was *contemptus mundi* incarnate.

Successive editions of Marist official documents laid down the requirements of the Brothers' dress code which had to be approved at every stage by the officials in the Roman Curia. In the *Constitutions* of the Marist Brothers Institute for the period extending from the time of approbation in 1863 to the 1908 internal review of the Institute's customs and general practices, the dress code is mapped out in minute particulars. Perhaps the best illustrations of this fastidiousness can be drawn from the 1881 'Trial' *Constitutions* that went directly to the Holy See for approval. A number of the articles of this highly formal document reveal the 'uniform' thinking prevailing among the shapers of Marist dress tradition at the time:

> Article 40: The Brothers' clothes shall be plain, modest, and conformable to evangelical poverty. They shall wear a triangular hat, a white rabat, a soutane of black cloth, closing in front with hooks and eyes to the middle, then sewn to the bottom (of the soutane); a mantle of the same cloth as the soutane, and long

enough to cover the arms stretched out; cloth or linen stockings, not knitted but sewn, and shoes with laces; those who have made the vow of Obedience shall wear, besides, a woollen cord, and the Professed Brothers a cross.

Article 41: There must be entire uniformity in the whole costume of the Little Brothers of Mary, both in the form of the clothes, and the quality of their material, as well as in the manner of wearing them.

Article 42: The Procurator-General and all those under him, whose duty it is to supply and procure the Brothers' clothing, are bound to follow exactly all that the Constitutions prescribe on the subject.

MARIST *Constitutions* 1881

Mary Ellen Roach and Joanne Eicher (1965: 61) refer to the dress and adornment of religious orders as "coercive." Needless to say, perhaps, the Marist Brothers' 'uniform' dress code was endorsed by the Vatican, and fully adhered to by members of the expanding, globalizing Marist Brothers Institute. By the end of the nineteenth century, the Institute membership had swollen to 7,180 subjects, in 733 Marist-owned establishments worldwide. From Canada to China, from Samoa to Spain (see Figure 5.1), the Marist "quasi-uniform" (Joseph 1986: 149–50), designed to be a universal symbol of the Marist global presence, was placed daily in classrooms on every continent before a Marist pupil roll

Figure 5.1 Arrayed in triumph. Photo-collage of 'the Marist Martyrs' (estimated at 174 Brothers) killed during the Spanish Civil War, 1936–9, exhibited at the Marist Brothers Generalate, Rome. Private collection.

of 94,770 students. Corporate success of this magnitude brought the Institute ever closer under the inspectorial eye of the Vatican bureaucracy. The quinquennial review and renewal of the Brothers' official regulatory codes became routine and a pretext for further elaboration and rationalization of dress norms (Keenan 2000).

Overt references to the 'magicality' of 'the Livery of Mary' are missing from the formal record. What was emphasized were the 'evangelical counsels'. The 1908 *Marist Directory* enjoins the Brothers to "cherish Poverty as their mother," and, accordingly, designs the following prescriptions, which endeavour to address the position of clothing in this "economy of salvation":

> Article 138: They shall have nothing of their own; everything of the Institute shall be in common, with the exception of clothing, the use of which shall be personal ...
>
> Article 139: Besides a copy of the Constitutions, the Brothers shall have the use of a Brass Crucifix, a Rosary, a New Testament with the Imitation of Christ, a Manual of Piety, a Roman Missal in common binding, a penknife, a pocketbook, a razor, and a travelling bag. These objects and their clothing are the only things they may take with them when they leave one House for another.
>
> Article 141: They shall not have, for personal use, anything that shuts with lock and key.
>
> MARIST *Directory* 1908

However, this use of the term 'personal' is somewhat ambiguous. In effect, it meant that the Brothers' religious habits—including socks and other intimate garments—were not inter-changeable between confrères. But the garments themselves were not *personally* chosen. They were issued.

The 1930 redaction of the *Rules of Government* flesh out the design of the Marist dress code in minute detail and excerpts from this high-point in the 'uniform' stage of the Brothers' dress tradition are revealing of just how far the Tridentine clerical mentality and regime could go to exercise close corporeal control over religious subjects:

> Article 69: They shall wear a white rabat, about four-and-three-quarter inches long, four inches wide, and having a slit of about one inch in the middle of the lower edge.
>
> Article 71: Cotton handkerchiefs shall be used, except when, through some facial weakness, linen ones are needed. In any case, they should not be of a gaudy colour.

> Article 72: The Brothers shall not use gloves without real necessity and in this case they shall wear black woollen gloves.
>
> Article 74: The Brothers shall wear laced shoes covering the whole foot, and these should be solid rather than fashionable. Each Brother ought to have two pairs.
>
> Article 80: Each Brother may be supplied with a soutane every eighteen months, a cloak every five years, and three pairs of stockings every year; and also two pairs of knee breeches and a hat every three years.
>
> Article 82: The Brothers should have their hair cut at least every two months, being careful to observe the rules of modesty befitting their state.
>
> MARIST Rules of Government 1930

By modern 'secular', and later Marist, standards all this is tantamount to a highly intrusive and a deeply depersonalizing regime. Clauses in the 1908 Marist *Inventory* exhibit an even more pernickety disposition. For instance:

> Article 618: The Brothers' shoes should be made of cow-hide leather, shall cover the whole foot, be fastened with mohair or cotton shoe laces, and have round toes regardless of fashions, times or places.
>
> Article 626: The Brothers' wearing apparel ... shall bear their admission number.
>
> MARIST Inventory 1908

Nothing much altered in the key components of the Brothers' uniform dress code from this point on, until that is, the Vatican II 'turn' (see below). Other than in countries with hard secularist and/or anti-clerical jurisdictions, throughout the global Marist world Brothers routinely wore the religious habit as 'a sign of consecration'—some say 'a sign of contradiction' to 'worldly' values—and 'a sign of witness' to 'Marian' simplicity. The Novice receives the habit consisting of: a black soutane (though a white soutane is available for hot climes); a rabat ('Geneva bands'-style: a white plasticized clerical collar, formerly starched linen); a cord containing three knots representing vows of Poverty, Chastity, and Obedience, which each Brother makes at 'First Profession.' A brass crucifix is presented to a Brother on making his Perpetual Vows in the Institute. With this set ensemble, the dress norms of the Brothers had stabilized, if they had not, indeed, frozen. This was an 'army issue' system, the kind of 'regulation dress' regime (see Figure 5.2) befitting the most 'carceral' of 'total institutions.'

The Tridentine hegemony was a far cry from the world in which Father Courveille was able to flaunt his 'retainers' in idiosyncratic garb. Was the uniform

Figure 5.2 Full Tridentine battle dress. Brother Joseph Vital (*b*. 1877, Damme, West Flanders), took the habit in 1895 and spent his Marist career in South Africa as a physical education instructor. Private collection.

an 'anthropologically strange' world away from the sacramental spirituality with which Champagnat's idea of 'the Livery of Mary' was sympathetic?

Expressive revolution, 1962–2017

Vatican II, the extensive movement to update and adapt Roman Catholicism to the modern era, including the religious life institutes of the Church, represents the 'unfrozen moment' in the dress history of the Marist Brothers. The times were propitious. Following the inspiration of his predecessor, John XXIII, Pope Paul VI—in pursuit of his advocacy for 'a noble simplicity' in ecclesiastical vesture, a reaction against the monarchical imperium of the Tridentine Church—sold off papal tiaras, cast aside red velvet slippers, dumped ermine-collared stoles, flamboyant cloaks, gaudy stockings, elaborate buckles, tasseled sashes, and all such triumphalist paraphernalia of ecclesial pomp. The critique of the hierarchical, reactionary, sumptuous sartorial power of the Tridentine Church found its secular cultural expressions in "profane" fancy dress, erotica, and the fashion marketplace (Cunliffe 1993; Keenan 1999a, 1999b). In Federico Fellini's 1972 movie *Roma*, svelte models parade on a runway displaying chasubles and mitres for a theatrical audience of nuns and clerics; while a stiff and starchy presiding prelate, an androgynous cardinal in crimson robes and 'cool shades,' falls asleep. The time for a sacred wardrobe overhaul was at hand.

The elected Marist Brothers' Superior-General charged with the Marist implementation of the Vatican II renewal charter for religious life within the Church, *Perfectae Caritatis,* (The Decree on the Adaptation and Renewal of Religious Life, 1965), was the Mexican Brother Basilio Rueda Guzmán, a qualified sociologist, who took a long-term 'realist' view on Marist dress. His 'measure' was functionality. He set his analysis within the context of the 'communalism' of the pioneer Marist Brothers. He wrote in one of his Circulars, "Project for Community Life":

> In the beginnings of the congregation, things for common use extended even to personal linen or underwear. Once washed it was sent to the linen-room, where each one went to take out his share, trying to get hold of articles which fitted him more or less. With a soutane to cover the lot, this did not raise problems of personal dignity which would be insoluble in western civilization at least.
>
> The "use in common" stays today at levels which are just as painful for persons of a certain temperament: tape-recorder, car, etc. I am not going to tell you at what point such and such an object should be in common; there is a matter there to examine.
>
> GUZMÁN 1979: 105

Guzmán and his General Council sought to replace the 'impersonalism' of the Tridentine model of 'the vowed life' by an orientation in keeping with the modernizing strategy of the Church at this time. In secular society, the "sixties" witnessed the "expressive revolution" (Martin 1981); and the counter-cultural movement in favour of communitarianism. At a time when the declining appeal and "senescensization" of religious life (Fuchs-Ebaugh 1977; Cada et al. 1979) were apparent, the Marist Brothers responded to the conciliar call to 'update, adapt and adopt' by conforming their dress code to the zeitgeist of freedom of self-expression (see Figure 5.3).

The enthusiasm for the renewal project was palpable. The initial trials "ad experimentum" allowed virtually total free dress choice; and radically foreshortened a complex, variegated dress tradition to the terse: "We wear a distinctive badge of the Institute" (*Draft Constitutions* 1985: 20). However, within two years, the Marist Institute pulled back from this radical minimalist sartorial libertarianism. A compromise solution was introduced considered to be more in keeping with the dialectical nature of the Church's renewal strategy in which *ressourcement* ('back to the roots') and *aggiornamento* ('adaptation to the signs

Figure 5.3 Airing post-conciliar differences. Gathering of Brothers attending Marist 'renewal' course, early 1974. Private collection.

of the times') were held together within an integrated theological and sociological framework. For the Brothers, this materialized as a 'dual' dress code in which the 'classical' option of distinctly traditional uniform religious attire was permitted alongside the 'modern' option of personally selected secular modern clothing. The 1987 Marist *Statutes* (nos. 61 and 61.3) specify as follows:

> Our habit is a type of attire, such as a suit, which is appropriate for a member of a lay Institute. Alternatively, it may be a soutane, with a Roman collar or Rabat, a cord or for the permanently professed, a crucifix ... The norms of the Province fix the details of dress. Whatever way we are dressed, we are always careful to avoid vanity or negligence.
>
> MARIST *Statutes* 1987

In the same vein, the 2007 Marist *Constitutions* repeat this verbatim, since when nothing substantial has changed in the Marist Brothers' *Rule*—the particular framework of precepts governing the life-world of any specific religious order—regarding the dress of the Brothers. With recent Institute membership of 3,270 (2014 Marist figures)—in stark contrast with 9,997 (1961 Marist figures) in their uniform heyday (Statistiques *Frères Maristes* 1967)—it would be naïve to infer from this correlation any causal connection between 'conservatism' in religious attire and recruitment to the Marist Brothers. The fact is that the Brothers' religious habit has become a 'Sunday best' option to be worn on special occasions such as jubilees and major feast days. At the canonization of Saint Marcellin Champagnat in Rome on 18 April 1999, and in 2017 throughout the worldwide events celebrating the bi-centennial 'birthday' of the founding of 'The Little Brothers of Mary' in 1817, many Marist Brothers chose the 'historic' dress option of 'the Livery of Mary,' their formal religious habit, for these memorializations. The "clothes of God" (Roach and Eicher 1979: 18) have assumed a privileged status within the individual Brother's personal wardrobe. For the better part of the working week, a Brother is likely to adopt attire appropriate to the social and cultural habitus in which he is immersed.

Around the Marist world today, one is likely to encounter Brothers in T-shirts and 'casuals,' baseball caps and sneakers, motley-colored clothing of all sorts. In recent years, a newly fashioned emblematic cross has been created and embossed on a badge for each Marist Brother to wear as a symbol of common identity around the world. The cross marks the French foundation of the Institute by using the inscription of the original French title, *Petits Frères de Marie* (Little Brothers of Mary). In the centre of the cross is a simple 'M' for Mary, patroness of the community. The 'M' is unique because it mimics a young person's handwriting, a 'remembrancer' of the Marist apostolic mission with youth. On the back are six small nail heads, highlighting the labor of the first Brothers who had to fabricate nails to sustain the original community and build their schools, chapels and residences. In this metallic "recall" of the hallowed time of Marist origins, artistically condensed within a "summarizing symbol" (Joseph 1986: 120), a variegated and convoluted sacred dress tradition, with its maximal expression in the religious uniform, has been minimized, miniaturized to a Marist-monogrammed tie-pin or lapel badge.

Conclusion: a two-state politics of the wardrobe

The tension between the dress traditionalists and the modernizers (Flannery 1989) appeared to have been resolved. 'Uniformitarians' could coexist alongside 'libertarians'; 'intransigents' and 'abolitionists' work, rest, and pray side by side. Dress choice—dress freedom—was given official sanction. A 'revolution from above' had taken place in this 'elaborated' version of the Marist dress code. The Vatican sartorial monopoly was broken; the great dress partition removed. But, again, we must emphasize: *cum permissu superioribus*—a 'top-down' resolution, an example of a more general approach to 'change' under-emphasized, perhaps, in the contested history of the Catholic Church (Stark 2016).

In terms of Isaiah Berlin's "two concepts of liberty" (Berlin 2002), the Brothers had won for themselves (as had other religious orders) both "negative freedom" meaning *freedom from* hegemonic dress control *and* "positive freedom" meaning *freedom to* make individual personal dress choices. Within the Marist *Fraternité*, the principles of dress *Liberté* and dress *Egalité* had established an irenic rapprochement (Keenan 2013). The Marist iteration of "two Catholic Churches" (Archer 1986) had been averted. And, more broadly still, the two great independent sartorial 'kingdoms'—the Religious and the Secular—found here two representative Marist sartorial tribes demonstrating that a constructive dress 'kula' was possible. In the contemporary global climate of 'wardrobe politics'—including the hijab question, faith symbols in the workplace, and transgender dress rights (Miller-Spillman et al. 2012)—these local 'experiments in peaceful living' within 'little traditions,' themselves within 'great traditions,' may have a wider point.

The partial 'secularization,' or better, perhaps, 'declericalization,' of the Marist dress code can be described in many ways—'detraditionalization,' 'vernacularization,' 'laicization,' 'informalization,' 'liberalization,' 'indigenization,' 'localization,' 'repersonalization'—depending on what best fits the 'discourse' in play. One might add, "subjectivization" and "the inward turn" (Taylor 1992); or, with the sixteenth-century Reformers' "dissolution of the monasteries" in mind, "delayed cultural Protestantization." However we describe it, the Marist attenuation of the strict uniform dress code represents the unlocking of the Tridentine sartorial 'iron cage.' The Marist Brothers avoided irreparable 'sectarian' splitting on 'the dress question' largely because of the institutionalization of a binary structural framework whereby the individual Brother could be, within his own conscience and inclination, authentically 'Marist' and 'modern' at the same moment, whether he wore the religious habit all or some of the time, routinely or rarely.

Two sartorial 'worlds,' each suffused with its own predominant principles: the 'Religious,' orientated around order, hierarchy, tradition, collective obedience, duty, and discipline; the 'Secular,' orientated around change, choice, self-expression, and individuality. The new Marist sartorial consensus no longer

Figure 5.4 Unity in diversity. Marist Brothers Institute Superior General and the Marist General Council, Rome, 1984. Private collection.

divided the Institute into two separate warring camps, "fashion" versus "anti-fashion" (Polhemus and Procter 1978). It was a case of tradition and modernity, collective and individual, history and present circumstances, working together in a non-zero sum twin-track accommodation of interests, commitments and worldviews. This "dual dress economy" (Keenan 2004: 55) where the sacred and the profane; the religious and the secular co-habit (see Figure 5.4) has both admirers and critics in the Marist Institute, in Vatican circles, and among the laity. Divisions are not uncommon between conservatives, moderates and liberals—and "indifferents," sartorial agnostics—within modern-day religious life at large on "the dress question" (Campbell-Jones 1979; Michelman 1999).

From the viewpoint of the *longue durée* of religious dress history, this seismic shift in the locus of dress 'power' from the 'imperative co-ordination' of the Marist Institute as a Vatican-sponsored organization to the body-self 'agency' of the individual Brother, is both a symbolic and a real step on the road to freedom of self-expression within a 'little tradition'. The so-called "subjective turn" brings a mixture of enthusiasm and resistance whether it surges up within secular or religious contexts, particularly those with long-standing collective traditions of conformity and obedience, Catholic or otherwise (Giddens 1991; Montemaggi 2017). Such may be the necessary price of liberty.

For how long the "unfreezing" of Vatican uniform dominion represented by this sartorial "two-state" hybridic structure will last is a matter of conjecture (Keenan 2002); and, even, perhaps, some concern, given signs of "retraditionalization" (Wittberg 1994) within society (Lilla 2016), the Church

(Hudson 2008), and religious life (White 2016) in the present day. Yet, could that Marist moment of sartorial dehegemonization contain lessons applicable in some measure to other contexts and settings in which the inclination towards uniform over-control seeks to impose its inflexible, domineering will upon the sovereignty—the sacrality—of the body-self, religious or secular?

Acknowledgments

I wish to record my gratitude to the Marist Brothers—Rev. Brother Justinian R.I.P., former Assistant Superior General, in particular—whose generosity gave me access to Marist archives and permissions to reproduce images.

References

Anderson, P. (2017), *The H-Word: The Peripeteia of Hegemony,* London: Verso.
Archer, A. (1986), *The Two Catholic Churches: A Study in Oppression,* London: SCM Press.
Avit, Frère (1972), *Abrégé des Annales de Frère Avit, 1789–1840,* Rome: Marist Generalate Archives.
Balko, A. (1976). "Champagnat as Craftsman," *FMS,* 19: 10, Rome: Marist Generalate Archives.
Balko, A. (1981), "New Light on Fr. Courveille," *FMS,* 46: 662–5, Rome: Marist Generalate Archives.
Bellone, G. B. (1982), *Cerchiamo l'autentico Champagnat,* Genova: Edizioni I.T.I.
Berlin, I. ([1958] 2002), "Two Concepts of Liberty," in Henry Hardy (ed.), *Isaiah Berlin: Liberty,* Oxford: Oxford University Press, 166–217.
Bogatyrev, P. ([1937] 1971), trans. R. Crum, *The Function of Folk Costume in Moravian Slovakia,* The Hague and Paris: Mouton.
Boulding, M. (1980). "Background to a Theology of the Religious Habit," *Downside Review,* 98: 110–23.
Cada, L. J., L. Fitz, R. L. Foley. T. Giardano and C. Lichtenberg (1979), *Shaping the Coming Age of Religious Life,* New York: Seabury Press.
Campbell-Jones, S. (1979), *In Habit: An Anthropological Study of Woking Nuns,* London: Faber and Faber.
Chastel, G. (1948), *Marcellin Champagnat,* Paris: E. Alsatia.
Churchill, W. (1948), *The Second World War: Volume 1—The Gathering Storm,* London: Cassell.
Colin, J. C. (1838), *Entrevue de J. C. Colin avec Mgr. Frayssinous, Récit Familier du Père Colin à ses Confrères,* vol. 1. Dupuy: Liullet.

Coste, J. (1963), trans. S. Fagan, *The Spirit of the Society of Mary,* Rome: Marist Generalate Archives.

Craik, J. (2005), *Uniforms Exposed: From Conformity to Transgression,* Oxford: Berg.

Crawley, E. (1931), "Sacred Dress," in Theodore Besterman (ed.) *Dress, Drink and Drums,* London: Harmondsworth, 139–64.

Cunliffe, L. (1993), "Get the Habit," *Vogue,* August: 136–7.

Douglas, M. (1973), *Natural Symbols: Explorations in Cosmology,* Harmondsworth: Penguin.

Durkheim, E. ([1912] 1915), trans. J. W. Swain, *The Elementary Forms of the Religious Life,* London: Allen and Unwin.

Eicher, J. and M. E. Roach-Higgins (1992), "Definition and Classification of Dress," in R. Barnes and J. Bubolz Eicher (eds), *Dress and Gender: Making and Meaning in Cultural Context,* New York: Berg, 8–20.

Farrell, K. B. (1983), *Achievement from the Depths: A Critical Historical Survey of the Life of Marcellin Champagnat (1789–1840),* PhD Thesis, University of New England.

Flannery, A. (1989), "This and That: The Habit Made Redundant?," *Religious Life Review,* July/August: 182–92.

Fuchs-Ebaugh, H. R. (1977), *Out of the Cloister: A Study of Organizational Dilemmas,* Austin, TX: University of Texas Press.

Furet, J.-B. (1856, 1947, 1989), *Life of Joseph Benedict Marcellin Champagnat,* Paris, Tournai, Rome: Society of St. John the Evangelist, Desclée & Co.

Gibson, R. (1971), *Father Champagnat: The Man and his Spirituality,* Rome: Marist Generalate Archives.

Giddens, A. (1991), *Modernity and Self-Identity: Self and Society in the Late Modern Age,* Cambridge: Polity Press.

Guzmán, B. R. (1979), "Project for Community Life," *Circulars* 27 (1), Rome: Marist Generalate Archives.

Hegel, G. W. F. ([1892] 1959), *The Logic of Hegel, 2nd edn,* Oxford: Oxford University Press.

Hosie, S. W. (1967), *Anonymous Apostle: The Life of Jean-Claude Colin,* New York: Morrow.

Hostie, R. (1972), *Vie et Mort des Ordres Religieux,* Paris: Desclée de Brouwer.

Hudson, Deal W. (2008), *Onward, Christian Soldiers: the Growth in Political Power of Catholics and Evangelicals in the United States,* New York: Threshold Editions.

Hume, L. (2013), *The Religious Life of Dress: Global Fashion and Faith,* London: Bloomsbury.

Joseph, N. (1986), *Uniforms and Non-Uniforms: Communication through Clothing,* New York and London: Greenwood Press.

Keenan, W. J. F. (1998), "Death Figures in Religious Life: Components of Marist Death Culture, 1817–1997," *Mortality* 3 (1): 7–26.

Keenan, W. J. F. (1999a), "Of Mammon Clothed Divinely: the Profanization of Sacred Dress," *Body & Society,* 5 (1), 73–92.

Keenan, W. J. F. (1999b), "From Friars to Fornicators: the Eroticization of Sacred Dress," *Fashion Theory*, 3 (4): 389–410.

Keenan, W. J. F. (2000), "Clothed with Authority: the Rationalization of Marist Dress-Culture," in L. B. Arthur (ed.), *Undressing Religion: Commitment and Conversion from a Cross-Cultural Perspective*, Oxford and New York: Berg, 83–100.

Keenan, W. J. F. (2002), "Twenty-First Century Monasticism and Religious Life: Just Another New Millennium," *Religion*, 32 (1): 13–26.

Keenan, W. J. F. (2004), "Dress Code Communication in Sociological Perspective," in Philip Hills (ed.), *As Others See Us; Selected Essays on Human Communication*, Dereham: Peter Francis Publishers, 36–58.

Keenan, W. J. F. (2006), "*Sacre Bleu*: Faith, Fashion and Freedom: Marist Foundation Garments 1817–1862," in Elisabeth Arweck and William J. F. Keenan (eds), *Materializing Religion: Expression, Performance and Ritual*, Farnham: Ashgate, 116–37.

Keenan, W. J. F. (2009), "Divinity and Power in Minute Particulars: Politics and Panentheism in the Implicit Religion of Marist Socks," *Implicit Religion*, 12 (2): 201–20.

Keenan, W. J. F. (2013), "Über kleine Freiheiten: Die Dualität der Bekleidungsfreiheit," in Clement Sedmak (ed.), *Gleichheit: Vom Wert der Nichtdiskriminierung*, Darmstadt: WBG, 203–26.

Lilla, M. (2016), *The Shipwrecked Mind: on Political Reaction*, New York: New York Review of Books Publications.

McGraw, R. (1983), *France 1815–1914: The Bourgeois Century*, London: Fontana.

McMahon, F. (1984), *Marist Milestones: A Champagnat Pilgrimage*, Rome: Marist Generalate, Archives.

McMahon, F. (1988), *Strong Mind, Gentle Heart. A Life of Blessed Marcellin Champagnat*, Drummoyne, NSW: Marist Brothers Publications.

McSweeney, B. (1987). "Catholic Piety in the Nineteenth Century," *Social Compass: International Journal of Sociology of Religion*, 34 (1/2): 203–10.

McVeigh, B. J. (2000), *Wearing Ideology: State, Schooling, and Self-Presentation in Japan*, Oxford: Berg.

Martin, B. (1981), *A Sociology of Contemporary Cultural Change*, Oxford: Blackwell.

Mayer-Thurman, C. C. (1975), *Raiments for the Lord's Service: A Thousand Years of Western Vestments*, Chicago: The Art Institute.

Mayo, J. (1984), *A History of Ecclesiastical Dress*, London: B.T. Batsford.

Michelman, S. O. (1999), "Fashion and Identity of Women Religious," in Linda B. Arthur (ed.), *Religion, Dress and the Body*, Oxford: Berg, 135–46.

Miller-Spillman, K. A., A. Reilly and P. Hunt-Hurst, eds (2012), *The Meaning of Dress*, London and New York: Fairchild Books.

Montemaggi, F. E. S. (2017), "The Authenticity of Christian Evangelicals: Between Individuality and Obedience," *Journal of Contemporary Religion*, 32 (2): 253–68.

Polhemus, T. and L. Procter (1978), *Fashion and Anti-fashion: An Anthropology of Clothing and Adornment*, London: Thames and Hudson.

Poupar Report (1823), *Enseignement Primaire. Rapport de l'Inspecteur Poupar* (Archives du Départmental du Rhône, T.-Vers-XXV) and Marist Generalate Archive.

Roach, M.E., and J. B. Eicher (1965), *Dress, Adornment and the Social Order*, New York: John Wiley.

Roach, M. E. and J. B. Eicher (1979), "The Language of Personal Adornment," in J M. Cordwell and R A. Schwarz (eds), *The Fabrics of Culture: the Anthropology of Clothing and Adornment*, New York, Paris, and The Hague: Mouton, 7–21.

Sester, P. (1981), *Tribute to the Founder, FMS* no. 49, Rome: Marist Generalate Archives.

Sester, P., ed. (1991–2), trans. Leonard Voegtle, *Letters of Marcellin J. B. Champagnat*, Rome: Marist Generalate Archives.

Society of Mary (1881), *Constitutions*, Rome: Marist Generalate Archives.

Society of Mary (1908), *Directory*, Rome: Marist Generalate Archives.

Society of Mary (1908), *Inventory*, Rome: Marist Generalate Archives.

Society of Mary (1930), *Rules of Government*, Rome: Marist Generalate Archives.

Society of Mary (1987), *Statutes*, Rome: Marist Generalate Archives.

Stark, R. W. (2016), *Bearing False Witness: Debunking Centuries of Anti-Catholic History*, New York: Templeton Press.

Statistiques Frères Maristes 1967. Rome: Marist Generalate Archives.

Taylor, C. (1992), *The Ethics of Authenticity*, Cambridge, MA: Harvard University Press.

Taylor, M. J., ed. (1968), *The Sacred and the Secular*, Englewood Cliffs, NJ: Prentice-Hall.

Thoreau, H. D. (1878[1854]), *Walden or, Life in the Woods*, Boston: James R. Osgood.

Turner, B. S. (1996), *The Body and Society: Explorations in Social Theory*, London: SAGE Publications.

White, H. (2016), "Springtime's Over, Ladies: Francis' Plans for the 'New Conservative' Religious Orders," *The Remnant*, 23 July.

Wittberg, P. (1994), *The Rise and Fall of Catholic Religious Orders: A Social Movement Perspective*, Albany, NY: State University Press, 1994.

Zind, P. (1969), *Les Nouvelles Congrégations Enseignantes en France de 1800 à 1830* St. Genis-Laval, Lyon: Centre d'Histoire du Catholicisme Français de l'Université de Lyon, Le Montet.

Part Three

Uniforming Leisure

In this section, uniform is addressed as an aspect of everyday life, particularly in relation to the rationalization and organization of cultural modernity. Here, uniform is understood as the deep codification of dress at certain historical moments, whether this concerns an increase in specialized dress as deemed appropriate for particular activities or the attempted production of new collective subjectivities, whereby a level of homogeneity is deemed desirable to mask existing differences and tensions. From Kemalist reforms in Turkey, as addressed by F. Dilek Himam, to the invention of leisure clothing in Britain as discussed by Geraldine Biddle-Perry, both were enabled by plans for the sartorial homogeneity of citizens. Uniformity made national identity somehow easy to read, but also demarcated neat divisions of time into work and leisure.

The desire for and imposition of order at times of accelerated change were fundamental responses to the pressures of modernity in many arenas, from modernist architecture to the mapping of territory, from social reforms to the regulation of time. As explored in this section, this ordering was manifest in regulatory clothing that was either encouraged through specific policies, or adapted through broader cultural norms that championed appropriate sartorial expression for specific activities or states of being. One clear instance of this, although not specifically addressed in the essays, was the elaborate code governing mourning dress in the second half of the nineteenth century, which included nuances of fabric and color and specialist garments to indicate the degree of bereavement. Whilst not appearing to be uniform in the conventional sense, being able to understand and partake in the wearing of codified dress indicated an understanding of the 'correct' ordering of specific cultures and a rationalized subjectivity.

The codification of dress also informed the commercial development of the clothing trade. If different clothes were deemed necessary for specific activities or situations, this indicates opportunity for manufacturers to produce an ever-wider variety of garments that could be marketed in response to new forms and gradations of leisure, from cycling in the late nineteenth century to motoring in the inter-war period to more recent spectatorship at home or away football matches and the baffling varieties of footwear designed for participants in a multiplicity of sports. It also led to the design of uniform 'leisure' clothing by those who would counter the excesses of capitalism, although also in the name of rationality, such as the Russian Constructivists. This was most famously through the work of Varvara Stepanova (1894–1958) who produced striking designs for *sportodezhda*, or sports costumes, in 1923. These genderless garments were intended to support not only free movement but also liberation from the tyranny of class difference as worn on the body. Within uniforming leisure then, we see the appearance of hyper-rationalization underscored by a commitment to the bottom line, whether it be a deep adherence to cultural norms, an increased profit margin, or a more utopian future.

6

Fashionably Rational: The Evolution of Uniformed Leisure in Late Nineteenth-Century Britain

Geraldine Biddle-Perry

The idea of 'leisure uniform' seems an oxymoron. Leisure infers a freedom from uniformity and an engagement in non-specific activities released from the constraints of everyday life. However, in his discussion of the historical meanings of leisure in Western culture, Chris Rojek 'de-centres' such a belief by demonstrating how the spatial and temporal dimensions of leisure are always instrumental to the economic apparatus and the class and social relations of industrial capitalism (1995). Modernity, he argues, did not just invent some indefinable, indeterminate thing called 'leisure.' Rather, the *concept* of leisure as 'free time' and a neutral space outside of work and domesticity became integral to the modern consciousness (Rojek 1995: 2). Social historian Peter Bailey evidences how, from the early nineteenth century, work and leisure were "no longer intertwined in the continuum of shared activities that characterised the daily and yearly round ... leisure was time clearly marked off from work, to be pursued elsewhere than in the workplace and its environs," but both were organized around the regulatory mechanisms of industrial capitalism and the productive tempo of the clock (Bailey 1978: 4). Max Weber's "Protestant work ethic" found expression in attempts to control individual and collective bodies through the dual concept of improvement, achieved through scientific rational advance, and "self-improvement," achieved through temperance, hard work, and useful play (2006). Recreation in Western capitalism was 'rationalized': it came to be seen as a reward for hard work that, like money, had to be both 'earned' and 'spent' wisely.

This essay explores the productive relations of leisure 'at work' in the construction of a modern sense of self in late nineteenth century Britain through a fashion historical lens. Previous research has examined how the spatial context of outdoor recreational leisure, particularly suburban club cycling, promoted sartorial display in a way that both maintained social distinctions and allowed a fluidity of interpretation and social aspiration that could be both problematic and potentially liberating (Biddle-Perry 2014a). New systems of identification and status recognition were discursively circulated through shifting style trends and a rapidly expanding mass market that reinforced existing hierarchies of status but also revealed cleavages within and between old and new social groupings. All the paraphernalia and coded rituals of deportment and dress that the regulation of work *and* leisure implied were always responsive to the external realities of social and economic competition and of massive demographic change (Biddle-Perry 2014b).

Rational recreational leisure participation was rooted in the sensibilities of middle-class Protestant asceticism that Weber (2006) theorizes was established as part of the religious reformation that took place in Northern European society from the sixteenth century. Work and leisure were progressively viewed as discrete activities whose productive pursuit required a shared moral purpose. Anti-Catholic religious belief was projected on to the everyday world and the actions of individuals within it through a concept of a religious 'calling' that usefully encompassed an ethical as well as spiritual obligation to create and maintain wealth and prosperity. The essence or 'spirit' of this form of modern capitalism was a belief that serving the greater glory of God on earth was a burden that could only be shouldered by spending one's life in sober utility, self-control, hard work, and the eschewal of luxury, wastefulness, self-absorption, and adornment. For an increasingly powerful middle class, rational recreation acutely synthesized political reform with new attitudes to fashionable consumption and a rapidly expanding mass market.

In this essay, the concept of rational recreation is developed in relation to two key nineteenth-century theorists, Georg Simmel (1964; 1904a; 1971) and Thorstein Veblen (1994), whose contemporary studies situated leisure, fashion, and dress as important forms of symbolic exchange in the new arena of modern life that the city and modern industrial capitalism was opening up. This frames a new approach to understanding the symbolic and material mechanisms of leisure uniformity in antithetical terms, that is, as the 'other' to working and competitive sporting bodies equally being formulated and fashioned. From the mid-nineteenth century, new forms of display and the acquisition of cultural and consumer 'knowledge' progressively marked out differences between classes and gradations of social status through the tastes and social mores of an emergent politically and culturally powerful bourgeoisie. The Victorian rational recreation movement incorporated ideas of social and economic improvement into a complex set of beliefs around the healthy body as a metaphor for more deep-seated understandings of different identities. The fashionable embodiment of such ideas always also implied a parallel system of status recognition to make clear distinctions between differently gendered and classed modern bodies.

Over the course of the nineteenth century, the wearing of distinctive forms of clothing specific to activity and environment became *de rigeur* for all types of sporting and recreational leisure activity (Cunnington and Mansfield 1969; Biddle-Perry 2014a, 2014b). This chapter explores the evolution of a modern leisure uniform whose purpose was to distinguish leisure time, space, and bodies as 'free' from the ideological, physical, and social constraints of everyday life while at the same time being compelled to take these as their reference point. This was an age in which the wearing of all kinds of uniforms was a vital construct in the invented traditions of class and nationhood that sought to channel and control the desires and actions of the newly enfranchised masses (Hobsbawm and Ranger 1983). As a potent instrument of social control, how was modern leisure rationalized as crucial to a new arena of consumer agency, and made uniform both ideologically and materially?

Rationalizing leisure

Leisure—by the very nature of its embodied form and function—provided a temporal and spatial forum for the constitution of new social bodies. The conceptual dimensions of modern leisure as it emerged in the nineteenth century became part of a whole discourse around competing ideas of healthy and moral citizenship, but it also arguably became fundamental to defining for the middle classes what it meant to *be* 'middle class'. Productive work and leisure staked out the parameters of their new political, economic, social and cultural territory in a new and expanding arena of fashionable status recognition. Religious conviction was harnessed to the political economy of an emerging professional and industrial middle class, and provided a platform from which to subdue the potentially dangerous democratic aspirations of the working classes *and* contest the historic socio-economic and cultural dominance of the aristocracy. This symbiosis between leisure and work functioned as a form of middle-class consciousness, so that "… in the enaction of their superior example ... they would be reminded of their own moral responsibilities" (Bailey 1978: 170–1). Across a range of political and religious affiliations, middle-class philanthropists, social reformers, and political activists sought to re-shape the working-class character by addressing what was seen as their appetite for worthless pleasure and idle amusement. Bailey argues: "Leisure constituted a problem whose solution required the building of a new social conformity—a play discipline to complement the work discipline ... pursued through the reform of popular recreations rather than their repression" (Bailey 1978: 5).

Attitudes and values were governed by the imperatives of work and a horror of the indolence, prodigality, and excess that characterized traditional 'sport' and gaming. There was a great deal of discussion by Sabbatarians and other cultural commentators about what types of sport and leisure might fall under the category of 'useful' by virtue of possessing some sense of purpose other than passing the time. This was motivated as much by middle-class guilt around hedonistic enjoyment and the potential subversion of the internal disciplines of thrift and industry, as it was about leading by example in the face of a feckless working class *and* parasitic ruling class. As Peter Bailey (1978: 76–7) points out, traditionally, it was the *abuse* rather than use of leisure time that had imprinted itself on the middle-class consciousness. Work and leisure action and its deportment had to conform to the same political and social ideological imperatives that were the mainstay of this new social order: the eschewal of aristocratic excess and working-class prodigality on the one hand, and on the other, a reinforcement of a growing non-manual/manual divide that from the mid-nineteenth century came to dominate British society along a fault line of middle-class cultural anxiety.

The critical approaches of Georg Simmel (1964; 1904a; 1971) and Thorstein Veblen (1994) have been the focus of widespread critique within fashion theoretical and historical studies since the 1980s and are central to contemporary approaches to fashion and dress as embodied social practices (Entwistle 2000: 98–102).[1] Understandings of top-to-bottom style diffusion as the causal feature of fashion change and the implication that social status barriers expressed through clothing were difficult or impossible to overcome are now seen as anachronistic (Crane 1993). Veblen's anti-fashion stance, it is argued, also trivializes fashion and fashion change as essentially feminine and thus superficial (Wilson 1985: 52–3). However, the mechanisms of these theories in the light of such critiques can still offer important insights into the relationship between new forms of consumerism and the processes of identification and display through which the classes, particularly the middle classes, were formed and re-formed into more homogenous social groupings (Simmel 1964). Both theorists were concerned with the ways in which the social reality of modernity entailed an ambiguous striving for social order and organization, and an engagement with the transitory and the new. Simmel explored these complexities in relation to two oppositional forces impelled by the experiences of the modern city: the search for uniformity and the desire for distinction. The metropolis offered individuals new opportunities for spectacle and display but the excessive array of goods to purchase, and a lack of the old social hierarchies and systems of identification that existed in traditional pre-industrial societies, constantly threatened to overwhelm and destabilize any sense of a coherent sense of self and its modern social relations. These potentially antagonistic forces, Simmel argued, could be overcome through the consumption of goods and services, particularly dress, that visibly articulated both collective conformity and individual differentiation. He concluded:

> Fashion is the imitation of a given example and satisfies the demand for social adaptation; it leads the individual upon the road which all travel, it furnishes a general condition, which resolves the conduct of every individual into a mere example. At the same it satisfies in no less degree the need of differentiation, the tendency towards dissimilarity, the desire for change ...
>
> SIMMEL 1904a: 138

Veblen's model of modern consumerism, like Simmel's, is effectively one of identification and demarcation, but one that affords primacy to the high cultural value and social status attached to leisure and consumption; and the classed power relations inherent in its mechanisms of comparison, aspiration and 'emulation.' Veblen's critique of a new and powerful 'leisure class' in America at the *fin de siècle* theorizes the acquisitive excesses of 'conspicuous consumption' that swiftly became obsolescent as they 'trickled down' from the upper classes and were taken up by those below them on the social ladder seeking to emulate their tastes and styles. However, the rational foundation of Veblen's satirical commentary also opens up an alternative discourse of modern leisure and fashionable consumerism by tracing its rise in terms of an evolutionary shift of power from the 'predatory' instincts of a pre-industrial aristocracy to the 'pecuniary' pursuits of an industrial middle class.

Veblen (1994) evidences how, in the eighteenth century, peer esteem and social status were allied with a sense of merit and concepts of honor through productive predatory activities such as hunting, military battles, and territorial conquest that wealth, land, and power have brought. However, the mere accumulation of such power and the acquisition of money, goods, and property were progressively seen as insufficient in themselves to differentiate their owners from those below them in the social hierarchy. This led to a gradual and "more strenuous insistence on leisure" as the measure of gentility by visibly making clear upper-class abstention from agricultural labor (Veblen 1994: 26–7). Superior cultural status was proclaimed through the acquisition of rare works of art and curiosities and the private pursuit of knowledge of "the dead languages and the occult sciences ... the latest properties of dress, furniture and equipage" (Veblen 1994: 29). Upper-class leisure and consumption via a process of 'selective sifting' assumed a 'symbolic utility' by usefully allying new forms of idleness and play with old forms of agricultural industry and the predatory culture of military conquest and traditional field sports.

It is this equation between 'selective sifting' of those aspects, traits, and habits of a previous predatory age that offer a symbolic utility *and* an imposition on the lower classes and orders that was the foundation for Veblen's arguments about the emergence of a new leisure class in the late nineteenth century. The "conspicuous consumption" of all the paraphernalia of a middle-class household was the means by which their reputation and social status was upheld: "... the utility of both alike for the purposes of respectability lies in the element of waste that is common to both" (Veblen 1994: 52). An upwardly mobile professional and industrial middle class selectively sifted the 'symbolic utility' of an aristocratic culture of leisured exclusivity to visibly communicate their status not as upper-class idlers, nor as lowly workers, but through their ability to afford a life of leisure through hard work and thrift.

A new, contested, landscape of modern leisure had emerged in which new forms of consumption and display were integral to the emergence of spectacularly fashioned classed and gendered, working and leisured bodies. But this latter contingency was a process fraught with difficulties for an aspirational middle class for whom traditional leisure pursuits were seen as "the weakness of an ill disciplined and animalistic working-class" and/or the "badge of a vicious and unduly privileged aristocracy" (Bailey 1998: 17–19). The concept of an aristocratic sporting and leisured heritage upon which to model and transform a new modern identity was problematic. While certain sections of the middle classes certainly did participate in such activities, a significantly greater number were far more likely to be driven by a puritanical eschewal of such activities (Holt 1989).

Samuel Smiles was one of the leading proponents of a Victorian reformist agenda; in his first book entitled *Physical Education* (1838) he railed against the "sham gentility" of a decadent and dissipated upper class. Smiles consistently emphasised the 'gentlemanly' qualities of power rather than refinement, and an independence of spirit evidenced in an unwillingness to be flattered or intimidated by these 'counterfeits.' Smiles advocated the "wholesomely cultivated mind and body, taught to endure, disciplined to obedience, self-restraint, and the sterner duties of chivalry" (cited in Haley 1978: 207). Essayist and philosopher Thomas Carlyle savagely attacked the dandy as a self-absorbed, grotesque relic of an outworn aristocratic order. Indebted to the martyrs of Protestantism, for whom the highest form of action was enduring with patience and stoical composure both physical and spiritual torment, the moral authority of Carlyle's new models of heroism arose by virtue of qualities of self-discipline and self-denial (Adams 1995: 21). The obligation to find fulfilling work and enjoy productive leisure activities was integrated into a model of rational recreation that expediently and, in Veblen's terms, 'selectively sifted' ideas about the human body and its moral deportment that were a mixture of traditional Christian belief and the various distillations of the findings of modern biological science (Park 1987: 7–34).

This struggle to reconcile a new model of middle-class manhood with older concepts of aristocratic masculine power constituted one of the founding symbolic oppositional discourses of Victorian culture (Adams 1995: 26–8). Smiles, in the most well-known of his treatises *Self Help* (1859), which sold over 20,000 copies in its first year, promoted the idea of the "self-made man" distinguished by a moral and physical "robustness" that marked him out as a member of a new gentleman class, an "aristocracy of Character rather than an aristocracy of blood" (Smiles 1859: 416).

Symbolic utility: honest, hard-working tweed

The theories of Simmel and Veblen are useful because they demonstrate an understanding of the mechanisms of modern industrial capitalism in relation to wider systems of social and symbolic exchange. These operate in a constant state of tension in relation to the new spaces of the modern city where a sense of self was formulated in the relationship between environment and self-presentation. For Simmel, the meaning of goods is located in a "dialectic of objectification": the life of the city and its complexities demand that people became more "specialised" in order "to give ones own personality a certain status within the framework of metropolitan life" (Simmel, 1971: 336). Veblen's rational critique seeks to expose the excesses of irrational conspicuous consumption and the strivings of a new leisure class to stand out from the crowd. Both schemas describe a contested landscape of bourgeois work and leisure in which the fashioning of each operated in relation to the other in the symbolic assertion of earned rather than inherited wealth, hard work and thrift rather than hedonistic profligacy and idleness. Antithesis was the driving force of nineteenth-century conspicuous consumption impelled by new systems of surveillance and the moral imperative of rationality in its widest sense. Let us now consider this antithetical impetus 'at work' in the fashionable production and consumption of new kinds of *specifically* leisured bodies.

The period after 1880 witnessed the widespread adoption of the tweed suit consisting of variations of 'Norfolk' jacket and knickers; this look became the predominant symbol of participation in all forms of recreational leisure, particularly with the booming popularity of recreational and club cycling. The arrival of a modern 'leisure uniform' sustained conceptions of both belonging to and freedom from the regulatory constraints of work and domesticity—in Simmel's terms, a dialectic of uniformity and difference. But how did such ambiguity come to be a crucial part of the new systems of status recognition that were the lodestone of Veblen's aspirational 'leisure class.' Veblen's evolutionary processes of 'selective sifting,' of both activities and consumerism goods seen to have a 'symbolic utility,' are useful here.

The agricultural revolution of the eighteenth century wrought radical changes to the rural landscape of the landed gentry. But the resulting larger, hedged fields, particularly after harvest, provided ideal conditions for fast chases on horseback and the shooting of game birds. Shooting—and progressively fox hunting—became the predominant sporting attractions of the large English country house and Scottish estates that were bought up by Lowland or English gentlemen for sport rather than agriculture and who replaced sheep and grazing land with deer forest and grouse moors (Birley 1993) (see Figure 6.1). Thus, while an aristocratic 'predatory culture' underwent significant changes, its roots remained in a preindustrial system of power and deference that, allied with an understanding of their concrete political and economic power, continued to be articulated through the concept of possession—of wealth, land, and knowledge. These elements were as Veblen argued, 'selectively sifted' for their 'symbolic utility' and embodied in action and deportment adaptive to a new landscape of upper-class sport and leisure.

This conceptual mix of the symbolic and the material is a useful one. As Mike Huggins argues, "[T]he fabric of estate landscape was shaped by aristocratic sporting pursuits quite as much as aesthetic and economic interests and

Figure 6.1 Royal shooting party including King Edward VII, by unknown photographer, c. 1890s. © National Portrait Gallery, London.

preferences, and they continued to exert traditional authority, and flaunt their wealth and status, through field sports" (Huggins 2004: 25). From the 1830s, modified versions of the traditional 'Shepherd's Check' of the Scottish Borders—collectively known as 'the Districts'—were developed in a range of heavy woolen fabrics and made up into new forms of sporting clothing: shooting jackets, knickerbockers and breeches, spats, boots, coats, overcoats, and capes designed for walking and stalking prey in the field rather than chasing them on horseback. Cloth and clothing were both descriptively territorial. 'Norfolk' and 'Fife' jackets, 'covert' coats and 'deerstalker' hats, 'Ulster' and 'Inverness' overcoats referenced these new upper-class sporting pursuits, the English and Scottish landscapes and their aristocratic title. Innovations in textile production allowed tweed to be produced in an almost infinite range of pattern and colors that equally embodied the land and the status of these new "Highland chiefs" (Gulvin 1973: 74). "Glenfeshie," for example, is described in a trade guide as "one of the bolder and most invisible of all the Districts" but "when seen in its proper environment," it reflected the red and gray granites of its namesake (the Glenfeshie estate); similarly the "Wyvis":

> ...is so unlike the other Gunclubs as to require a special description. It is extremely bold, about two and a quarter inches on the repeat. The ground is a deep fawn of the tint of withered bracken or dead beech leaves. The alternating colours, a solid dull brown green moss shade and a sprinkled bar of twist yarns of bright green, moss shade and grey.
>
> HARRISON 1956: 76

Prior to the 1830s and 1840s, the wearing of occasion- if not leisure-specific clothing, and the frequent purchase of tailor-made garments in the latest mode was something limited to only a privileged few. However, like those above them on the social scale, the middle class were also developing a new leisure culture in the context of industrial capitalism. The most prosperous and powerful of a rising middling class sought to 'buy into' the lifestyle of a traditional landed gentry with the purchase of new estates and the rebuilding of large country houses in addition to the luxurious townhouses they were remodeling. Many more who ranked a little lower down the socio-economic ladder were also increasingly socially and physically mobile and beginning to extend, like the aristocracy, their leisure domain. A number of spa towns and coastal resorts had rapidly expanded in England, at a faster rate of population growth even than manufacturing towns (Urry 1989). Scotland and the Scottish Highlands had also become fashionable through the popularity of the novels of Sir Walter Scott (these had achieved cult status with a new and growing reading public), and whose romanticized desirability was only further advanced with the visits of Queen Victoria and Prince Albert in the 1840s and their purchase of Balmoral Castle in 1848.

The rising upper middle and middle classes could not draw on a long history of enjoyment of traditional aristocratic and peasant rural 'sport,' nor the allied wealth, power, and cultural heritage of excess and individual performance that sustained its modern reformulation (Perrot 1981: 83). This new stratum of consumers needed to selectively sift strategies of sartorial exclusion according to a revised coded hierarchy of symbolic utility and they embarked on a process of sartorial and cultural territorialisation comparable in ambition and scope to that of the aristocratic class. Early cyclists took their sartorial cue from the predatory instincts of the upper classes; club uniforms were initially modeled on military tunics and breeches but within a few years this style was replaced by tweed Norfolks and knickerbockers (Figure 6.2). Equestrianism and the chivalric traditions were also a strong influence; pedals were referred to as stirrups, and the bicycle itself as a "steed" (Biddle-Perry 2014a).

Figure 6.2 Cyclist in tweed suit beside 'High Ordinary' bicycle with equestrian saddle. London Metropolitan Archive [Image 230832].

An article in the trade journal *Men's Wear* jingoistically concluded that while heavy and rather hot in summer, tweed was the best all-round fabric for cycling wear—"it stood the racket well" (Tayler 1908: 472). The fabric's association with aristocratic wealth and property and its links with Scottish thrift embodied the qualities of longevity and long term gain that was the *raison d'être* of the aspirant bourgeoisie. At the same time it offered a physical evocation of a British landscape that increasingly symbolized a distinctively bourgeois understanding of British identity, imperial power and masculine ideals (Anderson 2005). Promotional literature frequently invoked the natural landscape of Scotland and its flora and fauna in descriptions of the fabric's infinite variety of pattern and color combinations to highlight both its sporting heritage as a form of camouflage "in the field" and its fashionable credentials as an intrinsic element of upper-class informal urban attire (Anderson 2000).

Non-uniformity and distinction

The tweed suit's ambiguous facility to accommodate the performative dimensions that Simmel theorized as the need for both distinction and uniformity made it particularly suitable for its appropriation by middle-class recreationalists. As the natural landscape of leisure shifted from the rural to the urban and suburban in the second half of the nineteenth century, there was a gradual transition from large areas of broad color initially favoured by the sporting and fashionable upper-class consumer, to softer color effects and smaller and more muted patterns (Gulvin 1973: 6). The prestigious Cyclists' Touring Club (founded in 1878 as the Bicycle Touring Club) adopted the "West-of-England tweed" for outer garments consisting of a small gray check (Hoffman 1887). Smaller provincial and suburban clubs followed suit or opted for subdued District checks in shades of gray and their popularity meant that these progressively superseded the highly colored weaves popular in the 1870s (Gulvin 1973: 76). Rather than the bracken and heathers of the mountains and grouse moors, it was now the shades of the highways and byways of middle-class rational recreational leisure and tourism that colored tweed's designs and allowed their wearers to both blend in and stand out from the crowd.

Burberry's "Gamefeather Tweeds" employed "rich rare colourings, effects which appeal at once to those of artistic and sporting tastes," while their "Plus Beau Tweeds," were of the same nature and texture as the Gamefeather, but being only mixtures of black and white, are "quiet, unobtrusive, and selected generally by gentlemen whose tastes incline to grey" (*Men's Wear*, July 16, 1904: 27). Descriptors such as 'quiet' and 'natural' had gained much currency not just in promoting tweed's organic qualities but in implicitly referencing both the inappropriateness of the highly colored patterns of an upper-class sporting elite, and the 'loud' ready-made suits of brightly colored cheap check cloths now worn by the lower classes in the enjoyment of their 'leisure.'

The characteristic features of much working class clothing worn in their 'leisure time' was, like that of the middle and upper classes, about contrast to working attire, that had equally undergone considerable transformation and become more uniform. Manual laborers wore trousers, smocks, and collar-less shirts made of cheap ready-made fustian (a heavy linen or linen mix), heavy cottons like corduroy, moleskin, or 'beaver teen' in colors ranging from white, buff, and yellow to brown and blue, knitted Guernsey jumpers, cardigans that didn't show the dirt, while the rural classes wore an unbleached drill jacket called a "sloppy" (Crane 1993: 90–1). Overalls were required for workers in factories and heavy industries from about the 1870s to meet new legislative requirements; butchers, bakers, chemists, assistants and workers in other types of retail and trade premises similarly now wore stock coats and aprons of different colors (De Marly 1986). The use of uniforms and company livery expanded, particularly in the new industries of transport and communication. Those working for new public and private corporations and utilities such as the Fire and Police Service, the Water Board, the Post Office, say, or on the railways, all wore brightly colored and often ornate braided uniforms based on military uniforms to indicate ranks and gradations of employees (Crane 1993: 91). There was also an expansion in the use of much more clearly defined uniforms for domestic servants which were ever more fancy and decorative and often antiquarian in costume with breeches, colored tailcoats, and even powdered wigs to differentiate between master and servant and according to an expanding hierarchy of duties within the servant classes (Cunnington 1974).

In contrast with the neutral, discreet leisure wardrobe of higher social classes, and the drab colors and careworn or antiquarian outfits of their working lives, working-class leisure time was marked by high sartorial visibility, ornamentation, and fashionable novelty in clothes that embodied their (brief) respite *from* physical exertion and uniformed duty. Fancy suits and colored waistcoats were worn to the races and on days out, and contemporary social commentators warned against the wearing of coats cut on the lines of the "coster's Bank Holiday coat" with velvet trimmings (Shannon 2006: 146). The 'respectable' working classes similarly wore their antithetical Sunday best to embody their experience of the differential psychic and physical spaces of modernity. A parliamentary report on children's working conditions evidenced how Sunday was regarded as a day for enjoyment and pleasure for this social group: on Saturday night they "washed and laid out their best non-working clothes, prepared tea or coffee instead of gruel for breakfast and made a point of having a good lunch, looked forward to an afternoon tea, and invariably went out for a walk on Sunday evenings" (cited in Wigley 1980: 83).

According to these strict principles of antithesis, so central to a Victorian bourgeois rationale of symbolic utility, the most appropriate forms of leisure action and clothing for the middle classes were also those that offered the greatest contrast with a man's work; and in turn, the greatest contrast with the work and leisure of other men lower down the social scale, and of course women. The black business suit of the stockbroker, the industrialist, or the lowly clerk, might differ in cut, cloth, and quality but its adoption always reflected the interior cerebral rather than manual nature of their work, albeit sometimes at a greater financial cost for some then the financial reward for such work would logically allow (Breward 1999). The need to 'keep up' standards of dress and deportment assumed a huge significance in materially and symbolically underpinning the boundaries of gender and class at a time when they seemed increasingly under threat. In their symbolic assertion of earned rather than inherited wealth, hard work and thrift rather than hedonistic profligacy and idleness, the black business and tweed leisure suit *together* differentiated their wearers from both upper and lower classes alike. Stiff collars and neck ties, hard hats, shiny shoes, watch chains, tailored coats, and jackets embodied the constraints imposed by the maintenance of economic and cultural 'standards'; the tweed suit embodied both their escape and the superior status implied in what they were escaping from.

Fashioning freedom

The spatial context of outdoor recreational leisure promoted 'freedom' in a schema of sartorial display that maintained social distinctions but also allowed a fluidity of interpretation and social aspiration that could be both problematic and potentially liberating. The flexibility offered in the design of the ubiquitous Norfolk jacket gave all types of consumers 'room to manoeuvre' while still maintaining a sense of 'fitness for purpose.' Originally designed to accommodate the needs of an upper-class sporting elite engaged in a day's shooting or stalking across the moors, the Norfolk's formal design was open to interpretation. The provision for more generous pleats, pockets and pocket flaps, and extra buttons on the belt all allowed some variation in tailoring to suit the requirements of individual wearers in terms of their body shape and the needs of their different sporting activities. Thornton's tailoring guide proclaimed the jacket, "afforded greater scope for the introduction of novelties in both style and fitting qualities than any other garment in general wear..." (1911: 99). W.D.F. Vincent (another notable author of numerous 'Practical Guides' to pattern-cutting and tailoring) observed: "It matters not whether it is intended for fishing, walking, cycling, or equestrienne purposes; it is arranged in the same way," but the jacket's particular combination of tailoring innovation and uniformity of design gave it "characteristics peculiarly its own" (1904: 29–30). Thomas Holding, one of the founder members of the Cyclists' Touring Club, noted editor of *The London Tailor*, publisher of numerous other trade journals, and author of *The Camper's Handbook* (popularly referred to as the 'camper's Koran') recommended a jacket that accommodated a pocket on the left, "ten inches deep, ten inches across top, and at least twelve inches wide at the bottom, so that it may hold chops, groceries, or a rabbit if you poach;" adding that "on the cycle, I can carry my 'Campo' milk tin full inside this for a mile or two when off to a lonely Camping place" (Holding 1908: 215).

Popular trade guides and patented 'systems' of tailoring played a vital part in disseminating permutations in style and fashionable and popular taste. The mix of practical instructions, detailed patterns, and cutting directions as well as highly detailed and attractive illustrations, allowed very subtle differences in cut and style to be made visible to both consumer and trade alike; choice of fabric and style was a process of complex negotiation between client and craftsman (Breward 1999: 40–1). In an example from Thornton's *International System of Garment Cutting*, which offered bespoke tailoring to a burgeoning mass market, an aristocratic-looking masculine 'type' models a hunting ensemble of scarlet coat, breeches, and topper but this is followed on succeeding pages by the same figure dressed in distinct variations on the Norfolk and knickerbocker combination with matching cap, similarly posed but with the hunting crop now replaced by a golf club, a shotgun, a fishing rod, a walking cane, or a bicycle pump (1911: 56–9). It is the very non-specificity of the tweed suit, Fiona Anderson contends, that made it extremely popular with a broad urban middle class (2005: 290). A photograph of founder and first leader of the Labour Party, James Keir Hardie by Arthur Weston shows him in District-checked trousers, a dark jacket and waistcoat with a soft flannel shirt with collar and matching tie, accessorized with a tweed cap (Figure 6.3). Wearing the same outfit to take up his seat at the

Figure 6.3 Keir Hardie by Arthur Clegg Weston, c. 1892. © National Portrait Gallery, London.

House of Commons, Sarah Levitt argues, "His home-spun looking outfit thus conveyed the message 'I am your equal, a thinking man' to the middle class, whilst being identifiably socialist. It incorporated elements of working-class clothing, yet it was not working class" (1991: 184).

In the context of the tweed suit's political symbolism, much attention has been focussed within fashion historical studies on the Women's Rational Dress Movement and women's wearing of bifurcated garments in relation to wider battles for emancipation and suffrage. However, the majority of dress reformers were independently wealthy upper- and upper-middle-class women. 'Rationals' and even their more fashion-conscious adaptations were considered both subversive and unattractive by many mainstream consumers; they also often involved large quantities of heavyweight cloth being made up into designs involving complicated patterns of goring, pleating, kilting, and fastening that necessitated high quality, and hence expensive, bespoke tailoring skills. Popular writers on social etiquette such as Mrs Ada Ballin extolled the virtues of these "delightful," "lighter" costumes that nevertheless consisted of ankle-length garments that used up to a yard of material in each leg that were worn with lined knickerbockers underneath (Levitt 1986: 31). Nevertheless, it is important to acknowledge how such a look *because* of its notoriety and its links with an upper-middle and upper-class social elite might be seen as both highly fashionable and aspirational for popular consumers. Lady Harberton, founder of the Rational Dress Society that comprised leading figures in the women's suffrage movement, and women involved in other forms of political activism were all portrayed as active cyclists and Lady Harberton was president of the prestigious Cyclists' Touring Club (Wilson and Taylor 1989: 53–8). All kinds of products aimed at a mass market utilized the figure of a young woman in bloomers with her bicycle (see Figure 6.4). The majority of women might not choose to wear strict 'Rationals,' but that is not to say that they were somehow unaware of the subversive, political or fashionable possibilities nor the stylistic *cachet* this attached to their adaptation and appropriation by a mass market.

Like their masculine counterparts, aspirational mainstream female consumers swiftly appropriated tweed costumes designed for walking and other rural pursuits that were integral to the fashionable wardrobe of wealthy women enjoying the "autumn playground" provided by Scottish Estates during the shooting season (Taylor 2007). By the late-nineteenth century, lighter weight and cheaper woolen "tweeds" mass-manufactured in Northern England, were used for women's informal daywear— dresses and tailored costumes for morning and informal social occasions, for sporting and leisure clothing and progressively for

Figure 6.4 Young woman in rational dress advertising Elliman's Universal Embrocation. Wiki Commons File:Ellimans-Universal-Embrocation-Slough-Ad.png.

middle-class women following occupations like teaching and clerical work (Anderson 2006: 172–3). Fiona Anderson and Lou Taylor's work emphasises the links between gender and the multipurpose functional and fashionable nature of the cloth (Taylor 1999). From the 1860s, hundreds of different 'masculine' designs were 'feminized' by the use of lighter cloth and a different palette of colors—reds, deep ochres, oatmeal, myrtle green, moss—as well as novelty finishes such as astrakhan and bouclé trimmings that were tied into the shifts and changes of the Paris season as well as the sporting and social calendar.

Interaction between advances in pattern drafting and grading and stylistic change allowed manufacturers to produce and promote cheaper, yet still reasonable quality, ready-made tailored garments that became hugely popular with large numbers of women (Aldrich 2003). Tight-fitting complicated styles and heavy cloth had previously demanded a high level of tailoring skill that was beyond the capability of small dressmakers. The spread of the domestic sewing machine in conjunction with equally significant innovations in the nature of patternmaking and their dissemination in both shops and the popular press, like their menswear counterparts, emerged alongside the trend towards accessorization and the growing influence of leisure. The development of the simplified and less ornate tailor-made costume, the increasing popularity of the skirt (divided or otherwise) and feminized Norfolk jacket-and-blouse combination created a look that easily accommodated a diversity of individual body shapes and a broad spectrum of ideologies united in a desire for new kinds of 'freedom.' For their masculine counterparts the tweed suit represented freedom *from* work and the immediate coded hierarchies of the masculine workplace, yet for an expanding number of middle-class and lower-middle class women typists, shop assistants, and recreationalists, it also represented the freedom *to* work.

Decentering leisure clothing: 'symbolic futility'

The symbolic utility of the tweed Norfolk suit lay in combining hard-wearing material qualities with an almost infinite range and combination of colors, patterns, and designs to counter uniformity with distinction, social fellowship with individual agency, and conformity with idiosyncrasy. Holding contended that "a man can do anything in such a garment" (1908: 215). Humorously referring to what he described as "Ole Clo" (old clothes), he argued that the tweed jacket and various other 'democratic' accessories such as the tweed cap epitomized the spirit of camping and engendered the right attitude of mind in the campers that wore it:

> Comfort, freedom and happiness of mind are the first things in healthy Camping, and, therefore, our clothes should not oppress our minds. We should wear things that do not worry us in the care of them... It is better to be mistaken for a tinker, circus, bill-poster, or even a mendicant, than a clergyman, if we have comfort and freedom in our clothes. We are less conventional in these days, and a man is

admitted anywhere in a tweed suit, and in the lake district, in Ireland, and other places I have conducted religious services in churches thus clad.

HOLDING 1908: 215

The Cooperative Holiday Association (CHA), founded in 1891 by the Reverend T. A. Leonard to provide the working classes with access to the morally and spiritually uplifting influence of the countryside, did not have any specific rules of dress other than a lack of ostentation and the avoidance of any overt material display of economic and social advantage. Dressy clothes were deemed both unnecessary and suggestive of the conventions of urban life that the Association was anxious to get away from. The Reverend reminded members:

> We are plain folk and are expected to dress suitably and simply, so that poorer members are not made to feel out of place. While welcoming all and sundry who join us, we stipulate that there shall be no divisiveness or putting on of "side" by those who happen to be better off than others.

cited in SNAPE 2004: 147–8

The *Manchester City News* offered advice to any "business girls" considering holidaying with the CHA where "the normal 'rules' of fashion were suspended," and encouraged them to wear walking boots, short woolen skirts and woolen underwear, and to leave their jewelry at home (Snape 2004: 153). Describing her experience of a CHA holiday, a young female letter-writer to *Comradeship* (the Association's journal) recalls her impressions of her fellow companions:

> I think I can best describe it by the name of Bohemia for all its inhabitants lived the life of the free. All the ladies pinned up their skirts, wore stout-soled boots, carried sticks, went without headgear or wore men's caps. One woman (I hardly like to call her a lady) wore men's leather leggings, but then she was a suffragette. The men are fairly prim, contenting themselves by wearing soft collars and going about very often without coats or waistcoats... a more heterodox wild crew I never saw.

SNAPE 2004: 153

Recreational leisure in the outdoors provided an important milieu for middle-class bohemian fashions, particularly in relation to hats, which in the late nineteenth century were a primary signifier of social status and gender. In his autobiography, West End hatter Fred Willis described the "genuine bohemian" as the "type who took great pains with the carelessness of their dress;" they had taken to the "Austrian velour hat with avidity... Worn with a flowing bow tie and a corduroy coat it gave the wearer unquestioned right of entry into the Café

Royal or Rule's" (Willis 1948: 43). The wearing of bizarre, unusual, or "shapeless" hats had first enjoyed a vogue in upper-class sporting milieus (Mangan 1981: 171), but this trend swiftly became incorporated into 'tramping' and camping activities seen to have a potential for far more symbolic licence than for example suburban bicycling. An image of "A Pedestrian Trio" in *The Campers Handbook* (Holding 1908) shows different versions of millinery irrationality in the two seated figures at the front mixing and matching belted corduroys, leather gaiters, cotton drill 'sloppy' and collarless shirts, topped off with an out-of-shape old felt hat and a bizarre 'wideawake' style straw 'slouch'—ensembles that would not be out of place on the bodies of travellers or the agricultural and industrial laboring class.

Tamar Garb's (1998) exploration of the work of Impressionist artist Gustave Caillebotte in this period evidences how an artistic avant-garde were beginning to explore the complexities of bourgeois masculinity and the boundaries of masculine power exerted in their work and leisure. Many of Caillebotte's paintings depict working men—manual laborers figured in their tools, clothing, and the physical traces of work on their bodies and black-suited friends and contemporaries physically constrained in stuffy interiors. This, Garb argues, evidences how Caillebotte—in order to question privilege and class power as in any way essential—made constant connections between his work as a painter and the toil of various artisans and exposed the relationship between social hierarchy and appearance. In one portrait the family steward is dressed in a top hat and frock coat while Caillebotte himself, an extremely wealthy landowner as well as an artist, is photographed dressed in gardener's dark cotton 'sloppy' and belted drill trousers. There was also another important arena of experimentation Garb argues,

> ... that served as a bridge between the toiling bodies of the poor and the leisured bodies of the rich, which offered Caillebotte the perfect site for the expression of a physically revitalized masculinity. This was the sporting body, the body strained by the physical exertion that leisure could afford, the newly idealized body of the modern enfranchised male ...
>
> 1998: 46–7

This kind of sartorial licence was equally promoted through the ethos of egalitarian consumerism that was a significant part of holidaying with the CHA and key to the 'CHA experience': Spartan conditions (no carpeting, only cold baths in streams, water rather than hot tea on rambles often accompanied by two-hour lectures) and an idea of simplicity of lifestyle embodied in plain, functional clothes that served as a badge of membership and engendered a sense of self-identity as "CHA folk" (Snape, 2004: 150). But as social historian Robert Snape argues, what constituted appropriately simple clothing was imposed through an implicit understanding that always operated according to "its own hegemonic construct of social behaviour and taste" (2004: 149). CHA holidays were priced beyond the means of a significant number of working men and women and whilst free holidays were provided for some, participation in a CHA holiday did not extend to any "persons of intemperate, uncleanly or unpleasant habits" (Snape 2004: 152, 149).

Holding's *Camper's Handbook* is also peppered throughout with similarly ambiguous allusions to the democratic virtues of camping and the opportunities it offered "the poor clerk or workman" for both recreational and sartorial freedom (1908: 213). Thus, whilst suitable dress might be described as 'old clothes,' it would seem that they must be of a very specific type of 'old' jacket, waistcoat, underwear, nether garments, stockings, waterproofs, footwear, and headgear. All receive Holding's scrupulous attention and very detailed descriptions and arguably offer a very middle-class view of sartorial and economic 'poverty':

> The waistcoat should have ... a pocket with a flap to carry a few spare ten-pound notes you won't need, and a blank cheque, which, of course you never go without. These should be put in a thin letter case to keep off the perspiration and damp. Bank notes are liked best in a crisp condition.
>
> HOLDING 1908: 216

There is clearly an element of humor in Holding's last description, but the check and the bank account that went along with it might be handled by the 'poor clerk' most of his working life; whether he himself ever possessed one or a wallet with a few spare ten pound notes is extremely unlikely. Women could also wear old clothes, but these were equally subject to the economic and social ambiguities of Holding's sartorial prescriptions: they should be neither of an offensive color, nor "discreditably shabby ... [and] No woman of sense would don a new 'tailor-made' to go Camping in, and no such woman would go Camping in a ragged skirt" (1908: 224). Describing the symbolic expediency of the evolving middle-class wardrobe, Phillipe Perrot argues:

> Articles of clothing that originally fulfilled a real function in war, hunting, or work [have] degenerated into pure signification... The bourgeois clothing code, now legally free from sumptuary regulation, established itself as legitimate by hiding behind practical alibis and moral or aesthetic pretexts, as if to exculpate itself of the charge of gratuitousness.
>
> PERROT 1981: 10

The ability for mainstream consumers to mix and match and adapt new designs, fabrics, and fashions within an existing wardrobe allowed the potential for experimentation in relation to finances, political views, or participation in new forms of recreational activities to embody conceptions of freedom and social democracy through 'practical alibis.' For women, rational dress and its widespread contemporary critique in the press and popular culture provided a focus for a much wider and more far-reaching discourse around women's and girl's physiological development, female sexuality, and the educational, political, and property rights of a "New Woman" (Luck 1992). By the turn of the century, the New Woman in tailored skirt and blouse became the iconic figure of young or progressive femininity reproduced in posters, postcards, and on the stage (Ewing 1974: 20–2). For an expanding clerical class, the city offered a new arena for masculine display and opportunities for leisure with the potential to both confound and confirm contemporary anxieties about dress and attitudes to popular leisure and enjoyment in which both social aspiration and new understandings of 'professionalism' were central.

Within a very short time span, the choice of suitable recreational leisure clothing for specific forms of rational and healthy exercise, such as walking and cycling, was almost infinite in the possible combinations offered by various arrangements of Norfolk and semi-Norfolk jackets, worn with flannel shirts, or sweaters, various types of matching caps or 'soft felts'; these might be teamed with a variety of different cuts and designs of knickers, or knickerbockers, or breeches, or knickerbocker breeches that incorporated an equally diverse choice of fastenings and 'connectors'; socks or stockings or hose, gaiters, puttees, or spats, and various types of activity- and leisure-specific boots and shoes. Within another five years, their suburban sisters were now 'awheel' and wearing different versions of practical, shorter skirts, inter-changeable blouses, boleros, collars, neckties, jackets, hats, and boots (Jungnickel 2018).

The leisured bourgeoisie valorized the notion if not the reality of 'old clothes' to symbolize their freedom and their enjoyment of leisure; the working classes wore their old clothes to work in the dirty and dangerous spaces of large-scale Victorian industry while the residuum had no choice other than to wear old clothes. Through Veblen's processes of 'selective sifting' the symbolic utility of the sporting clothing of the upper classes and the working attire of the manual classes was incorporated into a new sartorial lexicon of middle-class leisure attire. However, while such clothing certainly was often materially more functional and less formal, the etiquette of what or what was not appropriate still operated according to the same culturally coded parameters of nineteenth-century uniformity and distinction. Cheap "cycle shop Norfolks" were things to avoid, they were "not Norfolks at all ... [but] mere jackets with artificial straps, sewn on to them. These straps do no good, and are questionable ornaments ... The pleats should 'work'..." (Holding, 1908: 224).

The wearing by the men and women of an expanding middle and lower middle class, of fashionably rational tweed suits, short walking skirts and boots, idiosyncratic knitted jumpers, soft collars and ties, 'tams' and boaters should not be confused with actual social change but rather be seen as a demonstration of the ways in which the symbolic and the material collided in the gradual and progressive negotiation of such change at an individual and collective everyday level. Understandings of personal improvement were incorporated into a complex set of beliefs around the healthy body as a metaphor for social advance that were swiftly embodied in leisure action and consumption as a key strategy of social inclusiveness but also of mobility.

Conclusion

This ambiguous notion of freedom was crucial to the construction of a Victorian professional and clerical class in relation to the occupational and social 'others' against which leisure time and leisure clothing was imaginatively formulated and economically afforded according to the social relations of Victorian propriety. It is important to recognize the role the uniform fashioning of specifically and visibly leisured bodies played in this kind of philosophical 'decentring' of leisure and the ideology of temporal and spatial freedom from the apparatus of bourgeois capitalism (Rojek 1995). The tweed suit in all its variations gave dreams of idleness or of paid employment, a desire for non-uniformity, irrationality, irregularity, neutrality, time-less-ness, and non-conformity, a tangible form through which they could be freely articulated.

For both men and women, leisure uniforms in their expression of collective fellowship and individual agency functioned to distinguish leisure as a discrete and separate activity enjoyed and experienced both free from but *always* in relation to the psychic and physical constraints imposed by the productive economic and class relations of industrial capitalism. If modernity invented the concept of leisure as productive 'free time,' it also invented a materially and symbolically functional leisure uniform of non-uniformity selectively sifted to embody the cost of such 'freedom.'

References

Adams, J. (1995), *Dandies and Desert Saints: Styles of Victorian Masculinity*. Cornell, NY: Cornell University Press.

Aldrich, W. (2003), "The Impact of Fashion on the Cutting Practices for the Woman's Tailored Jacket 1800-1927," *Textile History*, 34 (2): 134-70.

Anderson, F. (2000), "Fashioning the Gentleman: A Study of *Henry Poole And Co.*, Savile Row Tailors, 1861-1900," *Fashion Theory*, 4 (4): 405-26.

Anderson, F. (2005), "Spinning the Ephemeral with the Sublime: Modernity and Landscape in Men's Fashion Textiles 1860-1900," *Fashion Theory*, 9 (3): 283-304.

Anderson, F. (2006), "This Sporting Cloth: Tweed, Gender and Fashion 1860-1900," *Textile History*, 37 (2), 166-86.

Bailey, P. (1978), *Leisure and Class in Victorian England*, London: Routledge.

Bailey, P. (1998), *Popular Culture and Performance in the Victorian City*, Cambridge: Cambridge University Press.

Biddle-Perry, G. (2014a), "Fashioning Suburban Aspiration: Awheel with the Catford Cycling Club, 1886-1900," *The London Journal*, 39 (3), 187-204.

Biddle-Perry, G. (2014b), "The Rise of the World's Largest Sports and Athletic Outfitter: A Study of Gamages of Holborn, 1878-1913," *Sport in History*, 34 (2): 295-314.

Birley, D. (1993), *Sport and the Making of Britain*, Manchester: Manchester University Press.

Breward, C. (1999), *The Hidden Consumer: Masculinities, Fashion and City Life 1860-1914*, Manchester: Manchester University Press.

Crane, D. (1993), *Fashion and Its Social Agendas: Class, Gender and Identity in Clothing*, Chicago and London: University of Chicago Press.

Cunnington, P. and A. Mansfield (1969), *English Costume for Sports and Recreation from the Sixteenth to Nineteenth Centuries*, London: A&C Black.

Cunnington, P. (1974), *Costume of Household Servants: From the Middle Ages to 1900*, London: A&C Black.

De Marly, D. (1986), *Working Dress: A History of Occupational Clothing*, London: Batsford.

Entwistle, J. (2000), *The Fashioned Body: Fashion, Dress and Modern Social Theory*, Cambridge: Polity Press.

Ewing, E. (1974), *History of Twentieth Century Fashion*, London: Batsford Ltd.

Garb, T. (1998), *Bodies of Modernity: Figure and Flesh in Fin-de-Siècle France*, London: Thames & Hudson.

Gulvin, C. (1973), *The Tweedmakers: A History of the Scottish Fancy Woollen Industry 1600-1914*, Newton Abbott: David & Charles.

Haley, B. (1978), *The Healthy Body and Victorian Culture*, Cambridge, MA: Harvard University Press.

Harrison, E. S. (1956), *Scottish Woollens*, Edinburgh: National Association of Scottish Woollen Manufacturers.

Hobsbawm, E. and T. Ranger, eds (1983), *The Invention of Tradition,* Cambridge: Cambridge University Press.
Hoffman (Professor) (1887), *Tips for Tricyclists,* London: F. Warne.
Holding, T. H. (1908), *The Camper's Handbook,* London: Simpkin and Marshall.
Holt, R. (1989), *Sport and the British: A Modern History,* Oxford: Clarendon Press.
Huggins, M. (2004), *The Victorians and Sport,* New York: Continuum.
Jungnickel, K. (2018), *Bikes and Bloomers: Victorian Women Inventors and Their Extraordinary Cycle Wear,* London: Goldsmiths Press.
Levitt, S. (1986), *Victorians Unbuttoned: Registered Designs for Clothing Their Makers and Wearers 1839–1900,* London: Allen and Unwin.
Levitt, S. (1991), "Cheap Mass-Produced Men's Clothing in the Nineteenth and Early Twentieth Centuries," *Textile History,* 22 (2): 179–93.
Luck, K. (1992), "Trouble in Eden, Trouble with Eve: Women, Trousers and Utopian Socialism in Nineteenth Century America," in J. Ash and E. Wilson (eds), *Chic Thrills: A Fashion Reader,* London: Pandora, 200–13.
Mangan, J. (1981), *Athleticism in the Victorian and Edwardian Public School: The Emergence and Consolidation of an Educational Ideology,* London: Frank Cass.
Men's Wear Editorial, July 16, 1904.
Park, R. J. (1987), "Biological Thought, Athletics and the Formation of a 'Man of Character': 1830–1900," in J. Mangan and J. Walvin (eds), *Manliness and Morality: Middle-class Masculinity in Britain and America 1800–1940,* Manchester: Manchester University Press, 7–34.
Perrot, P. (1981), *Fashioning the Bourgeoisie: A History of Clothing in the Nineteenth Century,* Princeton, NJ: Princeton University Press.
Polhemus, T. (1984), *Streetstyle,* London: Thames and Hudson.
Rojek, C. (1995), *Decentring Leisure: Rethinking Leisure Theory,* London and Thousand Oaks, CA: SAGE Publications.
Rouse, E. (1989), *Understanding Fashion,* London: BSP Professional Books.
Shannon, B. (2006), *The Cut of His Coat: Men, Dress and Consumer Culture in Britain, 1880–1914,* Athens, OH: Ohio University Press.
Simmel, G. ([1903] 1964), "The Metropolis and Mental Life," in K. H. Wolff (ed. and trans.), *The Sociology of Georg Simmel,* New York: Free Press of Glencoe, 409–17.
Simmel, G. (1904a), "Fashion," *International Quarterly,* 10: 130–55 [available at www.modetheorie.de/fileadmin/Texte/s/Simmel-Fashion_1904.pdf].
Simmel, G. ([1904b] 1971), "On Individuality and Social Forms," in D. N. Levine (ed.), *Georg Simmel: On Individuality and Social Forms,* Chicago and London: University of Chicago Press.
Smiles, S. (1838), *Physical Education Or the Nurture and Management of Children,* London: Simpkin and Marshall.
Smiles, S. (1859), *Self-Help: with Illustrations of Character and Conduct,* London: John Murray.

Snape, R. (2004), "The Co-operative Holidays Association and the Cultural Formation of Countryside Practice," *Leisure Studies,* 23 (2): 143–58.

Tayler, S. J. (1908), "Cycling Dress," *Men's Wear,* March 21, 472–3.

Taylor, L. (1999), "Cloth and Gender: An Investigation into the Gender-specific Use of Woollen Cloth in the Tailored Dress of British Women in the 1865–1885 Period," in A. de la Haye and E. Wilson (eds), *Defining Dress: Dress as Object, Meaning and Identity,* Manchester: Manchester University Press, 38–43.

Taylor, L. (2007), "'To Attract the Attention of Fish as Little as Possible': An Object-Led Discussion of Three Garments, for Country Wear for Women, Made of Scottish Woollen Cloth, Dating from 1883–1908," *Textile History,* 38 (1): 92–105.

Thornton, J. P. (1911), *The International System of Garment Cutting, including Coats, Trousers, Breeches and Vests, with Diagrams and Full Instructions for Dealing with all Forms of Disproportion,* London: Thornton Institute.

Urry, J. (1989), *The Tourist Gaze,* London and Thousand Oaks, CA: SAGE Publications.

Veblen, T. ([1899] 1994), *The Theory of the Leisure Class,* Mineola, NY: Dover Publications.

Vincent, W. D. F. (1904), *The Cutters' Practical Guide to Cutting, Making, and Fitting, Lounges, Reefers, Norfolk, Sporting & Patrol Jackets: with Special Instruction on the Treatment of Disproportionate Figures,* London: John Williamson.

Weber, M. ([1904] 2006), trans. Talcot Parsons, *The Protestant Ethic and the Spirit of Capitalism,* London and New York: Routledge.

Wigley, J. (1980), *The Rise and Fall of the Victorian Sunday,* Manchester: Manchester University Press.

Willis, F. (1948), *101 Jubilee Road: A Book of London Yesterdays,* London: Phoenix House.

Wilson, E. (1985), *Adorned in Dreams: Fashion and Modernity,* London: Virago.

Wilson, E. and L. Taylor (1989), *Through The Looking Glass: A History of Dress from 1860 to the Present Day,* London: BBC Books.

7

Uniformity in Fashion Practices During the Modernization Period in Turkey

F. Dilek Himam

In Turkey, the modernization period of the early twentieth century saw the introduction of literature and media that presented the new fashions of the times, including photographs and illustrations of Western women and men. It was mainly the upper classes who began incorporating the modern, Western look into the way they dressed and several magazines of this era clearly described how to dress in a rational, standardized and Western way. Among those publications, the 1935 summer edition of the magazine *Yarım Ay* announced new autumn and winter dresses, hair and hat fashions in an article entitled "Dress, Hat and Hair Fashions of our Women for Autumn and Winter!"

> In this season, the God of War Mars and Goddess of Love Venus collided. Yes, now, mantles, overcoats and jackets like soldier jackets and hat pieces the same, as soldier caps are fashionable. However, it should be known that Mars can only control day fashions; but evening fashions are under the control of Venus. Evening dresses steal hearts like a night full of stars and eyes like a black velvet sky.... Dresses and overcoats look like military uniforms; arms are fluffy, shoulder lines are angular, buttons are trimmed and crosslined. Arms, cuffs, collars are made of black astrakhan, which is the most important fashion of this year...
>
> cited in TANYER 2006: 10

Yarım Ay magazine, published every fortnight, was not the only journal to promote changes in male and female dress in the modernizing Turkey of the 1930s and to identify a simplified, secular dress as prescribed by Kemalist ideology. Kemalism refers to reforms introduced by Mustafa Kemal Atatürk in the 1920s and 1930s, which were secular, statist and established the modern nation of Turkey. In *La Turquie Kemaliste*, the official propaganda publication that constructed the desired self-portrait of Republican Turkey, the most familiar images were unveiled women working next to clean-shaven men in educational and professional settings. Other images that proliferated included healthy children and young people in school uniforms, the modern architecture of public buildings in Ankara and other major cities, the spectacular performances of the national theater, opera, and ballet, and impressive scenes of agriculture, railroads, factories, and dams (Göle 1997: 5). Most symbolically, the Turkish project of modernization equated the nation's progress with the use of Westernized dress codes, underpinned by a desire for uniformity in appearance. The new dress culture of the Republican era had become deeply penetrated by the spirit of the time, and was activated as a form of social control, reflecting Diana Crane's (2000: 67) view that dress can be critical to reinforcing the project of modernity.

The modernization period in Turkey

In order to trace the modernity of fashion practices of the Turkish Republic, we need to take a step back to the early years of modernization, established under the Kemalist reforms introduced by Atatürk, who served as the first President of the Republic of Turkey from 1923 until his death in 1938. During this period, the nation was generally seen as the dominant social configuration. Kemalism's first aim was to nationalize Anatolia through a move from tradition to modernity, a transition thought to be achievable through nationwide education, industrialization, urbanization, and "civilization" (Kaya 2001:95). Thus, a universal civilization could be achieved by a high degree of rationalization (Kaya 2001:71) of the social world within the context of the early republican "civilizing mission." 'Civilization' could refer to various things: to *alafranga* (the European way) manners, to a society's level of technology, to its social customs, to the development of scientific knowledge and to greater uniformity in dress.

According to Ernest Gellner, the prominent theorist of nationalism, modern identity formation establishes a system that binds state and culture together: official ideology is propagated by the creation of museums, the writing of histories and various other forms of knowledge in order to educate citizens about what constitutes citizenship. "For Gellner, nationalism is a function of modernity and the process of modernisation, where education, technologies of communication and bureaucracy, the very structure of the modern state, are driven by rationalist, administrative imperatives" (Edensor 2002: 3). On this basis, modernization in Turkey was viewed simply as Westernization, on the assumption that the West was an advanced civilization and at the time, many argued that this could be attained by imitating the West (Gellner 1983: 10; 11–64).

Within this context, Turkish modernity is considered to have begun with the *Tanzimat* reforms, enacted between the 1830s and the First World War, when the impact of the European Industrial Revolution on the Ottoman Empire was particularly strong. With the establishment of the new Turkish Republic in 1923 from the ruins of the Ottoman Empire, a strong nationalist and corporatist discourse emerged under the ideological rule of Kemalist reforms. These reforms triggered a process of top-down, state-led, elitist modernization that sought to transform people's appearance, habits, living patterns, moral conduct, and worldview. The modernization process of the Republic of Turkey involved extensive reforms that introduced a radical program of secularization and uniformization. In the light of these developments, Turkey's adoption of Western ideas and institutions particularly in education, law, clothing, music, and the arts made the project of modernity appear feasible.

As discussed by İbrahim Kaya, in the process of Turkish modernization, Kemalism aimed to show the Anatolian masses the value of being a member of an imagined Turkish community and a feeling of confidence was needed to move society toward modernity; the nation was generally seen as the dominant social configuration of modern times, which accounts for the shift toward a nationalized collectivity in Anatolia (Kaya 2004: 43). Indeed, since Westernization is significant to the Turkish case, practices and experiences reflected a strong state as the main agent of modernization. During these times, events were shaped by the shock of worldwide depression, the overwhelming factor in the revision of economic policy, which forced the country to rely on internal sources and protectionist measures. This was clearly highlighted under the Etatism principle, as stated by Atatürk in 1932: "the principle of Etatism that we have chosen to follow is not in any way the same as in Collectivism or in Communism which seek to remove all instruments of production and distribution from the hands of individual enterprise and action in the economic field" (Okyar 1965: 98–101). In that sense, the state was interpreted as the controller of the industrialization process. At the Izmir Economic Congress (1923), it was clearly stated that industrialization was to be accomplished through new initiatives, while the government's main attention was directed to internal politics, and to major social and political reforms. In order to provide credit to facilitate this process, a new Industrial Incentives Law (*Teşvik-i Sanayi Kanunu*) was passed in 1927, explicitly calling for the building of "industrial plants for mass-production with the assistance of advanced machines, tools or mechanical equipment" (Bozdoğan 2011: 17–40).

Kemalist reforms also included the creation of a number of state institutions, including the National Economy and Savings Society (1929), which encouraged the public to use national products and to live economically. The Society also had a pedagogic mission, including "propaganda posters, the journal of *Economy and Savings*, preparation of brochures, educational materials, the institutionalization and celebration of Savings and National Products Week (*Yerli Malı Haftası*) ..." (Bozodoğan 2001: 137). New industrial plants—such as *Sümerbank* textile factories—were opened all over the country to support the national economy and, as state-led institutions, would produce affordable textiles for all kinds of citizens. All these practices provided the necessary ground for the formation of a common, collective, and uniform style of economical consumption shared by each member of the public.

During the modernization period, clothing that reflected traditional Ottoman norms changed in favor of a new 'civilized' persona, and new European-inspired 'modern' clothing for both sexes became symbols of modernity and progress; they sought to unify the nation by imitating the West. This period of the Republic was when modernization practices were represented through the more systematic and unified engagement of Turkish society. Under Atatürk, a number of reforms—from lifestyle to women's appearance, from cities to homes and kitchens—were launched to establish uniformity in daily social, educational, and cultural practices and products.

The mechanisms that established the Turkish Republic were legitimized under the dominance of Kemalist state policies, creating a unique discursive structure that advocated various modes of 'uniformity,' with principles of Kemalism established to provide the conceptual and contextual bases of uniformity. In the Kemalist discourse, the State is seen as an agent articulating the political, social, and cultural dynamics of an imagined Turkish community characterized as confident, civilized, and modern. Nationalism, on the other hand, advocates creating a community based on national unity, rather than race or religion. Hence, the Turkish nation-building project was not based on a racist and totalitarian ideology, but on the Kemalist project of shaping the multiracial and multicultural Ottoman-Turkish people into a uniform community connected by language, culture, and the national ideal.

While taking the initial steps of Kemalist reforms, the Turkish fashion and textile industry played a major role in constructing national uniformization and promoting social collectivity. The emergence of new forms of dress had a great impact on the standardization and modernization of fashion consumption. Local economies were organized to produce local Anatolian fabrics shared by male and female inhabitants of the new Turkey. The new citizen of the Turkish Republic was rejecting the old dress practices of the Ottoman empire and trying to adopt new dress items such as new outdoor dresses, sportswear, children's clothing, accessories, hats, stockings, and beachwear which were key visual elements in anticipation of creating 'a classless society,' according to the new state regulations.

Uniforming a nation

Among various definitions, according to symbolic interactionist Herbert Blumer, uniformity is reached "through consensus on a prevailing mode and its association with propriety, an orderly and regulated way to monitor and mark the shifting sands of social life, and the distillation of 'common sensitivity and taste' by the sanctioning of new modes and the rejection of old ones" (Blumer 1968: 344). Teuro Sekimoto's definition is more ideological, noting that "uniforms function as signs of the wearer's closeness to the state," as he goes on to say, "wearing uniforms is a convenient way for people on the fringes of the state machinery to distinguish themselves from the anonymous masses that have no uniform and are assumed to have no part in the working of the state and the nation" (Arthur 2000: 207). Linda B. Arthur highlights that "states have used varied forms of cultural codes to create powerful appearances of state control, nationality and group solidarity" (2000: 201). Brian McVeigh argues that "uniforms are used to socialize individuals ... to accept basic sociopolitical processes (hierarchization, categorization and standardization) generated by statist and capitalist projects" (McVeigh 2000: 11). In the most general sense, hence, the dynamics of uniformization is closely linked to power, standardization, unity, integration, solidarity, social control, and order.

Apart from these definitions, in ideological terms, the Kemalist modernization discourse could be distinguished by its theme of creating a unified collectivity and uniformity peculiar to Turkish modernization. In a great number of pioneering models and reforms in the early Republican period, a state-centered, national, civilized, secular, integrated, collective, and uniform understanding of modernization was adopted. Peoples' Houses (*Halk Evleri*) were founded in 1932 as state institutions, aimed at creating 'educational uniformity'. These institutions were established in anticipation of creating 'a classless society' by means of the social and cultural dynamics of uniformity, a project which had been further launched with an educational mobilization program (1937) for social change, better known as the Village Institutes (*Köy Enstitüleri*), to educate the public to join the nation (Yeşilkaya 1999: 72–8). Moreover, the process of standardization sought to erase numerous differences of class, gender, geography, and culture that were characteristic of 1920s and 1930s Turkey.

But how exactly did the fashion of the time enact the process of national uniformity? One of the miraculous solutions for this process was the establishment of dress reforms, which in the early Republic included a series of arrangements and regulations such as the hat-law (*şapka kanunu*) of November 1925, by which "the fez, the turban, and other forms of traditional garb with religious connotations were outlawed" (Bozdoğan 2001: 58). It also enforced in governmental and public venues the use of Westernized dress, adopted rapidly as uniforms by almost all Turkey's citizens, such as slim trousers, waistcoats, shirts, ties, jackets, brims, *redingots* (a kind of jacket embraced and copied as the Western equivalents mostly preferred by the middle-upper class) for men, and *à la garçonne* style shoes, dresses, gloves, headwear (*sıkmabaş*), and accessories for women. It also stipulated primary school uniforms (*önlük*) in educational institutions, as well as the legal obligation (December 1925) to wear dresses made of local fabrics (Himam and Pasin 2011: 159). These forms of dress functioned as a unifying symbol in the Turkish Republic, apparently erasing difference among class, race, religion, and gender, a phenomenon that was seen as important in creating a uniform society. Thus, Kemalist reforms aimed to create a feeling of collaboration among citizens, to foster a cooperative spirit and to gain a measure of social control. In order to introduce modern, Westernized, and civilized life styles to a traditional population, fashion had become an important instrument of modernizing regimes, and as Tim Edensor puts it, "a marker of national identity whose symbolic function is a badge of innovative modernity and national prestige" (2002: 108).

Apart from the dress reforms, in order to foster standardization the regime invested heavily in the creation of a national textile and apparel industry. Recipients of state funding, textile factories opened in the 1930s and produced a wide range of fabrics, dresses, uniforms, and accessories designed and produced in accordance with the regulations of dress reform.

Ideas of uniformity in Kemalist discourse were considered to be ideally expressed through the body of the individual, and the space s/he inhabits, both functioning analogously as 'uniforms.' Hence, the fashion practices of the time addressed the construction (and control) of an ideal Turkish citizen by producing stereotypical dress items, especially for women. For the Turkish experience of modernization, in addition to changes in fashion, liberating women was the most significant project in the transition to modernity; women were regarded in Turkey as particularly important agents in the formation of a modern society. According to the modernists, this was expressed in terms of the abolition of the veil, the establishment of compulsory co-education, the granting of women's suffrage, the social integration of men and women, and the participation of women in the public sphere (Göle 1997: 85, 86). In fact, as discussed by Emre Gönlügür, even in the postwar decades the female body continued to occupy the social imaginary as a veritable measure of progress (2014: 29).

Most symbolically, the Turkish project of modernization equated the nation's progress with the use of Westernized dress codes, enshrined in dress reforms. Such reforms affected the daily practices of an emerging modern nation-state in terms of gender equality, secularism, collectivity, and created a definite visual, social, and cultural profile for the modern Turkish man and woman who were now conceived as being more *unified*. During the modernization period, Turkish women were encouraged to adopt Western and what was thought to be civilized dress.

In Western societies in the years immediately following the First World War, a new image of woman, such as the "flapper" and the "*garçonne*," came to the fore (Paulicelli 2004: 236). This representation of modern Westernized women had strong connotations for Turkey's civilizational shift away from an Islamic society. Under the leadership of Atatürk, issues related to women and body image included the ideals that 'new' women should be modern, rational, married, monogamous, hard-working, uncomplicated, educated mothers and dedicated to the country. Many journals devoted pages to the proper etiquette of modern living (*Adab-ı Muaşeret Kuralları*), and described the expected behavior of the ideal man and woman. However, new daily life practices such as mixed-gender dining, walking, dancing, or the custom of men kissing a woman's hand were largely restricted to the new Republican elite, the pioneering agents of Turkish modernization. In that respect, these practices prepared the ground for the formation of a common and uniform style of consumption, promoted by the "state elite," the architects of Turkish national identity (Yavuz 1998: 19–41).

Fashion as agent of modernity

States have used varied forms of material culture, including dress codes, to exercise state control, to promote nationalism and group solidarity. In doing so, they have built their *esprit de corps* on the backs of their citizens through dress. In that sense, the clothing and fabrics of the early modernization era in Turkey effectively reactivated ideals of unity, integration, solidarity, social control, order, suppression of individuality, institutional branding, convenience, and standardization, all of which matched the aims of the regime. Fashion is a particularly illuminating window through which to observe mechanisms both of social control and of resistance. Besides, as a system projecting images and identities, fashion achieves two aims: first, it provides a visible narration of a given epoch; and second, it illustrates the contradiction of class and gender conflicts (Paulicelli 2004: 148). However, the emergence of what may be called 'modern fashion' in Turkey followed a well-defined, centrally sustained, state-sanctioned, unified culture, which was expected to permeate the entire population.

In the modernization period, uniform dress was mobilized to assert modern life against the divergent rules of dress for the cosmopolitan public of the Ottoman Empire. While defining the dress codes of men and women, the new clothing was classless and rational compared with the earlier period. At first, the wearing of the *fez* was forbidden and European clothing was recommended, for men brimmed hats were mandated in the sartorial strategies of dress reforms (Bal 1998), while for women Westernized clothing was promoted and visualized.

With the collapse of the Ottoman Empire and the establishment of the Turkish Republic, the country had more homogeneity, even with the presence of religious minorities, such as Christians and Jews. State and religion were separated in the new Republic and Atatürk's approach was to promote nationalism not based on race but citizenship (Bal 1998). Therefore, the clothing strategy of the modernization period disregarded differences of identity within the nation, promoting more standard, simple, classless, and homogeneous dress for every individual in the society. It was a quick and practical solution to the problems created by the objective to create a new identity and was attractive to a culture that sought to cut ties with undesirable parts of its past. Now the population of the new Republic had to unify around 'Turkishness' which, as defined by Atatürk, emphasized the centrality of a being a Turkish citizen, and took no account of the origins of its constituent people. In addition, these citizens could comfortably use these modern, Western, and functional garments without any reference to religion and race.

The early twentieth-century was not the first time laws prescribing particular forms of dress had been implemented. This is especially evident in the Turkish Republic's predecessor, the Ottoman Empire, founded in Anatolia during the fourteenth century by the Turkic Osmanlı dynasty. Sumptuary laws were designed to visibly distinguish between specific professions, ranks, status, and religious groups. For example, certain colors and garments were legally assigned to Muslims, Christians, and Jews respectively, intended to reinforce distinctions within the population. What made the clothing laws of the early twentieth century quite different from the old sumptuary laws was the enforcing of *uniformity* among the population as a visible manifestation of adherence to the ideologies of the state. Therefore, the early modernization practices of dress were critical to the construction of social and cultural solidarity.

New dress cultures that emerged after the modernization period provided such a framework, in which the clothing style of an ideal Turkish citizen corresponded with the homogenous, rational and refined characteristics of a modernized Turkey. Moreover, it affected the daily practices of an emerging modern nation-state in terms of gender equality, secularity, collectivity, and belonging, through which the visual, social, and cultural profiles of the modern Turkish man and woman were unified and desexualized. They both preferred plain outfits for working and socializing in shared private and public spaces, reflecting the characteristic idealizing of the relatively neutral Turkish citizen, whose dress reflected both global and local awareness of Turkishness in striking contrast with Ottoman dress customs.

Ottoman customs were deep-rooted and extended back the tradition of clothing laws to the beginning of the empire. Moreover, as elsewhere, Ottoman clothing laws gave a particular emphasis to head coverings, which typically designated honor and rank (Guindi 2000: 130). These head coverings like *yaşmak* (a kind of veil) were used with *ferace*-like outfits, which is a kind of outdoor dress that covers the whole body. These sartorial legislations were clearly defined in the Ottoman Empire to mark rank, gender and ethnicity. As an example of traditional Ottoman female dress, Figure 7.1 is a nineteenth-century photograph showing a woman from Smyrne (now İzmir City) wearing a *ferace* and with *yaşmak* on her head. The veil makes her eyes just visible; we do not see any more of her body. However, immediately after the establishment of the Turkish Republic, the 'Attire Reform' (*kıyafet devrimi*) meant that new modern women and men were seen together, similarly dressed in simplified, unified, and plain outfits. The Attire Reform initially focused on what was deemed 'civilized,' and fashionable clothing described as functional, simple, and comfortable. Both the

Figure 7.1 Woman with *ferace* and *yaşmak* from İzmir, Turkey. Nineteenth century, photographer unknown. Apikam archive. Author's collection.

government and local media promoted these sartorial ideals across Turkish society as an expression of national unity, homogeneity, and social integration, in stark contrast to the myriad of garments and headgear worn by different religious and occupational groups in the Ottoman Empire.

Even in the literature, the new civilized woman was emphatically prescribed. For example, Halide Edip Adıvar (1884–1964), a well-known Turkish novelist, nationalist, and political leader, embodied all of these civilized characteristics. In one of her novels, named *Yeni Turan* (first published in 1912 as a utopic novel to describe Turkey in 1930s), the idealized character, *Kaya* (meaning 'rock' in English) is not shown as a sexualized figure, and thus she is not endangered by any men in society. Likewise, another character *Ayşe* from a novel *Ateşten Gömlek* (1922) is fictionalized as maintaining her love of country above any romantic feelings (Ezer 2012: 81–90). The local press also promoted modern European or Western dress all over the country, which was a sign of a desexualized and secular Turkish citizen.

Fashion as a tool for Turkish modernization

The Early Republican modernization project in Turkey was a continuation of the Ottoman reforms, but in terms of national belonging, there were clear differences between Ottoman and Early Republican fashion. It was, however, after the proclamation of the Republic in 1923 that the dress of the 'new Turk' became a major visual symbol representing the transition to a modern, civilized society. In contrast, during the Tanzimat period, fashion rules had been regulated by the Sultan with special enactments called *ferman*. However despite these reforms, women were forbidden to show their faces in public, and it was obligatory to use *ferace* and *yaşmak*. The sartorial aspects of these regulations including the 'hat reform' in 1925 played an important role, and this fits with a tradition of introducing Western-style dress. In Turkish fashion history, the *fez*, a flat-topped, conical, brimless hat often accessorized on top with a tassel, and introduced during the sultanate of Sultan Mahmud II (Eicher 2011: 52), was originally considered 'modern' but during *Tanzimat* reforms, it was prohibited and replaced by the Western-style hat or cap.

In the Tanzimat period, 'palace' and royal women copied and adopted Western (mostly French) fashion styles. Traditional attire was worn with those new styles; for men this included jackets named as *redingot*, waistcoat, tie, *fez*, pointed-toe, high-heeled shoes, and for Tanzimat women, traditional *entari* (Ottoman dress), *kuşak* (belt), *salvar* (a bi-furcated baggy trouser), *ferace* and *yasmak* were complemented with Western accessories (like the corset, gloves, jewellery) and popular color palettes. In later reforms for Turkish women, traditional styles like the *kaftan* and *ferace*, or *yaşmak* (a thin veil that covered the face, worn in public) were replaced by a more modern Western look, including modern skirts, dresses, jackets, silk stockings, and shoes, and typically with a tight turban (*sýkmabaş*) covering the head. It also became obligatory to wear 'Westernized' clothing in

Figure 7.2 Turkish women with modern head coverings known as *sıkmabaş*. Turkey, c. 1920s. Author's collection.

public and in government offices. Across the nation, this type of dressing became widespread since it was strictly defined under the new regime. As seen in Figure 7.2, the hats named *sıkmabaş* were a local adaptation of standard 1920s *cloche* hats. In order to adapt new forms of dress, many women sought practical solutions, such as bell-shaped headwear like *sıkmabaş*. Instead of veils (*yaşmak* or *hijab*), some covered their hair only by using a headscarf tied under the chin, or some used umbrellas in order to hide their faces. However, *sıkmabaş* were an adaptation of modern Islamist Turkish women, not a religious-political symbol (Cronin 2014). In particular, hats or headcoverings were no longer differentiated in the Turkish Republic, as they had been in the Ottoman Empire. Hitherto, headwear represented variance in status dictated by gender, occupation, rank, and ethnicity whereas the new fashion blurred status while creating symbolic meanings of the new regime.

As argued by anthropologist Mary Douglas, a social structure, where people are required to display a high level of control, will utilize formality in key aspects of social behaviour (Douglas, 2002: 86). In that respect, a degree of uniformity in dress code and bodily grooming can be found in groups whose behavior is under a strong degree of control and this we find in the new Turkish citizen's habitus after the 1920s. With the development of the new reforms, there was a more unifying shift in dress regulations towards simplicity and cheaper fabrics, and greater uniformity in the clothing of both sexes compared with the luxurious, voluminous, and overlapped dresses of Ottoman dress culture. Under the Kemalist ideology, the veil or *çarşaf* (a long piece of fabric covering the body), *ferace*, and *yaşmak*—and in general all kinds of dress that concealed women— symbolized the old regime and thus dress became the marker of the sharp line between secularism and Ottoman roots. As noted by Hale Yılmaz, in the post-1922 period, the primary focus of the public debate on women's dress shifted to the abolition of primitive, foreign, and non-national (*gayri milli*) clothes and the adoption of modern clothing. The public debate no longer centered on the interpretations of *yaşmak*, *ferace*, and *çarşaf*, and Islamic requirements or Ottoman dresses. It was now a secular debate focused on the requirements of the society, while women's dress, their visibility, education, and employment and the regulation of male–female relations, continued to be perceived through local, tribal, and religious lenses. The other major shift was the Republican state's attempt to reach and reshape the entire population, including rural women, in its effort to create a modern and 'unified' nation out of a diverse Anatolian population. The dress reforms aimed at the erasure of all signs of 'backwardness' and difference, whether religious, tribal, ethnic, or local. Thus, the early Republican state's clothing regulations targeted women outside of the major urban centers as well (Yılmaz 2016: 87). These reforms also mandated primary school uniforms (black suits with white collars, known as *önlük*) in educational institutions, as well as the obligation to wear clothing manufactured with local fabrics. Regardless of age, children were required to wear identical black school uniforms as symbols of the new civilized modern generation (Himam 2016: 112–31).

Above all, the flourishing of department stores in Turkish major cities, in İstanbul or in İzmir, where exported goods were sold, saw the decline of traditional crafts in city centers; new fashions spread these new ideas throughout the country. The upper classes closely followed magazines and journals such as *İnci*, *Şükufezar*, and *Hanımlara Mahsus Gazete*, all of which featured Western dress and displayed a great passion for dress models from Paris. Dressmakers tried to imitate these models by using cheaper, affordable, and local fabrics while middle-income groups preferred street tailors and aristocratic families favored famous non-Muslim (*gayri müslim*) tailors such as the Greek Madame Fegara, Madame Kalivrusi, and Madame Galibe, as outlined in the memoirs of Leyla Açba (Açba 2010).[1] The material and fabrics of such clothing were mostly produced by local institutions after the 1930s. Before then, the Feshane Palace Factory and the Hereke Factory were the initial results of textile initiatives in Anatolia, with the establishment of palace factories by the government between 1840 and 1860. By the end of the nineteenth century, very precious carpets that continued the imperial tradition were woven in the workshops of the Kumkapı district of Istanbul (Arkas Art Center 2015). In the 1930s, Sümerbank textile factories had replaced this rich and substantial cultural heritage and started to produce affordable, cheap, durable, modern fabrics. These national institutions were supposed to produce new printed textiles in order to achieve the new mission to create civilized and standardized appearances, as discussed below.

Another significant change and an attempt to create uniformity in the modernization period was the rise of sportswear, including beachwear and pyjamas. The new dynamic structure of the Turkish Republic developed the concept of 'leisure activity', with the purpose of making daily life appear more energetic. Sport activities were of great importance, mostly among the upper classes and the women of these families became interested in horse-riding, tennis, and golf. However, swimming was soon to become more important than these activities. The state was attempting to create a healthy population; Atatürk himself defined the aim of the republic as "to locate and to cure a disease in a society is to improve the society through the necessities of the time" (Atatürk 1934)[2], thereby describing how a modern and healthy individual is a necessary element for a civilized society. To have a healthy body, to be vivacious and cheerful, and to be successful in various sporting activities were all a means to create national unity and the appropriate emotional atmosphere for unity (Himam 2013: 87, 88).

Some schools for young girls, such as *Kız Sanat Enstitüsü* (Girls' Institute), opened right after the foundation of *İnas Sanayi Sultani* in 1927 in order to educate modern Turkish females. Students were taught skills such as cooking soufflés and omelettes, gardening, creating artificial flowers, cake-making, embroidery, and millinery by European-educated instructors (Tanyer 2006: 20, 21). The objects produced in these institutions and the exhibitions or fashion shows also symbolized modernity and the success a developing country would bring. Above all, the emphasis given to local dress had, in fact, an immediate link to the massive initiatives undertaken by the regime in the field of fashion in the modernization era. In sum, all of these new schemes by the Kemalist regime encouraged the production of domestic traditions with Westernized tools, and aimed to boost national pride.

A rational shift in tailoring and fabric production

After the world economic crisis in the early 1930s, a rationing system was introduced for dress production and fabric consumption across Europe due to the scarcity of materials. Textiles were strictly controlled, and government campaigns (similar to Britain's wartime 'Make Do and Mend' campaign) encouraged women accustomed to discarding worn or outmoded clothing to re-make and update garments instead (Laver 2002). During the Republican era, with the establishment of the National Economy and Savings Society (*Milli İktisat ve Tasarruf Cemiyeti*) in 1929, the Turkish public were encouraged to use locally made products to live economically, and in order to provide credit to facilitate the economic development policies, and the government began to establish Public Economic Enterprises (*Kamu İktisadi Teşekkülleri*). These included several new industrial complexes in different sectors, and directly or indirectly served the construction of economic, cultural and social uniformities, to promote a new lifestyle and material culture. Most of these early-Republican state industries were geared towards import-substitution and the accompanying policies of 'national self-sufficiency,' which made no provisions for exports. The Sümerbank textile factories, supported by *Sanayii Maadin Bankası*, were initially established to produce affordable textile products, but as discussed below evolved into institutions that drove nationalization and modernization.

The modernization movement affected the daily practices of Turkish men and women in terms of sexual equality, secularism, collectivity, and belonging, as already mentioned. This led to their visual and social profiles being unified and desexualized, as both genders opted to dress in less ornamented, plainer clothes made of local fabrics, or—for a small minority—expensive European fabrics. Generally, the patterns of Republican times had simple cubical modules, controlled design in plainer colors, monochrome decorations and visual textures, and meandering lines which were made by textile designers of the period who drew on modernist design movements. In mass-produced textiles, very few patterns reflected the nation's Islamic roots, the Ottoman heritage or ancient Turkish civilizations (Himam 2016: 112–13). The first tailors, fashion and textile designers of the Turkish nation-building project tended to imitate many of the formal features of the modern capitalist and socialist design products of the period, since they used visual media as reference tools and models of modernization. New dress models representing equality were to eliminate divisions between the elite and the rest, as well as between genders, by means of unified textile patterns and almost prototypical dresses for both sexes.

Under the modernist regime, the direction taken by Turkish textiles and fashion divided into two: the first can be characterized as more traditional, and included home-based tailoring with regional handicraft products like weaving, felting, and knitting, ancient skills which continue even today in Anatolia; the other direction, characterized as 'modern,' was more Western, innovative, and industrial. Under the Kemalist reforms, major achievements in terms of production and experimentation with textiles were simple, contemporary, and domestically produced, or founded on national brands and industrial initiatives. Therefore, the establishment of state-led industrial factories was a significant milestone in the realization of state policies in Turkey; modern production and marketing processes grew rapidly as new factories spread across Anatolia. However, how exactly did the textile industry, women's dresses, and fashion practices in general enact a process of uniformization?

In the field of fashion and textiles, governmental attempts were also made to create a sense of Turkishness in fashion encouraging national products. As the economic crisis had a significant impact on world fashion, Turkey adopted a more rational, democratic, uniformed and collective approach to fashion involving the unification of styles and material culture based on Republican ideology. The *Sümerbank* factories played a key role in Turkish textile design history due to the significant number of designers and factory workers employed during the modernization era. Moreover, whether produced by tailors, at home or in factories, products that represented the typical design concepts of uniformity could be observed in fabrics and textiles. In continual production from the 1930s until the end of the 2000s, *Sümerbank* textiles strongly supported the modernization and standardization of the Turkish citizen until their privatization in the 1980s.

Due to the scarcity of textile design schools in Turkey, there was a shortage of qualified technical personnel, so that one of the nationalist missions of *Sümerbank* was to train competent staff, both for the company and for the country as a whole. *Sümerbank*'s educational mission in this field was one of the pioneering efforts in Turkey. *Sümerbank* Settlements, conceived as small factory towns, comprised not only spaces of production (factories) and support (warehouses, workshops, boilerhouse, water tower, garage, fire station) units, but also residences (family houses, single houses, dormitories), community spaces (cafeteria, social club, guest house, kindergarten, day-care center, hospital), recreation (bicycle park, swimming pool, sports fields), and education (*Sümer* Primary School) (Himam and Pasin 2011: 161). In these units, managers and the workers dressed in *Sümerbank* uniforms and shared a uniform and collective life style. Moreover, *Sümerbank* Settlements could be further considered "education centers" or "industrial schools," in Çağatay Doğan's phrasing, designed to teach workers in particular how to behave, think, inhabit, and dress in ways to reach the ideal of the uniform(ed) Turkish citizen. They became microcosms of the designed uniformity that would characterize the nation state (Doğan 2009: 78).

The production of *Sümerbank* fabrics (which involved reducing waste material and minimizing the use of dyes) contributed to the enactment of the Kemalist ideal of economical uniformity by means of design production. The fabrics and the dresses adopted a clear, democratic, simple, modern, and rational look that was devoid of any religious or Ottoman-Islamic connotations. Floral, geometric, and abstract adornments represented the traces of the nation-state ideal of the Kemalist discourse, derived from Anatolian's ancient cultural roots. Homogeneity and austerity were formally conceived in the equalized distribution of simple, geometric patterns on fabrics and their applications, as well as the absence of ornamentation on other fabrics, and many other qualities valorized by the modernist nation-state. The geometric articulation of fabrics, and square modules, were used in order to assign a uniform and modern outlook and lifestyle to the idealized Turkish citizen (see Figure 7.3).

The great symbolic value of local fabrics produced from the *Sümerbank* factories established in 1933 was derived from the attention given to ensuring uniformity and homogeneity visually, culturally, and socially through clothes and fabrics that symbolized secularism, collectivity, and belonging. Given their functionality, durability, and availability across the country, *Sümerbank* textiles were able to create a unique Anatolian fashion, which resonated with the desired collective identity of society. The making of an homogeneous, rational, and refined style of clothing for the new Turkish citizenry constitutes an important dimension of the desired social transformation. The clothes, which were mostly handmade from these fabrics, sewn at home by women or in local tailors' shops, were simple, functional, 'modern' designs reflecting the Republican pride of those who wore them. This can be seen clearly, for example, in an anonymous photograph of a group of women of different ages and different social classes, wearing exactly the same dresses made out of *Sümerbank* fabrics, with similar Westernized hairstyles and make-up in Figure 7.4. These products were promoted by various media (posters, magazines, and advertisements), which emphasized the expected visual expression of the uniform(ed) Turkish citizen.

In Ottoman Turkish culture, textiles were luxury goods, and included brocaded silks, velvets, and gold-embroidered fabrics. In particular, the *çatma*,

Figure 7.3 Example of a *Sümerbank* fabric with stylized flower patterns decorated with geometric abstract shapes. Designer unknown, *c.* 1950s. İzmir University of Economics, Faculty of Fine Arts and Design, Tudita archive.

seraser, and *kemha* fabrics were considered to be treasures, and the outfits made of precious materials and elaborate techniques symbolic of wealth and power. In contrast, in Republican Turkey, the concepts of practical and comfortable use were dominant in the dressing style of the uniformed Turkish citizen in daily life. From the 1930s, dresses and suits made with *Sümerbank* fabrics were commonly worn throughout the country. In time, *Sümerbank* was able to fulfill the nationalist aim of transforming the nation through modernist and uniforming collective strategies. Thus, by establishing a certain measure of control, hierarchy, standardization, unity and categorization, it was possible for Turkish citizens to become effectively socialized through *Sümerbank* fabrics. Clothes produced with them became a 'uniform' of sorts, a sartorial standard symbolizing the

Figure 7.4 A group of women wearing identical dresses with Westernized hairstyles and make-up. Photographer unknown, *c.* 1940s. Çağla Ormanlar Ok collection.

creation of a unified society. The typical striped and spotted *Sümerbank* pyjamas and monochrome school uniforms exemplified the standardization and unification of clothing in daily life. These fabrics were affordable for most income groups in the country.

Local provenance underlined the ideological purpose of *Sümerbank* fabrics through the usage of national raw material, which was financially appropriate for families and citizens from a wide range of income levels. On the other hand, some minor state elites, in particular those from high-income groups following global fashion trends, were able to distinguish themselves from the medium-and low-income groups of the uniform(ed) Turkish citizens wearing *Sümerbank* dresses. They used fabrics imported or brought from countries like France, and employed skillful tailors to produce imitation Western dress. To support this 'new look of the new Turk,' alternatives included a wide range of fabrics that people purchased in special stores and tailoring ateliers, at a time when a ready-to-wear garment industry did not yet exist in Turkey.

Twice a year the *Sümerbank* factory also gave dress coupons to its workers, which allowed the families of civil servants and *Sümerbank* workers to buy items of clothing and textiles that were usually subject to limitations. In relation to this, Şadiye Ölçer Aysal who was a *Sümerbank* employee mentions that "everybody was trying to build up a wardrobe despite shortages" (Himam 2017). Turkish citizens were building up a basic wardrobe like a tuxedo or suit for winter and summer use, or two pairs of shoes for two seasons. "People were copying the designs from certain magazines or with the help of tailors. A family would dress themselves from these fabrics for a long time. Moreover, even within families, children also wore identical *Sümerbank* pattern dresses" (Himam 2017).

Perhaps the most important context for the display of unified clothing and other material elements of Republican dress was that of grand social occasions and ceremonies. At Republican balls, held in famous hotels such as the Ankara Palas, people experienced the new culture of the modern Turkish Republic, including modern dances such as the tango, foxtrot, charleston and swing, wearing their rational and functional contemporary Western dress (Tanyer 2006: 6). Likewise, at *Sümerbank* balls that were organized in the factories, workers of all social strata were encouraged to wear *Sümerbank* clothes; women wore dresses made of typical cotton fabrics printed with small flowers, and men wore suits with neckties made of cotton *Sümerbank* fabrics. The process of standardization sought to erase the considerable differences of social class in the *Sümerbank* factories on such occasions.

Conclusion

A key objective of Turkish modernization was to teach Turks how to behave, live, and dress in accordance with the image of the idealized, modern, and refined citizen. In other words, these ideals became "microcosms of the uniformity of the nation" (Doğan 2009: 78). Different from the Western experience of modernity, the Kemalist model had to negate its own cultural precedents to promote 'the new', as distinct from the old and the traditional. Zafer Toprak states that "this new discursive style, in which civilization is considered as international and culture as national, led to the exclusion of the Ottoman living styles and norms" (Toprak 1988).

In that sense, when exploring fashion's role in Turkey, the dress practices of the modernization era do not simply reflect socio-political change, but rather express the desire for the functioning of an effective society. Throughout this process, a series of pioneering reforms were enacted in every aspect of social life that involved a state-centered, national, civilized, secular, collective, and uniform understanding of modernity. Fashion, as both practice and discourse, was effective in the modernization process, particularly in the formation of 'national' identity through images of uniformity. In that sense, fashion during the modernization era was a crucial medium for the construction of signs of new desires and patterns that also articulated the endlessly changing notions of beauty. In other words, the design concepts of uniformity were mostly reflected visually through the formal language of dress culture. Thus, the dress practices, textiles, and accessories adopted in the modernization period represent a critical medium for the advancement of national ideologies that attached to concepts of uniformity. This state-led parade of images of women in their modern dresses was justified by the rhetoric of liberation of the body/nation from the authority of tradition.

References

Açba, H. (2010), *Leyla Açba: Bir Çerkes Prensesinin Harem Hatıraları,* İstanbul: Timaş Yayınları.
Arthur, L. B., ed. (2000), *Undressing Religion Commitment and Conversion from a Cross-Cultural Perspective,* Oxford and New York: Berg.
Bal, İ. (1998), "The Turkish Model and The Turkic Republics," *Perceptions: Journal of International Affairs,* 3 (3).
Blumer, H. (1968), *Fashion, Encyclopedia of Social Sciences,* New York: Free Press.
Bozdoğan, S. (2001), *Modernism and Nation Building, Turkish Architectural Culture in the Early Republic,* Seattle: University of Washington Press.
Bozdoğan, S. (2011), *Industrial Architecture and Nation-Building in Turkey: A Historical Overview,* İstanbul: Aga Khan Trust and Istanbul Bilgi University Press.
Bozdoğan, S. and R. Kasaba (1997), *Rethinking Modernity and National Identity in Turkey,* Seattle: University of Washington Press.
Cronin, S. ed. (2014), *Anti-Veiling Campaigns in the Muslim World: Gender, Modernism and the Politics of Dress* (Modern Middle East and Islamic World Series), New York; Routledge.
Doğan, Ç. E. (2009), "Nazilli Basma Fabrikasi Yerleşimi: Tarihçe ve Yasami," in A. Cengizkan (ed.), *Fabrika'da Barinmak: Erken Cumhuriyet Dönemi'nde Türkiye'de Isçi Konutlari: Yasam, Mekan ve Kent* Ankara: Arkadaş Yayinevi.

Douglas J. D. (2001), "Gestus Manifests Habitus: Dress and the Mormon," in W. J. F. Keenan (ed.), *Dressed to Impress: Looking the Part*, Oxford: Berg, 123–39.

Douglas M. (2002), *Natural Symbols: Explorations in Cosmology with a New Introduction*, London: Taylor & Francis e-Library.

Edensor, T. (2002), *National Identity, Popular Culture and Everyday Life*, Oxford: Berg.

Eicher, J. B., ed. (2011), "Dress Reforms of the Early Twentieth Century in Turkey, Iran, and Afghanistan," in *Berg Encyclopedia of World Dress and Fashion: Central and Southwest Asia*, Oxford: Berg.

El Guindi, F. (2000), *Veil: Modesty, Privacy and Resistance*, Oxford: Berg.

Ezer, Ö. (2012), *Doğu, Batı ve Kadın: Üç Kadın Seyyahın Kaleminden: 1913–1930*, İstanbul: Kitap Yayınevi.

Gellner, E. (1983), *Nations and Nationalism*, Ithaca, NY: Cornell University Press.

Göle, N. (1997), "The Quest for the Islamic Self within the Context of Modernity," in S. Bozdoğan and R. Kasaba (eds), *Rethinking Modernity and National Identity in Turkey*, Seattle, WA: University of Washington Press

Gönlügür, E. (2014), *American Architecture and the Promise of Modernization in Postwar Turkey*, unpublished PhD thesis, University of Toronto.

Himam, D. (2013), "Femininity in the Public Sphere during the Early Republican Era and Swimsuits," in 5T *Turkish Design Society Meetings: Gendered Perspectives in Design*, İzmir, Yaşar University.

Himam, D. (2016), "Sümerbank: Fashion, Textiles and the Making of a National Material Culture," in *The Journal of Decorative and Propaganda Arts* 28, Miami Beach, FL: Florida International Board of Trustees, The Wolfsonian, Florida International University, 112–31.

Himam, D. (2017), Interview with Şadiye Ölçer Aysal (Sümerbank textile factory worker), İzmir.

Himam, D. and B. Pasin (2011), "Designing a National Uniform(ity): The Culture of Sümerbank within the context of the Turkish Nation-State Project," *Journal of Design History*, 24 (2): 157–70.

Kaya, I. (2001), *Social Theory and Later Modernities: The Turkish Experience*, PhD thesis, University of Warwick.

Kaya, I. (2004), *Social Theory and Later Modernities: The Turkish Experience*, Liverpool: Liverpool University Press.

Laver, J. (2002), *Costume and Fashion: A Concise History*, London: Thames and Hudson.

McVeigh, B. (2000), *Wearing Ideology: State, Schooling and Self-Presentation in Japan*, Oxford: Berg.

Okyar, O. (1965), "The Concept of Etatism," The Economic Journal, 75 (297), 98–111.

Ottoman Carpets from the Arkas Collection (1834–1930). Available online: <http://www.arkassanatmerkezi.com/En/article.aspx?pageID=209> [accessed February 22, 2018]

Paulicelli, E. (2004), *Fashion under Fascism: Beyond the Black Shirt*, Oxford: Berg.

Sekimoto, Teruo (1997), "Uniforms and Concrete Walls Dressing the Village Under the New Order in the 1970s and 1980s", in Henk Schulte Nordholt (ed.), *Outward Appearances: Dressing State and Society in Indonesia*, Leiden: KITLV Press.

Tanyer, T. (2006), *Cumhuriyet Dönemi Ankara'sının Sosyal Hayatından Sahneler,* Ankara: Vekam Yayın

Tanyer, T. (2006), *Cumhuriyet Dönemi Ankara'sının Sosyal Hayatından Sahneler,* Ankara: Vekam Yayın (7).

Toprak, Z. (1988), *Sümerbank,* İstanbul: Creative Yayıncılık.

Yavuz, M. H. (1998), "Turkish Identity and Foreign Policy in Flux: The rise of Neo-Ottomanism," *Middle East Critique: Critical Middle Eastern Studies,* 7 (12): 19–41.

Yeşilkaya, N. G. H. (1999), *İdeoloji ve Mimarlık,* İstanbul: İletişim Yayınları.

Yılmaz, H. (2017), *Becoming Turkish: Nationalist Reforms and Cultural Negotiations in Early Republican Turkey 1923–1945,* Syracuse, NY: Syracuse University Press.

Part Four

Uniforming Workers

What people wear at work can offer key insights into how specific institutions operate: how workers interact with their employers, colleagues, and others they may encounter in their workplace. Sartorial uniformity is now demanded in various work environments including business, retail, and hospitality, and denotes an increased interest in aestheticizing corporate culture. In this section, the chapters consider the significance of modern uniforms to work cultures, asking how they might be used to instil occupational identity and pride, or to coerce workers. An aesthetic of standardization in workwear has been widely interpreted as a technique to increase surveillance over the bodies of workers. This section focuses on the use of uniforms to embody a technical rationality that works to create images of unity and authority.

A discourse of uniformity in the workplace might emphasize the comfort and convenience of regulation clothing but the use of uniform is primarily about creating a more homogenized workforce. Uniform signifies the increased power and control employers have over the micro-territory of the worker's body. More recently, the promotion of dress codes has become critical to the commodification of labor. Aesthetic labor, a term used primarily in sociology and anthropology, explains how organizational cultures use aspects of appearance—including uniform—to discipline workers.

By enforcing uniform dress codes, organizations can *embody* the identity of the organization. These chapters raise questions about how organizational identity is constituted through clothing and whether the values designed into uniforms are inclusive or exclusive. At work, uniform is about image management and brand identity, but patterns of uniformity are rarely neutral; ideas of authority, integrity, and power are embedded in various kinds of uniform clothing, including the suit, as discussed in Samira Guerra's essay on uniforming the corporate body in the City of London. Once the notion of a 'classic' design is interrogated its 'professional formality' can betray the desire to bleach out inconvenient cultural and historical references. Thus, uniform is not the neutral outfit it is often claimed to be.

These chapters consider the tensions between visible uniformity, that is, the unifying character of sartorial uniformity, and invisible uniformity, the capacity for clothing to restrict workers' opportunities for self-expression. Whether or not uniforms compromise workers' agency, they are nonetheless promoted as essential to the operation of workplace duties. On the other hand, there is evidence that increasingly employers engage in consultations with their staff about new uniform designs, as discussed by Prudence Black in relation to the redesign of the uniform worn by the employees of Qantas Airlines. The chapters here consider what uniforms say about the bodies they adorn: their agency, how the service user perceives them, and the extent to which workers can negotiate dress codes. Debates on aesthetic labor draw attention to how uniforms make workers symbol-bearers of organizations, and ask whether that involves the suppression of identity markers concerning aspects of gender, sexuality, or race. While occupational uniforms might be intended to inspire conformity, and often coerce workers, there are also fascinating examples of resistance to restrictive workplace dress codes.

8

Uniforming the Corporate Body in the City of London

Samira Guerra

If the suit is considered to be the epitome of modern masculinity this "modesty and plainness in dress" (Kuchta 2002: 2) has not always been an aesthetic contrast to womenswear. Men's attire in the Middle Ages, until far into the eighteenth century, was colorful regardless of the wealth or social position of the wearer. A somber and unadorned form of menswear emerged at the beginning of the nineteenth century (Harvey 1995: 23). Interpreted by the psychologist John Carl Flügel as a "Great Masculine Renunciation" (1930: 111), the adoption of plain and sober dress for men reflected socio-political changes associated with the French Revolution. If adornment and decoration in menswear had been signifiers of social position, they had by this time become redundant. Flügel argued that for the modern man rigid and modest clothing "symbolise[s] his devotion to the principles of duty, of renunciation, of self-control" (1930: 133). Changes in men's clothing reveal their changing role in modern society. If menswear grants more seriousness and competence to men than women, then this might account for the widespread perception that fashion is inherently feminine (Breward 1999: 2; Craik 1994: 170; Wilson 2003: viii).

The globalization of Western forms of business wear is closely tied to the ways in which it embodies notions of authority, professionalism, legitimacy, integrity, and power. This makes the suit a pivotal costume to the success of corporate environments. This qualitative research explores questions of place, gender, and power through analysis of the relation between business wear, uniforms, and fashion using ethnographic data gathered in the City of London[1]. Sociologist Joanne Entwistle, describes the suit as "the standard 'masculine' dress" (2015: 37) in the white-collar workplace. Since corporate environments are male-dominated, this raises questions about how business wear works for women. Even though women have a range of options, shape- and color-wise, business wear is based on a masculine type of clothing. When women choose garments for business they are essentially mapping a masculine form onto the female body (Entwistle 2015: 37). This process is not unproblematic and, as this research will show, it can also be a source of anxiety for women in a business environment.

For the research, data is analyzed through literature on uniforms, the body and power in order to establish a framework to examine the *corporate body*. Through the work of sociologist Pierre Bourdieu, I consider what the uniformed body means in corporate environments. The philosopher Michel Foucault's work on power also furthers my exploration of the nature of corporate control through bodily practices of conformity and resistance in matters of clothing. Consisting of muted colors and restrained shapes business wear is often thought to embody conformity and represent a lack of individuality. This sartorial homogeneity resembles the uniform in that it works to standardize and control the body and dictates how the body embodies institutional power (Joseph 1986: 65; Fussell 2002: 177; Craik 2005: 134–5). Carrie Hertz criticises the interpretation many scholars make of uniform as "an idealized depiction of the garment and its functions" (2007: 53) instead of a focus what they do on an individual and interpersonal level. This research draws on interviews with individuals in corporate environments to examine this social dimension. The data addresses the corporate body, and asks what it is, how it looks and what it feels like. While recent academic literature sheds light on flight attendant uniforms (Black 2011, 2013), military uniforms (Peniston-Bird 2003; Tynan 2012, 2013) and school uniforms (McVeigh 2002; Dussell 2004) business wear remains an underexplored area. This research aims to add to the literature on occupational dress to argue that business wear is a category of uniform.

Occupational dress: business wear as uniform

Business wear is a type of occupational clothing. Sociologist Nathan Joseph (1986) divides occupational clothing into quasi-uniforms and standardized clothing. He argues that standardized clothing is often mistaken for uniform as there is not one distinct standard set of clothing, given and enforced by companies (Joseph 1986: 143–4). For Joseph, work apparel is standardized clothing that "denotes a membership in a diffuse, unorganized group" (1986: 144) without the use of strict dress codes, to offer wearers some sartorial autonomy. Corporations, however, are highly structured entities and not in fact the unorganized groups he suggests. What Joseph fails to acknowledge is that while individuals can choose between a black or navy blue suit, there is a measure of choice within the boundaries of accepted ideas of what business wear is, which is often elucidated by corporate dress codes. Individuals' agency does not start and end with what they choose to wear but also with what they choose *not* to wear, what fashion theorist Jennifer Craik calls the "other face" (2005: 4) of uniforms. While uniforms might represent a controlled, obedient body that follows regulation, uniformed bodies are equally inclined to transgress. Wearers' agency is the result of complex negotiation rather than autonomous choice. While Joseph's ideas about occupational uniforms are compelling, this research challenges them, by revisiting business wear from a new multi-dimensional perspective, taking into account contemporary forms of corporate control and the enforcement of dress codes.

Craik argues that occupational uniforms help in "establishing and maintaining a professional occupational persona" (2005: 126) and in her typology, corporate wear is a quasi-uniform that "may change arbitrarily [...] or be reasonably stable" (2005: 127). To work as a garment of authority, business wear must be characterized by "easily recognized vestimentary codes" (Craik 2005: 127). These codes are necessary to create the same meaning for wearers and the people around them. In highly corporate environments control and power are often exerted through "the enforcement of a uniform which enables the image and identity of the corporation to be literally em*bodied*" (Entwistle 1997: 316–7). What makes a uniform powerful is therefore its capacity to communicate within a given environment through bodily practices (Craik 2003: 134; Hertz 2007: 43; Entwistle 2015). Entwistle notes that clothing is "an important aspect in the management and discipline of bodies within the workplace" (1997: 316). The whole body—including self-presentation, behavior, enunciation, and diction—is governed by institutional control (Hertz 2007: 44). Thus, when studying uniforms, it is critical to consider how they embody specific identities and values.

Identifying the *corporate body*

The previous section established that control and its embodiment are crucial to the functioning of uniforms, particularly in the workplace. In this discussion, the theories of Bourdieu and Foucault are used to explore the meaning of the corporate body. The Foucauldian body is a non-material, intangible notion established in discourse rather than a corporeal, physical entity (Turner 1996; Entwistle 2015: 26–8). Bourdieu's ideas of embodiment and habitus are useful in addressing the reality of how actual bodies behave, but Foucault's theories of power and surveillance are more stringent when looking at corporate control since they deal with institutionalized power (Jenkins 2002: 123). Bourdieu is concerned with the ways in which societal strata are determined, maintained, and reproduced on a daily basis: his work deals with the "consumption and production of culture" (Rocamora 2015: 233). The concept of habitus is central to this idea describing as it does the condition of the individual in a cultural environment. The habitus consists of structure and agency: it is *opus operatum*, a structure of classification and schemata of perception. It is also *modus operandi*, the structuring structure of people's agency (Bourdieu 1984: 170-5). Consequently, the existence of different habitus necessitates the recognition of a system of classification to express difference.

Bourdieu's concept of habitus offers evidence of individuals' social positions in different realms of society, or *fields*, as Bourdieu calls them. Each field requires its members to possess a specific configuration of cultural, economic and social capitals to legitimize their access (Bourdieu 1983; Bourdieu and Wacquant 2006: 139). Clothing, and uniforms in particular, lend themselves to a Bourdieuan analysis. Habitus, fields and capitals are a useful lens through which to study fashion because sartorial appearance influences the representation of social, economic and political status, being closely related to prestige, influence, and power (Barnard 1996: 58–63). Bourdieu himself was concerned with fashion. In *Le couturier et sa griffe*, Bourdieu and Delsaut analyze the field of high fashion in France (1975) as they are interested in different sets of capitals, especially the "fashion capital" (Rocamora 2002: 343). This research explores questions of place, gender, and power through analysis of the relation between business wear, uniforms, and fashion by means of ethnographic data gathered in the City of London. Bourdieu's concepts are useful to consider how uniforms obtain meaning by revealing what they do and how they function on the body. What people think about business wear and how they perform their uniformed self is essentially about the habitus or corporeal practices (Entwistle 2015: 37).

Foucault is concerned with the origins of power and the ways in which it is exerted. A considerable part of Foucault's work revolves around a disindividualized kind of power exerted on behalf of institutions. To illustrate the functioning of this power in a quotidian setting, Foucault borrows Jeremy Bentham's idea of the panopticon (1991: 202, 205). The surveillance tower in the middle of the panopticon and its circular architecture allow omni-visibility and therefore perpetual control over individuals, to "see constantly and to recognize immediately" (Foucault 1991: 200). This enhanced visibility is due to the panopticon's unique architecture that facilitates the "normalizing gaze" (Foucault 1991: 184) as a means of control.

Individuals do not necessarily know if they are being watched but constant surveillance makes the individual aware that they could be watched at any time. Therefore power becomes automatic without its actual, perpetual exertion (Foucault 1991: 200-01). In the most ideal case its utilization becomes unnecessary and the outcome is a condition whereby "the inmates should be caught up in a power situation of which they are themselves the bearers" (1991: 201). Individuals do not simply experience disciplinary power but it is exerted on the body itself, leading to what Foucault calls "docile bodies" (1991: 138). This kind of power is more potent than physical punishment since it trains and disciplines the body and its behavior (Tynan 2015: 6).

There are studies of uniform that utilize a Foucauldian reading. In particular, the notion of the 'docile body' enables consideration of how restrictive clothing can be, as Jane Tynan argues in her study of how First World War British army uniforms transformed soldiers' bodies (2013). By means of a Foucauldian analysis she asks how visual and textual historical accounts of soldiers discursively shaped perceptions of lived masculinities during wartime (Tynan 2013; 2015). While uniforms are about disciplining bodies, Tynan observes that transgression and refusal to wear military uniforms also reveal wider attitudes about participation (2013: 87). Brian McVeigh's (1997) research addresses Japan as a uniformed culture to argue that the normalizing gaze governing the social environment ensures that people comply with a certain appropriateness of dressing. McVeigh studies the transformations that occur when people move in and out of uniform to reflect on how students negotiate between being and not being uniformed (1997: 191–6, 208–09). As with military and school uniforms, business wear similarly restricts the body and makes it visible to the normalizing gaze.

Entwistle (1997) also uses Foucault's "technologies of the self" (1988), this time to describe the agency of the career woman in relation to dressing for corporate environments. These technologies of the self undertake actions and make changes to the body and habitus in order "to attain a certain state of happiness, purity, wisdom, perfection, or immortality" (1988: 18). Entwistle speaks of the managed self that requires corporate control. Surveillance is not just directed to the quality of work done but reaches further into personal space by observing the woman's body (Entwistle 1997: 315–16). The enterprising self, denoted by notions of "internal self-management and relative autonomy" (Entwistle 1997: 316), allow the female worker to be proactive, and to realize the potential of power dressing. The enterprising self anticipates and internalizes what is expected, taking responsibility for success and embodies regulations without external control. Such a technology has become institutionalized since it is not only the businesswoman's objective but is also built into the corporate structure (Entwistle 1997: 318–22).

This research uses ethnographic fieldwork to explore lived experiences of corporate dressing. Entering the field in August 2015, I conducted observation in the areas of Liverpool Street, Bank, and St. Paul's in the City of London. I spent mornings, afternoons, and evenings there and joined people on their way to work, observed restaurants and cafés during lunchtime, and eventually took notes when people left their offices in the evening. I also observed the office of a trading company in London. Additionally, interviews captured the experiences of three business people who are required to wear business attire to work and are referred to as Heather, Maya, and Felix in the text[2]. Heather is in her thirties and employed as a market researcher by a trading company with UK headquarters in London, which is the office observed. When I interviewed Maya, she was at the end of a twelve-month trainee program in the internal audit department of a bank after graduating in finance. Felix has a trainee contract with a law firm on Old Broad Street in the City. The interviews were realized in a semi-structured manner, which meant that while some topics had to be covered, I left room for other topics to emerge during the interview.

Place: the office and the City as panopticon

According to a research report on the City, offices have become increasingly permeable; perceived as open-plan areas, these spaces enable collaboration and communication among colleagues (Katsikakis 2015: 37, 41). It is not just employees and their clothing that are representative for corporations; offices are also "now being managed as a corporate resource" (Katsikakis 2015: 41) to convey the desired image and corporate values. The office of the trading company I observed consists of three floors of open-plan offices and apart from certain structural supports the office is airy without any restricting walls. This architecture renders corporate bodies visible since there is no hiding place. The office is observable from any point much like Foucalt's panopticon; visibility here is a trap. Employees are aware that control can happen at any time. Thus, there is no need for perpetual surveillance to make individuals feel controlled. The power becomes automatic without needing enforcement to have an effect (Foucault 1991: 200–01). The corporate body created by the panoptic office is exemplified by Heather's response:

There are days like today when I'm wearing jeans. I wouldn't probably get up as much and walk around because I'm conscious of the fact that I'm wearing jeans and I don't want people to notice and it doesn't look professional [...]. I probably wouldn't dare to get up and talk to people if I had questions [...], probably just e-mail them to avoid getting up.

GUERRA 2015a

The dress code in the trading company forbids jeans, except on Fridays. The panoptic feel of the office space intensifies the inappropriateness of Heather's clothing, making her feel uncomfortable. Therefore she "assumes responsibility for the constraints of power" (Foucault 1991: 202) and controls herself by adapting her behavior. Heather's case of self-surveillance is an example of how invasive corporate control is and how it is exerted on the body, leading her to actively change her behavior in this situation.

The City is London's business and financial district where finance and insurance employees represent the majority of all workers (Katsikakis 2015: 5, 11). The observational data suggests that there is a consensus on appropriate work clothing. Most people in this area are dressed in a similar way, wearing tailored, unadorned suits or dresses in somber colors. The City induces sameness among its participants, creating a culture of uniformity. Business attire seems to govern individuals' movements and shapes their behavior. Men exhibit similar uniform gestures and embodiments while clad in business wear, putting the spare hand into the trouser pocket when talking on the phone or greeting a client with a firm handshake. Their habitus mirrors conventional values attached to the suit such as professionalism and authority, making everything about the appearance of these men look neat and controlled. On the one hand, being in the City has an influence on the *opus operatum* as it shapes the perception of what constitutes business wear. Those who are exposed to this corporate area develop a system of classification that enables them to identify what a successful embodiment of corporate wear should look like. On the other hand, new practices, such as their own embodiment of business wear, are produced through the *modus operandi* (see Bourdieu 1984: 170–5).

The way the body is controlled through garments therefore goes beyond the actual workplace. The City serves as an extension of the office where values concomitant with suits continue to be validated by the wider environment. In this way the City also functions as a panopticon. The normalizing gaze is shifted from superiors to participants in the *corporate field*. This has echoes of McVeigh's argument that, in Japanese society, the normalizing gaze operates through the social environment; here the corporate body is controlled by participants in the

City. This becomes evident when looking at data, gathered on the qualities of the City as a financial center, which shows that people tend to walk a lot in the City. When asked about moving around, answers focused on the fact that "you can stroll round the corner to meet your clients" (Lascelles 2003: 22). Being seen is of interest to firms because it gives their business credibility and improves professional relationships (Lascelles 2003: 27). Since there are many people in the streets, the individual never grasps the extent to which they are being controlled. The individual does not know when surveillance occurs as it could be at any given moment and there is an awareness that superiors, colleagues, and clients could potentially be everywhere. It is the combination of power being both "visible and unverifiable" (Foucault 1991: 201) that is crucial in this context. The normalizing gaze that individuals experience creates docile bodies obedient to rules in the corporate field. The possibility that people might run into clients on the way to lunch creates selves that are ready for business at all times. This includes being uniformed for business and constantly performing a corporate habitus. The office and the wider context of the City are spaces that facilitate surveillance due to their panoptic character. Space is an important variable that governs how corporate control is exerted on workers' bodies through social forces that shape the wider environments and not just when they are in the office.

Business wear and 'dress for success'

Discourses about clothing and gender circulate in corporate workspaces. Clothing that uniforms bodies consequently brings forth sameness. However, when it comes to performing gender, business wear very clearly distinguishes between male and female bodies (Entwistle 2015: 37). Craik argues that two kinds of uniforms exist for women: "quasi-masculine uniforms associated with instilling discipline, confidence […] and feminized uniforms that promote physical and emotional training in attributes of nurturing" (2003: 139). Since gender is a performative practice (Butler 1990: 25), it is sartorially produced within dominant cultural norms, as Heather points out:

> A lot of the women deliberately wear dresses. Not short dresses but they dress very girly type, wearing skirts and high heels, and I deliberately wear trousers. Just to make a point.
>
> GUERRA 2015a

In the context of dressing for success the appropriation of male clothing is "used to signify a particular status or position" (Barnard 1996: 116). How much business wear is perceived as predominantly masculine clothing becomes evident when shedding light on how individuals talk about business wear. Maya says that:

> Clothing actually has quite a big influence on your appearance, if people trust you or not [...]. When you audit them and you are wearing a suit people deem you more credible than if you walk around in ragged clothing.
>
> GUERRA 2015b

To adopt an authoritative position, Maya seeks legitimization in the way she dresses revealing that gender is reproduced through clothing and is actively negotiated by wearers. The suit is inherently masculine, bearing corporate notions and ideals, which are attached to and the property of the male body. Thus, the career woman is perceived as a female professional whose gender marks a difference from the orthodoxy of the corporate masculine body. The cultural construction of corporate wear as male clothing seems axiomatic and normalized because it is bound up with notions of masculinity. This difference also renders female bodies in corporate environments more visible. Both Maya and Heather are experimenting with gender boundaries and are clearly exploring what certain garments can embody. They also realize that certain types of clothing, and in this sense feminine business clothing, can appear sexualized, making it challenging for women to perform a professional self without gender designating their appearance and work. Heather tends to wear outer garments like trousers and blazers in muted colors and stays away from the brighter shades some of her colleagues wear. For her, the goal is to retain a subtle femininity to sartorially distinguish herself from men while not surrendering to the male gaze. The female body is hyper-visible to the corporation and to male colleagues because it is subjected to the normalizing male gaze: not only do superiors enforce the reproduction of corporate values but employees do so themselves when they control each other. Heather and Maya's behavior demonstrates that dressing closer to sartorial rules allows them to escape this heightened visibility and can be a means by which women seek privacy. Thus, succumbing to uniformity is not necessarily restrictive and oppressive for the body but can also act as a form of concealment.

Dressing for work as a project of the self gives women agency to decide how to perform gender and where to make use of power dressing, reflecting Entwistle's concept of the enterprising self. To be at eye level with her male

Figure 8.1 Male and female business wear. Getty Images [Image reference 612387512].

colleagues, Heather wears high heels when she is presenting, which makes her feel more powerful in a male-dominated environment. While it might feel empowering to simply add certain items, the technologies of the enterprising self integrate clothing far deeper into the career plan: "the career woman is told she must be calculating and cunning in her self-presentation" (Entwistle 1997: 318–19). This calculation manifests itself in Heather's perception of the representational function of business wear. For her, finding the perfect look is a challenge because her clothing represents herself and the company. Being and becoming the self in the corporate field is a constant negotiation of perceptions of the clothed self and the version imagined by the corporation. Clothing practices project the self through engagement with different garments, shapes, and colors to find what extraverts the self best (Woodward 2007: 157). In other words, the internalized cultural capital on fashion knowledge comes into conflict with corporate regulations and expectations. It becomes evident that Heather strictly divides her wardrobe between leisurewear and workwear when she says that:

> It's a conscious decision because when I'm at work I wear a blazer and when I'm out of it I don't want to wear a blazer [...]. It's very separate.
>
> GUERRA 2015a

Additionally, she and Maya report that it is common to change into leisure clothes when leaving work to take off the 'work uniform'. Maya elucidates that business wear "starts to annoy you. You keep waiting for the evening or the weekend to take it off" (Guerra 2015b). It therefore acts as a marker between private and professional life.

Sophie Woodward argues that work clothing makes women fit into the role of a professional, while there are efforts made to show the real self even when facing sartorial rules (2007: 143). The appropriation of the suit on a female body is not unproblematic and accounts from businesswomen shed light on how they deal with this issue. Dressing for power as a project of the self is hard work and requires incorporated cultural capital. While women use different strategies to dress for power, or for equality, the types of practices the women in this study engage in go beyond power dressing. Women's clothing practices, like power dressing 2.0, find women not simply emulating the male business suit but negotiating their femininity through sartorial practices that make them appear equal to their male colleagues. This also means incorporating one's own style and cultural capital with enforced dress codes and, thus, instead of simply imitating the power suit women search for their own empowering professional identity.

Power: obedience, resistance, and corporate control

The exertion of corporate power and lack of individuality that results from the wearer's compliance to dress codes and corporate rules of behavior poses questions about conformity and autonomy. In a society and an age where individualism is upheld, what does standardizing and restricting business attire do to wearers and their bodies? Does business wear look and function as a uniform on workers' bodies? And what happens if there is resistance to imposed clothing regulations? During rush hour, Liverpool Street station in London becomes a bustling place filled with people traveling to or from work. As it is in the vicinity of the business district, most travelers are business people in corporate attire. When standing on the ground floor looking down into the hall of the station, a seemingly never-ending swarm of suits can be seen walking in the same direction. Visually, they do not differ much from one another, giving a lasting impression of a large group of uniformed bodies.

This unifying character is not the only feature reminiscent of uniform, but here clothing also restricts the bodies of wearers. The strictness and seriousness of business is, thus, embodied in the dress code. Two dimensions exemplify this restriction: the bodily experience (what corporate control feels like) and how this restriction manifests itself through the dress code. With rigid cuts and inelastic fabrics, business wear constrains bodies, especially when the suits are tailored to the body so that they fit like a second skin, and allow only a little freedom to move. When asked about their most uncomfortable garment, the interviewees were quick to mention the blazer, as Maya explains:

> They are really impractical. And in the end I rarely wore them, never actually. Only when we saw a client. Because, you know, in winter it's really impractical under the coat, it feels really bulky. And in summer it's really hot.
>
> GUERRA 2015b

Maya dislikes blazers for functional reasons: the restrictive cuts of business wear can make her feel constrained and uncomfortable. She argues that these clothing restrictions are counter-productive since they can distract her from work. Likewise, Heather is not fond of blazers and confirms that it:

> ...does restrict you. When you're working and you've got a deadline you really want to be focused [...]. And when you're wearing like very stiff trousers, for example, or they've got a crease, some people don't mind it but I tend to think I wish I was just like [...], take my shoes off kind of thing and relax a little bit more and so I can get this done and focus and not feel uncomfortable.
>
> GUERRA 2015a

Heather's statement indicates that the ways in which the corporation exerts power is not only spatial. Since corporations control clothing, they control bodies, which means that discipline is easily exercised over the body through clothing. As Joseph argues, restrictive uniform clothing signifies the lack of power the person experiences by being exposed to the authority of the corporation (1986: 40). If there is no escape from surveillance, this suggests that business wear is a uniform to make the wearer part of the corporation and thus subject to corporate control.

The dress code is a manual that functions as a guideline for employees so that they know what to wear and what to avoid. The company I visited sets out its dress policy in their employee handbook and uses about one page of the thirty-seven-page long manual to explain what it expects from its employees in terms of clothing. Dress codes are not so concerned with what must be worn but focus instead on what is prohibited (Brunsma 2004: 15). In this sense the list of

Figure 8.2 Uniformity of business wear. Getty Images [Image reference 680449771].

unacceptable items is more detailed than the code itself. It specifically names items that are forbidden in the office such as denim, crop tops, or Ugg boots. Even if not explicitly written down, specific colors and cuts are known to be unacceptable, further constraining the choices a worker can make. Some rules are unsaid and have to be learned by participation in the corporate field. Felix discusses this fact when talking about ties. According to him, some ties are exclusively reserved for superior positions:

> What I would bring in at a later point, maybe like expensive ties because I don't know – There's this slightly stereotype. I think it's more pronounced in banking, as a trainee you can't have like a really expensive tie. It's like "Who do you think you are?—kind of thing.
>
> GUERRA 2015c

This anecdote is indicative of the hierarchy at play when it comes to clothing among City workers. Even though ties are part of the established dress code, there is some freedom for men concerning their shape, pattern, and color. Established businessmen set themselves apart from interns through their composition of capitals in the Bourdieuan sense. Since they have been working longer, they have a higher level of internal cultural capital, which refers to the knowledge and skills acquired that are specific to the corporate field. Being able to handle more challenging tasks they consequently receive higher pay than interns, which contributes to their higher degree of economic capital. Having established a career these businessmen in superior positions have connected to more business people throughout their career and therefore have more professional relations, which represents their social capital. Bourdieu argues that these accomplishments can become symbolic capital, also called distinction, if they are "known and recognized as self-evident" (Bourdieu and Thompson 1991: 238). Prestige is a manifestation of symbolic capital. The composition of capitals and how they are perceived within the social environment enables senior employees to distinguish themselves from interns. Due to this distinction, they profit from prestige and, hence, established businessmen are allowed to wear expensive ties to display their professional status, which reflects their position in the corporate field.

Given that dress regulations in corporate environments are particularly strict it is not always possible to dress the corporate self and think 'this is me.' Such issues are elucidated by moments of resistance. Since workwear does not mirror Maya's own clothing preferences, it feels like a costume to her. This state of discomfort has prompted her to employ strategies of resistance, to allow her to rebel against the imposed rules by introducing small, subtle changes to the dress code, such as more relaxed cuts or fabrics. Maya feels uncomfortable and tries to introduce her own personal style in a way that does not exceed the boundaries of the dress code. The strategy that she is employing is what anthropologist James C. Scott would call "everyday forms of [...] resistance" (1985). Looking at an oppressed peasant society in Malaysia, he discusses how powerless societies respond to the hegemony they are facing. He argues that instead of open revolt, which is usually unsuccessful due to their weak position, peasants deploy implicit strategies of insurgency such as false compliance or feigned ignorance. He calls such practices "weapons of the weak" (Scott 1985: 29). Similarly, Maya does not confront her boss but rather uses quiet forms of resistance. Constant efforts are being made to appear "ununiformed" (McVeigh 1997: 209) in a highly uniformed culture; the regulations that come with uniforms are always "imperfectly reproduced" (1997: 208) and "total socialization" (1997: 208) is not really possible.

To a certain extent, people are obedient but corporate control can never produce fully docile bodies because workers are ultimately subjects with their own agency (McVeigh 1997: 208). However, non-compliance with corporate dress codes does not go unnoticed and can have consequences, as Heather's example shows. Heather tells me that a former colleague experienced a rebuke after wearing revealing dresses and became the talk of the office. She was not directly approached by a superior but received a letter from Human Resources

(HR), stating that such clothing was not tolerated, a form of control that could be described as Foucauldian. Like control exerted in the panopticon, the individual is never watched by a visible person but knows control is coming from an anonymous agent in the tower. The fact that Heather's colleague was approached by a faceless HR department illustrates this disindividualized, panoptic power at work in her office environment (Foucault 1991: 202, 205). Foucault's notion of the panopticon illustrates how power operates in an institution, but also how it executes its control imperfectly. Therefore the lack of power that people experience is not equivalent to their agency, which they might use to deal with control on their own terms. Business wear uniforms bodies in terms of how it makes them look but also how it makes them feel. The feeling of control is evident on the bodies of City workers and the wearing of a corporate uniform is so invasive that it often clashes with their own perceptions of what they would like to wear. Above all, the lack of individuality paired with the feeling of constraint lead many to transgress in order to escape the regime of corporate power.

Conclusion

The corporate body is a restricted body. The ethnographic data presented reveals that an institutional focus on the clothed self in corporate environments addresses behavior, feelings, and perceptions of the body. How corporations control business people through clothing is inherently Foucauldian since power is exerted on the body by a faceless institution. The various ways in which wearers are subjected to power in the corporate field helps to explain how business wear functions as a uniform. If tailored business wear works like a second skin, this illustrates how invasive corporate surveillance is and how restrictive this power feels on the body. Spatiality has a controlling and corrective effect on business people due to the visibility of their bodies in the workplace. The office and the City function like a panopticon, surveilling and governing people's habitus by turning them into corporate, docile bodies. Corporate values are transferred from the office to the City where corporate control becomes social control. Heather's examples illustrate how the panoptic gaze operates in a closed corporate environment, and in particular how transgressive acts are communicated and admonished. To a considerable extent, individuals internalize dress codes and know what is expected from them in terms of clothing. Thus they assume the controlling function of the corporation to monitor themselves and each other. Such a normalizing gaze reproduces corporate values to become more powerful than the sole surveillance of a superior.

The suit, whose values of professionalism and authority are traditionally attached to masculinity, can pose difficulties for women and make them feel unsettled. As this research shows, men's body performances normalize the suit, so when women don a masculine garment it never really seems to fit on a female body. When deciding what works with their bodies, women are instead guided by their own preferences and notions of fashionability, making a considerable effort to negotiate gender expectations while trying to appear professional. Women do not just simply emulate a style of male clothing but they negotiate their own femininity in the workplace. By doing this, they are actively trying to shift the masculine values traditionally attached to the suit into their own realm. Crucial to this study is the finding that fashion and uniform often seem to be in conflict in the workplace but it is also clear that workers negotiate the emerging tensions through their own creativity in dressing. Therefore, they negotiate the relationship between fashion and uniform on the job.

Business wear in general requires constant negotiation between preferences and perceptions of the self, on the one hand, and corporate regulations, on the other. Strictly regulated environments are not just characterized by obedience but also by non-compliance, which indicates the boundaries of corporate control. The panoptic work environment is effective in creating docile bodies but only manages it up to a point, as individuals always remain subjects with their own habitus, no matter how stringently they are controlled. This means that while corporate regulations can induce submission they are equally prone to resistance. Uniforms appear to lack individuality, due to their tendency to standardize bodies, but this does not mean that wearers are devoid of agency. On the contrary, this is what makes the study of corporate uniforms fruitful: corporate bodies participate in a field where they negotiate their position using their own agency. Moreover, within the context of corporate rules and expected behavior, participants constantly negotiate between compliance and transgression. This research opens up the discussion on business wear to explore questions of embodiment and uniformity by drawing on the lived experiences of business people. Above all, the corporate body offers a good case study for considering how uniforms work as mediators of power.

References

Barnard, M. (1996), *Fashion as Communication*, London: Routledge.
Black, P. (2011), *The Flight Attendant's Shoe*, Sydney: New South Press.

Black, P. (2013), "Lines of Flight: The Female Flight Attendant Uniform," *Fashion Theory,* 17 (2): 179–96.
Bourdieu, P. (1983), "Ökonomisches Kapital, kulturelles Kapital, soziales Kapital," in Reinhard Kreckel (ed.), *Soziale Ungleichheiten (Soziale Welt Sonderband 2)* Göttingen: Verlag Otto Schwartz, 183–98.
Bourdieu, P. (1984), *Distinction: A Social Critique of the Judgement of Taste,* London: Routledge.
Bourdieu, P. and Y. Delsaut (1975), "Le Couturier et Sa Griffe: Contribution à une Théorie de la Magie," *Actes de la Recherche en Scienes Sociales,* 1: 7–36.
Bourdieu, P. and J. B. Thompson (1991), *Language and Symbolic Power,* Cambridge: Polity Press.
Bourdieu, P. and L. J. D. Wacquant (1992), *An Invitation to Reflexive Sociology,* Cambridge: Polity Press.
Bourdieu, P and L. J. D. Wacquant (2006), *Reflexive Anthropologie,* Frankfurt am Main: Suhrkamp.
Breward, C. (1999), *The Hidden Consumer: Masculinities, Fashion and City Life 1860–1914,* Manchester: Manchester University Press.
Brunsma, D. (2004), *The School Uniform Movement and What It Tells us About American Education: A Symbolic Crusade,* Lanham, MD: Scarecrow Education.
Butler, J. (1990), *Gender Trouble. Feminism and the Subversion of Identity,* New York: Routledge.
Craik, J. (1994), *The Face of Fashion: Cultural Studies in Fashion,* London: Routledge.
Craik, J. (2003), "The Cultural Politics of the Uniform," *Fashion Theory,* 7 (2): 127–47.
Craik, J. (2005), *Uniforms Exposed: From Conformity to Transgression,* Oxford: Berg.
Dussell, I. (2004), "Fashioning the Schooled Self," in B. M. Baker and K. E. Heyning (eds), *Dangerous Coagulations: The Uses of Foucault in the Study of Education,* New York: Peter Lang, 86–116.
Entwistle, J. (1997), "'Power Dressing' and the Construction of the Career Woman," in M. Nava, A. Blake, I. MacRury, and B. Richards (eds), *Buy this Book: Studies in Advertising and Consumption,* London: Routledge, 311–23.
Entwistle, J. (2015), *The Fashioned Body: Fashion, Dress and Modern Social Theory,* Cambridge: Polity Press.
Flügel, J. C. (1930), *The Psychology of Clothes,* New York: International Universities Press.
Foucault, M. (1988), "Technologies of the Self," in L. H. Martin, H. Gutman, and P. H. Hutton (eds), *Technologies of the Self: A Seminar with Michel Foucault,* London: Tavistock, 16–49.
Foucault, M. (1991), *Discipline and Punish: The Birth of the Prison,* London: Penguin.
Fussell, P. (2002), *Uniforms: Why We Are What We Wear,* Boston: Houghton Mifflin.
Guerra, S. (2015a), Interview with Heather (City worker), London.
Guerra, S. (2015b), Interview with Maya (City worker), London.
Guerra, S. (2015c), Interview with Felix (City worker), London.

Harvey, J. (1995), *Men in Black,* London: Reaktion Books.
Hertz, C. (2007) "The Uniform: As Material, As Symbol, As Negotiated Object," *Midwestern Folklore,* 32 1 (2): 43–58.
Jenkins, R. (2002), *Pierre Bourdieu,* Abingdon: Routledge.
Joseph, N. (1986), *Uniforms and Nonuniforms: Communication through Clothing,* Westport, CT: Greenwood Press.
Katsikakis, D. (2015), *Future Workstyles and Future Workplaces in the City of London,* Ramidus Consulting Limited, London: City of London Corporation and City Property Association. Available online: http: <http://www.cityoflondon.gov.uk/business/economic-research-and-information/research-publications/Documents/Research-2015/Future-workstyles-and-workplaces-in-the-city.pdf> [accessed: November 19, 2017]
Kuchta, D. (2002), *The Three-piece Suit and Modern Masculinity: England, 1550–1850,* Berkeley, CA: University of California Press.
Lascelles, D. (2003) *Sizing up the City: London's Ranking as a Financial Centre,* Centre for the Study of Financial Innovation, London: Corporation of London. Available online: http://www. longfinance.net/FCF/SizingUpTheCity.pdf [accessed: November 19, 2017]
McVeigh, B. (1997), "Wearing Ideology: How Uniforms Discipline Minds and Bodies in Japan," *Fashion Theory,* 1 (2): 189–213.
McVeigh, B. (2002), *Wearing Ideology: State, Schooling and Self-presentation in Japan,* Oxford: Berg.
Peniston-Bird, C. (2003), "Classifying the Body in the Second World War: British Men in and Out of Uniform," *Body & Society,* 9 (4): 31–48.
Rocamora, A. (2002), "Fields of Fashion: Critical Insights into Bourdieu's Sociology of Culture," *Journal of Consumer Culture,* 2 (3): 341–62.
Rocamora, A. (2015), "'Pierre Bourdieu: The Field of Fashion," in A. Rocamora and A. Smelik (eds), *Thinking Through Fashion: A Guide to Key Theorists,* London: I.B. Tauris, 233–50.
Scott, J. C. (1985), *Weapons of the Weak: Everyday Forms of Peasant Resistance,* New Haven, CT: Yale University Press.
Turner, T. (1996), "Bodies and Anti-bodies: Flesh and Fetish in Contemporary Social Theory," in T. J. Csordas (ed.), *Embodiment and Experience: The Existential Ground of Culture and Self,* Cambridge: Cambridge University Press, 27–47.
Tynan, J. (2012), "'Quakers in Khaki': Conscientious Objectors' Resistance to Uniform Clothing in World War I," in S. Gibson and S. Mollan (eds), *Representations of Peace and Conflict,* Basingstoke: Palgrave Macmillan, 86–102.
Tynan, J. (2013), *British Army Uniform and the First World War: Men in Khaki,* Basingstoke: Palgrave Macmillan.
Tynan, J. (2015), "Michel Foucault: Fashioning the Body Politic," in A. Rocamora and A. Smelik (eds), *Thinking Through Fashion: A Guide to Key Theorists,* London: I.B. Tauris, 184–99.
Wilson, E. (2003), *Adorned in Dreams: Fashion and Modernity,* London: I.B. Tauris.
Woodward, S. (2007), *Why Women Wear What They Wear,* Oxford: Berg.

9

A Cast of Thousands: Martin Grant and the New Qantas Uniform

Prudence Black

A new uniform for Qantas

During Sydney's Mercedes-Benz Fashion Week in April 2013, the international legacy airline Qantas unveiled their new uniform designed by Melbourne-born Paris-based, Martin Grant. Described as "the hostess with the mostest," famous Australian model Miranda Kerr opened the show in front of 300 guests at the Hordern Pavilion, at Sydney's Entertainment Quarter (Qantas 2013c). A Qantas promotional video shows the backstage preparation featuring Kerr in a silk dressing gown stripping down to black bra and underpants; a reminder to all that hers was a body unlike many of the 12,600-workforce destined to wear the uniform. The uniform wasn't rolled out until December that year, a week after Qantas announced it was planning to cut 1,000 jobs ("Qantas Rolls out New Uniform" 2013).

What decisions determine the timing of a new airline uniform? In 2013, Qantas was probably hoping the timing of the new uniform would provide for a 'good news' story. Historically though the appearance of a new uniform would often coincide with a new corporate branding campaign. In 1965, at the heart of the 'Jet Age,' Italian designer Emilio Pucci introduced a vibrant uniform for Braniff International challenging the view, aired in *Life* magazine, that "most airplane stewardesses are dressed as if they are travelling by bus in the year 1925" ("The Wild Hue Yonder" 1965). The new uniform was part of one of the most successful airline marketing campaigns ever, and along with the bold and bright uniform designs seven Boeing 727 jets were painted in matching colors. In 1974, Qantas used Pucci to design their new uniform as part of a program to internationalize the airline. Another reason for the introduction of a new uniform may have been to coincide with the fanfare surrounding the launch of a new fleet of planes. This was certainly the case with Qantas. New uniforms were designed in 1948 with the introduction of flight hostesses for the first time on the new Lockheed L749 Constellations, then again in 1959 with the first of the new Boeing 707 jet planes, and once again in 1971 for the Boeing 747 Jumbo Jets.[1]

And, so it was case for the Martin Grant uniform. Early in October 2011, Qantas announced the order for the new Boeing 787 Dreamliner plane, and CEO Alan Joyce revealed that a new uniform would be part of a bigger programme of renewal at the airline, including the revamping of the airline's lounges. The renewal was also part of a strategy to remove some of the negativity, which Qantas had accrued as a result of prolonged industrial unrest, culminating in the unprecedented grounding of 108 aircraft in twenty-two airports around the world on October 28 that same year (Cleary 2013). It is worth noting here that a new uniform can also be used to improve morale, a clear example of this being post-9/11 when United Airlines replaced the uniform for their 64,000 workers, albeit with a budget in mind, choosing Cintas, a large garment manufacturer who made uniforms for Starbucks and McDonald's (Adomaitis and Johnson 2005).

Not only is the timing of a new uniform strategic but the identity of the designer is equally important, particularly to garner long-term publicity. In the early years of Qantas, the selection of a fashion designer usually came from a recommendation made by the wife of the CEO, or someone in senior management, with the design process left in the hands of the senior 'flight hostess' (Black 2011). The designers selected were often highly regarded within the local fashion scene and capable of small-scale production but with the introduction of the Boeing 747s in the 1970s, which carried almost 300 extra passengers compared to the Boeing 707s, the uniforms had to be made on a much larger scale. Today, the Qantas uniform is one of the largest clothing contracts in Australia.[2]

The selection process

With the announcement of a new uniform in 2011, a group of Qantas representatives, including Charlotte Stockdale, fashion stylist and wife of Qantas designer Marc Newson, travelled to Paris Fashion Week to meet Australian designers who were exhibiting. The fact that they were hunting for somebody on the world stage suggested that they sought a designer with an international profile. Martin Grant and Colette Dinnigan (who had already designed a range of amenities for Qantas) were two of the designers they met to canvas interest for the new uniform. After this initial meeting, Qantas then asked two other well-known Australian designers, Josh Goot and Dion Lee to submit proposals. The group of four, asked to come up with a project for the uniform, were given the design brief to "provide a unique, functional and durable uniform, suitable for a premium airline operating across the world" (Qantas 2013b).

For the initial proposal, the designers were only expected to submit drawings but Grant decided to make a whole collection because he thought the corporate panel might not be, "…creative people necessarily. They have a hard time understanding a design concept and so it was very important for me to actually show them the clothes so that immediately they'd get a feel for what had been created" (Black 2014). This comment from Grant highlights the challenges that a fashion designer can face when working for a corporate client. Fashion designers, used to working and dealing with people in the creative industries, are far removed from the concerns of airline management, which typically involve regulations, timetable logistics, safety, fuel efficiency, and supply chains; they are less likely to understand the everyday practicalities of what it means to wear a uniform.

In March 2012, the initial presentation for the new designs was to a corporate panel made up of a senior management team and a senior executive team including Alan Joyce, Simon Hickey, and Olivia Worth, and a group of twelve employees from different areas of the company. Over the course of the project, the team of employees were asked to gather feedback from their co-workers and to bring comments back to the design team. This feedback happened right from the initial stages of the selection process. A broad-based consultative process regarding the Qantas uniform had begun in the early 1970s with the Pucci uniform; prior to that, the outfits had been designed in semi-secret to elicit surprise upon release (Black 2011). As Grant was to say later, feedback from the workers was important as "ultimately, they're the ones who have to wear the uniform every day and for the next ten years of their life in the company" (Black 2014). Understanding the longevity of an airline uniform is an important factor in the design process, as typically—given the vast expense—they are worn for an average of about ten years. Uniform projects are a challenge for any fashion designer such as Grant who was used to four collections a year. So, despite the prestige of winning a commission to design an airline uniform there is a distinct challenge in creating clothing that will remain 'fashionable' for a long period of time. This contingency is the antithesis of most of the briefs for designers who respond to fashion's fast turnover. Being too fashionable can also create problems;

the shortest-lived Qantas uniform was a burnt orange 'Coral' mini-dress, which lasted only two years (1969–71) because the flight hostesses (as they were called then) found their modesty compromised when they lifted their arms to place items in the overhead lockers (Black 2013). Other airlines adopted the miniskirt for their uniform but in 1971 when Canadian Pacific Air Lines introduced a midi-skirt to be 'on trend' there was a consumer—and ultimately sexist—backlash, with the result that a shorter skirt was reinstated (Sangster and Smith 2017).

Two months after the initial design concept presentation, in May 2012, Joyce announced Grant as the designer of the new uniform, at a press conference at the Park Hyatt Hotel at Circular Quay in Sydney. He described Grant's "elegant style as the perfect template for the new Qantas uniforms. His designs speak of a confident Australia, an Australia that is quietly proud, and an Australia that is heard everywhere in the world, what could be a better fit for Qantas?" (Qantas 2013c). Grant had the international reputation that Qantas wanted as he was well regarded in the industry, including ten years as artistic director of 'Barneys Private Label', Barneys New York, and 'Agnona' of the Ermenegildo Zegna group. In 2005, his place in Australia's fashion history had been acknowledged with a six-month exhibition of this work, *Martin Grant, Paris* at the Ian Potter Centre: National Gallery of Victoria (Jocic 2012).

Figure 9.1 Qantas cabin crew wearing Martin Grant uniform. Courtesy of Qantas, 2016.

Grant's uniform would be only the tenth official uniform design since Qantas began in 1920. His version, designed for 12,600 people, was to be worn in twenty-one different countries and at eighty locations. Thirty or forty different fabrics would be trialed, with seven or eight design iterations, for which they "created enough fabric that would take you from Sydney to Orange (250 km)," producing 400,000 garments distributed in uniform packages to 11,000 different postal addresses (Qantas 2013c). Grant was not the first international designer that Qantas had selected to design their uniform; as mentioned earlier, in 1974 Pucci designed a versatile uniform featuring a lightweight patterned synthetic jersey dress that could be worn on its own or underneath a two-piece suit.[3] It was a practical and popular uniform, with a dress that could be easily washed in the hand basin of a hotel bathroom. It was worn for thirteen years, until 1987, when, in the lead-up to the celebrations for the Bicentennial of Australia in 1988, a controversial decision was made to announce Yves Saint Laurent as the designer of the new Qantas uniform. Local designers thought the national carrier should support the Australian fashion industry and appoint one of their own. While Pucci and Saint Laurent could offer international credibility, there were also concerns about taking the manufacture of the uniforms off-shore, which meant that both uniforms ended up being made predominantly in Australia, and where possible using local wool.

No doubt aware of the controversy surrounding his appointment, Saint Laurent created a uniform which included a kangaroo-print shirt and skirt (which overseas passengers would frequently offer to buy) and a unisex style suit complete with Saint Laurent's signature military feature of gold buttons and gold braid rings on the cuffs of the jackets (see Craik 2015). The uniform wasn't popular with some of the crew, particularly male flight attendants who, while wearing the cropped jacket with the braided cuffs, were sometimes mistaken for bellhops as they waited in hotel lobbies for the airport bus (Black 2011). In the early 1990s, it was time to consider a new uniform. In response to criticism for appointing international designers, and the added factor that Qantas had moved from government-ownership to become a private company, it became important that the next two uniforms were commissioned to local designers: George Gross and Harry Watt designed the uniform in 1994, while Peter Morrissey followed with designs from 2003 through to 2013 (Black 2011). In the light of continued concern about supporting the Australian fashion industry, the selection of Grant was an exercise in diplomacy, solving the dilemma of finding an Australian designer while 'ticking the box' for international profile. For Grant, winning the opportunity to create the Qantas uniform made him part of an exclusive stable of world designers chosen to develop a whole new look for an aviation company.[4]

Martin Grant: the design process

Today Grant has a studio and showroom in Rue Charlot, in the Marais district in Paris, but he was originally from Blackburn, an outer suburb of Melbourne. He left school at the age of fifteen and when he was just sixteen joined a studio in Stalbridge Chambers, Little Collins Street, with other artists and designers, and there started his first ready-to-wear collection (Bagnall 1987). In 1988 he won Cointreau Young Designer of the Year but left fashion to study sculpture. After studying for twelve months he realized that "fashion was in a way a form of sculpture," and he "felt an affinity with fabrics" that he wished to return to, so in 1990 he moved to London, where he learned bespoke tailoring with Koji Tatsuno (Black 2014). In 1992 Grant moved to Paris, where he gained a reputation for making clothing that was classically tailored along simple lines. Grant described his immediate response to being announced as the designer of the new Qantas uniform as 'emotional'. Along with the fact that Qantas is an important part of Australia's history, Grant realized that the airline was a critical part of his own history, having lived overseas for twenty years. His time away from Australia coincided with Qantas' award-winning advertising campaign, which featured the song "I Still Call Australia Home," which was orchestrated to evoke feelings of nostalgia for Australians at home and abroad.[5]

Designing an airline uniform is a long and complex process, which may take up to two or three years, partly because it is a major investment for the company but also because it is important to get the technical aspects right. Grant felt that his own design style would suit the tight brief for a new uniform: "I'm more about evolution rather than revolution, so things can remain quite classic and don't really go out of date, and so the uniform is exactly that" (Qantas 2013a). He also acknowledged that designing a uniform is quite different to approaching a fashion collection, "It has to be something that's reasonably timeless. It has to be strong, it has to be punchy because you want them to be noticed, but you don't want it to go out-of-date" (Black 2014.) There are also some very practical elements when designing a uniform, such as "comfort, flammability, convenience" and "everyone has to look like a team ... since the employees are the face of the company" (Kwak 2013). A uniform has to represent the company, as ex-flight attendant Katya Noble, the Qantas 'Project Style' project manager, explains: "Along with the livery, the uniform ... is the single biggest touch point that we have with our brand (Qantas 2103c). For Grant, his own experiences as a seasoned traveler made him realize the importance of being able to recognize the airline staff you are traveling with as soon as you enter the airport.

Historically, a uniform, as the name suggests, is about creating 'one look.' In the introduction to *Uniform: Order and Disorder*, Francesca Bonami, Maria Luisa Frisa, and Stefano Tonchi suggest that "to make things uniform means to make them equal. Making individuals equal means abolishing distinctions of class and demographics" (2000: 14). Grant reiterates this when he says that with any uniform the aim is to "really get everybody looking as uniform as possible", with a design that works "right across the board even into the freight sections of the company" (Black 2014). The uniform, according to Michael Carter, "becomes the sartorial ideal against which departures are measured and, most importantly judged" (2017: 164). What Carter alludes to here is the importance of the uniform in articulating the values and standards of the organization. A soiled or ill-fitting uniform reflects not only on the individual, but on the whole organization.

One of the challenges of designing an airline uniform today is the diversity of roles people might occupy in an airline workplace. Once, it might have been the case that the flight and cabin crew had their own specially designed uniforms, as was the case in the 1960s when a number of international airlines, including Qantas, employed Japanese women and dressed them in traditional kimonos until this attire was deemed too expensive and an occupational health and safety issue (Black 2011;Yano 2011). The trend since the 1980s has been to dress the whole workforce in a range of mix-and-match garments from the same basic uniform scheme. This approach to dressing has removed some of the perceived 'glamor' and 'exoticization' of the cabin crew, whereby bespoke uniforms (for the female staff) have been replaced by a corporate uniform made for 'a cast of thousands.' There are exceptions to this, such as the 'Singapore Girls' flight attendant uniforms, which are still fitted individually to 'within an inch of their lives' in a modern version of Pierre Balmain's sarong-kebaya uniform from 1968.[6]

When Grant describes his personal challenge in designing the Qantas uniform, he views it as a shift from the field of making fashion "to create something that becomes iconic" (Qantas 2013a). With this in mind, he approached the design of the uniform in the very same way he did with other clothes in his collections: "I look at the codes, I look at things that have worked historically and remain powerful, and then you can draw on those elements" (Qantas 2013a). Other inspiration for the collection came from, "... all things that were Australian for example, different nature and fauna from Australia," but after reviewing the history of the Qantas uniforms alongside the corporate branding, he was clear that his initial designs were inspired by the Qantas company logo, which was a red triangle and the flying [winged] kangaroo (Black 2014). Qantas had used the kangaroo symbol on their aircraft since 1944 (adapted from the penny coin), then in 1947 graphic designer Gert Selheim modified the kangaroo to include wings, which appeared on the Lockheed L749 Constellation planes, which flew the famous long-haul 'Kangaroo Route' from Sydney to London. In the early 1980s, the wings were removed and the red triangle was introduced into the corporate design identity. Grant recalls that he was attracted to the red triangle for its strong graphic element and the kangaroo because it was 'ludique' (playful). For this reason, one of his early designs for a dress was a "kangaroo cloud" print, which was dark at the bottom and faded off to white at the top (Black 2014). He also designed another dress, one with an abstract print, which subtly referenced the Qantas logo, but after looking at it for a few months in his studio he tired of it, citing the fact that "prints can go out of style so quickly" (Black 2014). Removing the 'ludique' and patterned element from the uniform helped create a more sophisticated and international design, something in keeping with his own design philosophy.

Reflecting on the design process, Grant said there were no major battles over his ideas for designs and he thinks that may have been because he presented a version of the collection at the very beginning of the selection process. Having examples of the garments to show the various panels meant the options were clearly articulated: "They could see the options of going this direction or this direction, so they were the only things that really needed to be worked on" (Black 2014). There was some pressure to go with the patterned dress, but Grant convinced them not to make that choice. He prefers his clothes to have "a slight minimalism and classic pure lines. I don't like decoration, so it is much more about the form and the fit of the garments ... I decided to avoid the whole idea of a print and really just bring it back to the strong graphic quality to reflect the logo of Qantas which has stood the test of time" (Qantas 2013c). Once the idea of using a print was removed, conversations about the final designs turned to the strategic use of color. Here, it was critical to consider colorways used by other airlines; in particular it was important for him to move away from red and navy blue, a combination used by British Airways, Air France, and Japan Airlines.

The cut of the cloth

Grant flew back and forth to Australia six to eight times in one year and his time on board flights between Paris and Sydney became part of his research. He would talk to the cabin crew about what they wanted in a uniform and "one of the overriding things for the girls was they wanted glamor back in air travel, even asking for hats and gloves!" Comfort was another main requirement and the men wanted a lighter waistband (Kwak 2013). Associating glamor with the uniform means harking back to a time when airline hostesses and stewards (as they were called then) might sit on the edge of the seat and chat while you crossed continents, and layovers were spent in first-class hotels lounging by pools in exotic locations. Today, many flight crews are on short-term contracts and their time in the air is spent rebooting entertainment systems and selling scratch lotto tickets. Even when traveling with a legacy airline it is difficult to associate glamor with air travel (unless you are traveling Business or First Class). Flight attendants who seek a return to glamor are not acknowledging that flying then meant providing customer service on a Boeing 707 with a maximum of 100 passengers, compared with their experience today on the Airbus A380 with maybe in excess of 500 passengers. Airline companies often allude to a return to the days when flying was glamorous, and by selecting a Parisian designer, such as Grant, Qantas sought to provide that cache of glamor. Grant acknowledged this when in the uniform booklet (supplied to staff to show them how to wear the various components of the new uniform) he describes his uniform as:

> ...a classic suit for men and women. Great fit, close to the body without being tight, a narrow lapel...the attitude is slick but relaxed and comfortable. Sharp shapes in stretch comfort fabrics. The glamour of air travel.
>
> QANTAS 2103d

The suit was the main component of the new uniform. Anne Hollander suggests the suit represents "diplomacy, compromise, civility, and physical self-control" (1994: 83). But a suit also offers an egalitarian form: the standard components of the tailored jacket and trousers or skirt create a uniform appearance and the way it is worn also creates a type of 'professional' formality (see Peoples 2013). The fabric used in a suit usually determines the form; the Qantas uniform made of a wool mix is designed to hold its shape—it should not wrinkle or sag—and this 'holding of form' can shape demeanor and deportment.[7]

Experience in tailoring was another of the concerns when selecting a designer for the Qantas uniform, and it was a key reason why Grant won the design job.

His background in the craft of bespoke tailoring was important to Qantas, who wanted a uniform design that would be practical and look good worn across the whole company. His knowledge of tailoring enabled him to decide to make the suits more fitted than previous designs, explaining that "well-fit silhouettes that embrace the body shape are much more flattering than baggier suits that try to hide the body" (Kwak 2013). Along with the suit, the other main component of the uniform was a dress, which Grant described as a style that "skims the body, but it's not very fitted," which meant that with no fitted waistline, a separate belt was worn to define the waist (Kwak 2013). As the staff varied so much in height, there were no belt loops on the dress so that the belt could find the wearers' 'natural waist.' This was designed to improve the look and provide added comfort. Despite Grant saying the dress "is meant to hang and then be held in with a belt," they are quite fitted, and comments by staff at Qantas suggest that women have been encouraged to wear the dresses in a size that some feel is a bit tight (this is a problem especially as the body tends to swell during flight) (Black 2014). Another issue was the zipper on the back of the dress, which was too short, so some women had a longer zipper inserted, allowing them to step into it more easily when getting dressed (rather than pulling them over their heads). Incidentally, having uniforms altered or changing fabrics is a long-held tradition, and cabin crew would regularly visit tailors when travelling through Singapore on the 'Kangaroo Route.'

The dress has a round neck, in 'a classic colour,' French navy, with two wide diagonal bands featured across the chest in Qantas red, and fuchsia or ruby red. After trying lots of different colorways Grant settled on the red and fuchsia combination, "... it's really classic and beautiful—it harks back to couture ... it's very Yves St Laurent, which is ironic because Yves St Laurent designed the uniform for Qantas in the 1980s" (Black 2014). In selecting the colors, Grant commented:

> I tend to use the classic colours. Navy blue I think was the best. You needed a neutral colour, and suitable for both men and women. For me navy blue was the best option. Black tends to be a bit harsh and I don't know, it's got connotations of an undertaker or wedding or all of these things, whereas navy blue is even more neutral, it is more flattering to people. It's got red in it so it's actually not as harsh.
>
> BLACK 2014

Grant also considered gray but thought it a bit "too sad, too kind of boring business man" (Black 2014). He saw white as an obvious choice for the shirt.

There is no fuchsia used in the men's uniforms, although it was something he considered. Instead of the red triangle on the men's tie, Grant could have used the fuchsia pink but he was concerned that an association might be made with "Nazi Germany and the gays and now it's become the gay symbol, and flight attendants tend to historically also be a high percentage of gays and it was just too much red rag to a bull …" (Black 2014). Gender and sexuality are a consideration when designing for a workforce and a solution is often to create a uniform that is made up of a number of components, which can be worn in a range of combinations. While most airlines include the option of trousers for women, Virgin Atlantic Airways uniform protocol insists that female flight attendants must put in a personal request for permission to wear trousers, and in 2016—after a two-year dispute—British Airways female cabin crew, who had been employed on contracts from 2012 with stricter dress codes, were finally granted the right to wear trousers (female cabin crew could be exempted from wearing a skirt on medical or religious grounds). This was unusual because British Airways female cabin crew had worn trousers as part of their uniform since the 1970s. Other airlines, such as Ryanair and the Gulf carrier Etihad, allow the female cabin crew to wear dresses and skirts only. The use of a hijab has now become standard for most airlines, and in the case of Qantas a navy scarf can be worn for cultural, religious, and medical reasons.

For Grant, the key design elements were such that they could be incorporated into both the men's and the women's uniform. The design element was a bold diagonal stripe used on the dress (and repeated in a smaller scale on the men's ties) and, as he explained, it "was that sort of out of the box flash thing that they were particularly looking for. They wanted something that was very, very identifiable" (Black 2014). Creating a distinctive design is in keeping with the idea that an airline uniform has to be immediately recognisable and for Grant, "the bold diagonal stripe is about creating 'a visibility' you can't blend in either on or off the plane. Also, the position of the stripe across the top half of the body meant that it could be easily seen above the airline seats" (Black 2014). The dress is cut with a magyar-style sleeve (Grant calls it a 'kimono' sleeve), on the cross to allow more ease of movement, and worn just above the elbow. Without a shoulder seam the dress can fit different shoulder widths, which is an important consideration as the dresses are made up to a size 28 (Black 2014). Along with a range of sizes, the other consideration when it came to styling the uniform, was knowing that the average age for Qantas employees is forty-five, with many staff in their sixties. This demographic trend is older than many other airline companies; for example, Singapore Airlines require their iconic 'Singapore Girls' to retire at fifty.

Because of the very public promotion of a new Qantas uniform and the vast size of the order (thirty-five garment styles and 400,000 pieces of clothing), there were always questions about what fibers were to be used, and whether Qantas was supporting the national textile industry. Grant was well aware of these issues and thus made the decision, "for transeasonal versatility, I used Australian wool, since it's the most breathable fabric around. And because the items needed to be easy care, the dress can be washed and drip-dried" (Kwak 2013). The uniforms include fifteen different types of fabric, the suits are made from 80 percent Australian wool and 20 percent polyester, which Grant noted was a very high wool content compared to other uniforms.[8] While finances are a significant factor in decisions made about fabric selection, its performance is also important. In what was a very scientific process, 'hundreds and hundreds' of meters of fabrics were tested for the dress. The fabric had to be "shrink proof, and the dresses and tops had to be drip-dry, and they shouldn't crush when being worn and in suitcases, they also had to be non-flammable, breathable, anti-static and they shouldn't fade. In the end, the fabric selected for the dress was a 'beautiful quality' in 100 percent polyester, which could be manufactured in the exact colors required (something which was not possible with some of the other fabrics tested)" (Black 2014). The trench coat—one of Grant's signature garments—was a type of cotton, while the cotton shirts had a touch of polyester, and the knitwear was made from 100 percent wool. The shirts were made in Hawaii, while the rest of the uniforms were made in China and Vietnam.

Comfort and practicality are a major concern for cabin crew who were delighted to see the return of a woolen cardigan. It can be incredibly cold in sections of a plane and the cardigan can be worn on its own, or under the jacket if it was really chilly. Grant was sympathetic to the comfort of the cabin crew and remarked that he had wanted to respond to their concerns about comfort while on board, understanding that "small things like that are really important" (Grant 2014). The regulation of temperature is a key consideration for those tasked with designing a uniform, as Grant explained:

> The thing is when you're flying- particularly for the flight attendants, you're going through extreme heat changes, so in the aircraft to start with and also on the ground because if you're flying from Sydney to Dubai it might be winter in Sydney, and then you arrive in Dubai and it's 40 degrees and it's the same uniform. There's not a summer and a winter uniform because these people are literally flying across four seasons in a day so basically they have to be able to layer up.
>
> BLACK 2014

Cabin crew often wear protective clothing when preparing and serving food; in the 1930s the Qantas flight stewards wore white serving jackets and cummerbunds. Grant decided that rather than wear an apron – part of the previous Morrissey uniform – which "makes you feel like you should be cooking a barbeque in the backyard," he introduced a waistcoat for meal services. With calls for glamor and the desire to reintroduce a hat, the company conducted a survey about whether this headwear would be a popular choice. Cabin crew had not worn a hat since the Pucci uniform. The result of the survey was 50/50, and on that basis it was decided to include a hat, only to be worn when wearing the trench coat. It was, however, a challenge to find a hat that could be stored on board and does not take up too much room. The final design was a trilby style hat in a knitted fabric made from recycled bottle tops that could be rolled and put in a bag, and which once removed, springs back into the desired shape. The effect of wearing the trench with the trilby however, was more *Casablanca* espionage style than the desired contemporary glamor they had hoped for.

The decorative neck scarf is one of the distinctive features of many contemporary female airline uniforms. As well as being an identifiable element of the uniform design, the scarf has the added virtue of feminizing the suit. For Grant, the scarf was the hardest part of the collection to make:

> The problem is you'd think it would be the simplest thing ever to make a scarf, but for an airline company no because you can't just tie a knot. It has to have a safety release so that if somebody grabs the scarf they don't get strangled.
>
> BLACK 2014[9]

The safety issue around scarves and neckties arose in the 1970s when the airline industry was plagued with a number of highjacking attempts. Grant described the fuchsia pink scarf as "... the frivolous stylish element, but again it's an identifier. I think it's one of those things that you do really kind of identify. It's so visible" (Black 2014). Also, over the ten-year life span, elements of a uniform typically need refreshing, and a scarf is an easy and relatively cheap item to change. Grant suggested there were three elements of his uniform that could be easily changed:

> Usually after about five years they'll do just a little retouch of the uniform and that's why for me there were only those three elements that are major elements of the uniform that would be quite easy to change: the dress, the top and the scarf.
>
> BLACK 2014

What can happen is "if you change those three pieces the uniform could look entirely different, or it could just be slightly different. You'd keep all of the identifiers, so all of the suiting and the white shirting" (Grant 2014). This understanding of how a uniform works over time helps explain why Grant was the preferred candidate for the job. Katya Noble describes this in more detail:

> ... he really understood a uniform, he understood the need for it to have a uniformity and that when you change something over here then you in fact have to change something over there, so he understood how the jigsaw fitted together. So, you also need to design a uniform that is not only beautiful but also one that you can replicate year on year for much smaller quantities than what you launch with, so there is this whole supply chain side of things which is not glamorous in any way or form but it is something that is very important when creating the overall look and making sure that year on year you can maintain that look to the best of our ability.
>
> QANTAS 2103c

The economics of supplying a uniform and the decisions about how and when to change it also relate to issues around sustainability. In designing a new uniform, Qantas had to address the environmental problems with disposing of old uniforms. They were donated to the charity Mission Australia, which through its 'Soft Landing' program converted the uniforms into 100 tonnes of waste fiber to fill punching bags for gym use. The disposal of uniforms has been an issue for many airlines, but particularly in Japan, where there has been a black-market trade in current and old uniforms for fetish wear, and also for use in sex clubs. For this reason, and despite all their uniforms having identifying serial numbers, Japan Airlines created a policy of destroying all their uniforms. (Mayerowitz 2010). It is not unusual to see a uniform copied. Within a year of the display of the new Qantas uniform, a Chinese company had copies of the Grant uniform dress for sale ("Martin Grant copy uniforms" 2014). At one stage, copies of the Singapore Airlines uniform were available for sale at Singapore Airport, with the airline confident that these off-the-rack designs would never be confused with the bespoke uniforms worn by their cabin crew.

Nationalism and internationalism

Those with knowledge of French fashion recognize the Grant uniform as 'very French.' Grant's fashionable use of color blocking (bold segments of navy, red, and fuchsia), represented a move away from the wild flowers of the Pucci, the kangaroos of the Saint Laurent, and the boomerangs of the Indigenous-inspired 'Wirriyarra' Morrissey uniform.[10] There was a sense that the new uniform was designed with a degree of 'sophistication' in mind, that boomerangs worn across the bottoms of flight attendants were a bit kitsch, harking back to a fashion that had surfaced in the 1980s, which sought to champion an overt 'Australianness.'[11] Morrissey had already included and promoted Indigenous designs in his fashion collections, so it was no surprise to see the 'Wirriyarra' Indigenous print in his uniform. For Grant, the use of Indigenous design did not feel right and his reasons were that:

> ... there's a very, very small percentage of Indigenous employees in the company, and for me it was strange for a corporate company to actually take on board an Indigenous artwork to represent their company. To me it just didn't feel right.
>
> BLACK 2014

Grant, perhaps forgetting that Indigenous Australians had lived in the country for over 60,000 years, also thought that the use of distinctive Australian iconography "was really old-fashioned," stating that: "... Australia's a very young country and so it's always tended to harp on about Australian-ness ... for me it's just I think that time's moved on and I think Australia's also moved on. It's much more international now" (Black 2014). His designs were, for him, about connecting Qantas with a wider world:

> Qantas is an Australian company but it's also an international company. It's actually flying all over the world every day and so it's actually part of an international world. It's not just a parochial or small company that only exists in Australia, and so that for me was really important, to put it on that international stage ...
>
> BLACK 2014

Grant acknowledged that the technicalities of designing for a national airline were very specific:

> ... uniforms, when you look back, they really reflect an era and I find that fascinating because that's how fashion works but in airlines it's even more concrete somehow. It really is that challenge of coming up with something very fresh and contemporary, that next season won't look out of date. We're not talking about seasons we're talking about a whole period of time. I really do see Qantas as being sort of an ambassador for Australia. It feels like I'm contributing something to Australian history.
>
> QANTAS 2013a

Figure 9.2 Qantas pilots wearing Martin Grant uniform. Courtesy of Qantas, 2016.

In relation to international travel, the flight attendants in their uniform might be the first sense a tourist gets of a country as they embark on a flight, and it is for this reason, more than other forms of corporate dress, that airline uniforms are often designed with nationality in mind.

In April 2016, exactly three years after the Grant uniform was launched, Qantas unveiled a new uniform design for their workforce of almost 3,000 pilots. Once again, Grant designed the uniform and it came with a twenty-three-page guidebook containing strict instructions: no handlebar or horseshoe moustaches (the outline of the upper lip must be visible); no backpacks; no chewing gum; and jackets must be worn more regularly, including to and from work. It replaced a uniform that had been worn for thirteen years, introduced partly as a response to the increased number of female pilots and the need to design it around them, but also for the pilot workforce who were to increase with the long-awaited fleet of Boeing Dreamliners.[12] The criteria stated that uniforms must be comfortable and durable as pilots spend up to sixteen hours on an aircraft and like flight attendants, they need to be easily recognized on the plane and in airports. The shirt was a little looser, to make it easier to stretch up and manage the instrument controls on the roof of the flight deck, while the suit was more fitted than the previous uniform. Morrissey had previously replaced the double-breasted jacket with a modern single-breasted style. The new uniform included distinct male and female uniforms; the jacket for females more fitted at the waist with inverted tab pockets and was to be worn with a wider tie. Grant said the difference was only slight as the women "... don't mind having a uniform that's very close to the men's so I've just feminised it in the cut, the jacket is more fitted. Everything is more streamlined and tailored, the pants more narrow" (Sariban 2016). The new slim-fit single button suit seemed to suit the younger pilots but general comments suggest that many of the older pilots preferred the less fitted style of the previous uniform (Black 2017).

Conclusion

The new uniform is far removed from the military-style khaki pilot uniform from the 1930s, which included shorts and long socks but was similar to the double-breasted naval style uniform introduced in 1947.[13] Grant says "there was not an enormous amount that you can change in a pilot's uniform because there are so many historical codes involved; they're proud of their history, they're proud of where it comes from, and one of the places it comes from is the naval/military and that was one of the starting points for me in taking it back and reintroducing the white topped hat" (Qantas 2016). Pilots have high professional status and this may be one of the reasons that Grant suggests that the uniform has to remain traditional and not become subject to the vagaries of fashion. Respect for the profession can be maintained by referencing the uniform tradition.

Reflecting on its history, Grant thought that the most important feature of the uniform was the pilot's cap, again mentioning a return to the 'glamour of flying' and the days of the flying boats. The old-fashioned cap has created a mixed response from the pilots with some finding the call to the past misplaced and dated (Black 2017). The white cap with the navy peak is inherited from the period when a white cloth cap was placed over the hat to signal whether the pilot was travelling to the southern or northern hemisphere.[14] The removable cloth cover was eventually made of waterproof material, and this was then worn by all Qantas pilots until the early 1970s. Gone from the new cap is the badge that was referred to as 'scrambled eggs,' with its busy pattern of sprigs of gold leaves surrounding a red Qantas 'Q' topped with a coat of arms. This design has been replaced with a simplified and stark circular badge, featuring the 'Qantas Roo,' while sprays of Australia's national flower, the 'Golden Wattle,' decorate the cap peak. Despite the hint of nationalism the kangaroo signifies, the uniform resembles any other pilot's uniform, most of which tend to comprise a navy or black suit. While the Qantas pilots look like any other pilot the world over, the uniform worn by cabin crew and other staff is distinct, and while the Grant uniform might not clearly articulate a sense of Australian nationalism his style is not out of place in the international world of aviation. For the present time, with Qantas promoting itself as a global carrier, there is no desire to see the kangaroo or indeed Indigenous art dominate the design of the pilot or cabin crew uniform. In 2020, however, when Qantas celebrate their 100th anniversary, it is likely that there will be a return to national signifiers; perhaps then we can expect to see a new scarf with a koala print.

References

Adomaitis, A. D. and K. Johnson (2005), "Casual vs Formal Uniforms: Flight Attendants Self-Perception and Perceived Appraisals by Others," *Clothing and Textile Journal*, 23 (2): 88–101.

Bagnall, D. (1987), "A Fashion Hot House," *Vogue Australia*, March: 200–05.

Black, P. (2011), *The Flight Attendant's Shoe*, Sydney: NewSouth Press.

Black, P. (2013), "Lines of Flight: The Female Flight Attendant Uniform," *Fashion Theory*, 17 (2): 179–95.

Black, P. (2014), Interview with Martin Grant (fashion designer), Paris May 11.

Black, P. (2017), Anonymous Interviews with Qantas and Qantas Link pilots, June and July.

Bonami, F., M. L. Frisa, and S. Tonchi, eds (2000), *Uniform: Order and Disorder*, Milan: Charta.

Carter, M. (2017), *Being Prepared: Aspects of Dress and Dressing*, Sydney: Puncher and Wattman.

Cleary, A. (2013), "High Praise for Qantas Uniforms," *Australian Financial Review*, April 16. Available online: http://www.afr.com/business/transport/aviation/high-praise-for-qantas-uniform-20130416-jhz8j [accessed May 30, 2017].

Craik, J. (2005), *Uniforms Exposed: From Conformity to Transgression*, Oxford: Berg.

Hollander, A. (1994), *Sex and Suits: The Evolution of Modern Dress*, New York: Kodansha International.

Hughes, C. (2107), *Hats*, London & New York: Bloomsbury.

Jocic, L. (2012), "Precocious Style: The Fashion Design Council 1983–1993," *Art Journal 51*. Available online: http://www.ngv.vic.gov.au/essay/precocious-style-the-fashion-design-council-1983-93/ [accessed June 9, 2017].

Kennedy, S. (1991), *Pucci: A Renaissance in Fashion*, New York: Abbeville Press.

Kwak, C. (2013), "Lady Gaga Designer Takes on New Qantas Uniforms: An Interview with Martin Grant," June 23. Available online: http://www.cntraveler.com/stories/2013-06-23/ qantas-airlines-martin-grant-miranda-kerr-uniforms [accessed May 30, 2017].

"Martin Grant copy uniforms on sale to general public" (2014) *Airline Hubbuzz*. Available online: http://www. airlinehubbuzz.com/qantas-martin-grant-uniforms-sale-general-public [accessed May 20, 2017]

Mayerowitz, S. (2010) "Airline Uniforms Secretly Sold to Sex Clubs," March 3. Available online: https://abcnews.go.com/Travel/japan-airline-stewardess-uniforms-sold-sex-fetish-clubs/story?id=10002036 [accessed: May 25, 2017].

Peoples, S. (2013), "Embodying the Military: Uniforms," *Critical Studies in Men's Fashion,* 1 (1): 7–21.

"Qantas Rolls out New Uniform made Famous by Miranda Kerr, After Announcing 1000 Job Losses" (2013) *News.com.au*. Available online: http://www.news.com.au/qantas-rolls-out-new-uniform-made-famous-by-miranda-kerr-after-announcing-1000-job-losses/ news-story/4ba63c23ee914955cdd112a80672b8e8 9 [accessed May 17, 2017]

Qantas (2013a), "Martin Grant: The Inspiration." Available online: https://www.youtube.com/ watch?v=5DFb8Refwrs [accessed May 30, 2017].

Qantas (2013b), "Qantas Unveils New Uniform Designed by Acclaimed Australian Designer Martin Grant," *Qantas News Room*, April 16, 2013.

Qantas (2013c), *Runway to Runway–Qantas Sets Trends in Fashion*, December 12. Available online: https://www.youtube.com/watch?v=OLy7SCV6pWI [accessed May 30, 2017].

Qantas (2013d), "Top Tips for Perfecting Your New Look," in *Qantas by Martin Grant*.

Qantas (2016), "New Qantas Pilots Uniforms take to the Skies." Available online: https://dreamliner.qantas.com/accessibility/article/new-qantas-pilot-uniforms-take-to-the-skies/ [accessed June 3, 2017].

Sangster, J. and J. Smith (2017), " 'Thigh in the Sky': Canadian Pacific Dresses Its Female Flight Attendants," *Labor: Studies in Working-Class History,* 14 (1): 39–63.

Sariban, M. (2016), "Martin Grant's Qantas Pilot Uniform Make Their Runway Debut," *Vogue Australia*, 29 April.

"The Wild Hue Yonder: Pucci Dresses Airline Stewardesses for the Jet Age," *LIFE* Magazine, December 3, 1965: 76–77.

Yano, C. (2011), *Airborne Dreams: "Nisei" Stewardesses and Pan American World Airways*, Durham, NC: Duke University Press.

Part Five

Uniforming Fashion

The differences between uniform and fashion are at times subtle, and at other times stark. This section of the book explores the various ways in which fashion has inhabited uniform design. It also highlights uniformity as an emblem of fashion's modernity. In fashion, these seemingly endless references to uniform betray a desire to idealize the quintessential commonplace object with the result that since the end of the nineteenth century, designers have displayed a fascination with utility styling.

On the surface, uniform and fashion appear to be diametrically opposed: one offers a formula for fitting in while the other reflects the desire to be distinctive.

This section covers the various complex interactions between fashion and uniform to ask whether utilitarian dress embodies power or promises utopia. The emergence of modern uniform arose alongside the rise of the institution; these regulated environments required the incorporation of gendered performance into their daily practices. If regulation dress promotes a particular order of things, what social values does it carry? What lies behind the drive to rationalize subjectivity in this way? The chapters in this section explore the contradictions of uniform and consider how it creatively fashions and refashions the body.

This paradoxical side of uniform reveals the creative force of fashion at work in the making of military and civilian uniforms, which is often deployed in order to leaven the sterner aspects of regulation clothing. Many projects to design workwear in the twentieth century enlisted fashion to deflect from uniform's more authoritarian associations. For fashion consumers, uniform clothing had its attractions, which included its appeal to efficiency, rationality, and simplicity. Sartorial uniformity was also attractive to artists and designers, not least because, in the nineteenth and early twentieth century, it embodied utopian socialism. Later, the meaning of uniform was again transformed by its re-appropriation as symbol of social rebellion.

Both fashion and uniform represented the problems and opportunities of the machine age. Far from being viewed as a technique to suppress individuality, uniform represented freedom, and appeared to promise access to idealized forms of dress that would maximize human performance. Uniform can signify hierarchy and status, which no doubt makes it an attractive reference point for creatives in fashion design and media interested in the images of social power it can fabricate. The sense of order and authority that uniform embodied made it the clothing of a disciplinary society, yet this production line aesthetic also signified freedom and individualism in a new era of consumer choice. As discussed by Jane Tynan in her essay, there are many examples of uniform-fashion combinations that reflect the contradictions of post-war modernity.

Separating uniform and fashion obscures the extent to which they have developed a symbiotic relationship with a fascinating co-existence. Fashion–uniform interplays, such as the overalls discussed here by Djurdja Bartlett, also allow researchers to explore how individuals negotiate the competing incentives of conformity and transgression. Designers have appropriated the image and idea of uniform in ways that point to the complex nature of fashion itself, including the extent to which it has both a commercial and symbolic existence. This section explores the ongoing dialog between fashion and uniform, using historical and contemporary examples, to consider how these distinct body practices represent very different ideas of what it means to be modern.

10

Overalls: Functional, Political, Fashionable

Djurdja Bartlett

In terms of their flatness and economy of style, overalls are an extremely simple garment. Their current shape was developed from the robust trousers originally called 'waist overalls' launched by Levi Strauss & Co and other denim producers in the second half of the nineteenth century. When, in the 1910s, manufacturers, such as HD Lee Mercantile Company, started to offer all-in-one versions, overalls became widely acknowledged as the perfect workwear (Marsh and Trynka 2005: 24–38). In its strictly functional versions, the loose-cut outfit has been variably called 'overalls' or 'boilersuit,' as well as 'siren suit' during the Second World War. Its fashionable, often close-fitting version, borrows its name from sports, called a "jumpsuit," in reference to pilots' uniforms and parachutes (O'Hara Callan 1998). This basic, easy to mass-produce outfit faultlessly accompanied the accelerating industrialization processes, founded in the United States (US) and promoted through Frederick Taylor's 1911 ergonomic study *Principles of Scientific Management*. After carefully examining the physical gestures of workers, Taylor suggested that their repetitive and greatly simplified movements would be more efficiently employed in relation to time and expenditure of labor power. Three years later, Taylor's doctrine was duly applied at the assembly line at Henry Ford's factory in Highland Park, Detroit. As observed by Peter Wollen, Taylor's study "... heralded a new epoch in which the worker would become as predictable, regulated, and effective as the machine itself.... Fordism meant more than the mass production of standardized objects. It meant a new form of organization of production" (1989: 8). Accordingly, the masses who made up the semi-skilled workforce serving the moving assembly line sported overalls, an outfit which enabled the free movement of the body, and thus greatly assisted the efficiency and speed of the new age.

Utopian overalls

While they ideologically opposed capitalism, the early Bolsheviks were fascinated by American technology. In the 1920s, Americanization, from popular culture to architecture and machinery, stood for modernity in Western Europe as well, but the Soviets were particularly interested in its new model of industrialization. A machine-fascinated Bolshevik Alexei Gastev was one of the most prominent promoters of Soviet Taylorism. The Central Institute of Labour, which he founded in 1920, developed a programme of rhythmical economical movements for the factory floor, such as hammering and welding. The principles of Taylorism, industrial gymnastics, and industrial gesticulation were concurrently researched at the Institute of Rhythm in Moscow (see Bowlt 1996; Stites 1989: 145–55). In theater, Vsevold Meyerhold attempted to mechanize actors' movements through his system of biomechanics. In contrast to the psychologization of characters, as practiced in bourgeois theatre, biomechanics was articulated as the scientific and technical system of actors' movements, which stressed the most economical mechanized gesture (see Braun 2006).

Precisely due to the characteristics related to both technological modernization and modernity itself, overalls had been endorsed by the 1920s Russian Constructivists, a group of politically loyal artists, strongly supported by the Commissar of the People's Commissariat of Enlightenment, Anatoly Lunacharsky. Feeding on the concept of the American Taylorist stream-lined efficiency, the Constructivists, such as Alexander Rodchenko, Varvara Stepanova, and Liubov Popova, envisioned overalls not only as a strictly functional outfit, but moreover as an ideal socialist dress. The Constructivists fiercely rejected any form of decoration and embraced geometric abstraction as their exclusive visual language. The radically new lines of their dress designs visualized the radical nature of the Bolshevik project which aimed to totally transform the country, its culture and its citizens' opinions and looks (see Bartlett 2010: 13–62; for an overview of Constructivism, see Lodder 1983). Moreover, a series of sweeping political, social, and sartorial changes that the Constructivists called for was fuelled by pace, but they perceived time as rationalized and homogenized, with its rhythm choreographed according to the new progressive aesthetics.

Indeed, the Constructivists' modernist engagement with overalls did commence in the heart of the Russian 1920s modernism, Meyerhold's theatre productions. Led by the constructivist functionalist aesthetics, Popova did not design decorative theater costumes but work uniforms for the Meyerhold-directed stage play *The Magnanimous Cuckold* in 1922. She called her geometrically cut costumes *prozodezhda*. The word *prozodezhda* is an abbreviated combination of two words: *proizvodstvennaya* (production, industrial) and *odezhda* (dress). It is usually translated as 'production clothing' and intended them not only to allow total freedom of movement at the scene, but also to be worn by actors during rehearsals and in their everyday life. Additionally, Popova insisted that any distinction between men and women's costumes would be minimal, consisting only of "changing trousers to a skirt or culottes."[1] In 1922, Varvara Stepanova also designed the Constructivist costumes for the play *The Death of Tarelkin*. She used simple cuts and only two colors in geometric juxtapositions to achieve dynamic effects. Accordingly, the character Pakhom the porter looked like a moving piece of Constructivist art in his two-tone overalls.[2] Due to their radical theater costumes, both Popova and Stepanova acquired recognition and fame well outside their Constructivist artistic circle, among the large Moscow theatre audiences.

But staying true to the Constructivist ideals, Stepanova decided to take her uniformed clothes from the theatre experiment into everyday life experience as she sets out in her programmatic article "The Clothing of Today: *Prozodezhda*," published in the Constructivist journal *Lef* in 1923. Rejecting decorative pre-revolutionary fashions, Stepanova insisted on simplicity and functionality of the newly envisaged *prozodezhda*. She stressed that new clothing "is tested only through the process of working in it," and that "the clothing of today must be seen in action," further emphasizing that "clothing must cease to be craft-produced in favour of mass industrial production" (Stepanova 1923: 65). For her, the new industrial means would bring transparency to the relationship between clothes and their construction: "The stitching of a sewing machine industrializes the production of a dress and deprives it of its secrets" (Stepanova 1923: 65). Stepanova's *Lef* article was accompanied by a modernist drawing of sports clothing that geometricized both the body and the dress.

Apart from *prozodezhda* as work uniform, distinguished by profession and type of industry, Stepanova acknowledged its two other versions in her *Lef* article: *spetzodezhda*, special protective uniform, needed in certain jobs; and *sportodezhda*, sports clothing. Stepanova stressed universal traits in those clothes, and proposed that differences relating to different types of job could be accentuated by choice of fabric and slight changes in cut when it comes to work clothes. Colors, stripes, and emblems were supposed to differentiate uniforms meant for different sports. In this programmatic article, Stepanova did not specify the shape of her production clothes, neither did she divide them according to gender. They were never mass-produced, but four drawings of sports clothing that accompanied this article, demonstrated consistency with her radical theory. Stepanova's sports *prozodezhda* was worn by her students during the performance accompanying the event *An Evening of the Book in 1924* (see Lavrentiev 1988).

At the same time, the artist Gustav Klutsis also searched for a new socialist dress (see Tupitsyn 2004; Oginskaia 1981). For him, like his fellow Constructivists, dress had to be resurrected from the old world and re-designed for the new one precisely because it was an everyday object par excellence. In that sense, a new dress was ideologically as important as Eisenstein's avant-garde films, Meyerhold's modernist theater plays, Tatlin's futuristic *Monument to the Third International*, and other novel artistic practices promoting a new socialist state. Klutsis' two 1922 drawings of overalls were embedded in the early, vigorous Constructivist utopianism. As expected, prominent pockets stored tools in his overalls, which were designed for a highly qualified engineer, but those sophisticated instruments seemed to merge with the body underneath, to eventually reveal the engineer's internal organs, such as his heart and his lungs. In this sense, Klutsis contributed to the utopian vision of a new efficient man bordering on a machine.

But the Constructivists' embrace of overalls equally relied on the historical utopian rejections of dress as visible sign of gender, social, and class differences, and they imagined it as a class- and gender-neutral dress code. Such ideas were not novelty, neither in the West, nor in pre-revolutionary Russia. The typical characteristics of utopian socialist dress, advocated in theory and practice by the nineteenth century utopian socialist movement—simplicity, modesty, asexuality[3]—were influential in the Constructivist utopian narrative, almost as much as the latest news on the advancing machine age. By advocating that the concepts of simplicity and gender-neutrality could perfectly correspond to an industrially highly developed society, Alexander Bogdanov's 1908 science fiction novel *Red Star* was even more important. Bogdanov imagined a Marxian society on Mars that was about 300 years in advance of Earth in technology, ideology, and human behavior, with its citizens wearing androgynous, loose clothes, produced in the most technologically innovative ways.[4]

A utilitarian form of dress such as overalls fed the Constructivists' wild utopian dreams, burdened with noble, yet highly ideological principles. Likewise, as an easy-to-produce piece of clothing, overalls could have been mass-manufactured, or so the Constructivists hoped. In the end, Rodchenko was the only Russian Constructivist who wore *prozodezhda* in everyday life. Designed by himself, and sewn by Stepanova from woolen cloth in 1922, it was a proper worker's overall with big pockets to store tools, leather details, exposed stitching, and fastening done with metal buckles. In a photograph from that time,

Figure 10.1 Alexander Rodchenko in his *prozodezhda*, 1922. Rodchenko Family Archive. Courtesy of Alexander Lavrentiev.

Rodchenko proudly posed in his *prozodezhda*, standing in front of his folded spatial constructions, perfectly matching his radical outfit with his radical avantgarde art. He looked like an artist engineer, the role that the Constructivists imagined for themselves. One of his former students at VKhUMETAS, Galina Chichagova likened his appearance to the combination of the two highly regarded 1920s professions, accompanied with the correspondingly iconic images of overalls and leather jackets: pilot and motorist. Furthermore, Chichagova enthusiastically stated that she "immediately saw that this was a new type of man, a special one" (cited in Elliott 1979: 106).

By the mid-1920s, it was obvious that the Constructivist utopian ideals of the total redesign of dress had not materialized. Their dreams of catching up with the more advanced capitalist modes of production were broken by out-of-date machinery, shortages of raw materials, and lack of dyes. However, the members of a wider movement, known as International Modernism, continued to share and support the Constructivist aesthetic and drive for a new and better world throughout the 1920s. Integrating a novel geometric style with socially progressive politics, its various participants imagined an excessively rational universe, in which only an equally rational, mechanically produced dress could fit in. In the catalog of their 1929 exhibition *Civilized Woman* (Civilisovaná žena/Zivilisierte Frau), the members of the 1920s Czech functionalist modernism were all depicted in overalls, including their female colleague Božena Horneková (Horneková, Vaněk, and Rossmann 1929: 11).

The *Civilized Woman* project was initiated by the Bauhaus-educated Zdeněk Rossmann and realized in 1929 as an exhibition with its accompanying publication, in the Czech city of Brno, one of the strongholds of interwar International Modernism. Rossmann and his collaborators, from product designer Jan Vaněk to fashion designer Božena Horneková and journalist Milena Jesenská, shared the Constructivists' radical politics, as well as their anxieties, concerning fashion as a carrier of status and gender differences. Comparing fashionable women to "colourful parrots" and "decoratively adorned savages," Jan Vaněk, claimed that "only a woman who dresses in a civilized, cultivated and noble manner, would be welcomed among civilized men" (Vaněk 1929: 11). In order to become modern, a woman was supposed to dress like a man, as this rationalized dress style let her move freely, and enabled her to become civilized. Horneková designed a visionary collection based on women wearing trousers and overalls (Horneková, Vaněk, and Rossmann 1929: 87–91). In the photographs accompanying the catalog, this modernist woman wore leather overalls while piloting an airplane, but domestic help supported her sophisticated lifestyle, with even her maid sporting modernist overalls. Consequently, Hornekovás outfits executed for the exhibition *Civilized Woman* showed androgynous and functionalist, yet highly polished, clothes.

While modernist artists designed and promoted overalls, and consciously wore them in order to position themselves as socially progressive members of their respective societies in the 1920s, the uniformity of this outfit triggered some quite different reactions and emotions in the later periods, especially in the post-Second World War world, burdened with the accounts of destruction, post-Holocaust stories, and a totalitarian, Stalinist-type of socialism imposed on a large part of Europe. Those circumstances revealed a much cruder and gloomier version of modernity, which consequently affected both the arts and everyday life. In George Orwell's dystopian novel *Nineteen Eighty-Four*, published in 1949, the obligatory uniform of overalls symbolized such a darker side of modernity, in which individuality and free will were subjected to anonymous powers, guided by technical rationality.

In the words of Ursula K. Le Guin, "Every eutopia contains a dystopia, every dystopia contains a eutopia" (2016: 195). Indeed, overalls have existed in both: in utopia as an ideal outfit, and in dystopia as a cursed one. Julia, the heroine of

Nineteen Eighty-Four, hated the Big Brother-imposed rules that robbed her of her sexuality and femininity: short hair, a face without make-up, obligatory overalls. Talking to her secret lover Winston, she imagined her rebellion in sartorial terms: "And do you know what I am going to do next? I am going to get hold of a real woman's frock from somewhere and wear it instead of these bloody trousers. I'll wear silk stockings and high-heeled shoes! In this room, I'm going to be a woman, not a Party comrade" (Orwell 1984: 127). In the Soviet Union, the rise of Stalinism from the late 1920s tamed avant-garde utopianism into a homogenized industrial routine, by embedding the design, production and distribution of dress into its bureaucratic-led Five-Year Plans (see Bartlett 2010: 63–98). In 1931, according to the critic Alexei Fedorov-Davydov *"Prozodezhda* will unquestionably develop hand-in-hand with collectivization, with the elimination of individualism in everyday life and individual forms of labour" (1975: 138). In sharp contrast to Rodchenko's smart, hand-produced version, *prozodezhda* did become a mass-produced, ordinary clothing item. In the late 1940s, the new East European communist regimes attempted to repeat the Constructivist utopian experiment. Promoted in socialist media and propaganda posters, a new woman was increasingly depicted in overalls. Driven by ideological pressure, which, once more shaped perceptions of them as a class- and gender-neutral outfit, overalls were supposed to prevail over a feminine bourgeois dress. But the utopian aim to establish them as a uniformed female dress proved to be too radical an initiative at the everyday level, as women hated wearing overalls.

Functional overalls: work and sports

The characteristics such as simplicity, usefulness, and comfort have been crucial in promoting utopian versions of overalls. However, in contrast to their ideologically burdened uses in the early 1920s utopias, the contemporary American clothing companies relied on these notions while promoting their new workwear for the vast domestic market. Published in the *Saturday Evening Post* in 1917, The HD Lee Mercantile's advertisement boasted:

> Slip on a suit of Lee Union-Alls! You'll never wear anything else to work in. Such an improvement! Such convenience! Such service! It's the work garment men in all walks of life have been waiting for. The mechanic, the motorist, the farmer, the laborer, the man who does odd jobs about the home and works in his garden ... Cost no more, either, than old fashioned inconvenient, binding two-piece garments.
>
> see MARSH and TRYNKA 2005: 29

The ad continued with praise for the highest production quality and the excellent, hard-wearing fabrics used to make them, from khaki to denim and white drill, all of which supposedly pointed towards an undisputable durability of Lee Union Alls (Marsh and Trynka 2005: 29). This all-in-one, long-sleeved outfit was a significant improvement on the initial Levi's waist overalls, which sported suspenders attached to denim trousers with buttons. At the beginning of the twentieth century, both HD Lee Mercantile and JC Penney had been already producing bib overalls, consisting of trousers with a sewn-on bib, and with straps over the shoulders. Each new version contained ever more practical pockets, with the 1917 HD Lee Mercantile's overalls publicizing as many as eight big pockets.

Around that time, the forward-thinking Austrian architect and writer Adolf Loos saw the American worker in overalls as a new hero. Similar to the early Bolsheviks, Loos was not only impressed with American technological progress, but also perceived Americanization as a modernist project. Following his visit to America at the end of the nineteenth century, Loos saw his homeland as culturally and industrially backward, slow-moving, socially segregated, and aesthetically over-decorated. Loos did not concern himself with the challenging reality of the American working classes and the existing social inequalities. For him, America was a mythical country, a socially and culturally homogenous society, due to its advanced work methods executed by its capable, well-organized, and adequately clothed work force (see Stewart 2000). While he did not plot to bring down the existing political order like the Russian revolutionaries, he did want to modernize Austro–Hungary. And, in his 1908 article "Culture," Loos envisioned the man in overalls engaging with this urgent task of modernization. To strengthen his argument, Loos conveniently referred to one of the most famous literary heroes in the Germanic world, Goethe's Werther. In the eighteenth century, Werther enchanted his contemporaries with his desperately romantic love for Charlotte, and his equally romantic clothes. But, in the new world, Loos declared: "Charlotte will see her Werther approach in wide trousers that reach up to his armpits and are buckled over his shoulders. The American worker will have conquered the world. The man in overalls" (1998: 162).

Due to their durability, American soldiers in the First World War wore Lee's Union-Alls from 1917, and the army also provided the mechanic and supply units with Union-Alls. Historically, women started to wear overalls on the factory floor during that time. Women in masculine-style outfits performing man's manual work was initially a shocking sight, but the practice continued throughout the Second World War in the munitions factories and for agricultural labor. In an article published in *American Machinist* in 1918, the author wondered if "the Womanalls, now worn in munition factories and on other war emergency work were ugly"… and if "skirts necessarily hampered women's movements"? ("Skirts or Overalls for Women" 1918: 487; see also Steele 1989: 80). As stated by fashion historian Valerie Steele, working women themselves engaged in proposing overalls, and often preferred them to the wide, long skirts in which they had entered the workforce only a couple of decades earlier: "Many working-class women praised the new sartorial freedoms as well as the enhanced job opportunities. Said one ex-stenographer working in a World War One munitions factory: 'I should hate to go back to work in the old long skirts'" (Steele 1989: 78). A photograph of a special "feminine" trousered uniform from the July 1918 issue of *American Machinist* shows the overalls and cap developed by a committee of women workers (cited in Steele 1989: 80). The wide, loose trousers of this outfit vaguely resemble a long skirt.

It was seen as women's patriotic duty to temporarily replace men who were off to war, so positive images of the female workforce were presented in the contemporary media, which nevertheless aimed at keeping in balance the traditional gender difference. In the October 1917 issue of the French satirical weekly *La Baïonnette*, the illustrator and designer Paul Iribe depicted a pretty, overalls-clad woman in the munitions factory. Referring to the favourite holiday destinations of the rich, the caption sarcastically commented that not all the women were at Biarritz and Deauville. In the same issue, yet another drawing presented women in overalls at work in the munitions factory. Its author Leo Lechevallier envisaged them as attractive young women in coquettish berets, manning the machine in feminine kitten heels (*La Baïonnette* 1917: 632–3). Similarly, during the Second World War, as women were increasingly enrolled into the jobs that hitherto had been occupied by men, the British Ministry of Information tried hard to present overalls-wearing women as feminine. The long-established gender balance was suddenly disturbed, and the government not only attempted to cheer up women in their masculine-style clothes, but also to maintain the appearance of the conventional gender order. Thus, writing about women working in an anti-aircraft battery in the propaganda pamphlet *Eve in Overalls*, Arthur Wauters stated that women "wear exactly the same uniform as their men comrades, but they have not lost any of the allure of their sex" (1995: 17).

However, since class, culture, and education inform the production of femininity, several concepts of femininity co-existed in wartime, and new categories such as nationality and patriotism, entered into the game. In the US, Norman Rockwell's image showing a big, muscular woman in denim overalls received mass distribution on the cover of *The Saturday Evening Post* in

May 1943.[5] His heroine was eating a sandwich during her lunch break, with a rifle in her lap and her hard shoes crushing a copy of Hitler's *Mein Kampf*. Rockwell was at the time a popular artist of sentimentalized portrayals of American life, creating many cover illustrations in an idealistic manner for this popular magazine. Consequently, this hard-working woman, who deliberately renounced her femininity in order to perform her patriotic duty, became an iconic image, and, additionally, established overalls as a visual means of communicating the strength and determination of women in wartime America.

By designing overalls, American fashion designers also proved their patriotism, and indeed fulfilled the need for a new workwear. In 1942, the Sperry Gyroscope Company engaged Vera Maxwell, a pre-war pioneer of American sportswear, to create this type of outfit. Made of blue wool-treated gabardine, Maxwell's overalls were cleverly devised. With their "convertible collar, long barrel sleeves, front panels double tucked at waist, two button flap patch breast pockets, thirteen button drop seat with back placket concealed by topstitched back-contoured crossover self-belt, slash hip pockets, full-cut tapered pants, fix-stitched permanent crease" and some other carefully conceived details, Maxwell's overalls took into account the needs of women who would wear them, and was consistent with the military image of the Sperry Gyroscope Company.[6] Successfully supporting the American war effort with sophisticated technology devices, the company certainly wanted their highly skilled workforce dressed smartly and practically.

The media representations nevertheless differed, and often glamorized wartime work uniforms. An article, published in British *Vogue* in January 1942, attempted to adjust 'the new look' to the requirements of a military uniform:

> It's a look that does not jar with uniform—with women's uniform. Somehow, more and more, the eye unconsciously measures women up by this yardstick. Why does that shoulder-mane seem so out of date? Because it would look messy hanging on a uniform collar. ... Why does that heavy eye make-up seem overdone? Because it would racket with the simplicity of service clothes. The woman who could change instantly into uniform or munitions overall and look charming, soignée and right, is the smart woman of to-day
>
> "The New Look" 1942: 2

Even the so-called 'siren suit,' a one-piece outfit designed for use on the way to and in air-raid shelters, could be similarly glamorized. The Parisian haute couture collections, held in October 1939, and presenting the 1940 Spring Summer collections, included luxurious siren suits. In her 1954 autobiography, Elsa Schiaparelli reminisced how, after being forced to cut her workforce from 600 employees to 150, she nevertheless managed to design a collection in three weeks:

> This was the "cash and carry" collection with huge pockets everywhere so that a woman, obliged to leave home in a hurry or to go on duty without a bag, could pack all that was necessary to her. ... There was the Maginot Line blue, the Foreign Legion red, the aeroplane grey, the woollen boiler suit that one could fold on a chair next to one's bed so that one could put it on quickly in the event of an air-raid driving one down to the cellar. There was also one in white, which was supposed to withstand poisonous gas.
> SCHIAPARELLI 2007: 104–05 (see Blum 2003: 228–9)

During these presentations, another famous Parisian designer, Robert Piguet, showed his sophisticated overalls in iron-gray wool, with matching hooded cape in pink-, white-, and gray-checked fabric. Both Schiaparelli and Piguet's overalls were accompanied by flashlights and obligatory gas masks, but, although they would have been out of place in an ordinary cellar, they fitted perfectly into the shelter in the Paris Ritz, which had been furnished with fur rugs and sleeping bags from Hermès. And, indeed a scene, with Piguet and Molyneux's overalls in the Ritz's La Cave-Abri was depicted in the December issue of French *Vogue* in 1939 (*Vogue* Paris 1939: 22).[7]

The increasing interest in sports and healthy outdoor lifestyle required practical clothes, and in sports such as skiing and airplane piloting, they materialized as overalls. Skiing became an Olympic sport in 1924, which contributed to its rise in popularity. In the 1930s, two-piece ensembles, consisting of a tunic and trousers, turned into much more sensible overalls for both sexes. In the illustrations by Jean Pagès, published in American *Vogue* in December 1930, models confidently posed in their smart overalls, designed by Schiaparelli, Lelong, Lanvin, Jean Patou, and Jane Régny, while other skiers exercised and rushed down a slope in the background.[8] Following Charles Lindbergh's inaugural flight across the Atlantic in 1927, flying was regarded as the most exciting sport, and many members of the international elite became enthusiastic amateur pilots. One of them, Alicia Patterson, advised that: "... you can't fly around the country in your best clothes. You have to wear a flying suit, helmet and goggles" (1930: 60). In his leather overalls, Lindbergh turned into an aviator style icon, and female pilots not only appropriated his dress style, but attempted to match his endeavors. With her solo cross-Atlantic flight in May 1932, the

American Amelia Earhart became the most famous aviatrix. She was usually pictured in her flying uniform of overalls and leather jacket, and ultimately designed a jumpsuit featuring zippers and large pockets, just as she sported on her own outfit.[9]

Emilio Pucci's ski jumpsuit published on the cover of the British *Vogue* in January 1959, represented a significant development, as the designer printed his trademark colorful abstract pattern on elasticized gabardine. An aristocrat, but also an excellent skier himself, Pucci well understood that a ski outfit should provide total freedom of movement. With skiing evolving into a mass sport in the postwar period, new technologically advanced fabrics, like nylon and latex, were increasingly used in the mass production of skiwear, with the German company Bogner and some others entering the market from the early 1950s onward.

As overall prosperity emerged following the post-war deprivations, the early 1960s brought a new optimistic approach to life. Moreover, fueled by the forward-looking and successful space-related technological explorations, it seemed that modernity could finally live up to its noble promise of continuous human progress. The Space Age was marked by the Soviet Union's launch of Sputnik 1 in 1957, Yuri Gagarin's first manned space flight in 1961, Valentina Tereshkova becoming the first woman to pilot a space aircraft in 1963, and, finally, the Apollo 11 moon landing in 1969, when Neil Armstrong became the first man to walk on the moon. In the Soviet Union, the images showing Gagarin and Tereshkova in their futuristic, white cosmonaut suits in the stratosphere were the symbol of technological modernity, which also rekindled social utopian hopes and symbolically pointed toward the re-launch of socialism under Nikita Khrushchev. On the other hand, competing with the initial socialist victories in the space race, the US attempted to invent not only technologically more advanced versions for their cosmonauts, but also to design more visually appealing outfits. Scott Crossfield, one of the advisers to the US Air Force, suggested that a space suit should look "photogenic," even "glamorous," after spotting a "kind of silver lamé" fabric on the lab's floor of the Air Force contractor David Clark. That specific fabric—nylon with a vacuum-blasted aluminum coating—was indeed used in producing the early US space suit in 1957 (see de Monchaux 2011: 95). As explained by Nicholas de Monchaux, "... within a wider cultural understanding of the heroic 'space suit' throughout the 1940s and 1950s ... the silver space suit of the Mercury era seemed to relate to Flash Gordon ..." (2011: 104). During the Gemini era, challenged by scientific advances, the myth retreated, and so did the color silver. At that point, American audiences happily watched the

US astronauts exploring space in the scientifically verified, and easier to produce, white uniforms.

Glowing in its white and silver synthetic hues, the space suit became the ultimate overalls, functional and futuristic at the same time. Technologically-related advances in the development of new fabrics have continued to assist with designing and producing sports uniforms and workwear, while its looks have endlessly inspired fashion designers, especially those who creatively engage with sportswear. In this sense, André Courrèges was unique, an engineer by profession and an athlete himself. When engaged to design staff uniforms for the 1972 München Olympic Games, Courrèges clearly drew on the world of working clothes while designing loose overalls for manual activities, covering them with multiple pockets with zips (see Borgers 1993). Nevertheless, he also managed to include his already famous fashion item—the bodystocking—in two types of staff outfit, as well as creating the uniforms in his favourite colors: white, silver, light blue, and orange.

Fashionable overalls

From the 1920s, categories such as functionality, simplicity, and comfort increasingly migrated from the austere world of Russian and International Constructivism into the field of fashion. Additionally, in order to achieve a new modernist look, fashion relied on the avant-garde arts, such as Futurism and Cubism. As observed by fashion historian Richard Martin: "Cubism offered in fashion, as in art, a substantive and new manner of seeing, reasoned in dynamics of time and space, rendered with the volatility of modern life" (1998: 16). The Italian Futurist Thayaht (real name Ernesto Michahelles) proposed his all-purpose overalls—*la tuta*—in an advertisement published in the respected bourgeois newspaper *La Nazione* in Florence in June 1920. Thayaht designed his *tuta* as a simple outfit, to be cut along straight lines, fashioned from modest fabrics such as khaki and linen, and easy to make by oneself, following the instructions offered on the paper pattern he carefully devised. Thayaht's photographs and drawings pointed towards the construction of geometricized and flattened versions of both dress and body. There was the same economy of fabric consumption, of effort, and of energy in Rodchenko and Thayaht's overalls, but Thayaht was commercially minded. Indeed, only a couple of weeks after its launch, 1,000 *tuta* paper patterns had already been sold (Pratesi 2007; Morini 2007). Thayaht not only designed the *tuta*, but also wore it constantly himself.

Figure 10.2 Thayaht in his *tuta*, 1920. Courtesy of Photographic Archive of Prato Textile Museum [inv. n. 05.05.F06].

However, the *tuta* did not become an everyday dress for all sections of society, as envisaged by its designer in his launching slogan *Tutti in tuta* ("Everybody in tuta"). Instead, endowed with a modernist credo due to its novel, geometric cut, Thayaht's *tuta* was swiftly acknowledged in the world of Parisian haute couture, which, at the time, was equally modernist and eager to experiment.

From 1922, Thayaht practiced his new radical aesthetics at the Madeleine Vionnet fashion house in Paris, designing a series of tuta-style dresses, and minimalist air travel ensembles, nevertheless executed in the most refined fabrics. Adopting the modernist geometric visual language in her field of work, Vionnet herself relied on rectangles and circles when designing her high fashion dresses. In this, she shared modernity's interest in geometry as a progressive visual language with the Futurist Thayaht, and the utopia-driven Constructivists. However, the utopian dreams of deconstructing established dress codes and constructing a novel dress could materialize only in the field of fashion. As a modernist phenomenon itself, but unburdened by any messianic programs or manifestos, fashion both readjusted and transferred utopian ideas into the everyday. Its commercial nature enabled fashion and its practitioners to not only envisage new outfits in geometric shapes, but also to efficiently produce them, and sell them either as elitist clothes or mass sportswear.

Indeed, the Constructivist geometric aesthetic echoed in André Courrèges and Pierre Cardin's space age collections in the 1960s, an era which still dared to dream of a utopian society of the future. Embracing technology and science, both designers relied on man-made fibres, including vinyl and plastic, or the highly advanced fabrics that were usually used for aviation and sport. Equally, both Cardin and Courrèges showed overalls within their sartorial explorations of new expressions of modernity, brought on by the space age. Cardin's 1970 men's futuristic overalls fitted with his continuing space-inspired narrative of geometrically cut clothes designed to free the body. Around the same time, Cardin draped and gathered soft jersey knits into sculptural female overalls (see Längle 2005). In 1967, Courrèges launched his bodystocking, a very tight, knitted all-in-one jumpsuit, celebrating a fit and athletic body (see Guillaume 1998). Two years later, he honored the first manned moon landing with a range of mirror-disc-covered white overalls, photographed for American *Vogue* by Bert Stern.

Both Cardin and Courrèges designed unisex clothes, and thus the space trend embodied the earlier utopian ideas of simple, practical, and sexually neutral outfits for women. By fall 1971, the American designer Rudi Gernreich matched this approach in his work, but also extended it. He perceived "anonymity, universality, unisex, nudity as fact, and not as kick, and above all reality. By reality, I mean the use of real things: blue jeans, polo shirts, T-shirts, overalls" (cited in Luther 1999: 31). Around that time, Gernreich did design a series of overalls, of the practical, loose variety, such as a 1964 camel-hair aviator jumpsuit, to the striking evening examples covered in paillettes in the late 1960s, and a 1970 knitted version which enveloped the body like a glove. Gernreich ushered overalls into a new era. While fashionable, the space-age-related overalls were geometric and minimalist, clearly referring to their roots in utopian and avant-garde arts. In the 1970s, overalls acquired new extravagant shapes, were made in a range of new fabrics, and often turned into glamorous evening wear.

In the late 1970s, at the peak of the disco trend, a New York night club, Studio 54, commanded the latest overalls fashions. Here, American designers such as Halston and Stephen Burrows showed numerous versions of overalls as glamorous and sexually provocative evening wear. Halston excelled at making soft, unconstructed overalls in ultra-soft suede and the silky knit fabric known as 'liquid jersey,' while Stephen Burrows designed his revealing overalls in slinky, shimmering gold lamé, with a backless halter top.[10] Those luxurious versions could not be further away from the initial, basic and gender-neutral intentions of overalls, but this trend, which accentuated the female form, continued through to the end of the twentieth century. In the late 1980s, Thierry Mugler designed body-hugging overalls, which, due to their prominent shoulder pads, looked simultaneously sexy and menacing. In the early 1990s, Gianni Versace's overalls also showed an excessive body consciousness. In strong colors, from fuchsia to black, and embellished with gold accents, they also established an Italian version of unashamed glamor.

However, from the beginning of the twenty-first century, fashion designers started to refer to overalls' historical noble ideals. In his women's Spring/Summer 2003 collection, Yohji Yamamoto romanticized royal-blue militaristic jumpsuits by drawing on historical sources, such as August Sander's early twentieth-century photographs of anonymous German workers in overalls. In her attempts to update the Christian Dior fashion house, its designer Maria Grazia Chiuri relied on very simple denim overalls in her Autumn/Winter 2017 collection. Moreover, some designers have been reclaiming overalls for men. By offering the masculine-style overalls in brown (*Vetements* in collaboration with Levi's, Spring/Summer 2017), dark blue (Louis Vuitton, Spring Summer 2018), and khaki (Prada, Spring/Summer 2018), fashion designers investigated whether overalls, after their previous androgynous and highly sexualized female versions, could dress a man in search of his new male identity.

The most diversified ways in which contemporary fashion designers have appropriated such a basic piece of clothing like overalls, points to the complex nature of fashion, which stretches beyond the commercial. While he did not refer to fashion in the context of clothing, Boris Groys's musings on the phenomenon in his work *On the New*, seem to encapsulate the multifaceted relationship between overalls, utopia and fashion: "For fashion is radically anti-utopian and anti-totalitarian: its constant shifts attest that the future is unpredictable and cannot escape historical change and that there exist no universal truths that might completely determine the future" (Groys 2014: 49).

In contrast to their ever-changing fashionable versions, overalls became a sartorial symbol of social rebellion in the late 1960s and 1970s. Embellishing them with peace badges and other anti-war insignia, young men turned overalls into a peace-promoting uniform while protesting against the Vietnam War. When in the 1970s, women challenged their position and role in society, they often wore overalls on feminist marches. Elizabeth Wilson emphasized that feminism was innovative in pioneering thrift-shop styles and retro-chic. In this context, variously accessorized dungarees and boilersuits could be, and had been, redefined as "fashionable" and "sexy" (Wilson 1985: 240).

Overalls carrying a radical political message have again reappeared at the end of the twentieth and the beginning of the twenty-first century. Working outside the fashion system, progressive artists Maura Brewer and Abigail Glaum-Lathbury from the Chicago- and Los Angeles-based Rational Dress Society, have attempted to re-position overalls in an ecologically different social and sartorial environment. Understanding that the political potential of utopian dress is diluted or abandoned at the moment when fashion translates the categories of functionality, simplicity, and gender-neutrality into fast-fashion items, these artists have tried to retrieve the original, genuine meanings of these notions in order to design and offer their overalls through a new, radical practice. They introduced their project, *Jumpsuit*, in 2016, and envisioned it as an "ungendered mono-garment to replace all clothes in perpetuity" (Stafford 2016). Their jumpsuit comes in only two colors—black and white—and can be made in over 200 sizes, customized to a person's individual body type. The artists sell their overalls online, and have additionally devised paper patterns that can be downloaded from their website. This is a return to the beginning, which started with the Russian science fiction writer Alexander Bogdanov's 1908 novel *Red Star*. Only now, due to the incredible technological advances in production, distribution, and communication, is this a potential reality, or at least one of its possibilities.

References

Bartlett, D. (2010), *FashionEast,* Cambridge, MA: MIT Press.
Blum, D. E. (2003), *Shocking!: The Art and Fashion of Elsa Schiaparelli*, New Haven, CT: Yale University Press.
Bogdanov, A. ([1908] 1984), *Red Star: The First Bolshevik Utopia*, L. R. Graham and R. Stites (eds), Bloomington, IN: Indiana University Press.
Borgers, W. (1993), "Fashion at the Games," *Olympic Review;* N 308, June 1993: 256–63. Available online: http://library.la84.org/OlympicInformationCenter/OlympicReview/1993/ore308/ORE308o.pdf [accessed: December 5, 2017]
Bowlt, J. (1996), "Body Beautiful: The Artistic Search for the Perfect Physique," in J. Bowlt and O. Matich (eds), *Laboratory of Dreams: The Russian Avant-garde and Cultural Experiment*, Stanford, CA: Stanford University Press, 37–58.
Braun, E. (2006), Meyerhold: *A Revolution in Theatre,* London: Methuen.
"C'est toujours Paris qui crée la mode" (1936) *Marie Claire,* Paris, November 10: 10–11.
"*Dark Skiing Suits Are Smartest*" (1930) *Vogue*, New York, December 22: 47–8.

Elia, A. (2014), "The Wardrobe of the Modern Athlete: Activewear in the 1930s," in P. Mears and G. B. Bayer (eds), *Elegance in an Age of Crisis: Fashions of the 1930s*, New Haven, CT: Yale University Press.

Elliott, D, ed. (1979), *Alexander Rodchenko, 1891–1956,* Oxford: Museum of Modern Art.

Fedorov-Davydov, A. (1975), *Russkoe i sovetskoe iskusstvo*, Moscow: Iskusstvo.

Groys, B. (2014), *On the New*, London: Verso Books.

Guillaume, V. (1998), *Courrèges*, London: Thames & Hudson.

Horneková, B., J. Vaněk, and Z. Rossmann, eds (1929), *Civilisovaná žena/Zivilisierte Frau (Civilized Woman)*, Brno: Jan Vaně K.

La Baïonnette (1917), Paris, October 4: 632–3.

Längle, E. (2005), *Pierre Cardin: Fifty Years of Fashion and Design*, New York: The Vendome Press.

Lavrentiev, A. (1988), *Varvara Stepanova: A Constructivist Life,* London: Thames & Hudson.

Le Guin, U. K. (2016), "Utopiyin, Utopiyang," in *Utopia Thomas More*, London: Verso, 195–98.

Lodder, C. (1983), *Russian Constructivism,* New Haven, CT: Yale University Press.

Loos, A. ([1908] 1998), *Ornament and Crime*, Riverside, CA: Ariadne Press.

Luther, M. (1999), "Looking Back at a Futurist," in P. Moffitt (ed.), *The Rudi Gernreich Book,* Cologne: Taschen, 10–35.

Marsh, G. and P. Trynka (2005), *Denim: A Visual History of the World's Most Legendary Fabric*, London: Aurum.

Martin, R. (1998), *Cubism and Fashion*, New York: The Metropolitan Museum of Art.

Mirabella, G. (1994), "Geoffrey Beene Interview," in J. Abbott Miller (ed.), *Geoffrey Beene Unbound*, New York: The Museum at FIT, 2–8.

Monchaux de, N. (2011), *Space Suit: Fashioning Apollo*, Cambridge, MA: The MIT Press.

Morini, E. (2007), "La Tuta: da antimoda a haute couture", in: *Thayaht: Un artista alle origini del Made in Italy*, Prato: Museo del Tessuto Edizioni: 24–33.

Oginskaĩa, L. (1981), *Gustav Klutsis*, Moscow: Sovetskiii khudozhnik.

O'Hara Callan, G. (1998), *Dictionary of Fashion and Fashion Designers,* London: Thames & Hudson.

Orwell, G. ([1949] 1984), *Nineteen Eighty-Four*, Harmondsworth: Penguin.

Patterson, A. (1930), "Flying for fun," *Vogue*, New York: 59–61; 154.

Pratesi, M. (2007), "1920. Thayaht inventa la Tuta e nasce il Made in Italy," in *Thayaht: Un artista alle origini del Made in Italy*, Prato: Museo del Tessuto Edizioni, 12–23.

Sarabianov, D. V. and N. L. Adaskina (1990), *Popova,* New York: Harry N. Abrams.

Schiaparelli, E. ([1954] 2007), *Shocking Life,* London: V&A Publications.

"Skirts or Overalls for Women" (1918) *American Machinist*, September 12: 487.

Stafford, Z. (2016), "Tired of the tyranny of fashion? Wear a jumpsuit every day," *The Guardian*, June 2, 2016; Available online: https://www.theguardian.com/fashion/2016/jun/02/jumpsuit-rational-dress-society-fashion-clothing-vogue [accessed June 5, 2016]

Steele, V. (1989), "Dressing for Work," in C. Brush Kidwell and V. Steele (eds), *Men and Women Dressing the Part*, Washington, D.C.: Smithsonian Institution Scholarly Press, 64-92.
Stepanova, V. (Varst) (1923), "Kostium segodniashnego dnia—prozodezhda," (Today's clothing: Prozodezhda), *Lef*, N 2: 65-68.
Stewart, J. (2000), *Fashioning Vienna: Adolf Loos's Cultural Criticism*, London: Routledge.
Stites, R. (1989), *Revolutionary Dreams: Utopian Vision and Experimental Life in the Russian Revolution*, Oxford: Oxford University Press.
"The New Look" (1942), *Vogue* London, January.
Tupitsyn, M. (2004), *Gustav Klutsis and Valentina Kulagina*, New York: International Center of Photography and Göttingen: Steidl.
Vaněk, J. (1929), "Žena konečně civilisovaná" (The Woman Is Finally Civilized), in B. Horneková, J. Vaněk and Z. Rossmann (eds), *Civilisovaná žena/Zivilisierte Frau (Civilized Woman)*: Brno: Jan Vaněk, 7-13.
Veillon, D. (2002), *Fashion under the Occupation*, Oxford: Berg.
Vogue Paris (1939), December.
Wauters, A. (1995), *Eve in Overalls*, London: Imperial War Museum.
Wilson, E. (1985), *Adorned in Dreams: Fashion and Modernity*, London: Virago.
Wollen, P. (1989), "Cinema/Americanism/the Robot," *New Formations*, N 8, Summer 1989: 7-34.

11

Utility Chic: Where Fashion and Uniform Meet

Jane Tynan

If "uniforms shape who we are and how we perform our identities" (Craik 2005: 4), could the same be said for fashionable dress? Uniform, a more specialized form of clothing than fashion, is designed for a specific occupation within an institutional setting; its widespread use since the nineteenth century reflects the critical role it has come to play in the display of social identities. The uniform symbolizes the institution the wearer represents, but also impacts how social roles are performed. Fashion, on the other hand, is a social practice associated with change, creativity, and individual liberty. Historian Paul Fussell sums up the dilemma that uniform represents: "everyone must wear a uniform, but everyone must deny wearing one, lest one's invaluable personality and unique identity be compromised" (2002: 5). This encapsulates ongoing tensions between fashion and uniform, whereby the pressure to fit in clashes with the drive to be distinctive. This chapter focuses on those complex interactions between uniform and fashion, military and work uniform; it looks to the militarizing of civilian life from the mid-1850s onwards in order to understand what gave rise to the prominence of uniforms in everyday life. Further, the discussion explores the ongoing dialog between uniform and fashion; it considers what inspiration fashion finds in uniform and whether it represents power, or promises utopia.

Fashion has profoundly shaped uniform design. For instance, the first uniform for the British Admiralty, introduced in 1748 for commissioned officers, imitated the Macaroni style, a masculine fashion of the time known for its continental flavour. When in 1827 the Admiralty replaced this style of uniform, it drew directly from contemporary fashions. Technological changes drove uniform design for the British Navy but dandy styles of the 1820s and 1830s were also an influence (Miller 2007: 9). The eventual regulation of military and naval uniforms was of critical importance to their development, but nonetheless officers continued to have their uniforms tailored to reflect current fashions. This was the case for the most utilitarian military uniforms worn by the British on the western front in the First World War; they too were fashioned by aesthetic considerations. The Norfolk jacket, for instance, began its life as a sportswear staple—as did the trench coat—for the leisure classes in late nineteenth century England. These designs, originally created for sport and leisure, suited the wet muddy conditions of the trenches. Despite a rational and utilitarian appearance, even the design of British First World War uniforms drew on various civilian fashionable styles.

During wartime, women's civilian clothing was in turn influenced by military uniform: at the time of the Boer War, many advertisers celebrated the popularity of khaki cloth for civilian fashion and the First World War saw military details transposed onto women's clothing, particularly through the adoption of khaki and trench coat styles. When leisure wear for both men and women became associated with shirking during the First World War, fashion sought out the safety of military styling to send out a patriotic message through a visual language of military participation (Tynan 2013a). In the twentieth century, fashion and uniform have had many playful interactions, each representing very different ideas of what it means to be modern. Elsa Schiaparelli, an Italian designer associated with surrealism, was one of the first designers to look to the uniform for inspiration. In spring 1940, she created designs based on camouflage taffetas and 'trench' brown, and in so doing was one of the first designers to appropriate camouflage for fashion. Later in 1962, when her high fashion business folded, her salon created the New York Preen designs for nurse's uniforms. Despite her reputation for surrealist designs, Schiaparelli also embraced utilitarian design and adapted military styles for fashion.

Uniform styling has long held a fascination for fashion designers, from the military trench coat first worn by officers in the First World War, Coco Chanel's sailor suits, Yves Saint Laurent's pea coat, to the ubiquitous use of camouflage on the contemporary catwalk. Not all fashion historians, though, agree that war stimulates creativity in fashion. According to James Laver, "the war, as all wars do, had a deadening effect on fashion, and there is little to record until the conflict is over" (1969: 229). Like many art and fashion historians, Laver believed that war was incompatible with art and design innovation. My discussion challenges this view. I examine how fashion inhabited uniform design, but also how uniformity became part of the logic of fashion, both in terms of its production and consumption. Laver's perspective, though, misses a more subtle point: while war might appear to deaden the accessibility of fashion, it does introduce utility into fashionable dress.

Uniforms and modernization

Historically, uniform schemes were thought to be a corrective to the excesses of fashion. The European sumptuary tradition in the Middle Ages established the practice of categorizing people through the clothes that they wore (Maxwell 2014: 47). Restricting inappropriate consumption was to regulate social groups, particularly town-dwellers and religious minorities, but the practice also extended to the colonies, where visible hierarchies were based on race rather than class. Sumptuary laws in various regions, primarily in medieval Europe, reflected the power and authority of the state and in colonial contexts involved transforming or erasing local forms of dress. This is where sumptuary laws prefigured proto-nationalism by demanding the outward display of rank and position (Maxwell 2014: 57). Uniforms enabled social control, but patriotic nationalists, who sought new forms of citizenship based on collective power, also adopted them. The French Revolution itself created nationalist uniforms and revolutionary symbols such as tricolor cockades and red caps. These experiments with uniform that arose from Enlightenment thought flourished through the modern age to endure both authoritarian and utopian social structures. At certain points since the mid-nineteenth century, uniform has been advanced as a solution to various social problems, particularly to redress power imbalances; it has thus been imbued with the values of democracy and equality.

In the modern world, both fashion and uniform have laid claim to an ideal world but each have a distinctive attitude. In many modern institutions, there were real efforts to play down fashion when designing uniforms for work. Florence Nightingale, a social reformer who was called upon to improve the poor conditions in British army hospitals during the Crimean War, "insisted that her nurses wear uniforms of plain gray tweed wrappers for winter and printed cotton for summer, along with check aprons and white caps" (Bates 2011: 160). For Nightingale, adopting uniform was an opportunity to diminish the influence of fashion on nurse's dress. She was dismissive of fashions such as crinolines and hair-pads and sought practicality and humility in the clothing worn by her nurses; she also sought a secular approach to uniform, omitting, as she did, any religious references from their dress.

Nightingale's "discourse of anti-fashion with moral overtones," which was evident in these first uniforms, reflected the values of middle-class Victorian society, in particular those articulated by the clergy and social reformers (Bates 2011:160). In nineteenth-century Britain, in particular, the vogue for uniform satisfied the desire amongst social reformers for rationality and modesty. The

Lutheran minister Theodor Fliedner, whose pioneering Kaiserwerth Deaconess Institute in Prussia was instrumental to the modernizing of nursing, in part achieved this through the adoption of uniforms (Hardy and Corones 2017). Nightingale visited the Prussian Institute and wrote about it enthusiastically. While fashion did have a part to play in the development of nurses' uniforms, the styles favored were modest and practical, and the new "uniformity of their dress was the mark of their status as independent and educated" (Hardy and Corones 2017: 529). Uniform, critical to the modernization of nursing, had a complex relationship with modern fashion. Rational dress modeled on fashion mediated the challenges of creating a new generation of trained nurses that might potentially threaten older practitioners.

This all-female occupation was to use the uniform to re-create the image of nursing by mixing elements of both domestic service and feminine fashion, while retaining current ideas of feminine respectability (Bates 2011: 175–6). Thus, even uniform schemes devised by social reformers—who were often hostile to fashion—clearly made concessions to fashionable dress. Pioneers sought to reproduce specific kinds of social identities; in this case, Fliedner saw fit to adapt the contemporary dress of married middle-class townswomen from the lower Rhineland, to establish nurses, often unmarried and working class, as respectable professionals so they could work in public without censure. Both models of nursing uniform demonstrate that these experiments drew on fashion in order to establish, create and reproduce a 'new femininity.' More significant, though, were the ways in which fashion could leaven the more austere, masculine values built into uniform design. A few fashionable details can usefully dilute the stern masculine uniform aesthetic, a technique that also offers a comforting reference point to the social values of the day. In Second World War recruitment, combining uniform and fashion showed how "effective the military was at using the designer uniform to establish group identity" (Ryan 2014: 428) for women serving in the US Navy and Coast Guard. Thus, to separate uniform and fashion can obscure how significant their relationship was in meeting the aesthetic needs of liberal democracy.

Uniforms and surveillance

The emergence of modern uniforms were, amongst other things, a means by which the rational needs of the institution could meet the social and psychological needs of gendered performance. What women experience in uniform depends upon context: nurses in the nineteenth century uniform identified them with their public service role, but later in the twentieth century uniforms were the focus of complaints that they sexualized women in the workplace, particularly for airline, retail, and catering staff. If uniform can liberate women by offering them an official role in the public sphere, it can equally be oppressive and the source of their objectification. Uniform schemes conjure up an image of imposed authoritarian systems that deny the wearer's agency, but this might just be a caricature; after all, uniforms have been 'fashioned' for a variety of reasons. Equally, the image of fashion as dictatorial requiring compliant uniformity of its followers might also be a myth. What both of these images obscure is the extent to which democratic ideals drove the regulation of appearances in various institutions in the nineteenth century. Emerging uniform schemes symbolized a convergence of utopian and utilitarian ideals. It was only later that they would be interpreted as authoritarian.

In schools, uniforms were often part of a whole aesthetic system that incorporated the design of classrooms and clothes, instructional materials and the ordering of objects (see Stephenson, this volume). It was egalitarian discourse that saw the uniform become a symbol of "economic, hygienic and democratic attire in tune with the expansion of mass schooling" in Argentina and the US at the start of the twentieth century (Dussel 2006: 181). Here, uniform creates an austere image in contrast to the waste commonly associated with fashion and luxury. Combined with British Victorian values of morality and virtue, the school uniform embodied new models of citizenship based on active work on the self (Dussel 2006: 186). Performing citizenship daily gave clothing a role in the discipline of schoolchildren and the regulation of their bodies could be achieved by regular checks to see whether they were 'properly dressed.' Uniform was thus not only a form of clothing but a means by which institutions could locate deviance in the bodies over which they had power. By the 1890s, once uniform was widespread it was thought to be part of a system of social control, but uniform schemes also emerged from a desire for restraint and equality. Patriotic nationalists saw uniform projecting an image of collective power, but later when establishing institutions they also might have employed them to impose collective discipline.

This perspective on uniform is well documented by sociologists and historians who draw on the work of French philosopher Michel Foucault. For Foucault, modern institutions subjected the body to a "normalising gaze" (1991, 1990, 2001), a model that has been adopted to consider how uniform clothing is used in various contexts to embody collective disciplines. The anthropologist Brian McVeigh examines what Japanese high school uniform means through the concept of the "normalising gaze," which for him became central to the maintenance of strategic schooling as part of a nationalist economic project (1997: 195). Here, uniform inscribes bodies to reflect particular constructions of citizenship. Daniel Purdy also finds Foucault's ideas compelling to contrast two modes of visibility—the tactical and the fashionable—in his work on the eighteenth-century Prussian army uniform (2003: 23–45). His account of the development of a soldierly aesthetic suggests that simplicity was instrumental to a disciplinary field of vision, but he also concludes that Foucault misses the role of the erotic in the construction of the military body (Purdy 2003). Modern uniforms offer a system to mark—and make visible—bodies for classification and discipline. As McVeigh and Purdy suggest, uniform orders people within disciplinary structures, but projects such as these often enlist fashion to deflect from sterner aspects; its magical qualities can appear to recreate and transform the body.

Much analysis of modern uniform emphasizes discipline and control, omitting the driving force of the erotic, as Purdy points out, an aspect of uniform that is, however, clearly present in many fashion images. Despite the currency of analyses that characterize uniform as surveillant, it would be foolish to ignore the pleasure many people take in wearing uniform. The new nurse's outfit, as discussed, enabled women to perform a public role, and as one young nurse in the 1930s on an all-male ward put it, "my uniform gave me a feeling of security and authority" (Hardy and Corones 2017, 528). In a contemporary study of white-collar masculinity in the US, men who were not troubled by conformist tendencies in their work lives were also likely to demonstrate a "strategic embrace of conformity" in dress to increase their chances of upward mobility (de Casanova 2015: 86). This was particularly the case with the men's suit and, as such, its history is complicated by gender and class politics that made it a site of struggle between democratic ideals and the conformity demanded in a disciplinary society.

A sartorial embodiment of Western democracy, the men's suit is a good example of a civilian uniform, perfectly embodying that compromise between democracy and discipline. By the late nineteenth century "democracy had found its apposite expression in the properly fitted suit," a powerful symbol of the various compromises that integrated capitalism with democracy in US society (Zakim 2003: 218). In many areas of civilian life uniform embodied new models of citizenship based on active work on the self, whereas fashion held connotations of an old world based on hereditary privilege and excess. New ideals embodied in the suit were, however, infused with sexism, arising as they did from the patriarchal assumption that manly modesty was a show of leadership and public spirit, a virtue not expected nor sought from women. The 'Great Masculine Renunciation,' a term given to the pattern of change men's dress underwent from fashionable display to plainness and austerity, has been widely documented as an anti-fashion movement. The term, invented by the psychologist John Carl Flügel to describe what he saw as the clear break from the fashionability of masculine dress in the nineteenth century, described the adoption of more austere clothing habits by men, best exemplified by the suit. Fashion historian Christopher Breward argues against this conventional reading of nineteenth-century masculinity in Britain, by looking to the range of men's consumption practices from 1860–1914, which found them engaging with fashion in less conspicuous ways than women (Breward 1999). Fashion would always upset the ideals built into the suit:

> Elite understatement was still a fashion statement; inconspicuous consumption still a form of consumption, however inverted or opposed to luxury it may have been. And once renunciation became fashionable, it lost its social cachet... anti-fashion lost its occult status, its ability to stand outside and above the world of fashion...with the great masculine renunciation it was now even more difficult to distinguish between men of principle and men of fashion.
>
> KUCHTA 2002: 174–5

When we ask whether the conventional suit is uniform or costume, it is clear that it straddles both; this is perhaps why debates in fashion history regularly engage with, and never resolve, questions about the tensions between conformity and individuality. Often, it is hard to draw the line between uniform and fashion.

Work uniforms in fashion and popular culture

Uniform in civilian life has become significant to our ideas about work. For instance, we make distinctions between manual and skilled workers by reference to the shirt collar. These distinctions between white- and blue-collar workers first emerged in the US in the 1920s. Those who were uniformed became known as blue-collar workers, due to the color of their workwear, while those in the professions, who wore suits and white shirts, were referred to as white-collar workers. These established dress codes formed the basis of class and gender differences largely thought to be common sense (Tynan 2016). Our social environment teaches us to "look for uniformity in the clothing of a group such as military and police and to overlook differences" (Joseph 1986: 115). Thus, we are taught to expect public servants to be dressed in this way. Regulation dress embodies the interests of the institutions that set it to work and promotes the idea that we can discern clear visible differences between people according to the public role they perform.

Uniforms ascribed social status to people who took on particular roles, professions and sporting activities in the nineteenth century. Once established, outfits that once marked status and conferred authority upon wearers became a sign system for fashion designers to raid for new trends and looks. Workwear has long been of interest to fashion designers, photographers and stylists. Furthermore, in many cases, workwear became leisurewear. Blue jeans went from being a garment "associated exclusively with hard work to one invested with many of the symbolic attributes of leisure" (Davis 1989: 348). Denim jeans were first created as workwear for farm laborers and miners in the western states of the US in the nineteenth century. By the 1960s denim jeans had taken on an entirely different set of meanings: casual, counter-cultural, and symbolizing the non-conformist outsider. Since then, denim jeans have become a staple for a

Figure 11.1 Katharine Hamnett Spring/Summer 1997 collection. Photograph by Niall McInerney, Bloomsbury Publishing Plc.

range of social classes. Simultaneously a fashionable item and a uniform, through age and wear this garment transforms into a highly personal item.

More recently, the streetwear label *Vetements* appropriated part of the uniform worn by the courier and parcel shipping company, DHL. The yellow T-shirt carrying the DHL logo was distinctive but ordinary, and for *Vetements* to sell a straight copy for a high-fashion price tag prompted various arms of the media to publicly wonder how such a mundane item could become a fashion trend (Cochrane 2016). *Vetements* have a distinctive approach to fashion that involves a rejection of glamor; their apparently humble name simply translates as 'clothing' and they identify as a 'design collective' rather than a fashion label. It is as if the illusions of post-war capitalism have faded, and along with it some of the early signs of stability, embodied by the work uniform. Now that Western models of work are more precarious, work uniforms are paraded as pastiche in the form of capitalist kitsch on the twenty-first century catwalk.

Post-war consumerism altered the traditional meanings of uniform, particularly for women. If young contemporary designers are appropriating uniform codes for the catwalk, then it is worth reflecting on why the fashion industry was first called upon to 'fashion' public service uniforms. In the case of airline staff, this new era required fashion designers to improve the image of the original 'stewardesses' who in the 1930s were nurses whose main role was to guarantee the safety of passengers. In Chapter 9 of this book, sociologist Prudence Black explores this 'fashioning' of uniform, through the Australian airline Qantas, and finds that post-war uniforms were highly charged, both culturally and socially; they articulated "how the profession was designed into existence through the appearance of these professional women" (2013:181). Like the creation of the nurse's uniform in the mid-nineteenth century, airline uniforms became prone to fashion changes in order to cope with the social anxieties ignited by the sight of working women. Fashion and uniform came into contact because they relieved the problems each caused the other. A uniform with military styling was thought to guarantee the safety role of the crew while the fashion treatment was deployed in an effort to normalize these women as professionals, even if some of the designs served to emphasize their sexuality in ways that might undermine their status.

Uniform signifies hierarchy and status within a closed social system, something that makes it attractive to fashion designers, journalists, and stylists keen to appropriate its sense of stability. Returning to the situated meanings of uniform brings into focus just how perfectly these uniform-fashion combinations embodied post-war modernity. The sense of order and authority that uniform conveyed made it the clothing of a disciplinary society, yet a new era of consumer choice sought to be represented by ideas of freedom and liberation. The new airline uniform for Qantas, with just enough military connotations, a cool modernist aesthetic, but also a strong sense of style and creativity, hit the right note to embody the age: "This new manifestation of the uniform created tension between control and release, stillness and dynamism that contributed a great deal to the mid-twentieth-century perception of the flight hostess as an eroticized glamorous figure" (Black 2013: 187). Regulated clothing embodies 'aesthetic labor,' a term used to describe the demand to make employees, particularly in service roles, look good and sound correct. Uniforms are designed to project a specific kind of power, but also a sense of restraint, a guarantee that the wearer will control their impulses in order to take care of customer needs first. Fashion/uniform interplays balance the competing demands for creativity and control. This calculated balancing of the dynamic creativity of fashion with the discipline and restraint of uniform sought to combine the traditional image of public service with a consumer desire for gratification. Uniform–fashion combinations were ideal to represent the contradictions of post-war society in the West.

Uniform and subcultures

Military uniforms first appeared as counter-cultural symbols in the post-war period when the issue of army surplus saw more military clothing spill onto the streets. Army clothing, adopted by various youth subcultures emerging in this period, became a symbol of establishment power that young people sought to challenge. Playing with the meanings of military uniform by disorganizing its signs and symbols was key to its power as street wear. Homoerotic depictions of men in uniform had also been in evidence within popular culture throughout the twentieth century, but became more explicit by the 1970s, when images started to play with the 'straight' ultra-masculine identity that uniforms project; police, army, and navy uniforms have all been used to challenge hegemonic masculinity. Military uniform had a certain power, which made it an ideal target for young people to dramatize and desecrate.

From the 1960s onwards, the fashion media favored images of uniformed bodies that emphasized sexual deviance and the most sensational aspects of war. Given the very real military conflicts taking place, this raises questions about the ethical basis of such images, but fashion editors and photographers are clearly excited by the dangers of war. In addition, such fashion images can always be

Figure 11.2 Jean Paul Gaultier, Spring/ Summer 1996 collection. Photograph by Niall McInerney, Bloomsbury Publishing Plc.

given ambiguous status and so are commonly interpreted as anti-war messages. Some fashion designers focus their interest on styles of military spectacle by referencing red coats, military lace, and elaborate headdresses. Such pre-modern styles of military dress recall a golden age when fashionability was a weapon on the battlefield. I focus on the appropriation of modern versions of military uniform in fashion and the values that they represent. There is something completely different at work with the fashionable appropriation of *modern* military uniforms, particularly the popular references to utility and combat issue.

By appropriating military clothing, kit, and symbols in their advertising, fashion designers convey an atmosphere of risk and transgression, so critical to a youth fashion market (Tynan 2013). For instance, French designer Jean Paul Gaultier has, particularly in the 1990s, referenced police, navy, and military uniform for their social and sexual power (Figure 11.2). This complex semiotic game would not be possible had it not been for the popularity of homoerotic images of uniform already present within pornography. In addition, whatever the reasons for the emergence of military references in streetwear, youth style that involves military clothing is now commonplace and returns regularly in fashion. In both pornography and youth style the military uniform suggests deviance. In the 1990s, British designers Katherine Hamnett and *Red or Dead* tapped into this rebellious attitude with their creative interpretations of military uniform. Maharishi, a youth-orientated British fashion label, which started out calling itself 'Pacifist Military Design', is a contemporary version of this. Maharishi appears to reference the DIY subversions of army surplus clothing popularized by youth subcultures in the 1970s and 1980s. 'Military chic' can be subtle and complex, a postmodern interplay of meaning rather than a direct reference to military uniform itself. What it does represent, though, is the militarization of popular culture. This is particularly notable in US society since the end of the Second World War, reflecting the interdependence of the military and the economy, which has made fashionable military clothing important identity markers (Davies and Philpott 2012: 52).

When uniform is referenced in fashion design and media, it clearly offers an opportunity for people to play with ideas of conformity/transgression. This chimes with my analysis of developments in the design of nurse and airline uniforms: the lure of transgression and playfulness was just as important as the incentive to conform. Their combined power mixed the benefits of liberation and discipline, playing with tensions between conformity and individuality that have long occupied fashion and dress historians. Can uniform clothing inspire spiritual or psychological uniformity? Or is uniform simply about power and domination? If uniform was invented as a corrective to the worst excesses of a fashion society, then is the appropriation of uniform by contemporary fashion a similar impulse in an age of austerity? When uniform is appropriated by fashion, it can be an act of resistance to the established order. Might it also be a sign of the dissolution of modern social structures represented by the stability of the uniformed citizen? Various popular images reflect this, but does this postmodern play that divests uniform of its power and authority indicate crisis? The fetishizing of Japanese schoolgirls in uniform demonstrates the importance of the military-style uniform to post-war Japanese society, but also the extent to which it has become an anti-establishment statement (Kinsella 2002: 219). In contemporary Japanese culture, uniformed characters are rarely conformist but instead are tragic, heroic and "shown to experience characteristic modes of dysfunctionality, disconnection, despair, or desire, which symbolize the political tensions and complications of modernity in Japan" (Kinsella 2002: 219). Thus, in the second half of the twentieth century, it is not clear whether the uniform represented conformity or resistance, or indeed whether now, in its new disorderly forms, it embodies the very complexity of contemporary subjectivity. The uniformed citizen in Japan has run its course in terms of an ideal, to transform into a sexualized and disorderly being, embodying all the anxieties of the age:

Schoolgirls in uniform have been elected the living metaphors of a widespread anxiety about the dissolving of citizenship and of the social subject in their entirety as they vanish into the financial interstices of the economy.

KINSELLA 2002: 236

What happens when the image of the uniform is desecrated by fashion or popular culture? Is the eroticizing of the uniform dramatizing a wider anxiety about the stability of social identity? Representations of uniform, particularly military uniform, are often highly eroticized. Uniforms suggest authority, but people in uniform are also untouchable. Add to that the fact that many wearing uniform (police and military) mete out punishment, or have control over our bodies (health professionals), and it is clear why uniforms form part of erotic fantasies. The uniform enables role-play in sexual relationships, where people can be consumed by the role suggested by the clothing (Steele 1996: 180). The fashion media has appropriated the fetishist's cult of uniform, with the result that we are accustomed to seeing women and men wearing styles that reference military and naval uniforms (Steele 1996: 180). By evoking fantasies of dominance and submission and representing the aestheticization of violence, the uniform injects images with a certain excitement and sense of danger. Fashion is a game of appearances whereby uniforms are highly charged socially, psychologically, and culturally.

Conclusion

Fashion media regularly returns to military themes, and workwear continues to be a source of fascination; uniform thus forms a significant part of the contemporary fashion scene. Is it really that surprising, though, to find military ideals of fitness, obedience, discipline, and control of eternal interest to the fashion industry? Uniform does what fashion does: it controls, manipulates, and transforms the body appearing to confer upon it new powers. If, historically, uniform schemes were a corrective to the excesses of fashion, then in the post-war period fashion has clearly tempered its more masculine and militaristic aspects. What is striking, though, is that separating uniform and fashion does not enrich our understanding of how these very different approaches to clothing have dressed the body in modernity.

Institutions saw uniforms as part of a whole aesthetic system that ordered objects and people. However sinister that sounds, it was an egalitarian discourse that saw the uniform become a symbol of a new economic rationality and the extension of rights such as education and health. Uniform provided solutions for utilitarian social reformers, but fashioning those uniforms helped to mediate many of the challenges that these radical societal transitions posed. Uniform did not necessarily become authoritarian until it became a key part of the iconography of fascist regimes, and even then fashion played a part. Indeed, French fashion appropriated aspects of Italian fascist uniforms in the mid-1930s, an early instance of designers displaying a fascination with the aesthetic side of fascism (Paulicelli 2004: 107). Uniform is not, therefore, an entirely rational form of dress but has always been 'fashioned' by current concerns and novelties. Fashion gives uniform a sense of time and place. Debates in fashion history often grapple with questions of conformity and individuality, which is clear from the ways in which the men's suit was interpreted and understood as neither a uniform nor a fashion, but possibly both. Fashion and uniform have been in constant dialog, but each represent very different ideas of what it means to be modern.

What uniform–fashion experiments did was to combine the best of both worlds, but the instability of the resulting designs reflected all the contradictions of post-war Western society. Those contradictions have only deepened, particularly when we witness the once stable uniform subject to scenes of disorder and confusion in contemporary fashion photography, whereby violence and catastrophe and the abuse of power is eroticized for effect. The hint of violence, too, is never far from fashionable depictions of military uniform, a reminder of just how highly charged this symbol has become. Is the routine use of military references in fashion part of a creeping militarization of popular culture? Is the fashioning of uniform in popular culture a sign of the instability of the idea of the uniformed citizen, or its ubiquity? Does the fascination with the uniformed citizen represent nostalgia for a time when this figure embodied dreams of democracy? That utopian dream now seems distant. The uniformed citizen, no longer taken seriously, is perhaps doomed to be a dysfunctional anti-hero now we find uniform divested of its authority. An object of postmodern play, the uniform, once a sign of stability, is now re-fashioned and paraded in ever more grotesque forms, and appears to embody all the fears and anxieties of the age.

References

Bates, C. (2011), "'Their Uniforms All Esthetic and Antiseptic': Fashioning Modern Nursing Identity 1870–1900," in I. Parkins and E. M Sheehan. (eds), *Cultures of*

Femininity in Modern Fashion, Durham, NC: University of New Hampshire Press, 151–79.

Black, P. (2013), "Lines of Flight: The Female Flight Attendant Uniform," *Fashion Theory,* 17 (2): 179–95.

Breward, C. (1999), *The Hidden Consumer: Masculinities, Fashion and City Life 1860–1914,* Manchester: Manchester University Press.

Cochrane, L. (2016), "Scam or Subversion? How a DHL T-shirt became this year's must-have," *The Guardian,* April 20. Available online: https://www.theguardian.com/fashion/2016/apr/19/dhl-t-shirt-vetements-fashion-paris-catwalk [accessed January 18, 2017]

Craik, J. (2005), *Uniforms Exposed,* Oxford: Berg.

Davies, M. and S. Philpott (2012), "Militarization and Popular Culture," in K. Gouliamos and C. Kassimeris (eds), *The Marketing of War in the Age of Neo-Militarism,* London: Routledge, 42–59.

Davis, F. (1989), "Of Maids' Uniforms and Blue Jeans: The Drama of Status Ambivalences in Clothing and Fashion," *Qualitative Sociology,* 12 (4): 337–55.

De Casanova, E. M. (2015), *Buttoned Up: Clothing, Conformity and White-Collar Masculinity,* Ithaca, NY: Cornell University Press.

Dussel, I. (2006), "When Appearances Are Not Deceptive: A Comparative History of School Uniforms in Argentina and the United States," *Paedagogica Historica,* 41 (1–2): 179–95.

Foucault, M. (1990), *The History of Sexuality,* vol. *1,* London: Penguin.

Foucault, M. (1991), *Discipline and Punish: The Birth of the Prison,* London: Penguin.

Foucault, M. (2001), *Madness and Civilization: A History of Insanity in the Age of Reason,* London: Routledge.

Fussell, P. (2002), *Uniforms: Why We Are What We Wear* Boston: Houghton Mifflin.

Hardy, S. and A. Corones (2017), "The Nurse's Uniform as Ethopoietic Fashion," *Fashion Theory,* 21 (5): 523–52.

Kuchta, D. (2002), *The Three-Piece Suit and Modern Masculinity: England 1550–1850,* Berkeley, CA: University of California Press.

Kinsella, S. (2002), "What's Behind the Fetishism of Japanese School Uniforms?" *Fashion Theory,* 6 (2): 215–37.

Laver, J. (1969), *A Concise History of Costume,* London: Thames and Hudson.

Maxwell, A. (2014), *Patriots Against Fashion: Clothing and Nationalism in Europe's Age of Revolutions,* Basingstoke: Palgrave Macmillan.

McVeigh, B. (1997), "Wearing Ideology: How Uniforms Discipline Minds and Bodies in Japan," *Fashion Theory,* 2 (1): 189–213.

Miller, A. (2007), *Dressed to Kill: British Naval Uniform, Masculinity and Contemporary Fashions 1748–1857,* London: National Maritime Museum.

Paulicelli, E. (2004), *Fashion Under Fascism: Beyond the Black Shirt,* Oxford: Berg.

Purdy, D. (2003), "Sculptured Soldiers and the Beauty of Discipline: Herder, Foucault and Masculinity," in M. Henn and H. A. Pausch (eds), *Body Dialectics in the Age of Goethe*. Amsterdamer Beiträge zur neueren Germanistik, Amsterdam, vol. 55: 23–45.

Ryan, K. (2014), "Uniform Matters: Fashion Design in World War II Women's Recruitment," *The Journal of American Culture*, 37 (4): 419–29.

Steele, V. (1996), *Fetish: Fashion, Sex and Power*, New York: Oxford University Press.

Tynan, J. (2013), "Military Chic: Fashioning Civilian Bodies for War," in K. McSorley (ed.), *War and the Body*, London: Routledge.

Tynan, J. (2013a), *British Army Uniform and the First World War: Men in Khaki*, Basingstoke: Palgrave Macmillan.

Tynan, J. (2016), "Status," in A. Palmer (ed.), *Cultural History of Dress and Fashion in The Modern Age*, Vol. 6. London: Bloomsbury, 131–50.

Zakim, M. (2003), *Ready-Made Democracy: A History of Men's Dress in the American Republic, 1760–1860*, Chicago: University of Chicago Press.

Part Six

Uniforming the Military

Military spectacle drives the management, discipline, and morale of soldiers. This section examines military uniform to consider how, on one hand, it functions as a visual representation of military values and, on the other, is integral to the technology of warfare. In a civilian context, uniform clothing makes the status of the wearer explicit, but does leave room for ambiguity. In military contexts, however, it is highly codified, having a range of very specific functions. The visual appearance of army clothing encodes hierarchy and military status; it is a primary site of ritualized training and the discipline of recruits. Most of all, military uniform distinguishes combatants from civilians in war zones. This section considers what military uniform actually does for troop morale, how it trains soldiers to think in particular ways and why it is used to determine legal questions in armed conflict.

These chapters draw attention to the ways in which uniform promotes regulated behavior, both to hide vulnerability in combat, but also to make soldiers from ordinary civilians. Clothing, body, and performance come together in military dress. One of the questions this research raises is what relationship women have to uniform in the masculinized setting of the army as explored in Stephen Herron's essay about gender and uniform in the Ulster Defence Regiment. Military service is a key cultural symbol of manhood, evident in the rules and regulations pertaining to women soldiers, which can be designed to keep them away from front line action. Women are often thought to be disruptive to the army, an assumption that legitimizes sexist jokes, harassment, and career restriction. Clothing has a special place in these debates; it is critical to presenting a particular image of the military unit, to those in and out of uniform. Here, the military institution and civil society can conspire to restrict full participation in army life, for those considered by virtue of their gender or sexuality, or both, to be unsuitable for active service. Various symbolic and ritual characteristics of the army, often material and visual, embed these values in the military institution.

These chapters also highlight a key question about the role of uniform in the military: when is a soldier a soldier? This question arises for scholars of International Relations, particularly since a recent 'aesthetic turn' has seen efforts within the discipline to redress a lack of research on visual cultures. This is the focus of Amin Parsa's chapter about the role uniform plays in legitimating killing in war zones. The reality is that on the battlefield, abstract knowledge of enmity takes on a visual form; attached to uniforms are rights and responsibilities, both legal and social. Regulations regarding what can be worn and when forms the basis of principles of distinction in armed conflict as agreed rules of engagement give military uniform its visual and material power. Technologies of deception, such as camouflage, are of particular interest here, being as they are an instance of military actors mediating the boundaries of legal and illegal violence. Uniforms mask soldiers from themselves and others in intriguing ways. This section explores the significance of military uniform, in order to ask how it has become culturally meaningful, inside and outside the army, and why it is so critical to questions of power and public truth in war and conflict.

12

Military Uniform and Lethal Targeting in International Law on Armed Conflict

Amin Parsa

There is a rich literature on military uniform as instrumental to establishing an institutionalized army, to attracting recruits, to instilling order and discipline, and to forging professional soldiers from ordinary citizens (Foucault 1995; Craik 2003; Münkler 2004; Tynan 2013; Peoples 2014). There is, however, much less research on the central role that military uniform plays in the international law of armed conflict, specifically its foundational principle: to distinguish between civilians and combatants.

International law of armed conflict is structured on three major principles: distinction, proportionality, and precaution. Yet it is the principle of distinction that the International Court of Justice takes as the single principle upon whose structure the whole body of international law of armed conflict is composed (International Court of Justice (ICJ) 1996). This is because this principle pertains to the characteristic activity of armed conflicts, that is, the use of lethal force in order to target enemy combatants and military objectives. The principle of distinction in its treaty codification reads:

> In order to ensure respect for and protection of the civilian population and civilian objects, the Parties to the conflict shall at all times distinguish between the civilian population and combatants and between civilian objects and military objectives and accordingly shall direct their operations only against military objective.
>
> Protocol Additional to Geneva Conventions, Protocol I 1977: Article 48

There is some distance between the protective impetus of this principle as is set out in the Geneva Conventions and its application during the course of an armed conflict. The law itself does not do much to bridge this gap, nor for that matter does it offer practical guidelines for soldiers, caught in the heat of the battle, on how to make a distinction between civilians and combatants, or on how to recognize a target amongst a mass of bystander civilians. Nor do such guidelines exist for international organizations, whose function is to oversee or evaluate the correct application of laws during armed conflicts. The fundamental questions here are; how can law create practical processes that facilitate soldiers in making the distinction during armed conflict and create a system of evaluation upon which it can judge the legality, or for that matter the legitimacy of every case, of lethal targeting? This chapter, in a way, will explore questions of legitimacy in lethal targeting in armed conflict. It does so, however, by attending to the unique and overlooked material functions that the military uniform plays in the operability of international law of armed conflict.

To set the claim of this chapter clearly and from the outset: law of armed conflict secures its own viability through a series of material interventions in the battlefield's organization to create distinctively visible categories of targets and non-targets. Law of armed conflict initially divide human and non-human objects present in the battlefield into two distinct categories of lawful and unlawful targets. Lawful human targets are known as combatants and non-human lawful targets are referred to as military objectives. The rest are non-targetable protected entities known as civilian population and civilian objects. From an operational point of view, then, law of armed conflict facilitates this categorization by imposing certain material requirements of visibility for objects and individuals that, under the law, can be lethally targeted. In the end, whom or whatever remains outside the legal requirements of visibility for targets is spared from deliberate lethal targeting.

The legal requirement of visibility, as far as targeting enemy combatants and protecting the civilian population is concerned, is predominantly carried out by the material and immaterial acts of the military uniform. For law of armed conflict, wear or non-wear of the military uniform is the threshold on the ground that determines whether an individual is a targetable combatant. Soldiers then also have the exclusive right to use lethal violence against his or her adversary, or against a protected, non-targetable civilian. Whenever an individual wearing a military uniform is spotted in the battlefield, international law assumes the lawfulness of the subsequent targeting, unless proven otherwise. It is through this simple visual function that military uniform realizes the ambitions of laws of armed conflict's most significant principle in protecting civilians during war.

Nicholas Mirzoeff uses the term 'visuality' to describe the relationship between visualization and re-ordering of fields of perception as a means to legitimize and instrumentalize power and violence (2011b). Mirzoeff defines visuality as a policing of perception, which orders fields of visibility by claiming the exclusive authority over both what is to be seen and how it is to be seen in any given configuration. Visuality, as such, refers to the configuration of practices and regulations—which are not necessarily perceptual or material—that order and control the affective registry of individuals in relation to what they see in every given context (Mirzoeff 2011b). The chief function of visuality is to safeguard the possibility of using the monopolized violence and exercising power whilst lending authority and legitimacy to that exercise in such a way that the relation between power and authority ultimately comes to seem self-evident and natural (Mirzoeff 2006, 2011a, 2011b). What follows is a re-systematization of a series of legal obligations from the point of view of the military uniform, whereby it functions to legitimize acts of targeting by creating distinctive forms of visibilities in the battlefield. This will then show how the military uniform, which starts as work attire, can become an active object that reconciles the ambitions of the principle of distinction, as an abstraction in the law, with its actual application during armed conflict by combatants. These legal obligations, which collectively hold together the principle of distinction and by extension the whole body of law of armed conflict, are namely: the combatant's obligation to self-visualize by wearing distinctive insignia, the prohibition of perfidy and the prohibition of the wearing of protected uniform emblems or uniforms of the opposing army. The defining characteristic of each of these obligations is that they are generated to fit with the features of military clothing.

Uniform, given its distinctive materiality on the surface, creates visually recognizable categories of people. This basic visual function makes it possible for the law of armed conflict to discriminate in the use of lethal force. However precise, given its materiality, a military uniform can be feigned, reproduced, or stolen and can also be worn by an adversary. Furthermore, uniforms can be—and indeed are—manipulated to trick the onlooker regarding what he or she sees. That is clearly the case with camouflaged uniform, which, instead of creating a clear visual distinction between soldier and background, is designed to hide its wearer from view. Furthermore, uniforms can be taken off and replaced by clothing that does not signify violence, for example, civilian clothing. These visual characteristics of military uniform have forced the law to adopt various obligations and prohibitions which form the legal structure that puts the principle of distinction into motion in the real world.

Knowledge-vision and the obligation of self-visualization

In order to understand the function of military uniform in the context of the law of armed conflict, we first need to unpack the basic operation of the principle of distinction. As already mentioned, according to this principle, it is only the combatant category that can be deliberately targeted: "It is only the soldier who is himself seeking to kill who may be killed" (Sitaraman 2009: 1757). Article 4 of the Third Geneva Convention of 1947 (hereinafter GCIII) broadly defines combatants as members of the armed forces and members of militia or volunteer corps who form part of such armed forces. To begin with, the very emergence of the category of combatant as the only legitimate target, is itself connected to the history of the development of the nation-state and its institutionalized army, in which military uniform played a key role. Within the strategic understanding of war, combatants are targetable since they represent the militarized willpower of the adversary in fulfilling its political objectives. This is most famously captured by the Prussian military theorist, Carl von Clausewitz, who made the link between war efforts and the achievement of political goals. In his seminal work, *On War*—published originally in 1832—which still acts as a point of departure in many strands of war studies, Clausewitz writes: "war is an act of force to compel our enemy to fulfil our will" (2000: 264). Accordingly, the use of force, launching of attacks, and targeting are means to an end, that is the submission of the enemy to our will (Mansfield 2008: 34). Within this dynamic, then, targets are those who constitute the formation of a willpower, which in turn blocks the realization of its enemy's political objectives.

The idea of a war in which violence is exercised discriminately only against combatants, in order to uphold the principle of distinction, becomes tenable only if we understand Clausewitz's observation in connection with the historical development of the nation-state and its institutionalized professional army. Prior to the emergence of the professional institutionalized state army, wars were characteristically long in duration, waged against the enemy estate and the population as a whole without discrimination, and, most significantly, were intended to not necessarily break the enemy's political will but to wear them down (Münkler 2004: 36 and 42–5). Once wars were "statised" (Münkler 2004), that is, made the exclusive prerogative of states, in the mid-seventeenth century, the state army emerged as a symbolic embodiment of a nation's political willpower. Concentration of a state's willpower in its army—the power to resist, defend, and invade—resulted in the operational transformation of the conduct of war. From this point onwards, war was transformed from the plunder and brutalization of an entire enemy population and its property to an organized and structured confrontation between professional armies, each representing the willpower of a particular political arrangement. Hence the famous maxim of Clausewitz applies: "war is policy with other means"[1] (2000: 280).

Law of armed conflict in Article 43(2) of the 1977 First Protocol Additional to the Geneva Conventions (hereinafter API) has internalized this relation between nation-state, its political intentionality, and the institution of the army and its members, by granting combatants the exclusive right to participate in hostilities, and to use weapons and weapon systems in order to injure and kill, while enjoying immunity from prosecution for such acts (Bothe et al. 1982: 243). This is why combatants can be legitimately targeted once they have been spotted in a battlefield, whether they are using their weapons or not. In fact, combatants are targetable even whilst they sleep (Schmitt 2009: 316; Solis 2010: 188). Moreover, law of armed conflict also adopted the Clausewitzian understanding of the enemy willpower as the main target. Accordingly, during an armed conflict every act of targeting should yield a definite and direct "military advantage" (Article 51(5)(b) of the API), a requirement that has been reflected in international law as early as 1868 in the St. Petersburg Declaration. Accordingly the only acceptable military advantage an army can seek is to "[weaken] the military force of the enemy" (Declaration November 29–December 11, 1868).

This criterion for lawful targeting I refer to as 'knowledge' of targetability; in other words, the realization that an individual contributes to an enemy's willpower and in so doing forms an antagonistic relationship with the adversary's fulfilment of political objectives. Here, 'knowledge' is the answer to the simple question of who the human targets are according to the principle of distinction. And what makes *them* a legitimate target, as opposed to civilians? Yet it is one thing to know that law permits the use of violence against adversarial armed forces and it is quite another to discern one from amongst the civilian population in the heat of the battle. The knowledge of targetability needs to be grounded concretely in order to operationalize the principle of distinction outside of the law book. This is where the military uniform enters the scene. The second paragraph of Article 4 of the GCIII provides some direction in this regard. This paragraph goes on to include into the category of combatants: "Members of other militias and members of other volunteer corps, including those of organized resistance movements, belonging to a Party to the conflict providing they fulfil four requirements." Most important for us is the requirement of having a fixed distinctive sign recognizable at a distance."[2] This requirement refers to the practical necessity that an individual's contribution to the willpower of the adversary—that is, the criterion of knowledge—needs to be perceptible for soldiers materially, if it is going to be a functional criterion for lawful targeting. Therefore, the characteristic of a lawful target is its visual distinguishability from non-targets. The requirement that combatants be visually distinguishable in Article 4(2) of the GCIII is even clearer in Article 44(3) of API:

> In order to promote the protection of the civilian population from the effects of hostilities, combatants are obliged to distinguish themselves from the civilian population while they are engaged in an attack or in a military operation preparatory to an attack.
> Protocol Additional to Geneva Conventions, Protocol I 1977: Article 44(3)

The International Committee of the Red Cross—as the organization entrusted by the international community to preserve and supervise the application of the Geneva Conventions, and a prominent authority in providing widely regarded interpretations of these conventions—in its commentary to the Geneva Conventions, refers to this "requirement of visibility" as a "fundamental obligation" (Pilloud et al. 1987: 527) that has reached the status of customary international law (Henckaerts and Doswald-Beck 2005: 384).[3]

One could say, then, that the lawful target is produced only when the abstract knowledge of enmity takes on a visual and material form. This is the second criterion of operability of the principle of distinction, to which I refer to as the requirement of 'vision.' As a result, the obligation of the principle of distinction is twofold. On the one hand, during attacks combatants must distinguish between lawful targets and civilians, while on the other hand, the whole operation of this first obligation depends on all combatants visibly distinguishing themselves by wearing fixed distinctive signs recognizable at a distance. Military uniform is that "fixed distinctive sign recognizable at a distance" as per Article 4(2) of the GCIII definition. The reason that Article 4 does not mention uniform by name has to do with maintaining the basic function of the military uniform in creating a visual distinguishability rather than a dismissal of the uniform as a material obligation. In fact, the wearing of military uniform as a distinctive and recognizable sign by regular forces "were deemed, by the 1874 Brussels Conference and the 1899 and 1907 Hague Peace Conferences, to be inherent in the regular armed forces of States" (Pilloud et al. 1987: 234–5).

Furthermore the replacement of uniform with a "distinctive and visible sign" in the second paragraph of Article 4 of the GCIII had to do with the growing worry of the drafters of the Geneva Conventions regarding the development of new technologies of deception and concealment, such as camouflage (Bothe et al. 1982: 465). The main source of concern was that new technologies might in the long run result in the production of military uniforms belonging to different armies that look more and more like one another and, as a result, undermine the visual function of the military uniform. Therefore drafters decided to insist on visual distinguishability rather than on the uniform itself (Pilloud et al. 1987: 465). This episode stands out as an example of how uniform and the modes of (in)visibility it produces effectively determined the wording of the law of armed conflict.

The targetability of a uniformed individual is presupposed with no further processing needed on the part of the onlooker. This is because military uniform binds the two elements of knowledge, enmity and distinctive visibility, into a material form distinguishable upon sight. As a result, military uniform makes the abstract knowledge of targetability concrete by what Sharon Peoples (2014) refers to as managing interpretation and perception to make certain kinds of associations self-evident. Targeting without knowledge of enmity is nothing but a random attack. The same applies to targeting with the required knowledge but without any visual distinction (Parsa 2017). Without uniform, the principle of distinction would not be operable. Reliance of the principle of distinction on military uniform in determining the boundaries of legal and illegal violence cannot be exaggerated. The role of uniform in authorizing the use of lethal force is such that international law even warns civilians against wearing clothes that may resemble a military uniform in color or pattern. The commentary to API notes:

> [A] journalist risks losing effective protection (even if he does not lose the *right* to protection to which civilians are entitled) if he closely follows a military unit engaged in action or if he gets too close to a military objective, since these are both legitimate objectives for attack. In the same vein, if he wears clothing, which too closely resembles military uniform, he will incur risks of a similar nature. In all these cases he therefore acts at his own risk: in exposing himself to danger in this way he would forfeit protection *de facto*.
>
> PILLOUD et al. 1987: 922

In the midst of a battle, military uniform—or other types of clothing that may resemble army clothing—can effectively remove individual legal protection and expose one to lawful lethal attack. In this sense, the immediate result of wearing a uniform, during an armed conflict, is to have one's body displaced from legal normativity, in which arbitrary deprivation of life is prohibited and punishable as murder, to another normativity in which lethal violence can be lawfully exercised against the said body.

Attached to the uniform are rights, privileges, and responsibilities. Combatant immunity in killing and injuring the adversary has already been mentioned. Additionally, if a civilian who is taking a direct part in hostilities is captured, he or she will not enjoy the privileges of prisoner of war status and can be prosecuted for crimes such as murder. Prisoner of war status is privileged and reserved for uniformed combatants only. Predictably, if a member of an armed force, a combatant, engages in warfare wearing civilian clothing without military uniform, that combatant can be prosecuted for the crime of perfidy (Article 37 of the API), a crime that aims to discourage unlawful deception of the enemy through the abuse of the legal and military connotations of civilian clothing, as opposed to the military uniform. Furthermore, crimes committed by a uniformed soldier during an armed conflict can result in the investigation of war crimes, whereas if a civilian commits the same crime, it results only in criminal proceedings. In other words, the military uniform is also the threshold that determines the applicable law on a particular body during an armed conflict. A materially sensitive re-organization of the law of armed conflict illustrate how other regulations that pertain to lethal targeting result from varying modes of visibilities and invisibilities embodied by military uniform.

Perfidy: wearing protected uniforms and camouflage

Military uniform shapes the law of armed conflict, as it pertains to lethal targeting, beyond the obligation to self-visualize as a combatant. The inherent logic of materiality is that the object at hand simultaneously inhabits both its potential for doing and undoing its original purpose. As Paul Virilio observes, "the invention of the ship was also the invention of the shipwreck" (2007: 10). Military uniform, as much as it is an instrument to create visibility, also prompts the making of forms of invisibilities in warfare. Given its material condition, military uniform can easily be taken off and replaced by civilian clothing. A military uniform can also be hijacked by an adversary and worn illicitly to create a false sense of trust. Moreover, technologies of deception and camouflage are multibillion-dollar businesses intended to subvert the visual function of the military uniform. This means that uniform, in each instance of (in)visibility that it potentially produces, is also a source of many more legal obligations, which in turn further shape the boundaries of lawful targeting. As the military uniform has the legal authority to determine which human body is a legitimate target, and it demonstrates the extent to which the law trusts it as signifier of the legality of violence, then it follows that such authority might be used by parties to a conflict in order to disadvantage an adversary. We regularly hear about non-state rebel groups in breach of international law and endangering civilian populations by attacking whilst wearing civilian clothes; they refuse to visibly distinguish themselves as fighters. However, the benefits of undoing the visibility of the military uniform is far too great for its use to be confined to non-state rebel groups. State armies are also regularly manipulating the visual requirements of the law of armed conflict.

In February 2002, *Médecins Sans Frontières* released a report in which it criticized the international coalition forces' targeting operations in Kandahar, Afghanistan (Kelly and Rostrup 2002). The report, published in *The Guardian* newspaper, claimed that US military forces had regularly operated whilst in civilian clothes—T-shirts, baseball caps, and jeans—and at times with concealed weapons. Others noted similar incidents in which US Special Operation Forces participated in hostilities dressed in traditional Afghan civilian attire (Solis 2010: 221). Another well-known episode concerns the Colombian Army's 'Operation Jaque' in July 2008. In an effort to free several hostages, most notably former presidential candidate Ingrid Betancourt, from the Revolutionary Armed Forces of Colombia (FARC), the Colombian military forces masqueraded as civilian members of an imaginary international humanitarian Non-Governmental Organization (NGO). The Colombian military forces dressed in civilian clothes—some wearing Che Guevara T-shirts and others wearing emblems resembling those of the International Committee of the Red Cross—flew into the FARC military base in a military helicopter painted in white and bearing the emblem of a fictitious NGO. As a result, the Colombian army freed hostages and managed to arrest the FARC commander of the camp, Gerardo Aguilar Ramírez (Brodzinsky and Davies 2008).

The above examples show how easy and effective it is for armies to operate without regard to the legal obligations of self-visualization by wearing military uniform. Law of armed conflict, mindful of such possibilities and in order to secure the authority of the military uniform as the signifier of lawful target, set out further prohibitions and punishments based on whether combatants wear or fail to wear the military uniform. 'Perfidy' refers to prohibited acts of creating forms of visibilities or, for that matter, invisibilities that:

> invite the trust and confidence of an adversary to lead him to believe that he is entitled to, or is obliged to accord, protection under the rules of international law

applicable in armed conflict, with intent to betray that confidence, that is to kill, capture or injure the adversary.

Protocol Additional to Geneva Conventions, Protocol I 1977: Article 37(1)

This prohibition is a customary rule of international law and given its detrimental effects on the visual order that protects civilians from harm breaking it can amount to grave breaches of the law of armed conflict, particularly if they result in killing or seriously injuring enemy forces (Article 85 of the API). Moreover, according to the Rome Statute of the International Criminal Court, treacherous injuring or killing of the adversary is a war crime (Rome Statute July 1, 2002, Article 8(2)(b)(xi) and Article 8 (2)(e)(ix)). Some relevant acts of perfidy that involve undoing the legal aesthetics of the military uniform are: feigning the intent to negotiate or surrender under the white flag of truce; feigning civilian, non-combatant status; and feigning protected status by the use of signs, emblems, or uniforms of the United Nations or of neutral or other states not parties to the conflict (Article 37 (1) of the API). Each of these actions invite and obtain the adversary's trust, because they either obscure the legal and political associations originally intended by distinctive visuals of uniforms and signs (such as the white flag of truce) or by hiding the willpower of the adversary, represented in the color and pattern of the military uniform (by wearing of civilian clothes or uniform of the neutral third party). It must be noted that such manipulations of uniform visibility constitute perfidy if done with the intention to kill, injure, or capture. The mere wearing of civilian clothes without participating in attack is not necessarily considered perfidy but nonetheless results in the loss of combatant status and its privileges, as is typically the case with spies and saboteurs (Article 46 of the API).

Wear of enemy uniform or protected uniforms

Once law depends upon the targetability of the military uniform, then forms of deception can arise from various practices around uniform-wearing. Just as replacing a military uniform with civilian clothing can provide protection, wearing an enemy uniform can provide unparalleled access. The possibility of wearing enemy uniform is another way in which the laws of armed conflict are written based on the uniform's visualization possibilities. On April 2, 2014, a Taliban suicide bomber who wore an Afghan police uniform killed six police officers and left four more wounded in Kabul's green zone (Latifi 2014). Similarly, so-called 'green-on-blue attacks' are constant in Afghanistan, and involve using the trusted uniforms of the enemy or allied forces in order to infiltrate protected areas before launching an attack. The color code here refers to the mapping system of International Security Assistance Force (ISAF) forces in Afghanistan. Blue refers to friendly forces, red to hostile, yellow to unknown, and green to neutral forces—in this case, Afghan national security forces (Defence R & D Canada September 2005).

These abuses of uniform are dealt with in other Articles of the Geneva Conventions. Accordingly, it is prohibited to use "the flags or military emblems, insignia or uniforms of adverse Parties while engaging in attacks or in order to shield, favour, protect or impede military operations" (Article 39(2) of the API). Inflicting serious injury or death on an adversary while wearing the enemy uniform, signs, or emblems constitutes a war crime (Article 8(2) (b)(vii) of the Rome Statute). Even though wearing the enemy uniform, rather similar to acts of perfidy, can certainly invite the trust of the enemy, there is a reluctance by international law commentaries, especially that of the International Committee of the Red Cross and state practices, to equate use of enemy uniform with perfidy (Henckaerts and Doswald-Beck 2005: 215). There is no conclusive debate on why such acts are not perfidious. However, going back to the knowledge-vision construction, perfidy endangers civilian lives by disrupting

Figure 12.1 Full-length image of British army soldier with gun by graffiti on wall. John Vlahidis/EyeEm. Copyright Getty Images [Image ref: 898334748].

the link between the visual meaning of clothing in wartime and established knowledge of how adversarial militarized willpower is represented. In contrast to perfidy, a fighter who wears enemy uniform still operates within the knowledge and visual framework of the targetability of uniform. In other words, a Taliban fighter who wears the ISAF military uniform may very well be mistaken by other Taliban fighters as an enemy target and as such invites not so much protection, but attack. The distinction between perfidy and the wearing of enemy uniform highlights this neat function of the wear or non-wear of military uniform.

Camouflage

The dependency of lawful targeting on modes of visibilities strongly links targeting to technologies of both seeing and deception. Training to target comprises the preparation of combatants to see, detect, and aim, and correspondingly this also involves equipping them with the techniques of concealment. The enemy uses both techniques to hide, and they need to be applied in order to be able to target the adversary first. "[T]raining in concealment [is] inseparable from training in observation: the practice of one invariably demand[s] knowledge of the other" (Wiseman 1951–3: 167; Forsyth 2013: 1038). Not surprisingly, then, the art of concealment and camouflage boomed during the First World War, just as aerial surveillance became integral to modern warfare. Rapidly developing technologies of vision, mainly centered on aerial reconnaissance, aerial photography, and industrialized cartography (Gregory 2015), turned the battlefield into what Virilio refers to as a "field of perception" (Virilio 1999). In response, new strategies of defense developed around artistic practices of camouflaging forces and weapons systems. This is a period in which zoologists, biologists, and artists worked together with armed forces to develop techniques to reduce the stark visibility of the military uniform.

On the British front, artists such as Solomon J. Solomon and Norman Wilkinson, zoologists and biologists such as Graham Kerr and Hugh Cott (Forsyth 2013), and American artists and naturalists such as Abbott Thayer, proved critical to the development of camouflaged uniform (King 2014). In principle, camouflage is the representation of the background as a foreground and enables techniques that can conceal objects and deceive the eye regarding movement. The more advanced digital camouflage combines artistic intervention with scientific methods in order to not so much blend the object with the background but to incorporate the neurophysiology of the human eye to deceive the brain and eye to "interpret patterns as part of the background" (King 2014; Campbell-Dollaghan 2014). Article 37(2) of the API permits use of such deceptive techniques under the category of permitted ruses of war:

> Ruses of war are not prohibited. Such ruses are acts which are intended to mislead an adversary or to induce him to act recklessly but which infringe no rule of international law applicable in armed conflict and which are not perfidious because they do not invite the confidence of an adversary with respect to protection under that law. The following are examples of such ruses: the use of camouflage, decoys, mock operations and misinformation.
>
> Protocol Additional to Geneva Conventions, Protocol I 1977: Article 37(2)

For armies to give soldiers permission to wear camouflaged uniform may appear to contradict the whole function of uniform according to the law of armed conflict. Camouflage appears to undo my argument regarding the dependency of the legal use of violence on the visual discernibility of the uniform. If uniform plays such a central role in constructing the architecture of legality in wartime, specifically because of the visibility it creates, then how is it possible that the same law permits practices that reduce the visibility of the military uniform? Camouflage uniform does reduce target visibility, and it may very well deceive the onlooker about what is seen, but once spotted, a camouflaged uniform works no differently than an ordinary one. It still clearly transmits the relation of the wearer with the adversary's militarized willpower. Camouflaged uniform is still an enemy uniform and can only conceal the body of the target; it does not visibly associate a body with a hostile polity. No matter how much it is obscured, the distinctive color and patterns of the adversarial uniform testify to the political antagonism against which, under the circumstances of an armed conflict, international law authorizes the use of lethal violence.

Conclusion

Military uniform is a logistical instrument for armed conflict, not only in so far as it enables the organization of an army and preparation for the battlefield, but also because the central principle by which laws of armed conflict operate depend upon it. The idea of protecting civilians during armed conflict and permitting the use of lethal violence solely against a defined category of individuals is only made possible when the military uniform is used to make a clear visual distinction between bodies. Uniform distinguishes the embodiment of the state's militarized and political willpower from civilian bystanders. Uniform acts as a bridge between the law in principle and the law in operation. In this sense, international law's authority in declaring some violence lawful and others unlawful is a by-product of the ways in which military uniform organizes the battlefield, into bodies upon whom violence can be exercised lawfully and those that must be protected from lethal targeting.

Did the targeted individual wear military uniform or civilian clothing? At the time of targeting, did the civilian's attire resemble a military uniform? Did the attacking combatant use lethal force while wearing a military uniform? What national army or international organization did the uniform signify while the combatant was operating? Was the uniform worn lawfully by an authorized member of a national army or was it abducted and worn by an enemy or participating civilian? These questions, together with other regulations not related to wear of uniform, form the process by which the principle of distinction can grant or refuse legal authority to an act of targeting. Military uniform brings together a whole host of regulations in the laws of armed conflict that together make authorization of the use of lethal violence in wartime possible. Without military uniform, the principle of distinction and its constellation of rules would be inoperable, and the legality of every act of lethal targeting in armed conflict would remain uncertain. In other words, the laws of armed conflict, through their power to legitimize wartime violence, operate as a mode of visuality organized by military uniform.

References

International Court of Justice (ICJ) (1996), Legality of the Threat or Use of Nuclear Weapons, Advisory Opinion.
Bothe, M., M. M. Eaton, K. J. Partsch, and W. A. Solf (1982), *New Rules for Victims of Armed Conflicts: Commentary on the Two 1977 Protocols Additional to the Geneva Conventions of 1949*, The Hague: Nijhoff.
Brodzinsky, S. and C. Davies (2008), "Colombia Hostage Rescue: The Audacious Plot that Freed World's Most Famous Captive," *The Guardian* (accessed February 11, 2016).
Campbell-Dollaghan, K. (2014), "The History of Invisibility and the Future of Camouflage," *GIZMODO* (accessed February 11, 2016).
von Clausewitz, C. (2000) *On War, The Book of War*, New York: Modern Library.
Craik, J. (2003), "The Cultural Politics of the Uniform," *Fashion Theory: The Journal of Dress, Body and Culture*, 7 (2): 127–47.

Declaration, The St. Petersburg, (November 29–December 11, 1868), *The St. Petersburg Declaration on Renouncing the Use, in Times of War, of Explosive Projectiles Weighing under 400 Grams.*

Defence R & D Canada (September 2005), *Commented APP-6A - Military Symbols for Land Based Systems: NATO's Current Military Symbology Standard.*

Forsyth, I. (2013), "Subversive Patterning: The Surficial Qualities of Camouflage," *Environment and Planning A,* 45 (5): 1037–52.

Foucault, M. (1995), *Discipline and Punish: The Birth of the Prison,* New York: Vintage Books.

Gregory, D. (2015), "Gabriel's Map: Cartography and Corpography in Modern War," in P. Meusburger, D. Gregory, and L. Suarsana (eds), *Geographies of Knowledge and Power,* New York: Springer.

Henckaerts, J. M. and L. Doswald-Beck (2005), *Customary International Humanitarian Law Vol. 1, Rules,* Cambridge: Cambridge University Press.

Kelly, M. and M. Rostrup (2002), "Identify Yourselves: Coalition Soldiers in Afghanistan Are Endangering Aid Workers," *The Guardian,* February 1, 2002 (accessed January 26, 2016).

King, A. (2014), "The Digital Revolution: Camouflage in the Twenty-First Century," *Millennium/ Journal of International Studies,* 42 (1): 397–424.

Latifi, A. M. (April 2, 2014), "Taliban Suicide Bomber Disguised in Police Uniform Kills Six in Kabul," *Vice News* (accessed February 11, 2016).

Mansfield, N. (2008), *Theorizing War: From Hobbes to Badiou,* Basingstoke: Palgrave Macmillan.

Mirzoeff, N. (2006), "On Visuality," *Journal of Visual Culture* 5 (1): 53–79.

Mirzoeff, N. (2011a), "The Right to Look," *Critical Inquiry* 37 (3): 473–496.

Mirzoeff, N. (2011b), *The Right to Look: A Counterhistory of Visuality,* Durham, NC: Duke University Press.

Münkler, H. (2004), *The New Wars,* Oxford: Polity Press.

Parsa, A. (2017), *Knowing and Seeing the Combatant. War, Counterinsurgency and Targeting in International Law,* PhD Dissertation, Faculty of Law, Lund University.

Peoples, S. (2014), "Embodying the Military: Uniform," *Critical Studies in Men's Fashion,* 1 (1): 7–22.

Pilloud, C, Y. Sandoz, C. Swinarski, and B. Zimmermann, eds (1987), *Commentary on the Additional Protocols of 8 June 1977 to the Geneva Conventions of 12 August 1949,* Geneva: Nijhoff.

Protocol Additional to the Geneva Conventions of 12 August 1949, and Relating to the Protection of Victims of International Armed Conflicts 1977 (Protocol I).

Schmitt, M. N. (2009), "Targeting and International Humanitarian Law in Afghanistan," M. N. Schmitt (ed.), *The War in Afghanistan: A Legal Analysis,* Newport, RI: U.S. Naval War College.

Sitaraman, G. (2009), "Counterinsurgency, the War on Terror, and the Laws of War," *Virginia Law Review,* 95 (7): 1745–1840.

Solis, G. D. (2010), *The Law of Armed Conflict: International Humanitarian Law in War*, Cambridge: Cambridge University Press.
Statute, Rome (July 1, 2002), Rome Statute of the International Criminal Court.
Third Geneva Convention Relative to the Treatment of Prisoners of war (August 12, 1949), Geneva.
Tynan, J. (2013), *British Army Uniform and the First World War: Men in Khaki*, Basingstoke: Palgrave Macmillan.
Virilio, P. (1999), *The Politics of the Very Worst*, New York: Semiotext(e).
Virilio, P. (2007), *The Original Accident,* Cambridge: Polity Press.
Wiseman, D. J. C. (1951–53), *Special Weapons and Types of Warfare, Volume III: Visual and Sonic Warfare*, London: War Office.

13

Military Uniforms and Women in the Ulster Defence Regiment

Stephen Herron

Academic research on the integration of women into the military remains in its infancy. More specifically, the participation of women in the military and the multiplicity of meanings that women in uniform can convey has been sidelined. This chapter, based on previous anthropological fieldwork, explores the role uniforms play in contributing to the performative characteristics of military operations, by transmitting particular kinds of messages to soldier and outsider. The focus of the discussion is an analysis of the Ulster Defence Regiment (UDR), a locally recruited regiment of the British Army who operated in Northern Ireland during what is commonly known as the 'Troubles,' a period of sectarian violence in Northern Ireland in the latter part of the twentieth century. Particular attention is paid to the symbolic characteristics of uniforms with respect to the 'Greenfinches,' as female UDR soldiers were nicknamed, and how their clothing both incorporated and challenged traditional masculine identities within this military context. By drawing on Erving Goffman's performances (1959) and Pierre Bourdieu's (1977) theory of symbolic violence, this chapter examines the cultural complexity of uniforms worn by female soldiers and considers the role of cartoon sketches featuring female soldiers, which were placed in UDR magazines during the Regiment's existence.

The creation of the UDR

Formed in 1970 as a replacement for the mainly Protestant/Unionist-controlled Ulster Special Constabulary (USC), the UDR has often been regarded as a controversial regiment of the British army, viewed with both affection and hatred by sections of the Northern Ireland population and further afield. Recruited within Northern Ireland and operational only during the 'Troubles' meant that a UDR soldier's killer could also be their neighbor. The Regiment was placed under the control of the British Army in order to avoid controversies that dogged the role of the USC, and in the hope that it would prove more appealing to both Catholic and Protestant. At the time when the Regiment became operational, on April 1, 1970, it had 2,440 members, of which 946 were Catholics. Perceived targeting of local Catholics, coupled with allegations of collusion with Loyalist paramilitaries, alienated the UDR from large sections of the population, but the Regiment was held in high esteem and even affection by many others, which mirrored the deep divisions that existed in Northern Ireland as a whole. Unable to rid themselves of continued controversies, the UDR merged with the Royal Irish Rangers in 1992 to form the Royal Irish Regiment, ending its twenty-two-year existence. Responsible for killing six civilians and two members of the Irish Republican Army (IRA), the Regiment also suffered as a result of the troubles, enduring the deaths of 197 UDR officers and soldiers, while a further sixty-one ex-soldiers were killed after they left the Regiment (UDR Association 2011).

Following the formation of the Ulster Defence Regiment in 1970, it took another three years before women were recruited. With the Regiment's manpower and resources becoming increasingly strained following a dramatic rise in Troubles-related incidents (1972 witnessed the largest number of incidents and deaths in a single year during the Troubles), in 1973 it was decided to approve the introduction of women into the Regiment. Insurgents in Northern Ireland also began to see the strategic benefit of using women in operations, most notably as transporters for bomb-making equipment and as look-outs for their male counterparts. In response, and to enable UDR soldiers to search females, women were recruited. Consequently, the UDR would be the first regiment in the British Army to recruit females as front line infantry soldiers.

Women normally resident in Northern Ireland between the ages of eighteen to fifty, and in some cases fifty-five, were eligible to apply for enrolment (Ulster Defence Regiment 1983), requiring one eight-hour duty per week, which could take place either during the day or night. At these early stages, Greenfinches' principal duties consisted of searching civilian women, acting as radio and telephone operators, and carrying out clerical and administrative tasks. Women initially served as part-time soldiers, which extended to full time as the structure of the Regiment changed. Structural changes were combined with increased operational roles including mobile and foot patrols. As the Regiment became more professionalized, the numbers of female soldiers in the Regiment also grew. Statistics show that by the early 1980s there were approximately 750 women serving against an overall membership of 6,000. This made up 11.5 percent of the Regiment's strength (Ulster Defence Regiment 1983). However, despite membership growth, integrating women into this heavily masculinized environment was difficult. The practices and symbols they applied to distinguish male and female soldiers, as well as soldiers and outsiders, draw attention to the fluidity and complexity of the military's symbolic and ritual characteristics and especially to the performative characteristics of the military environment.

Military operations as performances

Previous anthropological research into symbols and rituals in military contexts have demonstrated their wide-ranging impact. These works have included research into military uniforms (Lomsky Feder and Ben Ari 1999; Maček 2001) and the role of military language (Partridge 1948; Murray 1986; Cohn 2000; Gavriely-Nuri 2010). Particular focus has been placed on research into ritual and symbolism in military parades and public commemoration events (Schwartz 1982; Zerubavel 1995; Jarman 1997; Azaryahu 1999; Ben-Amos 2003). A major theme arising from research on military parades and events is their performative characteristics. For Don Handelman (1998), public events are constituted through their intentionality (or design) and their practice (or performance). However, research into the performative characteristics of the military should not be restricted to highly formalized public rituals, an approach that fails to address the impact of symbols and rituals in the field of combat, where the military is designed primarily to function. Ritual and social conflict are intrinsically linked and often ritual is designed as a response to specific instances of social conflict (Turner 1957; Gluckman 1962).

Performances, as viewed by Goffman, are the "activity of an individual which occurs during a period marked by his continuous presence before a particular set of observers and which has some influence on the observers" (Goffman 1959: 22). In many respects, viewing the military operation as a performance is an extension of what happens when training soldiers. The capacity to learn is closely connected to the ability to perform these same tasks. Soldiers require a series of symbolic and ritualistic characteristics to be on display in order to turn these physical acts into military acts. Goffman's work on presentations of the self provides important clues regarding the complex range of actions, emotions and interactions taking place between the soldier and insurgent or civilian. These encounters, which could be described as scenes, involve the performer facing a

Figure 13.1 UDR soldiers on parade at Steeple Camp, Antrim, Northern Ireland. Remembrance Sunday, 1970. Photograph by Len Kinley. Wikimedia Commons: File [Soldiers_of_UDR_on_parade_at_Steeple_Camp, Antrim.jpg].

series of problems on how to communicate a particular image of themselves to their audience. These numerous 'fronts' which involve the use of dramatological devices and equipment, ranging from clothing, body gestures, language, gender, age, and insignia of rank are "part of the individual's performance which regularly functions in a general and fixed fashion to define the situation for those who observe the performance" (Goffman 1959: 22), and are required to promote dramatic realization. However, this also requires considerable effort on behalf of the soldier as highlighted by Arlie Hochschild's concept of emotional labor, whereby one suppresses inner feelings "in order to sustain the outward countenance that produces the proper state of mind in others" (1983: 7). UDR soldiers used emotional labor to suppress their feelings; facial and bodily displays of emotion were vital in order to "coordinate self and feeling so the work becomes effortless" (Hochschild 1983: 8), enabling them to have a commanding presence and maintain control on operational duty. Military operations act as a filter through which other symbolic and ritual characteristics can be on display, both visually and non-visually. This is most vividly illustrated by uniforms, and the multiple roles and meanings they have for both soldiers and outsiders, especially in how they shape female soldiers' conceptions of military life.

The examination of women in the military provides insights into the connections between militarism and sexuality by highlighting "the ways in which a militarized society penetrates into the very texture of women's lives" (Amott 1984: 7). Often "the military has been defined traditionally as a masculine institution; it may be the most prototypically masculine of all social institutions" (Segal 1995: 758). My focus on the connection between the military and women, however, is not only about analysing it as a male preserve; it considers identities created in the military institution, but also those that are negotiated and challenged, within a particular set of social contexts and structures. Focusing on the experiences of UDR women allows for analysis into the Regiment's power to shape, control, and recast the lives of women who served in order to ask how they variously accepted and challenged their positions.

Previous research has shown the complexities facing women in the military. Cynthia Enloe (1983) draws attention to the military as a patriarchal institution while Karen Davis (2007) highlights how women's ability to perform in leadership roles in combat is constantly questioned and compromised. Emphasis has also been placed on the marginalization of women from mainstream military activities (Howes and Stevenson 1993; Segal 1995; Enloe 2000) and on the distinctions made between women and men in the military, particularly in relation to their roles and responsibilities. Meira Weiss (1999) highlights how female soldiers are often described as "non-combatants" in a definition shared cross-nationally, for example, in Germany (Tuten 1982; Segal 1995: 760) or the UK (Goldman 1982; Campbell 1993). According to Mady Segal (1995), when the military require women, their roles are diminished and de-valued. A process of cultural amnesia takes place which fails to recognize the contribution of women, and in the aftermath of conflict, female soldiers are reconstructed as minor players. Segal further argues that the greater the importance placed on actual fighting, especially ground combat, the less participation by women, whereas peacekeeping roles and those resembling domestic policing are likely to have greater female participation.

Segal's interpretation of women's military roles provides an interesting reference point when examining the contribution of the Greenfinches and their place within the military establishment, especially as the UDR were the first regiment in the British Army to recruit females as front line infantry soldiers. While many nations currently conscript men, few require women to serve in the military (Howes and Stevenson 1993; Segal 1995). Therefore, the mobilization and experiences of women in the UDR offers a case study through which to explore how they constructed their identities within a masculinized social context. Bourdieu's (1977) description of "symbolic violence" provides a conceptual basis for such analysis. Understanding that such symbolic or everyday violence encompasses the implicit, legitimate, and routine forms inherent in particular social, economic, and political formulations, provides a basis upon which to examine the extent to which UDR Greenfinches were forced, often unknowingly, to accept their conditions, or how female soldiers' complicity with the military environment perpetuated their positioning in the Regiment.

By concentrating specifically on female UDR soldiers and the uniforms they wore, this discussion demonstrates how the symbolic and performative characteristics of the military are not only prevalent in the physical act of soldiering. They are implanted throughout the military structure as is evident in cartoon images and sketches in UDR magazines, which will be examined below. The sexual imagery and innuendos in such sketches form the basis for arguing that such visual imagery showcased both the attitude of male soldiers towards their female counterparts and the extent to which female soldiers were prepared to both challenge and perpetuate such attitudes.

Uniforms: a very public camouflage

Military uniforms symbolize the multiplicity of meanings at play in an armed force. Accordingly, their study can help to "explore both the individual and collective identities that the dressed body enable" (Hansen 2004: 372). Like all clothing, their key characteristic is that they both touch the body and face outward towards others. However, the paradox of military uniform is that it is designed to camouflage and conceal the soldier from the enemy in hostile environments, while at the same time it offers a very visual representation of a military force, immediately recognizable to outsiders.

Uniforms play an important role in contributing to the performative characteristics of military operations by transmitting particular messages to the outsider, which the military hope they will accept, most notably regarding military power and authority. The public "are asked to believe that the character they see actually possesses the attributes he appears to possess, that the task he performs will have the consequences that are implicitly claimed for it" (Goffman 1959: 28). Soldiers, consequently, use uniforms not only to construct their appearance but also to shape identity, reinforcing the experiential dimension and the quality of clothing, which in turn is influenced by the situation and structure of the wider social context (Woodward 2005). As a result, "clothing, body and performance come together in dress as embodied practice" (Hansen 2004: 373). Yet the subjective and social characteristics of uniforms may lead to "considerable ambiguity, ambivalence and therefore uncertainty" (Hansen 2004: 372). Such uncertainty is reinforced by the fact that military uniforms act as a multi-layered symbolic transmitter. While the uniform may in a general sense act as a symbol, within this lies a further layer of smaller, yet equally important symbols, shown below, which combine to give a uniform its potency and symbolic power.

For example, on the UDR cap is a badge, which depicts a harp framed by the Maid of Erin and surmounted by a crown created during the reign of the current Queen of the United Kingdom. The harp, a symbol traditionally associated with Ireland, has historical resonance as Irish regiments have worn it for centuries. While the harp framed by the Maid of Erin denotes the Irish aspect of the Regiment, the crown symbolizes the authority of British rule. Combining the Irish and British symbols acted as a visual representation of the political unification between Northern Ireland and Great Britain and reminds outsiders of the political position and objectives this regiment had in the Northern Ireland conflict. It also symbolized the actions they undertook as a legitimate force, which had been enshrined in law. In other words, such symbols helped to justify and professionalize the Regiment.

Uniforms are particularly important in demonstrating the professionalism and competency of a military force when on duty. For UDR soldiers, the provision and wearing of the correct uniform was integral to army life and imperative for the Regiment to be recognized as a professional force. Yet, as illustrated by my (Herron 2013) research with former UDR soldiers, during the Regiment's infancy a number of them did not have access to full uniform, and until they had, did not feel themselves to be soldiers. The symbolism of the uniform was thus as important as its functionality. Uniforms instilled a sense of confidence and security in the minds of the soldiers who wore them. They acted as a metaphorical border between the danger and uncertainty of the outside world and the controlled and regulated arena of a military body. By putting on the uniform, these soldiers were about to enter a special behavioral frame (Bateson 1972; Handelman 1977) but did so in the knowledge that this in turn increased their risk of identification by the enemy.

Uniforms: symbol of a soldier's control

Writing about reservists in the Israel Defense Forces (IDF), Edna Lomsky Feder and Eyal Ben Ari (1999) observe that new recruits putting on uniforms are donning disguises, or wearing masks. As such, soldiers during their stint of duty were temporarily not themselves, but people placed in special circumstances, a situation which may allow or demand from them a certain type of behavior. Uniforms had the role of masking soldiers both from others and from themselves; they enabled a temporary separation between the personal identity of the user and the action undertaken. Uniforms therefore had a paradoxical role. On one level they were designed to camouflage soldiers, yet they were also designed to announce themselves clearly to outsiders. Uniforms had a dual purpose, to both hide the soldier, but also to bring him or her into view.

Ben Ari and Lomsky Feder's work stresses how uniforms transform a soldier into a performer in the military arena. Like the use of costumes in a play, the uniform acts as a cloak, masking personal identity and transporting the person into a new world which is likely governed by rules that are different than those of civilian life (1999: 175–6). Just as uniforms are designed to protect soldiers physically from the dangers of conflict, these costumes also protect their identity, their role as a social being, and as a whole person in the social world separate from the trials and traumas of conflict. Yet the circumstances for UDR soldiers were even more complex. As a locally recruited army, the ability of UDR soldiers to escape the perils of life in the military did not end when they removed the uniform. When carrying out fieldwork with former UDR soldiers, I (Herron 2013) uncovered the complexity facing their daily interactions when I discovered that they thought it safer to be on duty than off duty and out of uniform. Consequently, for my research (Herron 2013) it emerged that instead of uniforms acting as a metaphorical boundary between military and everyday life, for a number of soldiers wearing a uniform actually gave them a sense of control over their own destiny, which they could not achieve in their private life. Ivana Maček (2001), who carried out research into soldiers' experiences of war in Sarajevo, postulates that for soldiers, uniforms were representative of a collective ideal that disguised and denied individuality. Instead, soldiers saw themselves as interchangeable, the same as every other soldier and part of a collective structure fighting on behalf of a particular side and for an ideal. This emphasis on how uniforms stress collectively and apparently deny individuality should not be seen in a wholly negative light. For UDR soldiers, who were living in an everyday environment of uncertainty and change, the predictability and certainty that being part of a collective body brought them was a source of much comfort and strength.

Goffman's (1959) argument concerning impression management takes the idea of disguise further. In many respects, uniforms and military symbolism are a vital part of deception tactics used operationally by soldiers to manipulate both insurgents and the wider civilian population in counter-insurgency contexts. Uniforms and equipment are designed to create the impression of power and authority. However, UDR soldiers were in reality made vulnerable by the unpredictability of the conflict and responses of insurgents and the wider population. Consequently, soldiers were not fully convinced by the power they sought to portray in these performances. For Goffman, such impression management holds two important distinctions: expressions given and those given off. While individuals can control expressions given, others can access both impressions given and given off. As such, when the performer has no belief in their own actions or in the responses of the audience, they are forced to engage in actions that manipulate and cover such impressions.

Such actions once more highlight Hochschild's (1983) concept of emotional labor and the need to distance one's own feelings but also to regulate bodily and facial displays. Emotional labor is important to understand how soldiers cope because if unsuccessful they might be viewed by others, including the public, insurgents, and fellow soldiers, as unable to withstand the pressures of operational duty. As Susan Martin (1999) argues, regarding police officers, their ability to engage in emotional labor affects how other officers and citizens view them. Similarly, UDR soldiers had to engage in a process of emotional management, which covered their inner feelings in order to obtain the acceptance and compliance of others. Yet, for such emotional labor to be effective in transmitting certain messages to others also required symbols, such as the uniform, to hide the vulnerability of soldiers in hostile areas, thus demonstrating "the potentially infinite cycle of concealment, discovery, false revelation and rediscovery" (Goffman 1959: 8) in these performances.

The changing style of uniforms

When the Regiment was first founded, uniforms consisted of a simple infantry kit with flak jackets, tin helmets, olive-green field dress, green jacket trousers, and khaki shirts. The green berets worn by members led to their unofficial title, 'Green Tops.' Soldiers were issued DMS (Directly Moulded Sole Boots) boots. In order to seal the gaps between soldiers' trousers and boots, they wrapped puttees—tightly bound strips of cloth—around their ankles. Trousers, which were called 'denims' or 'lightweights,' were originally olive green and not fireproof.

Figure 13.2 A platoon of UDR soldiers march past Mahon Road Barracks, Portadown, Co. Armagh, Northern Ireland c. 1970s. Photograph by Thunderer. Wikimedia Commons: File [11_UDR_March_Past.jpg].

Original body armor was also basic in design, consisting of a flak jacket worn over their uniform. This flak jacket was layered kevlar ballistic fabric that felt like padding; the detachable pockets and webbing to hold equipment was light order. This was primarily because soldiers were never too far away from base so they did not need to carry equipment. The supply of white winter duffel coats underlined the makeshift nature of the Regiment in the early days, and while it would keep a soldier warm and concealed in the Arctic, they made soldiers an easy target in the green, grassy slopes of Ireland. Weaponry was also outdated. Soldiers were issued with Second World War surplus .303 Lee Enfield rifles and Bren guns.

However, the growing length and intensity of the Troubles coupled with an increasingly professional enemy meant that uniforms changed to become more orientated to counter-insurgency. This saw the original army kit adapted and developed until it became what was termed 'Combat Soldier 95,' which was introduced in late 1990. This was a form of patterned uniform similar to the version used by the contemporary British military and consisted of trousers and shirts, with body armor worn under the uniform. With ceramic plates embedded inside, Combat Soldier 95 became known as 'Northern Ireland body armor,' because it was adapted to meet the challenges of insurgency threats. Soldiers' helmets also changed to no longer use tin, and had a visor in place for public-order incidents. Weaponry was also upgraded from a basic self-loading rifle (or SLR) to what became known as the SA 80. Furthermore, baton guns were issued and if soldiers were involved in public-order duties, they would have riot shields, batons, and fire extinguishers. Towards the end of the UDR's existence, soldiers were issued with shin guards, elbow pads, and shoulder pads for public order duties.

As attention to soldiers' kits grew, so did the effect of operational location on uniforms. Specific urban and rural kits were designed. For example, in an urban area a patrol was never far from base, but in rural areas soldiers could be miles away, and because of the danger posed in areas such as South Armagh, military vehicles could not be used to the same extent. Therefore, rural soldiers had to be self-contained. This required them to carry large amounts of equipment and supplies, enough to keep them out on duty for at least twenty-four hours. The changing design and functionality of uniforms had a significant effect on external perceptions of the Regiment. In the UDR's formative period, it was perceived as a body of relatively untrained locals but altering the uniform helped to improve perceptions of professionalism both within and outside the Regiment. Yet the perceptions of women in the Regiment would underline the complexities and struggles they faced when integrating into a heavily masculinized environment. Just as uniforms project an image—make an impression—they also project inwardly affecting the confidence and attitudes of soldiers.

Greenfinches, uniforms, and weapons

While uniforms are the visible representation of a military force, and used in order to project individual and collective identities, for Greenfinch soldiers their purpose was even more complex. Not only were they designed to distinguish soldier from civilian, but their uniforms also helped to reinforce gender differences. Kjeld Galster and Marie-Louise Nosch (2010) refer to the historical connotations of military uniforms whereby their aesthetic appeal can have a significant impact on soldiers' morale. Galster and Nosch observe how military leaders throughout history have used the masculine design of military uniform and noted its impact upon soldier and civilian. Referring to Hugo Boss's line of Nazi uniforms during the 1930s, Galster and Nosch highlight this as one example of the importance military leaders placed on uniforms historically to display particular (masculine) images.

With respect to the UDR Greenfinches, during the early years of the Regiment, uniform kit consisted of a khaki skirt (which would later become a piper green skirt), white blouse, green pullover, green beret, and black shoes. Such kit was not compatible with the demands placed on frontline infantry soldiering, especially counter-insurgency operations in rural areas. Therefore, uniforms helped to restrict women's operational roles, relegating them to more supportive functions, thus reinforcing the view that they were not 'real soldiers.'

Furthermore, if we understand that the purpose of a military force is the engagement of violent acts, then, soldiers require weaponry to be successful. However, UDR Greenfinches were denied the opportunity to carry weapons on patrol. Only male soldiers on patrol were allowed to handle weapons, and the only time that female soldiers carried them was on a firing range and in non-combat scenarios. To understand attitudes towards women soldiers carrying weapons, it is important to appreciate the symbolic power attributed to the weapon itself. The weapon "is a perceptual instrument that organizes prospects, frames a historical landscape before itself: a political spectacle of targets as moral objects" (Feldman 2001: 55). A weapon's ultimate power does not just rest with its physical impact upon the human body, but in the responses of actors and audiences to its potential capabilities, which in turn make it an icon-making device.

The lack of willingness to allow women to carry arms was related to the symbolism associated with weaponry, especially sexualized and gendered characteristics. Carol Cohn (2004) argues that phallic worship was an important part of the arms race, whereby "missile envy" was a significant motivating factor

Figure 13.3 Ulster Defence Regiment Greenfinch in semi-formal skirt wearing old-style 'flak jacket' body armor c. 1970s. Photograph by Ronnie Gamble. Wikimedia Commons: File [UDR_Greenfinch.jpg].

in nuclear build up. The language and imagery associated with defense technology consists of sexual imagery, which has been a central part of all warfare, and once more illustrates a male-centered approach in military culture. Phallic references to missiles ranged from language that emphasized their exceptional thrust to weight ratio to the depth of their penetration capabilities. This sexual imagery, as demonstrated by Cohn's example of phallic worship, illustrates women's complex position, particularly their relationship with weaponry and how that might affect them in a male dominated military environment. Greenfinch soldiers, who had already blurred distinctions between male and female through their role on the front line of operations, were perceived to be in danger of further blurring this boundary if they were allowed to carry weapons.

Weiss argues that the history and experiences of female nurses in the Israeli army "reflects and re-affirms this patriarchal order of the military and society" (1999: 282). Military service acts as a "key symbol" (Ortner 1973) of manhood and is codified along a binary structure, based on good/evil, front/home, combatant/non-combatant, victory/defeat. However, Weiss highlights how the experiences of these nurses challenged the idea that men were ideally in arms while women stayed at home, because these nurses took on double shifts working both at home and in the army. While female UDR soldiers were accepted (just), to undertake military tasks that fulfilled a caring or supporting function for their male counterparts, to be in possession of a weapon was less acceptable. Because a weapon or gun is the piece of equipment soldiers use to enact violence and inflict death and injury on others, it is therefore a highly symbolic instrument military men use to express accepted forms of masculinity. Allowing women to carry arms not only brought into question the femininity of female soldiers, but challenged the masculinity of male soldiers. It was argued that the weight of a gun, apparently too heavy for women soldiers to carry, would in turn affect their ability to shoot the gun properly and might also hinder them in keeping pace with a patrol, especially over rough terrain. Because Greenfinches often undertook supportive roles, including scribing or radio duties, carrying a gun was also thought to restrict their movement and ability to carry out these duties effectively. Yet this overlooked the fact that female soldiers were already carrying considerable amounts of heavy equipment, from rucksacks and radios, to the uniform itself, while on duty.

Furthermore, deep-seated cultural attitudes towards women within the military structure made their participation in the armed forces disruptive to a force modeled on a masculine ideal, which is primarily why Greenfinch soldiers did not carry weapons. Their lack of weaponry was also defended on the basis of arguments about social cohesion. This was premised on the belief that for the military to maintain operational effectiveness, armed forces required cohesion among personnel. According to Rachel Woodward and Trish Winter (2004), the main issue affecting women is not their stamina or fitness but perceptions that their very presence is disruptive to the cohesiveness of a fighting team. For Woodward and Winter, traditionally women are seen in the military as a disruptive force whose presence challenges the status quo of a deeply masculine environment. Such attitudes reflected how symbolic violence permeated operative undertakings by soldiers. These forms of violence, however, can often be misrecognized as something else, usually positive; for example, restricting women from taking a fully active part in military operations was defended on the basis that it would enhance social cohesion in operative units. Because at least one Greenfinch, who would be unarmed, accompanied each UDR patrol this required a male soldier to be present with them to provide cover and protection, which was a source of frustration for both male and female soldiers. Forcing women soldiers to rely on the protection of men not only underlined their inferior status, but also reinforced the dominant position of men as leaders and protectors.

As female soldiers lost their individuality, this contributed to the tendency to sexualize them. Michael Kimmel (2004) argues that people who are admitted into an organization, but who are recognizably different from the large majority of members, might become hyper visible as members of their category but be completely invisible as individuals. The prevailing attitude in the regiment towards women and weapons was a vivid example of how such views could impact upon females' ability to immerse fully in the structure of military life. Women soldiers' perceived weaknesses, operational liabilities, and the distraction they apparently posed to male counterparts placed them outside the mainstream military establishment and thus they became a source of ridicule and criticism. Such issues are further demonstrated in cartoon sketches shown in regimental magazines, which demonstrate how women were both sexualized and ridiculed as operational liabilities.

Cartoon sketches and sexism

Uniforms, weapons, and symbols associated with the UDR functioned as a collective acceptance of women's role in the military. These symbolic instruments of the state had a performative purpose beyond their operational role. They reinforced broader gender stereotypes both within the military and in the wider community, as they were influenced by past, present, and future relationships between soldier and civilian, man and woman as "the emotional life of feeling and thinking selves is normally marked by past, present and future interactions with others" (Svašek 2008: 97). Consequently, audiences for these performances, be they soldier or civilian, were exposed to repeated examples of gender stereotyping. This section thus focuses on a "little genre of everyday life" (Barber 1997), namely cartoons, and "the use of visual iconography drawn from a satirical cartoon" (Manning 2007: 184). One of the most visual methods by which the UDR characterized women as sexualized beings was through cartoons and captions in their regimental magazines and publications. Such images are a commentary on the experiences of female soldiers and offer insights into their relationship with their male counterparts. This is because images do not simply derive from a fund of stored impressions but are dependent upon the situated contexts of the creator and reader in everyday life.

The power of cartoons to visually embody a prevailing discourse relating to specific cultural and social dynamics is shown by Josh Greenberg (2002), who proposes that images in political cartoons condense claims or mini narratives about putative problem conditions. They draw upon and reinforce 'taken for granted' meanings of the world. These cartoons provide meta-languages for discourse about the social order by constructing idealizations of the world, positioning readers within a discursive context of meaning making and offering readers tools for deliberating on present conditions. Analyzing the cartoon sketches displayed in UDR magazines shows how such images situate attitudes towards women within the context of everyday life and how universal values are exploited to persuade readers to identify with the image and intended message of the sketches. They demonstrate how such cartoons are constructed against the backdrop of assumptions about the social world. The form and content of such pictures represents a particular viewpoint about who their readers are and what they will find interesting, informative and humorous.

Robert Jarvenpa (1976), for example, highlights the visually expressive power of cartoons and their roles in American-Finnish ethnic slurs and how analogous forms of visual joke appear in reference to Finnish-Americans or 'Finns' in the western Great Lakes region. Jarvenpa refers to cartoon images, which include the drawing of a Smithala and Wessinen One-Shot Finnish Revolver. The brand name is a Finnicized pronunciation of a prominent American manufacturer of handguns. The crux of the joke, however, lies in the gun's peculiar construction. The barrel is mounted backwards so that a single shot is sufficient to dispatch the unfortunate user of this weapon. Unmistakably, the viewer is told that the Finn is stupid, incompetent, and potentially self-destructive. Jarvenpa provides an excellent example of the visual power of cartoons in projecting specific messages, and, in a similar vein, UDR cartoons, in their portrayals of women, were designed to reflect internal conventions regarding women's role in the Regiment, and furthermore, reveal dominant views held about women in the wider society. To achieve this, sketches were designed according to wider cultural understandings of humor, and specifically black humor. At this point, it should be noted that cartoons displayed in UDR magazines often made fun of the Regiment itself. John Darby highlights that cartoons produced by the British army in Northern Ireland were "often designed to show themselves as the butt of their own cartoons" (1983: 93). Furthermore, UDR cartoons primarily focused on internal aspects of the force, rather than questions about the conflict in Northern Ireland. Darby highlights, in relation to the police in Northern Ireland, that their cartoons principally have themes that are about "constabulary rather than paramilitary duty" (1983: 102)

Two cartoons sketches as seen in UDR magazines are analyzed here to examine their hidden (and unhidden) messages. Inspiration is taken from the methodological schema adopted by Ray Morris (1989; 1991; 1992a; 1992b; 1993; 1995) who highlights the formats cartoons use to establish social goals. These are attained by first establishing the source of the cartoon, such as the newspaper or magazine; second, by constructing a specific frame and agenda to create or excite interest in a problem or issue; and third, by constructing a normative agenda against which newsreaders may evaluate the cartoon's characters in moral terms. Finally, these goals are achieved by promoting a desire for action by ensuring the message portrayed in the cartoons resonates with the lived experiences of the audience. First, by being displayed in the UDR magazine, the cartoon designers present themselves as mediators who can accurately reflect the interpretation and attitudes towards women that were existent in the Regiment. This is primarily because this magazine was produced for and circulated amongst members only. Women are the primary targets in these cartoons, and their presence routinely represented as a distraction to men and most likely to impact upon their operational effectiveness (Ulster Defence Regiment 1983).

The first cartoon depicts a UDR sergeant inspecting female troops lined in formation for a parade and kit inspection. However, the women in this picture, while they do wear military uniform, have their regulation blazers and blouses removed. Parade inspections, which are usually associated with respect, authority, and formalized types of behavior, on this occasion appear to expose unmilitary behavior, such as untidiness, disobedience, and a lack of discipline. This reinforces the view that women are a disruptive presence in the military. Female soldiers are shown in a state of partial undress, with the sergeant then depicted holding up a telescope to inspect their bodies. Accompanying him is a sketch of another male soldier, reinforcing the impression that men inspect women, accompanied by the phrase "Girls! Girls! He wanted a 'kit inspection'." This cartoon depicts women as sexualized beings, which serves to highlight their difference, both physically and in terms of their capability, from their male counterparts. Furthermore, this image implicitly suggests that because women in the military distract men, they could, in turn, subsequently undermine the effectiveness of the force. To place greater emphasis upon this, a photograph of a male UDR soldier was placed beside the sketch with the accompanying phrase "wanted a quick look myself and now I've seen it all!" (Ulster Defence Regiment 1983) Attaching a photograph of a soldier to this picture not only reinforces the idea that females are distracting, but also shifts the messages in such cartoons from the realm of fiction to reality, suggesting that this is an issue with real material consequences.

The second cartoon is set in an operative environment rather than the formalized occasion of a kit inspection, but in this sketch the themes brought into focus in the first picture are revisited and extended. The cartoon, entitled 'A Pressing Problem' (Ulster Defence Regiment 1988) pictures a UDR platoon on operation, located in a field, where two male soldiers are seen in camouflage hiding in mobile hedges. They are spying on two female soldiers urinating in the field, who are shown hunkered down with their underwear around their ankles. The multi-layered meanings represented in this picture reveal very particular views of both women and men. Firstly, in relation to women, they are represented once more as a distracting force, who, on this occasion, are thought to be diverting male soldiers from their military duty. Furthermore, they are represented as reducing the operational effectiveness of the force by failing to concentrate on their duty as soldiers because they are urinating. This implies that while male soldiers can urinate quickly, the process for women can cause more difficulty, and because of this, they may have to rely on other soldiers to act as lookouts for signs of danger. In turn, the cartoon sketch reinforces the sexist view that women, and their perceived lack of military abilities, hindered the operational effectiveness and strength of the UDR, principally because they always had to be looked after. Also this picture demonstrates women soldiers' apparent inability to take their training on board and apply these skills in practice. In the picture, it shows women urinating in the middle of an open field, in direct contrast with the men who, while they may be spying on the women, are at the same time demonstrating their ability to use the skills gained in training; they use the environment and countryside to their strategic advantage, especially in the art of concealment. The messages portrayed in these cartoons of women as sexualized beings and a hindrance to operational effectiveness, uncovers how gendered identities are constructed and represented within the Armed Forces and the role of symbols, including uniforms. Designed to be both a reflection of political and popular culture and a mechanism to shape perceptions and popular narratives, these visible representations demonstrate how symbolic acts of violence permeate the military establishment.

Conclusion

This chapter sought to illustrate the importance of the symbolic and ritual characteristics of the military with reference to the locally recruited UDR, a regiment that operated only in Northern Ireland during the Troubles. Having established the performative roles the UDR undertook when on operational duty, using the work of Goffman, this discussion moved on to examine the role uniforms played in presenting a particular image of the soldier both to those in and out of uniform. The symbolism associated with the military uniform had particular connotations for women soldiers. Greenfinches were restricted from engaging in physical combat, which was a form of symbolic violence during which the actions, both visible and invisible, of the military, combined to shape attitudes and behavior towards women. From uniform restrictions to cartoon sketches, various factors combined to shape the life of a Greenfinch soldier. However, for such military actions to succeed in shaping attitudes towards women relied on the acceptance, either knowingly, or unknowingly, of female soldiers.

While the actions undertaken by female soldiers and their male counterparts draw attention to the performative characteristics of soldiers on duty, they also highlight the fluid and marginal states UDR soldiers often found themselves in. Their struggles to form a permanent identity in a social and geographical environment in constant flux suggests that further exploration is needed in terms of the symbolic and ritual characteristics of the military, especially in operational contexts. This has particular ramifications for contemporary forms of conflict, which has taken on increasingly asymmetric, unpredictable and localized forms.

References

Amott, T. (1984), "Bloodless Coup," *The Women's Review of Books*, 1 (5): 7–8.
Azaryahu, M. (1999), "The Independence Day Parade: A Political History of a Patriotic Ritual," in E. Lomsky-Feder and E. Ben-Ari (eds), *The Military and*

Militarism in Israeli Society, Albany, NJ: State University of New York (SUNY) Press, 89–116.

Barber, K., ed. (1997), *Readings in African Popular Culture*, Bloomington, IN: Indiana University Press.

Bateson, G. (1972), *Steps to the Ecology of Mind*, San Francisco: Chandler.

Ben Amos, A. (2003), "War Commemoration and the Formation of Israeli National Identity," *Journal of Political and Military Sociology*, 31 (2): 171–95.

Bourdieu, P. (1977), *Outline of a Theory of Practice*, Cambridge: Cambridge University Press.

Campbell, D. (1993), "Women in Combat: The World War II Experience in the US, GB, Germany and the Soviet Union," *Journal of Military History*, 57: 301–23.

Cohn, C. (2004), "Sex and Death in the Rational World of Defence Intellectuals," in B. E. Schmidt and I. W. Schröder (eds), *Anthropology of Violence and Conflict*, New York: Routledge, 354–63.

Darby, J. (1983), *Dressed to Kill: Cartoonists and the Northern Ireland Conflict*, Belfast: Appletree Press.

Davis, K. D., ed. (2007), *Women and Leadership in the Canadian Forces: Perspectives and Experience*, Winnipeg: Canadian Defence Academy Press.

Enloe, C. (1983), *Does Khaki Become You? The Militarization of Women's Lives*, Boston, MA: South End Press.

Enloe, C. (2000), *Manoeuvres: The Militarization of Women's Lives*, Berkeley, CA: University of California Press.

Feldman, A. (2001), "Violence and Vision: The Prosthetics and Aesthetics of Terror," in V. Das, A. Kleinman, M. Ramphele, and P. Reynolds (eds), *Violence and Subjectivity*, Berkeley, CA: University of California Press, 46–78.

Galster, K. and M. L. Nosch (2010), "Textile History and the Military: An Introduction," *Textile History*, 41 (1): 1–5.

Gavriely-Nuri, D. (2010), "Rainbow, Snow, and the Poplar's Song: The 'Annihilative Naming' of Israeli Military Practices," *Armed Forces and Society*, 36 (5): 825–42.

Gluckman, M. (1962), *Essays on the Ritual of Social Relations*, Manchester: Manchester University Press.

Goffman, E. (1959), *The Presentation of the Self in Everyday Life*, London: Penguin Books.

Goldman, N. L., ed. (1982), *Female Soldiers: Combatants or Non-combatants?*, Westport, CT: Greenwood Press.

Greenberg, J. (2002), "Framing and Temporality in Political Cartoons: A Critical Analysis of Visual News Discourse," *Canadian Review of Sociology and Anthropology*, 39 (2): 181–98.

Handelman, D. (1998), *Models and Mirrors: Towards an Anthropology of Public Events*, New York: Bergahn Books.

Hansen, K. (2004), "The World in Dress: Anthropological Perspectives on Clothing, Fashion, and Culture," *Annual Review of Anthropology*, 33: 369–92.

Herron, S. (2013), *The role and effect of violence on the Ulster defence regiment in south Armagh*, PhD Thesis, Queen's University, Belfast.

Hochschild, A. H. (1983), *The Managed Heart: Commercialization of Human Feeling*. Berkeley, CA: University of California Press.
Howes, R. H. and M. R. Stevenson, eds (1993), *Women and the Use of Military Force*. London: Lynne Rienner Publishers.
Jarman, N. (1997), *Material Conflicts: Parades and Visual Displays in Northern Ireland*, Oxford: Berg.
Jarvenpa, R. (1976), "Visual Expression in Finnish-American Ethnic Slurs," *The Journal of American Folklore*, 89 (351): 90–1.
Kimmel, M. and A. Aronson, eds (2004), *Men & Masculinities: A Social, Cultural, and Historical Encyclopedia*, Santa Barbara, CA: ABC-CLIO.
Lomsky Feder, E. and E. Ben Ari (1999), *The Military and Militarism in Israeli Society*, Albany, NY: SUNY Press.
Maček, I. (2001), "Predicament of War: Sarajevo Experiences and Ethics of War," in B. E. Schmidt and I. W. Schröder (eds), *Anthropology of Violence and Conflict*, London: Routledge, 197–224.
Manning, P. (2007), "Rose-coloured Glass? Colour Revolutions and Cartoon Chaos in Postsocialist Georgia," *Cultural Anthropology*, 22 (2): 171–213.
Martin, S. E. (1999), "Police Force or Police Service? Gender and Emotional Labor," *The ANNALS of the American Academy of Political and Social Science*, 561 (1): 111–126.
Morris, R. (1989), *Behind the Jester's Mask*, Toronto: University of Toronto Press.
Morris, R. (1991), "Cultural Analysis Through Semiotics: Len Norris' Cartoons on Official Bilingualism," *The Canadian review of Sociology and Anthropology*, 28 (2): 225–54.
Morris, R. (1992a), "Cartoons and the Political System: Canada, Quebec, Wales and England," *Canadian Journal of Communication*, 17,(2): 253–58.
Morris, R. (1992b), "Editorial Cartoons and the Reproduction of Capitalist Order," in M. Grenier (ed.), *Critical studies of Canadian Mass Media*, Toronto: Butterworths, 145–54.
Morris, R. (1993), "Visual Rhetoric in Political Cartoons: A Structuralist Approach," *Metaphor and Symbolic Activity*, 8 (3): 195–210.
Morris, R. (1995), *The Carnivalization of Politics: Quebec Cartoons on Relations with Canada, England and France, 1960–1979*, Montreal and Kingston: McGill-Queen's University Press.
Murray, T. (1986), "The Language of Navy Fighter Pilots," *American Speech*, 61 (2): 121–29.
Ortner, S. (1973), "On Key Symbols," *American Anthropologist*, 75: 1338–46.
Partridge, E. (1948), *A Dictionary of Forces' Slang 1939–1945*, London: Secker and Warburg.
Regimental Association of the Ulster Defence Regiment (2011), *The Ulster Defence Regiment roll of honour*. Available online: http://www.udrassociation.org/Roll%20of%20Honour/roll_of_honour_index.htm [accessed May 25, 2011].
Schwartz, B. (1982), "The Social Contexts of Commemoration: A Study in Collective Memory," *Social Forces*. 61: 374–403.

Segal, M. W. (1995), "Women's Military Roles Cross-nationally: Past, Present and Future," *Gender & Society,* 9 (6): 757–75.
Svašek, M. (2008), "Postsocialist Ownership: Emotions, Power and Morality in a Czech Village," in M. Svašek, *Postsocialism: Politics and Emotions in Central and Eastern Europe,* Oxford: Berghahn Books, 95–114.
Turner, V. (1957), *Schism and Continuity in African Society,* Manchester: Manchester University Press.
Tuten, J. M. (1982), "Germany and the World Wars," in N. Goldman (ed.), *Female Soldiers: Combatants or Non-combatants?,* Westport, CT: Greenwood Press.
Ulster Defence Regiment (1983), *10th anniversary of the Greenfinches,* Belfast: Ulster Defence Regiment.
Ulster Defence Regiment (1988), *15th anniversary of the Greenfinches,* Belfast: Ulster Defence Regiment.
Weiss, M. (1999), "Engendering the Gulf War: Israeli Nurses and the Discourse of Soldiering," in E. Ben-Ari and E Lomsky-Feder, *The Military and Militarism in Israeli Society.* Albany, NY: SUNY Press, 281–301.
Woodward, S. (2005), "Looking Good: Feeling Right-aesthetics of the Self," in S. Kuchler and D. Miller (eds), *Clothing as Material Culture,* Oxford: Berg, 21–39.
Woodward, R. and T. Winter (2004), "Discourses of Gender and the British Army," *Armed Forces & Society,* 30 (2): 279–302.
Zerubavel, Y. (1995), "The Multivocality of a National Myth: Memory and Counter-memories of Masada," in R. Wistrich and D. Ohana (eds), *The Shaping of Israeli Identity: Myth, Memory and Trauma,* London: Frank Cass, 110–28.

Conclusion

In this brief conclusion, we seek to summarize the most salient points made by the preceding chapters, interwoven with perspectives on the future development of research on uniform. The scope of this book demonstrates the variety of ways in which uniforms were worn in response to social changes from the mid-1800s to the present day. It highlights various uniform schemes that emerged as a result of both technological advances and the visuality that shaped public life. On one hand, institutions could see how uniformity might erase local, ethnic, political, and spiritual allegiances and practices in favor of a unified and authorized identity. On the other, where there was a desire in civil society to rupture these hegemonic structures, voluntary groups also saw that uniform clothing could make their case for liberty and freedom. This book has explored the multivalent meanings of uniform, which is revealed as a lens through which we can view the many faces of modernity.

Uniform represents the fusing of the body and material dress. What fashion history misses in its focus on consumerism in matters of clothing is the extent to which the history of dress has involved masses of citizens voluntarily wearing uniform. The interdisciplinary approach of this book avoids positing uniform as an idealized form of dress to instead highlight the social, cultural, economic, and political contexts for its emergence in various regions and historical moments. Uniform was primarily adopted as a modern form of dress due to the increased role image played in public life. Image technologies emerge with the official desire for more centralized structures, which were often achieved through the use of surveillance. Uniform was a solution to the desire for people management driven by this rationalized, centralized and disciplinary structure. At various points, uniform schemes were ideologically burdened, as they were adopted to fulfil utopian visions of socialism, to advance commercial capitalism, or to embody forms of ethnonationalism. While some of the work here emphasizes these tendencies in Europe and North America in the twentieth century, the essays as a whole seek to uncover uniform as a multifaceted phenomenon with various manifestations depending on where it is found. What is clear is the contingency of uniform: it can only be understood through the situated cultural contexts, body practices and political discourses that give it life. This collection of essays highlights the very real challenges to understanding uniform as a cultural category.

The lack of certainty about what constitutes uniform is not the problem it first appears to be. Sartorial uniformity has extraordinary visual, material, and symbolic power, but that too can break down and lose its potency. In each essay, authors ask what activates clothing to make it potent in political and social discourse. This volume explores how and where uniform mediates relationships between public and private worlds to reveal the interconnected concerns of dress, gender, and citizenship in modernity. It attempts to place uniform in various historical contexts from its origins in company livery, through its high point as part of the structuring experience of modernity, to the way it has endured in more diffuse forms in postmodernity. As this volume demonstrates, uniform as an object of study is increasingly of interest to researchers in a range of disciplines. In anthropology, where questions of materiality highlight relationships between material and social worlds, the surface qualities of the uniform are shown to be particularly effective in reproducing social and cultural meanings. By examining a widely worn item such as uniform, anthropologists can utilize its materiality to access how institutions work, to consider how social values are encoded in clothing, but also to determine how designers and makers engage with regulation. Researchers in anthropology and sociology are increasingly examining the social significance of the various materializations of uniform.

New interest in uniform has also arisen from the 'aesthetic turn' in International Relations. Military uniform may be viewed as an aesthetic element in the art of warfare, but it also has strategic value; it promotes regulated behavior, hides vulnerability in combat, and disciplines soldiers. Crucially, on the battlefield, uniform shapes the laws on armed conflict. Clothing, body, and performance come together in military dress but only recently have scholars of International Relations given uniform any serious attention as a culturally meaningful image and object. So too have scholars in sociology and business studies become more interested in what 'aesthetic labor' means for workers in terms of uniforms and workplace dress codes. Various academic disciplines now see how meaningful the study of uniform is to the history of the body in modernity. Uniform touches on a range of academic disciplines as it represents a visual and material force in the modern world with an infinite variety of examples.

The uniforming of political movements as explored in the first section by Annebella Pollen and Li Li drew attention to the complexities of clothing in public life. While uniform may appear to have a rigid design aesthetic, like all clothing it also has the capacity for artifice and illusion. If the body in motion gives life to the uniform, this is evident in relation to politics and revolution, which often shapes its most potent images. Future work on this area might reckon with more recent political organizations and events, for example the style of various right-wing groupings that have had a stronger public presence in the US and elsewhere in recent years. Reporting on the dress of a large number of participants in the 'Unite the Right' rally in Charlottesville, Virginia in August 2017, one commentator from *GQ* magazine observed "scores of white men dressed in crisp polos and khakis, turning the uniform of business-casual blasé into a white-hot statement." Here, the desire to take a collective stance saw participants improvising a uniform from their leisurewear wardrobe to express a particular form of patriarchal white supremacy.

In the next section on how uniforms operate in institutions, William J. F. Keenan and Kate Stephenson revealed how regulatory dress asserted group identity in specific educational and religious settings, often as an attempt to mitigate against the mutability of the modern body and its perceived excesses. Within contemporary culture, the renewed focus on school uniform in Britain is worthy of further analysis. In the popular press, particularly 'successful' schools are often identified as those with stringent dress codes while at the same time stories about the exclusion of pupils for being imperfectly uniformed are published with routine commentary, bemoaning the overly strict imposition of regulations. Uniform is thus presented as a clearly identifiable fulcrum around which pivot competing values involving individual choice and a perceived 'common good.'

Uniformity in clothing is often associated with modernization projects, with its implications of progress, rationality, and the adoption of technocratic solutions to social problems. Uniform was clearly integral to official efforts to modernize in various regions and often reflected a statist approach to human organization. In the section on uniform and leisure, the widespread adoption of codified dress preoccupies F. Dilek Himam and Geraldine Biddle-Perry, both of whom explored uniformity as part of the creation of an 'imagined community.' They highlighted tensions between the modern uses of uniform on the one hand to express collective fellowship, and on the other to manage and control citizens, pointing to contradictions that arise with the regulation of leisure clothing. The pattern to democratize fashion has not subsided, and now surfaces in the vogue for luxury urban sportswear. The contradictions of utility and luxury deserve more attention from future researchers who might explore what leisurewear—with its tendency for uniformity—means in a globalized age.

Nowhere is the uniform more conspicuous than in the workplace, as discussed in the section on uniforming workers. With its aesthetic of standardization, prescribed dress codes represent the implicit demands for conformity. Sartorial uniformity reflects commodified labor, which Samira Guerra explored in her ethnographic study of corporate dress in the City of London. Prudence Black examined the key considerations in the creation of airline uniform, a study that raises questions about how this form of clothing can create and sustain a dialog with fashion design, at a time when glamor has become part of the corporate image. This is clear from recent collaborations between fashion designers and transport companies: Christian Lacroix designed uniforms for Air France in 2000, Vivienne Westwood for Virgin Airlines in 2014, and Wayne Hemingway gave Transport for London a whole new look in 2015.

The interplay of fashion and uniform was a theme addressed by Jane Tynan and Djurdja Bartlett, who looked at how uniformity became an emblem of fashion's modernity. On the surface, uniform and fashion appear to be diametrically opposed but, as these essays reveal, projects to design workwear in the twentieth century often enlisted fashion to deflect from the more authoritarian associations of uniform. For fashion consumers, uniform clothing had its attractions, which included its appeal to efficiency, rationality and simplicity. Further study on the ongoing dialog between fashion and uniform within contemporary culture has the potential to offer insights into what these distinct body practices represent in the digital age.

Military uniform is the reference point for much uniform design. Indeed, the uniform might have its clearest role in distinguishing combatants from civilians in war zones. Essential to the functioning of army discipline, military uniform has become part of the technology of warfare as was evident in the last essays in the final section of the volume by Amin Parsa and Stephen Herron. These chapters raised questions about what role military uniform plays on the battlefield; why it is used to determine legal questions in armed conflict; and how masculinized design can limit women's full participation in the military. Clothing, body, and performance come together in military dress; thus, gendered performance is a key question for those exploring the social and cultural meaning of uniform in military contexts. So too, technologies of deception, such as camouflage, highlight critical tensions between visibility and invisibility for combatants. This returns us to the first essay by Pollen, where she argued that uniform is primarily about constructing a sense of power and authority where none before existed. What emerges from this collection of essays is the sense that uniform can simultaneously project material and symbolic power primarily for political, social, and religious groups and institutions.

As suggested above, this volume is not exhaustive in terms of how uniform clothing might be studied in the future. Further research might focus on the ways in which uniform and fashion have co-habited historically. Sartorial proscription is particularly evident in the workplace, where the drive for normalizing standards of behavior has generated public debate on workers' agency in relation to what they wear. There is much work to be done on dress policies; created to promote an image of unity and authority, they can also be coercive in seeking to stabilize gender, sexuality, and class in the workplace. If dress regulation is about discipline and control over bodies, particularly those that threaten the status quo, how do public and private companies reconcile this with equality legislation? Companies might demonstrate their commitment to equality and diversity through policy documents, but further research would reveal exactly how that bears out. How are the limits of social identity drawn with regard to workers' appearance? This is a particularly vexed question in relation to race, which deserves much more research on whether standardized dress is implicated in hegemonic structures to encode whiteness. Further research on uniform could feed into wider debates on the role of visual and material culture in perpetuating inequalities. Uniforms and standardizing dress codes have been shown to regulate behavior by systematically testing whether bodies are exceeding cultural norms.

To interrogate what uniform means in the twenty-first century, researchers might look to new kinds of uniforms, particularly those created for the precarious worker under neo-liberalism. What kinds of current political forces seek to normalize power over bodies, and how does that manifest in clothing for work and leisure? It might be tempting to believe that dominant political forces are solely responsible for dreaming up new uniforms, but as discussed, urban sportswear, which is valued by young people for its uniformity and utility, is increasingly marketed as luxury fashion. There are similar patterns in the clothing choices of youth activists for street protest. Future scholars might further explore how civil disobedience has utilized uniform and what dissenters do to improvise their own outfits. Does clothing, with a certain uniformity, for instance, embolden activists to resist authority? Future scholars might also consider the relationship between surveillance technology and street clothing, particularly how youth groups and activists—such as Anti-Fascists—create their uniforms of protest to resist the gaze of surveillance cameras. Collective identity has been expressed through symbolic systems of dress, historically, in order to embody a range of styles and identity positions in modernity and postmodernity. Uniform still has extraordinary potency today and—as object and image—is ever more critical to public discourse.

Notes

Chapter 1

1 Hermann Broch, *The Sleepwalkers,* 1986 (first pub 1932), London: Pantheon Books.

Chapter 3

1 Mao's poem "Wei nü minbin tizhao" (Inscriptions for the Women Militants) in *Mao zhuxi shici* (*Poems by Chairman Mao*; Mao 1969). Translation is mine.
2 'Class enemies' was a loosely defined phrase encompassing a wide range of social groups which were viewed in be in opposition to the 'proletarian class' or 'revolutionary mass of workers, peasants and soldiers.' When the Cultural Revolution began, the 'five black elements' consisted of former landlords, former rich peasants, counterrevolutionaries (who had resisted the Communist Party's rule), bad elements (who had committed crimes) and rightists (who were accused of attacking the Communist Party in the 1957 political campaign). 'Capitalist roaders' and 'revisionists' referred to Mao's opponents in the Communist Party who advocate economic reforms instead of 'class struggles.' 'Four olds' include 'old ideologies, old cultures, old habits, and old customs.'

Chapter 6

1 See for example, Elizabeth Rouse, *Understanding Fashion* (London: BSP Professional Books, 1989), who outlines the major problems with such an approach in terms of the diverse reasons that instigate fashion change and in the light of new understandings of sub-cultural fashionable innovation, and correlated changes in production after the Second World War. For arguments relating to how styles also 'bubble up' from the street and the culture of minority and low-status groups, see Ted Polhemus, *Streetstyle* (London: Thames and Hudson, 1984).

Chapter 7

1. Leyla Açba was maid of honor to Emine Nazikeda Kadınefendi, the first wife of the last sultan of Ottoman Empire, Sultan Vahideddin. She served Kadınefendi from 1919 to 1924, and following her exile from İstanbul, she moved to Sivas. For more information, see H. Açba and L. Açba: *Bir Çerkes Prensesinin Harem Hatıraları* (İstanbul: Timaş Yayınları, 2010).
2. For more information, see Atatürk's *Discourse and Statements* (1934), Chapter 2, p. 262. For more on healthcare reforms in Turkey, see V. Yılmaz, *The Politics of Healthcare Reform in Turkey*, Palgrave Macmillan, 2017.

Chapter 8

1. The City of London refers to the financial district in the capital city of the United Kingdom which hosts many of its trading and financial firms.
2. I obtained their consent to record the interviews, which I later transcribed. Their real names were changed to protect their privacy.

Chapter 9

1. The flight hostesses joined flight stewards who had worked as cabin crew with Qantas since 1938.
2. Other large corporate contracts for uniforms include the main banks and national organisations such as Australia Post.
3. Emilio Pucci designed uniforms for Braniff Airlines from 1965 to 1977 as part of Alexander Girard's 'The End of the Plain Plane' design scheme.
4. For example, in 1985 Japan Airlines had 7,830 submissions to become the designer to replace the Hanae Mori uniforms. Other designers of airline uniforms include: Sir Hardie Amies, Howard Greer, Christian Lacroix, Christóbal Balanciaga, Edith Head, Ralph Lauren, Jean Louis, Pierre Cardin, Oleg Cassini, André Courrèges, Christian Dior, and Vivienne Westwood.
5. Qantas first used the Peter Allen song "I Still Call Australia Home" in a $3 million campaign to coincide with the 1998 Commonwealth Games.
6. In 1993 a wax model of the 'Singapore Girl' was installed in Madame Tussaud's, London.
7. I would like to thank Michael Carter for reminding me of this feature of the suit.
8. The polyester in the mix helps the fabric dry quicker and last longer.
9. Pilots always have ties with elastic or velcro fastenings.

10 Despite the busyness of the 'Wirriyarra' print, Grant thinks it is "quite calm . . . quite discreet, with its tone on tone colours." Martin Grant interview with the author, 11 May 2014.
11 A distinct Australian style was seen in the fashions of surfwear companies like Mambo, and the colorful knits of Jenny Kee and Linda Jackson at Flamingo Park.
12 Sharelle Quinn and Ann Bennett became Qantas' first female pilots in 1985. In 2016, females represented only 4 percent of Qantas pilots.
13 The exception was during the Second World War, when the pilots reverted to a khaki uniform.
14 See the image of Danish Airlines crew from 1938 wearing a similar cap in Clair Hughes, *Hats* (Bloomsbury: London: New York, 2017), 88.

Chapter 10

1 Popova was the author of both set designs and costumes, and the play premiered in April 1922. See Sarabianov and Adaskina for Popova's Manifesto, and her *prozodezhda* drawings (1990: 379 and 246–47, respectively).
2 The play *The Death of Tarelkin* was directed by Meyerhold and his "laboratory assistant," Sergey Eisenstein. For an overview, see Lavrentiev 1988: 68–72. Stepanova's overalls design for Pakhom the porter, and the photograph of the actor wearing them, are reproduced on p. 71.
3 The idea that fashion is the enemy of true equality had been strongly advocated by nineteenth-century socialist and liberal thinkers and writers, such as Charles Fourier, Robert Owen, and Henri Saint-Simon.
4 Alexander Bogdanov was a trained scientist, economist, philosopher, and close collaborator of Lenin in the early years.
5 Rockwell's illustration was *The Saturday Evening Post*'s cover on May 29, 1943. It became known as 'Rosie the Riveter,' as Rockwell drew the name 'Rosie' on his heroine's lunch box. Representing women who tirelessly worked in munitions and war supplies' factories, Rosie the Riveter had turned into a cultural icon.
6 The original of this Maxwell's overalls is in the collection of the Museum of the City of New York. Inventory information: Museum of the City of New York: Vera Maxwell. [Jumpsuit: Rosie the Riveter], 1942. Museum of the City of New York, 85.95.4.
7 The drawing of Piguet's ensemble was also published in: "C'est toujours Paris qui crée la mode", *Marie Claire*, Paris, November 10, 1939, pp. 10–11. For these collections, see also Veillon 2002: 8–9.
8 *Vogue*, New York, December 22, 1930, pp. 47–8.
9 In 1934, the US Rubber Company, the creators of Lastex, engaged Amelia Earhart to design a modernist sporty collection, which was offered at American department

stores. For an overview on aviation as sport, and Amelia Earhart's collection, see Elia 2014: 217–8.

10 The Metropolitan Museum in New York contains a number of Halston's overalls in their dress collection, as well Burrows' slinky gold number, and a minimalist Beene version.

Chapter 12

1 This phrase is widely known as "war is politics by other means," but there are differing translations of *On War*. Due to the differing qualities of the translations, I mainly rely on the Modern Library's compilation, entitled *The Book of War*, which includes both Clausewitz's *On War* and Sun-Tzu's *The Art of War*.

2 The other three requirements are: that of being commanded by a person responsible for his subordinates; that of carrying arms openly; that of conducting their operations in accordance with the laws and customs of war.

3 In simple terms, customary international law refers to international legal obligations that states have regardless if they have signed and ratified treaties or conventions in which such obligations are mentioned.

Select Bibliography

Adams, J. (1995), *Dandies and Desert Saints: Styles of Victorian Masculinity*. Cornell, NY: Cornell University Press.
Adomaitis, A. D. and K. Johnson (2005), "Casual vs Formal Uniforms: Flight Attendants Self-Perception and Perceived Appraisals by Others," *Clothing and Textile Journal*, 23 (2): 88–101.
Aldrich, W. (2003), "The Impact of Fashion on the Cutting Practices for the Woman's Tailored Jacket 1800–1927," *Textile History*, 34 (2): 134–70.
Anderson, D. and D. Killingray, eds (1991), *Policing the Empire: Government, Authority and Control, 1830–1940*, Manchester: Manchester University Press.
Anderson, F. (2000), "Fashioning the Gentleman: A Study of *Henry Poole And Co.*, Savile Row Tailors, 1861–1900," *Fashion Theory*, 4 (4), 405–26.
Anderson, F. (2005), "Spinning the Ephemeral with the Sublime: Modernity and Landscape in Men's Fashion Textiles 1860–1900," *Fashion Theory*, 9 (3): 283–304.
Anderson, F. (2006), "This Sporting Cloth: Tweed, Gender and Fashion 1860–1900," *Textile History*, 37 (2): 166–86.
Anderson, P. (2017), *The H-Word: The Peripeteia of Hegemony*, London: Verso.
Arthur, L. B., ed. (2000), *Undressing Religion Commitment and Conversion from a Cross-Cultural Perspective*, Oxford and New York: Berg.
Ash, J. (2009), *Dress Behind Bars: Clothing as Criminality*, London: IB Tauris.
Barnard, M. (1996), *Fashion as Communication*, London: Routledge.
Barthes, R. (2006), *The Language of Fashion*, Oxford: Berg.
Bartlett, D. (2010), *FashionEast*, Cambridge, MA: MIT Press.
Bates, C. (2011), "'Their Uniforms All Esthetic and Antiseptic': Fashioning Modern Nursing Identity 1870–1900," in I. Parkins and E. M. Sheehan. (eds), *Cultures of Femininity in Modern Fashion*, Durham, NC: University of New Hampshire Press, 151–79.
Ben Ari, E. and E. Lomsky Feder (1999), *The Military and Militarism in Israeli Society*, Albany, NY: SUNY Press.
Biddle-Perry, G. (2014), "The Rise of the World's Largest Sports and Athletic Outfitter: A Study of Gamages of Holborn, 1878–1913," *Sport in History*, 34 (2): 295–314.
Biddle-Perry, G. (2014a), "Fashioning Suburban Aspiration: Awheel with the Catford Cycling Club, 1886–1900," *The London Journal*, 39 (3): 187–204.
Black, P. (2011), *The Flight Attendant's Shoe*, Sydney: New South Press.
Black, P. (2013), "Lines of Flight: The Female Flight Attendant Uniform," *Fashion Theory*, 17 (2): 179–95.

Blumer, H. (1968), *Fashion, Encyclopedia of Social Sciences*, New York: Macmillan and Free Press

Bonami, F., M. L. Frisa, and S. Tonchi, eds (2000), *Uniform: Order and Disorder*, Milan: Charta.

Bourdieu, P. (1977), *Outline of a Theory of Practice*, Cambridge: Cambridge University Press.

Bourdieu, P. (1984), *Distinction: A Social Critique of the Judgement of Taste*, London: Routledge.

Bowlt, J. (1996), "Body Beautiful: The Artistic Search for the Perfect Physique," in J. Bowlt and O. Matich (eds), *Laboratory of Dreams: The Russian Avant-garde and Cultural Experiment*, Stanford, CA: Stanford University Press, 37–58.

Braun, E. (2006), *Myerhold: A Revolution in Theatre*, London: Methuen.

Breward, C. (1999), *The Hidden Consumer: Masculinities, Fashion and City Life 1860–1914*, Manchester: Manchester University Press.

Breward, C. (2001), "Manliness, Modernity and the Shaping of Male Clothing," in J. Entwistle and E. Wilson (eds), *Body Dressing*, Oxford: Berg, 165–81.

Breward, C. (2003), *Fashion* Oxford: Oxford University Press.

Brunsma, D. (2004), *The School Uniform Movement and What It Tells us About American Education: A Symbolic Crusade*, Lanham, MD: Scarecrow Education.

Burman, B. (1995), "Better and Brighter Clothes: The Men's Dress Reform Party, 1929–1940," *Journal of Design History*, 8 (4): 275–90.

Canning, K. (1999), "The Body as Method? Reflections on the Place of the Body in Gender History," *Gender and History*, 11 (3): 499–513.

Colville, Q. (2003), "Jack Tar and the Gentleman Officer: The Role of Uniform in Shaping the Class- and Gender-Related Identities of British Naval Personnel, 1930–1939," *Transactions of the Royal Historical Society*, 13: 105–29.

Coupland, P. M. (2004), "The Black Shirt in Britain: The Meanings and Function of Political Uniform," in J V. Gottlieb and T P Linehan (eds), *The Culture of Fascism: Visions of the Far Right in Britain*, London: I. B. Tauris, 100–15.

Craik, J. (2003), "The Cultural Politics of the Uniform," *Fashion Theory*, 7 (2): 127–48.

Craik, J. (2005), *Uniforms Exposed: From Conformity to Transgression*, Oxford: Berg.

Crane, D. (1993), *Fashion and Its Social Agendas: Class, Gender and Identity in Clothing*, Chicago and London: University of Chicago Press.

Crawley, E. (1931), "Sacred Dress," in T. Besterman (ed.), *Dress, Drink and Drums*, London: Harmondsworth, 159–64.

Cronin, S, ed. (2014), *Anti-Veiling Campaigns in the Muslim World: Gender, Modernism and the Politics of Dress*, Durham Modern Middle East and Islamic World Series, London: Routledge.

Cunnington, P. (1974), *Costume of Household Servants: from the Middle Ages to 1900*, London: A&C Black.

Cunnington, P. and A. Buck (1978), *Children's Costume in England 1300–1900*, London: A&C Black.

Cunnington, P. and A. Mansfield (1969), *English Costume for Sports and Outdoor Recreation; From the Sixteenth to the Nineteenth Centuries*, London: A&C Black.

Davidson, A. (1990), *Blazers, Badges and Boaters: A Pictorial History of School Uniform*, Horndean, Hants.: Scope Books.

Davis, F. (1989), "Of Maids' Uniforms and Blue Jeans: The Drama of Status Ambivalences in Clothing and Fashion," *Qualitative Sociology*, 12 (4): 337–55.

Davis, K. D., ed. (2007), *Women and Leadership in the Canadian Forces: Perspectives and Experience*, Winnipeg: Canadian Defence Academy Press.

Davis, M. (2000), *Fashioning a New World: A History of the Woodcraft Folk*, Loughborough: Holyoake Books.

De Casanova, E. M. (2015), *Buttoned Up: Clothing, Conformity and White-Collar Masculinity*, New York: Cornell University Press.

de Marly, D. (1986), *Working Dress: A History of Occupational Clothing*, London: Batsford.

Drakeford, M. (1997), *Social Movements and their Supporters: The Green Shirts in England*, Basingstoke: Macmillan.

Dussel, I. (2006), "When Appearances are not Deceptive: A Comparative History of School Uniforms in Argentina and the United States," *Paedagogica Historica*, 41 (1–2): 179–95.

Dussell, I. (2004), "Fashioning the Schooled Self," in B M. Baker and K. E. Heyning (eds), *Dangerous Coagulations: The Uses of Foucault in the Study of Education*, New York: Peter Lang, 86–116.

Edensor, T. (2002), *National Identity, Popular Culture and Everyday Life*, Oxford: Berg.

Eicher, J. and M. E. Roach-Higgins (1992), "Definition and Classification of Dress," in R. Barnes and J. Bubolz Eicher (eds), *Dress and Gender: Making and Meaning in Cultural Context*, New York: Berg, 8–20.

El Guindi, F. (2000), *Veil: Modesty, Privacy and Resistance*, Oxford: Berg.

Elliott, D., ed. (1979), *Alexander Rodchenko, 1891–1956*, Oxford: Museum of Modern Art.

Enloe, C. (2000), *Manoeuvres: The Militarization of Women's Lives*, Berkeley, CA: University of California Press.

Entwistle, J. (1997), "'Power Dressing' and the Construction of the Career Woman," in M. Nava, A. Blake, I. MacRury, and B. Richards (eds), *Buy this Book: Studies in Advertising and Consumption*, London: Routledge, 311–23.

Entwistle, J. (2000), *The Fashioned Body: Fashion, Dress and Modern Social Theory*, Cambridge: Polity Press.

Evans, E. J. (2001), *The Forging of the Modern State: Early Industrial Britain, 1783–1870*, London: Routledge.

Ewing, E. (1974), *History of Twentieth Century Fashion*, London: Batsford Ltd.

Ewing, E. (1977), *History of Children's Costume*, London: Batsford Ltd.

Falasca-Zamponi, S. (2002), "Peeking Under the Black Shirt: Italian Fascism's Disembodied Bodies," in W. Parkins (ed.), *Fashioning the Body Politic*, Oxford: Berg.

Featherstone, M. (1991), *The Body: Social Process and Cultural Theory*, London: SAGE Publications.
Fine, B. (2002), *The World of Consumption*, 2nd edn., London: Routledge.
Finnane, A. (2008), *Changing Clothes in China: Fashion, History, Nation*, New York: Columbia University Press.
Flügel, J. C. (1930), *The Psychology of Clothes*, New York: International Universities Press.
Forty, A. (1986), *Objects of Desire: Design and Society 1750–1980*, London: Thames and Hudson.
Foucault, M. (1988), *Technologies of the Self: A Seminar with Michel Foucault*, London: Tavistock, 16–49.
Foucault, M. ([1977] 1991), *Discipline and Punish: The Birth of the Prison*, London: Penguin.
Fussell, P. (2002), *Uniforms: Why We Are What We Wear*, Boston: Houghton Mifflin.
Giddens, A. (1991), *Modernity and Self-Identity: Self and Society in the Late Modern Age*, Cambridge: Polity Press.
Goldman, N. L., ed (1982), *Female Soldiers: Combatants or Non-combatants?*, Westport, CT: Greenwood Press.
Green, N. L. (1997), *Ready-to-Wear and Ready-to-Work: A Century of Industry and Immigrants in Paris and New York*, Durham, NC: Duke University Press.
Guppy, A. (1978), *Children's Clothes 1939–1970: The Advent of Fashion*, Poole: Blandford Press.
Haley, B. (1978), *The Healthy Body and Victorian Culture*, Cambridge, MA: Harvard University Press.
Hall, D. E. (2006), *Muscular Christianity: Embodying the Victorian Age*, Cambridge: Cambridge University Press.
Hansen, K. (2004), "The World in Dress: Anthropological Perspectives on Clothing, Fashion, and Culture," *Annual Review of Anthropology*, 33: 369–92.
Hardy, S. and A. Corones (2017), "The Nurse's Uniform as Ethopoietic Fashion," *Fashion Theory*, 21 (5): 523–52.
Harvey, J. (1995), *Men in Black*, London: Reaktion Books.
Herbert, M. S. (1998), *Camouflage Isn't Only for Combat: Gender, Sexuality and Women in the Military*, New York: New York University Press.
Hertz, C. (2007), "The Uniform: As Material, As Symbol, As Negotiated Object," *Midwestern Folklore*, 32, 1 (2): 43–58.
Himam, D. and B. Pasin (2011), "Designing a National Uniform(ity): The Culture of Sümerbank within the context of the Turkish Nation-State Project," *Journal of Design History*, 24 (2): 157–70.
Hobsbawm, E. and T. Ranger, eds (1983), *The Invention of Tradition*, Cambridge: Cambridge University Press.
Hollander, A. (1994), *Sex and Suits: The Evolution of Modern Dress*, New York: Kodansha International.
Holt, R. (1993), *Sport and the British; A Modern History*, Oxford: Clarendon Press.

Holt, R. (2006), "The Amateur Body and the Middle-class Man: Work, Health and Style in Victorian Britain," *Sport in History*, 26 (3): 352–69.
Hume, L. (2013), *The Religious Life of Dress: Global Fashion and Faith*, London: Bloomsbury.
Jarman, N. (1997), *Material Conflicts: Parades and Visual Displays in Northern Ireland*, Oxford: Berg.
Joseph, N. (1986), *Uniforms and Nonuniforms: Communication Through Clothing*, Westport CT: Greenwood Press.
Kaiser, S. (1998), *The Social Psychology of Clothing: Symbolic Appearance in Context*, New York: Fairchild Publications.
Keenan, W. J. F. (1999), "From Friars to Fornicators: The Eroticization of Sacred Dress," *Fashion Theory*, 3 (4): 389–410.
Keenan, W. J. F. (2001), *Dressed to Impress: Looking the Part*, Oxford: Berg.
Kidwell, C. and V. Steele (1989), *Men and Women: Dressing the Part*, Washington D.C.: Smithsonian Institution Scholarly Press.
Kinsella, S. (2002), "What's Behind the Fetishism of Japanese School Uniforms?," *Fashion Theory*, 6 (2): 215–37.
Küchler, S. and D. Miller, eds (2005), *Clothing as Material Culture*, Oxford: Berg.
Kuchta, D. (2002), *The Three-Piece Suit and Modern Masculinity; England, 1550–1850*, Berkeley, CA: University of California Press.
Laver, J. (1969), *A Concise History of Costume*, London: Thames and Hudson.
Laver, J. (2002), *Costume and Fashion: A Concise History*, London: Thames and Hudson.
Lehmann, U. (2000), *Tigersprung. Fashion in Modernity*, Cambridge, MA: MIT Press
Levitt, S. (1991), "Cheap Mass-Produced Men's Clothing in the Nineteenth and Early Twentieth Centuries," *Textile History*, 22 (2): 179–93.
Lipovetsky, G. (1994), *The Empire of Fashion: Dressing Modern Democracy*, Princeton, NJ: Princeton University Press.
Martin, R. (1998), *Cubism and Fashion*, New York: The Metropolitan Museum of Art.
Maxwell, A. (2014), *Patriots Against Fashion: Clothing and Nationalism in Europe's Age of Revolutions*, Basingstoke: Palgrave Macmillan.
Mayo, J. (1984), *A History of Ecclesiastical Dress*, London: B.T. Batsford Ltd.
McVeigh, B. (2002), *Wearing Ideology: State, Schooling and Self-presentation in Japan*, Oxford: Berg.
Miller-Spillman, K. A., et. al. (2012), *The Meaning of Dress*, London and New York: Fairchild Books.
Miller, A. (2007), *Dressed to Kill: British Naval Uniform, Masculinity and Contemporary Fashions 1748–1857*, London: National Maritime Museum.
Miller, D. (2010), *Stuff*, Cambridge: Polity Press.
Myerly, S. H. (1996), *British Military Spectacle; From the Napoleonic Wars through the Crimea*, Cambridge, MA: Harvard University Press.
Parkins, W., ed. (2002), *Fashioning the Body Politic*, Oxford: Berg.
Paulicelli, E. (2004), *Fashion Under Fascism: Beyond the Black Shirt*, Oxford: Berg.

Peniston-Bird, C. (2003), "Classifying the Body in the Second World War: British Men in and Out of Uniform," *Body & Society*, 9 (4): 31–48.

Peoples, S. (2013), "Embodying the Military: Uniforms," *Critical Studies in Men's Fashion*, 1 (1): 7–21.

Perrot, P. (1981), *Fashioning the Bourgeoisie: a History of Clothing in the Nineteenth Century*, Princeton, NJ: Princeton University Press.

Petersen, T. B. and V. Riisberg, (2016), "Pockets, Buttons and Hangers: Designing a New Uniform for Health Care Professionals," *Design Issues*, 32 (1): 60–71.

Polhemus, T. (1984), *Streetstyle*, London: Thames and Hudson.

Polhemus, T. and L. Procter (1978), *Fashion and Anti-fashion: an Anthropology of Clothing and Adornment*, London: Thames and Hudson.

Pollen, A. (2015), *The Kindred of the Kibbo Kift: Intellectual Barbarians*, London: Donlon Books.

Richmond, V. (2013), *Clothing the Poor in Nineteenth Century England*, Cambridge: Cambridge University Press.

Rocamora, A. and A. Smelik, eds (2015), *Thinking Through Fashion: A Guide to Key Theorists*, London: I.B. Tauris, 233–50.

Roche, D. (1994), *The Culture of Clothing: Dress and Fashion in the "Ancient Regime"* (trans. Jean Birrell), Cambridge: Cambridge University Press.

Rouse, E. (1989), *Understanding Fashion*, London: BSP Professional Books.

Ryan, K. (2014), "Uniform Matters: Fashion Design in World War II Women's Recruitment," *The Journal of American Culture*, 37 (4): 419–29.

Sangster, J. and J. Smith (2017), "'Thigh in the Sky': Canadian Pacific Dresses Its Female Flight Attendants," *Labor: Studies in Working-Class History*, 14 (1): 39–63.

Schuessler Poplin, I. (1994), "Nursing Uniforms: Romantic Idea, Functional Attire or Instrument of Social Change?," *Nursing History Review*, 2: 153–67.

Schwarz, R. A. (1979), "Uncovering the Secret Vice: Toward an Anthropology of Clothing and Adornment," in J. M. Cordwell and R. A. Schwarz (eds), *The Fabrics of Culture: The Anthropology of Clothing and Adornment*, The Hague: Mouton Publishers, 23–46.

Shannon, B. (2006), *The Cut of his Coat: Men, Dress and Consumer Culture in Britain 1860–1914* Ohio: Ohio University Press.

Simmel, G. (1904), "Fashion," *International Quarterly*, 10: 130–55.

Snodgrass, M. E. (2015), *World Clothing and Fashion: An Encyclopaedia of History, Culture and Social Influence*, London: Routledge.

Steele, V. (1996), *Fetish: Fashion, Sex and Power*, New York: Oxford University Press.

Stepanova, V. (1923), "Kostium segodniashnego dnia – prozodezhda," (Today's clothing: Prozodezhda), *Lef*, N 2: 65–68.

Stites, R. (1989), *Revolutionary Dreams: Utopian Vision and Experimental Life in the Russian Revolution*, Oxford: Oxford University Press.

Streicher, R. (2012), "Fashioning the Gentlemanly State: The Curious Charm of the Military Uniform in Southern Thailand," *International Feminist Journal of Politics*, 14 (4): 470–88.

Styles, J. (2007), *The Dress of the People: Everyday Fashion in Eighteenth-century England*, New Haven, CT: Yale University Press.
Synott, J. and C. Symes (1995), "The Genealogy of the School: an Iconography of Badges and Mottoes," *British Journal of Sociology of Education*, 16 (2): 139–52.
Tonchi, S. (2010), "Military Style," in V. Steele (ed.), *The Berg Companion to Fashion*, Oxford: Berg, 507–08.
Tynan, J. (2013a), "Military Chic: Fashioning Civilian Bodies for War," in K. McSorley (ed.), *War and the Body*, London: Routledge.
Tynan, J. (2013b), *British Army Uniform and the First World War: Men in Khaki*, Basingstoke: Palgrave Macmillan.
Tynan, J. (2018), "Codes: Police Uniform and the Image of Law Enforcement," in I. Ward (ed.), *A Cultural History of Law in the Age of Reform*, Vol. 5, London: Bloomsbury, 55–71.
Ugolini, L. (2011), "The Illicit Consumption of Military Uniforms in Britain, 1914–1918," *Journal of Design History*, 24 (2): 125–38.
Veillon, D. (2002), *Fashion Under the Occupation*, Oxford: Berg.
Wauters, A. (1995), *Eve in Overalls*, London: Imperial War Museum.
WBG, 203–26.
Wilcox, C. (2010), "Military and Civil Uniforms in Australia," in M. Maynard (ed.), *Berg Encyclopedia of World Dress and Fashion*, Vol. 7, Australia, New Zealand and the Pacific Islands, Oxford: Berg, 195–201.
Williams-Mitchell, C. (1982), *Dressed for the Job: The Story of Occupational Costume*, Poole: Blandford.
Wilson, E. (1985), *Adorned in Dreams: Fashion and Modernity*, London: Virago.
Wilson, E. and L. Taylor (1989), *Through The Looking Glass: A History of Dress from 1860 to the Present Day*, London: BBC Books.
Woodward, S. (2007), *Why Women Wear What They Wear*, Oxford: Berg.
Yagou, A. (2011), "Foreword: Uniforms in Design-Historical Perspective," *Journal of Design History*, 24 (2): 101–04.
Zakim, M. (2003), *Ready-Made Democracy: A History of Men's Dress in the American Republic 1760-1860*, Chicago: University of Chicago Press.

Index

Açba, Leyla 147, 284n.1
Action (newspaper) 32, 42
Adivar, Halide Edip 144
'aesthetic labor' 17, 159–60, 230, 278
Afghanistan 247, 249
agbadas (robes) 13
"Age of Shirts, The" (Chesterton) 25
"aggiornamento" 87, 98–9
Agnona 182
Air France 186–7, 280
Airbus A380 plane 187
alafranga 136
Albert, Prince 76, 118
Alexei Fedorov-Davydov 207
"ambiguous masks" 43
American Machinist 208–9
Anatolia *see* Turkey
Anderson, Fiona 123, 125
Ankara Palas hotel, Turkey 154
Apollo 11 moon landing 212
Argentina 225
Ari, Eyal Ben 261
Armstrong, Neil 212
Army Comrades Association 23
Arthur, Linda B. 139
Atatürk, Mustafa Kemal 135–8, 141–2, 148
Australia 3, 180–7, 190, 192–3, 195–6, 229, 284n.2, 285n.11
Austro-Hungary 208
"autumn playground" 124

Bailey, Peter 109, 112
Ballin, Ada 124
Balmain, Pierre 185
Balmoral Castle 118
Balston, Rev. 73, 80
Ban Wang 60–1
Barneys Private Label 182
Bartlett, Djurdja 5, 200, 201–17, 280
Battle of Cable Street (1936) 27
Benedictine Boulding 90

Bentham, Jeremy 164
Berlin, Isaiah 101
Betancourt, Ingrid 247
Biddle-Perry, Geraldine 4, 107, 109–31, 279
Black, Prudence 5, 160, 179–95, 229–80
black shirts 26, 28
    see also British Union of Fascists
blazers 42, 70, 75, 169, 172, 270
"bloods" 78
blue-collar workers 227
'Blueshirts' *see* Army Comrades Association
bodystockings 213, 215
Boeing aeroplanes
    707 180, 187
    727 179
    747 Jumbo Jet 180
    787 Dreamliner 180, 194
Boer War 222
Bogdanov, Alexander 204, 217, 285n.4
Bogner 212
Bolsheviks 5, 202, 208
Bonami, Francesca 185
Boss, Hugo 265
Bourdieu, Pierre 162–4, 167, 173–4, 255, 259
boy scouts *see* Scout Association
Boy's Brigade 43
Braniff International Airline 179, 284n.3
Breward, Christopher 227
Brewer, Maura 217
Britain *see* United Kingdom
Britain First 44
British Admiralty 221
British Airways 186, 189
British Army 6, 14, 165, 223, 255–6, 259, 270
British Empire 67, 72
British Navy 221
British Union of Fascists 23, 26, 28, 30
Brussels Conference (1874) 244
Burberry 120

'burqa ban' 24
Burrows, Stephen 215–16
business wear 161–76

Cable Street, Battle of (1936) 25
cadet corps 75–6
caesaro-papist bureaucracy 90
Café Royal 127–8
Caillebotte, Gustave 128
Camisards 25
camouflage 11, 119, 222, 238, 241, 245–6, 250–1
Camper's Handbook, The (Holding) 122, 129
Canadian Pacific Air Lines 182
capitalism 2, 18, 108–10, 115, 118, 131, 202, 226, 277
'capitalist kitsch' 5
Cardin, Pierre 215, 284n.4
Carlyle, Thomas 115
çarşafs 147
Carter, Michael 185
Cavaliers 25
Central Institute of Labour (Soviet Union) 202
Champagnat, Jean-Baptiste 88
Champagnat, Marie-Thérèse 88
Champagnat, Père Marcellin Joseph Benedict 88
Chanel 16
Chanel, Coco 222
Chang, June 58
Chartered Associations (Protection of Names and Uniforms) Act 1926 (UK) 31
Charterhouse school 67, 70, 77
Chesterton, A. K. 42
Chesterton, G. K. 25
Chiang Kai-shek 52
Chichagova, Galina 205
children
    fetishizing uniformed Japanese schoolgirls 232
    school uniforms 3, 67, 74–6, 79, 81–3, 136, 140, 147, 153, 162, 165
    working conditions 121
China 23, 49–54, 57–9, 62, 190
Chiuri, Maria Grazia 216
Christian Dior fashion house 216
Christianity 44, 66, 70, 91–2, 115, 142

Cintas 180
City of London 4, 159–76, 280
Civil Examination system (China) 51
Civilized Woman (exhibition 1929) 206
Clarendon Report (1864) 72–3
Clark, David 212
'class enemies' 53, 57, 60, 283n.2
Clausewitz, Karl von 242–3
"Clothing of Today, The: *Prozodezhda*" 203
Cohn, Carol 266–7
Cointreau Young Designer of the Year Award 184
collectivism 137, 207
Colombia 247
colonialism 12–13
'Combat Soldier 95' 264
combatants 5, 237, 239–44, 246–7, 250, 280
communism 38, 52–7, 59, 137
Communist Youth organizations 28
communitarianism 98
Comradeship (journal) 127
Confucianism 52
Conservative Red Guards 58
    see also Red Guards
Constitutions (Marist Brothers) 93–5, 99–100
Constructivism 5, 108, 202–7, 213–15
consumerism 112–13, 116, 128, 229, 277
Cooperative Holiday Association (CHA) 127
corporal punishment 52, 71
Cott, Hugh 250
Council of Trent 88
Courrèges, André 213, 215
Courveille, Father Jean-Claude 91–2, 96–7
Craik, Jennifer 43
Crimean War 223
Crossfield, Scott 212
Cubism 213
Cultural Revolution (China) 3, 23, 49–62
cycling 108, 110, 116, 119, 122, 128, 130
Cyclists' Touring Club 120, 122, 124

Daily Worker 43
dandyism 15, 17
Davis, Karen 259
Death of Tarelkin, The 203, 285n.2

Decline of Aristocracy, The (Ponsonby) 63–4, 70
Delsaut, Yvette 164
democracy 130, 223–4, 226, 234
denim jeans 208–10, 216, 228, 263
Dinnigan, Colette 180–1
DMS (Directly Moulded Sole Boots) 263
"docile bodies" 165, 168, 174–6
Douglas, Major C. H. 34, 40
Douglas, Mary 146
dress codes
    City of London 162–3, 167, 171–5
    conclusions 278–81
    introduction 4–6, 16–17
    Marists 87–90, 93–6, 98–9, 101
    overalls 204, 214
    public schools 72–4, 76
    Qantas 189
    Turkey 136, 141–2, 146–7
    utility chic 227
    workers 159–60
"dual dress economy" 102

Earhart, Amelia 212
Easter Rising (1916) 13
Economy and Savings (journal) 138
Edensor, Tim 140
egalitarianism 57
Eicher, Joanne 94
Eisenstein, Sergei 204
Enlightenment 54, 202, 223
Enloe, Cynthia 259
Entwistle, Joanne 161, 163, 165, 169–70
equestrianism 118
Etatism principle 137
Etihad 189
Eton collars 4, 81
Eton jackets 73, 80–1
Eton school 67, 73–5, 80
European Industrial Revolution 137
European Red Falcons 41
Eve in Overalls (pamphlet) 209

Fair, Henry 41
FARC forces 247
fascism 15, 38, 41, 234
fashion
    and cultural practices 9
    dictatorial image of 225
    a form of communication 7–8
    military 53, 75
    a new identity 59–62
    uniforms 16–18, 57, 83, 213–15, 226
Feder, Edna Lomsky 261–2
Fedorov-Davydov, Alexei 207
Felix 166, 173
Fellini, Federico 97
ferace 143–5, 147
ferman (enactments) 145
Feshane Palace Factory 148
fez 140, 142, 145
"field of perception" 250
Finnane, Antonia 58
First World War 7, 23, 36, 137, 141, 165, 208, 222, 250
Five-Year Plans 207
"flappers" 141
Fliedner, Theodor 224
Flügel, John Carl 9, 161, 227
football 68–9, 70, 108
Ford, Henry 201
Fordism 201
Foucault, Michel 12, 15, 162–8, 175, 225–6
France
    and Camisards shirts 25
    Christian reconversion of 91
    export of fabrics to Turkey 153
    and Italian fascist uniforms 234
    Restoration era in 92–3
    Revolution 6, 89, 161
    uniforms as a militant threat 24
François, Frère 93
Freeman, Luke 12
Frisa, Maria Luisa 185
Furet, Brother Jean-Baptist 88, 92
Fussell, Paul 221
Futurism 213

Gagarin, Yuri 212
Galster, Kjeld 265
Garb, Tamar 128
"*garçonnes*" 140–1
Gastev, Alexei 202
Gaultier, Jean Paul 231
Gellner, Ernest 136–7
Geneva Conventions 239, 243–5, 248–9, 251
    1947 (GCIII) 242
    Article 43(2), 1977 First Protocol (API) 243

gender 3, 5, 8–10, 14–17, 51–2, 56, 92, 70, 108, 111, 114, 121, 125, 127, 141–3, 146, 160, 168, 176, 199, 203, 206–9, 216, 237, 258, 265–9, 278, 280–1
Germany 24, 26, 30, 42, 50, 76, 189, 216, 259
Gernreich, Rudi 215
Girl Guides 31
Glaum-Lathbury, Abigail 217
Glenfeshie 117–18
Goethe, Johann Wolfgang von 208
Goffman, Erving 90, 255, 257, 262–3, 272
Golding, Paul 44
Gönlügür, Emre 141
Goot, Josh 181
Gramsci, Antonio 11
Grant, Martin 179–96, 285n.10
Graves, Robert 77
Great Leap Forward 57
"Great Masculine Renunciation" 9, 161, 227
Green Shirts 28, 32, 36–40
  see also Social Credit Party
'Green Tops' 263
'green-on-blue attacks' 249
Greenberg, Josh 269
Greenfinches 255–6, 259–60, 265–7, 272
Gross, George 183
Groys, Boris 216
Guerra, Samira 4, 159, 161–76, 280
Guild of Youth 28–9, 31
Guzmán, Basilio Rueda 98

habitus 100, 146–7, 163–5, 167–8, 175–6
Hague Peace Conferences (1899/1907) 244
Haileybury school 78
Halston 215, 286n.10
Hamnett, Katherine 231–2
Han Chinese 51
Handelman, Don 257
Hanýmlara Mahsus Gazete (magazine) 147
Harberton, Lady 124
Hargrave, John 33–7, 40
Harrow school 67–9, 74, 81
Harvey, David 1
hat-law 1925 (Turkey) 140

HD Lee Mercantile Company 201, 207–8
Headmasters's Conference (1869) 74
Heather 166–70, 172, 174–5
Hemingway, Wayne 280
Hereke Factory 148
Herron, Stephen 5–6, 255–72, 280
Hertz, Carrie 162
Hickey, Simon 181
Himam, Dilek 4, 107, 135–55, 279
Hobsbawm, Eric 6–7, 78
Hochschild, Arlie 258, 263
Holding, Thomas 122, 126–7, 129
Hollander, Anne 187
Honig, Emily 60
Horneková, Božena 206
Huggins, Mike 116–17
Hurry, Colin 36
Hurstpierpoint school 78
Hussars 75
Hyam, B. 81

"I Still Call Australia Home" 184, 284n.5
Imperial Fascist League 28–9
İnas Sanayi Sultani 148
İnci (magazine) 147
Independent Labour Party Guild of Youth 28–9, 31
India 12–13
Indian Mutiny 12–13
industrial capitalism 109–10, 115, 118, 131
Industrial Incentives Law 1927 (Turkey) 138
Institute of Rhythm, Moscow 202
International Committee of the Red Cross 244, 247, 249
International Court of Justice 239
international law 5, 239–52
International Modernism movement 205–6
International System of Garment Cutting (Thornton) 123
Inventory (Marist Brothers) 96
Ireland 23, 32, 144, 261, 264
Iribe, Paul 209
Irish Republican Army (IRA) 256
Irish Volunteers 14
ISAF forces 249–50
Islam 141, 146–7, 149, 151

Israel Defense Forces (IDF) 261
Italian Fascisti 28
Italy 15, 25–6, 28–9, 42, 216
Izmir Economic Congress (1923) 137

Japan 50–2, 59, 165, 167, 185–6, 192, 225–6, 232
Japan Airlines 186, 192
Jarvenpa, Robert 269–70
JC Penney 208
Jesenská, Milena 206
John XXIII, Pope 97
Joseph, Nathan 93, 162–3, 172
Journal of Design History 2
Joyce, Alan 180–2
Judaism 27–8, 42, 142–3
Jumpsuit 201, 212, 215–17

Kaiserwerth Deaconess Institute, Prussia 224
"kangaroo cloud" (print) 186
'Kangaroo Route' 186, 188
kangaroo symbol 186, 196
Kaya, İbrahim 137
Keenan, William J.F. 3–4, 65, 87–103, 279
Keir Hardie, James 123
Kemalism 4, 135–41, 147–8, 150–1, 154
Kensington Fascists 28
Kerr, Graham 250
Kerr, Miranda 179
"kerygma" (spiritual power) 92
Khrushchev, Nikita 212
Kimmel, Michael 268
Kindred of the Kibbo Kift 33, 36
Kiz Sanat Enstitüsü (Girls' Institute) 148
Klutsis, Gustav 204
knickerbockers 70, 117–18, 124, 130
Ku Klux Klan 24

La Baïonnette (magazine) 209
La Cave-Abri (Ritz) 211
La Nazione (newspaper) 213
La Turquie Kemaliste (publication) 136
la tuta (overalls) 213
Lacroix, Christian 280
Lancing school 78
laobaixing (common civilian) 54
Laurent, Brother 91
Laver, James 222

Le Guin, Ursula K. 206
League of Unemployed 36
Lechevallier, Leo 209
Lee, Dion 181
Lef (journal) 203
Legion of Blue and White Shirts 28
leisure uniforms 109–31, 279–80
leisurewear 170, 228, 279–80
Leonard, T. A. 127
Levi Strauss & Co 201
Levitt, Sarah 124
Li Li 3, 23, 49–63, 279
Lin Biao 57–8
Lindbergh, Charles 211
Little Brothers of Mary (1817) 89, 94, 100
Little Red Book (Mao Zedong) 57–8
Liu Shaoqi 57–8
Liverpool Street Station, London 166, 171
"Livery of Mary" (religious dress) 92, 95, 97, 100
Locker-Lampson, Commander 26, 28
Lockheed L749 Constellation planes 180, 186
London Metropolitan police 15
London Tailor (journal) 122
Long March 59
Loos, Adolf 208
Louis XIV, King 25
Lunacharsky, Anatoly 202

Macaroni style 221
Macdonell, A. G. 30
Maček, Ivana 262
McVeigh, Brian 139, 165, 167, 225–6
Madame Fegara 147
Madame Galibe 147
Madame Kalivrusi 147
Madeleine Vionnet fashion house, Paris 214
Magnanimous Cuckold, The (Meyerhold) 202–3
Maharishi 232
Mahmud II, Sultan 145
Malagasy Independence Day 12
Malaysia 174
Manchester City News 127
Manchurian monarchy 50–2
Mao Zedong 3, 49–62

Marcellin Champagnat, Saint 89–90, 100
Marist Brothers 4, 87–8, 97–102
Marist Directory (1908) 95
Marist dress history
    expressive revolution 97–101
    foundation livery 90–3
    liberalization 87–90
    Tridentine uniform 93–7
Marist Institute 98, 102
Marist Society 91, 93
Marist Statutes (1987) 99
Marlborough school 76, 78
Martial Arts Society 51
Martin Grant, Paris (exhibition) 182
Martin, Richard 213
Martin, Susan 263
Maxwell, Vera 210
Maya 166, 169, 171–2, 174
Médecins Sans Frontières 247
Mein Kampf (Hitler) 210
men 6, 31, 54, 60, 74, 128, 15, 139, 161, 215, 226, 256, 260
Men's Wear (journal) 119–20
Mercedes-Benz Fashion Week (April 2013) 179
Meyerhold, Vsevold 202, 204
Middle Ages 6, 161, 223
Middle Class Culture in the Nineteenth Century (Young) 79
military uniforms
    camouflage 11, 119, 222, 238, 241, 245, 250–2
    in China 45–6, 53–4, 59, 62
    as counter-culture symbols 230–4
    enemy 10, 240–3, 246–50
    introduction 239–41
    and lethal targeting 246–50
    perfidy 241, 246–50
    principle of distinction 239, 241–5, 252
    recent origin of 10
    Ulster Defence Regiment 5, 237, 255–72
Miller, Daniel 7
Mirzoeff, Nicholas 240–1
Mission Australia (charity) 192
modernism 16, 89, 202, 206
modernity
    Chinese 55
    conclusions 277–8, 280, 282
    institutions 65
    introduction 1–4, 11, 16, 18
    leisure 107
    Marists 102
    Nineteenth-Century Britain 113, 121
    overalls 201–2, 212–15
    Turkey 136–42
    uniform and fashion 199–200
    utility chic 229–33
modernization 4, 52, 87, 135–55
Montmorency, Lionel 68
Monument to the Third International (Tatlin) 204
Morrissey, Peter 183, 191, 193–4
Mosley, Sir Oswald 26–7
Mugler, Thierry 216
Muscular Christianity 66, 70
Mussolini, Benito 26

Napoleonic Wars 10
nation-states 11, 23–4, 141, 143, 151, 242–3
National Economy and Savings Society (Turkey) 138, 149
National Socialists 26
neo-liberalism 281
New Army (China) 50
New York Preen designs 222
Newson, Marc 180
Nicholls, J. 80–1
Nicolson, Harold 76
Nigeria 13–14
Nightingale, Florence 223
Nineteen Eighty-Four (Orwell) 206–7
Noble, Katya 184–5, 192
Norfolk jackets 116–18, 122–3, 126, 130–1
Northern Ireland 6, 255–6, 264, 270, 272
Northern Ireland body armor *see* Combat Soldier
Nosch, Marie-Louise 265

Old Red Guards 58
    see also Red Guards
Olympic Games (1972) 213
On the New (Groys) 216
On War (Clausewitz) 242, 286n.1
'Operation Jaque' (Colombian Army) 247

Opium Wars 50
Orwell, George 206
Ottoman clothing laws 143
Ottoman Empire *see* Turkey
overalls 5, 120, 200–17, 285nn.2,6, 286n.10
Oxford and Cambridge boat race 69

'Pacifist Military Design' *see* Maharishi
Pagès, Jean 211
panopticon 90, 164, 166–8, 175
Parsa, Amin 5, 238, 239–54, 280
Pasenow, Joachim von 1
Patterson, Alicia 211
Paul VI, Pope 97
Peoples' Houses 140
People's Liberation Army (PLA) 3, 49–50, 55–62
Peoples, Sharon 245
Perfectae Caritatis 98
'performances' (Goffman) 257
Petits Frères de Marie see Little Brothers of Mary (1817)
phallic worship 266–7
Physical Education (Smiles) 114–15
Piguet, Robert 211
police
    cadets 43
    uniforms 14–16
political uniforms 26, 40
Pollen, Annebella 3, 23, 25–7, 256, 279–80
Ponsonby, Arthur 70
Popova, Liubov 202–3, 285n.1
postmodernism 200, 232, 234, 278
Principles of Scientific Management (Taylor) 201
prison uniforms 14
prisoner of war status 246
"Project for Community Life" (Guzmán) 98
"Protestant work ethic" (Weber) 109
Protestantism 115
prozodezhda 203–5, 207, 285n.1
Public Economic Enterprises (Turkey) 149
Public Order Act 1936 (UK) 3, 25–44, 38
public schools 4, 67–83
Public Schools Act (1868) 67, 71
Pucci, Emilio 179, 181, 183, 191, 193, 212, 284n.3
Purdy, Daniel 226

Qantas uniforms
    choosing the cloth 187–92
    design 182–6
    nationalism/internationalism 192–6
    new 5, 179–80
    selection 180–4
Qing dynasty 50
Qiu Jin 51–2, 59

race 3, 10, 14, 17, 138, 140, 142, 160, 223, 281
Rae Yang 60
railways 16–17, 120–1
Ramírez, Gerardo Aguilar 247
Ranger, Terence 6
Rational Dress Society 124, 217
Recollections of Rugby 69, 83
Red Detachment of Women 49, 54
Red Detachment of Women (film) 49–50
Red Guards 23, 49–50, 55–62
Red Star (Bogdanov) 204, 217
'red summer' (1966) 55
Religious Superiors 87, 88–90
Republican Revolution 59
Roach, M. E. 94
Roche, Daniel 50
Rodchenko, Alexander 202, 204–5, 207, 213
Rojek, Chris 109
Roma (Fellini) 97–8
Roman Catholic Church 4, 87–8, 90, 97
Rome Statute of ICC 248–9
Rossmann, Zdeněk 206
Roundheads 25
Rouse, Elizabeth 283n.1
Routledge's Handbook of Football (1867) 69
Royal Army Medical Corps 50
Royal Irish Rangers 256
Royal Irish Regiment 256
    see also Ulster Defence Regiment (UDR)
Royal Navy 10
Rugby and Harrow jackets 81
Rugby school 67, 69, 73, 81
Rule's 128
Rules of Government (Marist Brothers) 95–6
Russia 3, 50, 108, 204
Ryanair 189

SA 80 rifle 265
Sabbatarians 112
sacred dress 87, 100
St John Ambulance 31
Saint Laurent, Yves 183, 193, 222
St. Petersburg Declaration (1868) 243
Sanayii Maadin Bankasi 149
Sander, August 216
Sarajevo 262
Saturday Evening Post 207, 285n.5
Savings and National Products Week (Turkey) 138
Schiaparelli, Elsa 211, 222
school uniforms
    conclusions 279
    institutions 65–6
    introduction 3–4
    public schools 67, 74, 76, 79, 81, 83
    Turkey 136, 140, 147
    utility chic 225–6
    and workers 162, 165
Scott, James C. 174
Scott, Sir Walter 118
Scout Association 41, 43, 65–6
Second Vatican Council *see* Vatican II
Second World War 201, 208–9, 224, 232, 264
Segal, Mady. W. 259
Sekimoto, Teuro 139
'selective sifting' (Veblen) 114, 116, 130
Self Help (Smiles) 115
Selheim, Gert 186
sexism 226, 268–72
sexuality 10, 17, 130, 160, 189, 204, 207, 229, 237, 258, 281
shooting season 124
Shrewsbury school 67
Simmel, Georg 17, 110, 112–13, 115–16, 119
Singapore Airlines 189, 192
'Singapore Girls' uniforms 185, 189
Sino-Japanese War (1938–45) 52
siren suits 211
Skiing 211–12
Sleepwalkers, The (Broch) 1
"sloppy" drill jackets 120
Smiles, Samuel 114–15
Smithala and Wessinen Revolver 269
Snape, Robert 127, 129
Social Credit Party 28, 32–3, 39–40
social class 16, 121, 151, 154, 229

Social Credit system 32–3
socialism 199, 206, 212, 277
Socialist Education International 41
Society of Mary 90–1
soldiers 10–13, 50, 54–5, 58–9, 165, 208, 237–40, 255–72
Solomon, Solomon J. 250
Some People (Nicolson) 76
Song Binbin 56
South Armagh 265
Soviet Taylorism 202
Soviet Union 5, 202, 207, 212
Space Age 212, 215
Sperry Gyroscope Company 210
spetzodezhda 203
Spider Eaters (Rae Yang) 60
sport 26, 29–30, 67–71, 74–7, 108, 110–20, 128, 130, 148
sportodezhda 108, 203
Sputnik 1 212
Stalin, Joseph 87, 206–7
Stalinism 207
Steele, Valerie 209
Stepanova, Varvara 108, 202–4
Stephenson, Kate 3–4, 65, 67–85, 279
Stockdale, Charlotte 180
Stowe School 75
Strafgesetzbuch (Criminal Code) 24
Streicher, Ruth 13
Studio 54 (night club) 215
subcultures 230–3
suits 70, 75, 81, 120–1, 131, 152, 154, 167, 171–2, 188, 211–12
Şükufezar (magazine) 147
Sümerbank textile factories (Turkey) 138, 148–51
sumptuary laws 6, 90, 129, 143, 223
Sun Yat-sen 57
surrealism 222

Tacey, Charles 38
Taiwan 53
Taliban 248, 250
Tanzimat reforms (Turkey) 137, 145
Tatlin, Vladimir 204
Tatsuno, Koji 184
Taylor, Frederick 201
Taylor, Lou 125
Tereshkova, Valentina 212
Thailand 13

Thayaht 213–14
Thayer, Abbott 250
theory of symbolic violence (Bourdieu) 255
Thornton's tailoring guide 122
Tiananmen Gate Tower 56–7, 60
Tonchi, Stefano 185
Toprak, Zafer 154
Transport for London 280
Tridentine Catholicism 88–90, 92–8, 101
Tsinghua University 55
Turkey
    fashion and modernity 142–8
    modernisation in 136–9
    tailoring and fabric 149–55
    uniforming 139–41
Turkic Osmanlý dynasty 143
tweeds
    Gamefeather 120
    Plus Beau 120
    suits 116, 119–24, 126–7, 131
"two concepts of liberty" (Berlin) 101
Tynan, Jane 5, 165, 200, 221–36, 280

UDR cap badge 261
UDR magazines 255, 260, 269–70
Ulster Defence Regiment (UDR)
    cartoon sketches and women 268–72
    creation 255–7
    Greenfinch uniforms 265–8
    military operations 257–60
    public camouflage 260–1
    uniform style 263–5
    uniforms as symbols of control 261–3
Ulster Special Constabulary (USC) *see* Ulster Defence Regiment (UDR)
Ulster Volunteers 14
'Ultramontane' Church 92
Ultramontanist model 93
Union-Alls (Lee) 207–8
'Unite the Right' rally (2017) 279
United Airlines 180
United Empire Fascist Party 28
United Kingdom
    and Ireland 14
    mass clothing production in 16–17
    nineteenth-century masculinity in 227
    and the Opium Wars 50
    and the Public Order Act 1936 (UK) 3, 25–44, 38
    state of army hospitals 223
    uniformed political movements in 23–4
    Victorian rationality and modesty 223, 225
    women as "non-combatants" 259
United Nations 248
United States
    and Americanization 202, 208
    and Eton jackets 81
    expansion of mass schooling in 225
    and Finnish-Americans 269
    and freedom of expression 24
    and militarization of popular culture 232
    right-wing groupings in 279
    and the Space Age 212
    white-collar masculinity in 226
    and woman in overalls 209
    women serving in the forces 210
U.S. Navy and Coast Guard 224
utopianism 204, 207

Vaněk, Jan 206
Vatican II 87, 89, 96–8
Veblen, Thorstein 110, 112–16, 130
Versace, Gianni 216
Vetements 216, 229
Victoria, Queen 118
Village Institutes 1937 (Turkey) 140
Vincent, W.D.F. 122
Virgin Airlines 189, 280
Virgin Mary 90–1
Virilio, Paul 246, 250
visuality 66, 240–1, 252, 277
VKhUTEMAS 205
Vogue (magazine) 210–12, 215
Volunteer Movement (1859) 75

Watt, Harry 183
Wauters, Arthur 209
Weber, Max 90, 109–10
Weiss, Meira 259, 267
Wellington College 76
wenzhi binbin 57
West-of-England tweed 120
westernization 137
Westminster school 61, 67
Weston, Arthur 112
Westwood, Vivienne 257

white-collar workers 209–10
Wild Swans (Chang) 54
Wilkinson, Norman 231
Willis, Fred 116
Wilson, Elizabeth 199
Winchester school 67, 73
Winter, Trish 268
Winterton, Lord 27
'Wirriyarra' Morrissey uniform 193, 285n.10
Wollen, Peter 201
women
    and business wear 161–2, 168–71
    Chinese feminism 54
    civilian clothing in wartime 222
    and Constructivist thinking 203
    cultural practices associated with 9
    emancipation of in China 52, 59
    experiences in uniform 259, 267, 269
    and girls' public schools 67, 81
    liberation in Turkey 136, 138, 141–3, 145–8
    'make do and mend' in Turkey 149
    in military uniform 10
    as "non-combatants" 259
    and nursing 9–10, 224
    in overalls 215–17
    and power dressing 171
    and rational dress 124–5, 130, 217
    as Red Guards 23, 49, 55–6
    and the Space Age 212
    in the Ulster Defence Regiment 265–72
"Women Militias" (Mao Zedong) 53
Woodcraft Folk 41–3
Woodward, Rachel 268
Woodward, Sophie 171
workers
    blue-collar 227
    discipline and control in the workplace 17–18
    introduction 159–60
    and workwear 227–30
Worth, Olivia 181
Wyndham Lewis, D. B. 39–40

Yamamoto, Yohji 216
Yan'an uniform 57
Yarim Ay (magazine) 135
yaşmaks 143–7
Yeni Turan (Adivar) 145
Yilmaz, Hale 147
Young Communist League 28, 41
Young, Linda 79
Young Pioneers 28–9, 41

Zhou Enlai 58
Zouaves regiment 75